Studies in Diplomatic History

Essays in memory of David Bayne Horn

Professor of Modern History
in the University of Edinburgh

Edited by
Ragnhild Hatton
and M. S. Anderson

ARCHON BOOKS
1970

Published throughout the world, except the United States,
by Longman Group Ltd.

First published in the United States by Archon Books, 1970

SBN 208 01039 4
Printed in Great Britain

CONTENTS

[1] This contribution will form part of a study of Mussolini's foreign policy to be published by Macmillan.

NOTES ON CONTRIBUTORS

M. S. ANDERSON, M.A., PH.D. (Edinburgh); Reader in International History in the University of London; author, *Britain's Discovery of Russia, 1553–1815* (London, 1958); *Europe in the Eighteenth Century, 1713–1783* (London, 1961); *The Eastern Question, 1774–1923* (London, 1966).

SIR HERBERT BUTTERFIELD, M.A. (Cambridge), F.B.A.; formerly Regius Professor of Modern History in the University of Cambridge, Master of Peterhouse and President of the Historical Association; author, *The Peace Tactics of Napoleon, 1806–1808* (Cambridge, 1929); *The Statecraft of Machiavelli* (London, 1940); *George III and the Historians* (London, 1957) and numerous other works.

ALICE CARTER, M.A. (London); Lecturer in History, London School of Economics and Political Science; author of articles on seventeenth- and eighteenth-century English financial, religious and legal history and Anglo-Dutch relations, and of *The English Reformed Church in Amsterdam in the Seventeenth Century* (Amsterdam, 1965).

DIETRICH GERHARD, DR. PHIL. (Berlin); Professor Emeritus of History, Washington University, St Louis and of the University of Cologne; author, *England und der Aufstieg Russlands* (Munich, 1933); *Alte und neue Welt in vergleichender Geschichtsbetrachtung* (Göttingen, 1962) and of many articles on comparative history.

G. C. GIBBS, M.A. (Liverpool); Lecturer in History, Birkbeck College, University of London; author of articles and contributions on Parliamentary influence and control over British foreign policy in the eighteenth century and on the influence of the press during that period.

RAGNHILD HATTON, CAND. MAG. (Oslo), PH.D. (London); Professor of International History in the University of London; author, *Diplomatic Relations between Great Britain and the Dutch Republic, 1714–1721* (London, 1950); *Charles XII of Sweden* (London, 1968); *Europe in the Age of Louis XIV* (London, 1969).

DENYS HAY, M.A. (Oxford); Professor of Mediaeval History in the University of Edinburgh; author, *Polydore Vergil* (Oxford, 1952); *Europe: the Emergence of an Idea* (Edinburgh, 1957); *Europe in the Fourteenth and Fifteenth Centuries* (London, 1966); editor, *English Historical Review*, 1958–1965.

V. G. KIERNAN, M.A. (Cambridge); Reader in History in the University of Edinburgh; author, *British Diplomacy in China, 1880 to 1885* (Cambridge, 1939); *The Revolution of 1854 in Spanish History* (Oxford, 1966); *The Lords of Human Kind: European Attitudes to the Outside World in the Imperial Age* (London, 1969).

ANDREW LOSSKY, B.A. (London), PH.D. (Yale); Professor of History, University of California at Los Angeles; author, *Louis XIV, William III and the Baltic Crisis of 1683* (Berkeley–Los Angeles, 1954) and contributions on Russian and French history and diplomacy.

C. A. MACARTNEY, M.A., D.LITT. (Oxford), F.B.A.; Fellow of all Souls College, 1936–65, formerly Professor of International Relations in the University of Edinburgh; author, *The Magyars in the Ninth Century* (Cambridge, 1930); *October Fifteenth: a History of Modern Hungary, 1929–1945* (Edinburgh, 1956); *The Habsburg Empire, 1790–1918* (London, 1969).

JAMES N. M. MACLEAN OF GLENSANDA, B.LITT. (Oxford), PH.D. (Edinburgh); Lecturer in History in the University of Edinburgh; author, *Reward is Secondary. The Life of a Political Adventurer and An Inquiry into the Mystery of Junius* (London, 1963).

W. MEDIGER, DR. PHIL. (Göttingen; Professor of History, Technische Universität, Hanover; author, *Moskaus Weg nach Europa* (Braunschweig, 1952); *Mecklenburg, Russland und England-Hannover, 1706–1721* (Hildesheim, 1967).

I. H. NISH, M.A. (Edinburgh), PH.D. (London); Lecturer in International History, London School of Economics and Political Science; author, *The Anglo-Japanese Alliance: the Diplomacy of Two Island Empires, 1894–1907* (London, 1966); *The Story of Japan* (London, 1968).

STEWART OAKLEY, M.A. (Oxford), PH.D. (London); Lecturer in History in the University of East Anglia, formerly Lecturer in History in the University of Edinburgh; author, *The Story of Sweden* (London, 1966) and of several articles.

GUIDO QUAZZA, DR. ÈS LETTRES; Professor of History in the University of Turin; author, *L'equilibrio italiano nella politica europea alla vigilia della guerra per la successione polacca* (Turin, 1944); *Le riforme in Piemonte nella prima metà del Settecento* (Modena, 1957); *Il problema italiano e l'equilibrio europeo, 1720–1738* (Turin, 1965).

MICHAEL ROBERTS, M.A., D.PHIL. (Oxford), F.B.A.; Professor of Modern History in the Queen's University of Belfast; author, *Gustavus Adolphus: a History of Sweden, 1611–1632* (London, 1953–58); *Essays in Swedish History* (London, 1967); *The Early Vasas: a History of Sweden, 1523–1611* (Cambridge, 1968).

ESMONDE ROBERTSON, M.A. (Edinburgh); Lecturer in History in the University of Edinburgh; author, *Hitler's Pre-War Policy and Military Plans, 1933–1939* (London, 1963).

JOHN C. RULE, A.B. (Stanford), PH.D. (Harvard); Professor of History, University of Ohio; author of articles on French history in the later seventeenth and early eighteenth centuries; editor of and contributor to *Louis XIV and the Craft of Kingship* (Columbus, Ohio, 1970).

HENRY L. SNYDER, B.A., PH.D. (University of California at Berkeley); Associate Professor of History, University of Kansas; author of many articles on English history in the reign of Queen Anne, and at present editing the Marlborough-Godolphin correspondence for the Clarendon Press.

EDITORIAL NOTE

This volume was intended and went to press as a collection of studies in honour of D. B. Horn on his retirement from active teaching at Edinburgh University, which was to have taken place in June 1970. His sad and unexpected death in August 1969 has unfortunately transformed it into a memorial volume. It is some consolation to know that he was aware before his death that the volume was in preparation and that he himself supplied information helpful to the making of the Bibliography.

The editors wish to thank all the contributors who made the volume possible; in particular they wish to acknowledge the help of Professor Horn's colleague over many years, Professor Denys Hay. They desire also to give thanks to the Editor of the *Historische Zeitschrift* for permission to have Professor Dietrich Gerhard's lecture translated; to Michael and Brigitte Hay for the main work on this translation; and to Mr Francis Guercio for the translation of Professor Guido Quazza's contribution.

In essays dealing with the period before 1752 each contribution indicates whether the dating is in New Style (ten days ahead of the Old Style in the seventeenth century and eleven days ahead in the eighteenth century) or Old Style – the former being more suitable on the Continent in general, the latter for Britain and Sweden. Double dating, or the letters N.S. or O.S., are given where necessary to avoid ambiguity. Where Old Style is used, the year is still reckoned from 1 January, not 25 March.

M.S.A.
R.M.H.

ABBREVIATIONS USED IN FOOTNOTES

A.A.E.	Archives du Ministère des Affaires Étrangères, Paris.
A.M.O.N.	*Archives de la Maison d'Orange-Nassau*, 4th series, ed. Th. Bussemaker (Leiden, 1908–17).
A.N.	Archives Nationales, Paris.
A.R.A.	Algemeene Rijks Archief.
B.M. Add. MSS.	British Museum, Additional Manuscripts.
B.N.	Bibliothèque Nationale, Paris.
Bod. Lib.	Bodleian Library, Oxford.
B.M.	British Museum Library, London.
C.P.	Correspondance Politique, A.A.E.
D.A.	Dresden Archives (Sächsisches Landeshauptsarchiv, Dresden).
D.R.A.	Dansk Rigsarkiv, Copenhagen.
F.O.	Foreign Office Papers, P.R.O.
G.A.A.	Gemeente Archief, Amsterdam.
G.A.R.	Gemeente Archief, Rotterdam.
G.L.	Gothenburg, Landsarkivet.
H.A.	Hanover Archives (Niedersächsisches Staatsarchiv, Hannover).
H.M.C.	Historical Manuscripts Commission.
H.T.	*Historisk Tidskrift* (Stockholm).
J.H.C.	*Journals of the House of Commons.*
J.H.L.	*Journals of the House of Lords.*
N.L.S.	National Library of Scotland.
Pam. dipl. snosh.	*Pamiatniki diplomaticheskikh snoshenii drevnei Rossii s derzhavami inostrannymi* (St Petersburg, 1858).
P.R.O.	Public Record Office, London.
R.A.	Riksarkivet, Stockholm.
Recueil	*Recueil des Instructions données aux Ambassadeurs et Ministres de France depuis le Traité de Westphalie* (Paris, 1884–).
Sbornik	*Sbornik imperatorskogo russkogo istorischeskogo obshchestva* (St Petersburg, 1867–1916).

S.P.	State Papers, P.R.O.
S.R.O.	Scottish Record Office.
S.T.	Staten Generaal papers, A.R.A.
S.T., N.G.B.	*Sekai taisen kankei, Nihon gaikō bunsho* (Tokio, 1936–).
S.U.P.H.	*Den Svenska Utrikes Politikens Historia* (Stockholm, 1950–61).
U.U.B.	Uppsala University Library.

Papers referred to from other collections:

Blenheim MSS., the property of the Duke of Marlborough, Blenheim Castle, Oxfordshire.

Brydges Papers (Stowe Collection), Huntington Library, San Marino, California.

Burnet Letters, Bodleian Library, Oxford.

Clarendon Papers, the property of the Earl of Clarendon, Bodleian Library, Oxford.

Evelyn MSS., the property of the Trustees of the Evelyn Heirlooms, Christ Church, Oxford.

Finch-Hatton MSS., Northampton Record Office.

Longleat MSS., the property of the Marquess of Bath, Longleat, nr. Bristol.

Macartney Papers, Public Record Office, Northern Ireland.

Methuen Papers, Kenneth Spencer Research Library, University of Kansas.

Morrison Papers, Mitchell Library, Sydney.

Newdigate Newsletters, Folger Shakespeare Library, Washington.

Portland (Harley) Loan, the property of the Duke of Portland, British Museum Library.

Somerset Letters, Boston Public Library.

Spencer MSS., the property of the Earl Spencer of Althorp.

Wade Papers, Cambridge University Library.

Whitelocke Papers, the property of the Marquess of Bath, Longleat, nr. Bristol.

I

DENYS HAY

David Bayne Horn
1901–1969

The most remarkable aspect of David Horn's career was its consistency. He was faithful throughout to Edinburgh, to diplomatic history and to the eighteenth century. Yet this fidelity rested on an accident, or rather on one of those circumstances which seem to steer a man despite himself towards his real purposes. At school the talented boy saw himself as a scientist and, having accumulated a proper number of Highers in a spread of subjects, he concentrated on chemistry. It was to study this subject that he came to Edinburgh University in 1918. At that point he was confronted with a timetable clash: Chemistry and Latin initially coincided, so Maths it had to be, along with British History as a sort of makeweight. And a chemist thus became a historian. This and similar stories carry a moral: awkward timetables have their compensations.

Why Edinburgh University? To this there is a short answer. Edinburgh was a good university and able Scottish boys looked no further; at that time – and indeed to some degree still – Scottish universities were not competing with those in England. For an Edinburgh lawyer, as the boy's father was, to send an intelligent youth to another Scottish centre, let alone to England, was a highly unusual course of action. Family indecision, such as it was, derived from an uncle who, having graduated in Arts and Divinity, had failed to get a New College Chair and advised a career as a barrister. The Horns lived for a while in the New Town (hence David's attendance at the Edinburgh Institution, as Melville College was then called). It was inevitable that David Horn should then go to the Old College, that detached portion of Georgian Edinburgh south of Princes Street, and midway between Dublin Street, where he had spent some of his early years, and Liberton, to which the family returned later on.

Edinburgh University after the First World War was (like many other contemporary establishments) relatively small and intimate and, especially as one moved into honours work, one saw a lot of the other students in one's own and adjacent years. This was encouraged also by the curriculum. There were very few options and so classes were filled by people who soon knew each other very well. One such contemporary of David Horn's was later to become his wife: he married Barbara Scott in 1929. Until very recently, when the History Department has been removed from its home in the Old College to a new building, a list of medallists in History was maintained on a great board in the British History classroom and on it the names may be read of the future partners.

Honours in History meant, to a large extent, honours in British History; and British History meant English History. This was a tradition going back to the first holder of the Chair of History, Sir George Prothero, and it was maintained by his successor, Sir Richard Lodge.[1] Lodge was a dominant figure in university life, Dean of the Faculty of Arts, one of the handful of men in the place who had his own telephone. His teaching consisted of magisterial lectures at two levels: the survey class in British History (the Romans down to 1832) and a final year course on European history in the eighteenth century. Tutorials were handled by junior members of the department. These classes of Lodge's seem to have underpinned the whole edifice of Edinburgh history: the rest of it was, as might have been expected, mainly constitutional. Some students did, of course, take Scottish History; and other options open to the connoisseur were Ancient History, History of Art and Indian and Colonial History. The speciality chosen by David Horn, as by many of his contemporaries, was Economic History: the lecturer was J. F. (later Sir Frederick) Rees. Diversification had been provided by the 'outside subjects' taken in the first year (Horn took Latin and Maths), but the history subjects as such had an extraordinary concentration on the political, legal and constitutional affairs of England and on modern England at that.[2]

Staff-student relationships were virtually non-existent so far as the

[1] See Horn's own account in his review of *Sir Richard Lodge. A Biography by his Daughter, Margaret Lodge* (1946) in *Scottish Historical Review*, XXVII (1948), 77–85.

[2] It may be of interest to record the classes attended by David Horn in 1918–22.

Year I. Latin, Mathematics, British History (55 B.C.–A.D. 1688).

Year II. Economic History, British History honours (to 1660), Mackay Lectures (British History in the eighteenth and nineteenth centuries), Political Economy.

professor was concerned. David Horn recalled speaking to Lodge twice as an undergraduate: once he daringly rang him up prior to his freshman year to consult him as Dean; and once in his final year, after returning to the class after a fortnight of illness, Lodge asked him if he felt better. If Lodge was distant, often engaged on university matters, his lecturer, D. P. Heatley, was a tower of strength and it was to Heatley that Horn constantly returned when one got him to talk of his undergraduate days. Lodge was numinous, inspirational; but a student could take counsel with Heatley. Between them Heatley and Lodge did nine-tenths of the teaching. Tutorials (here Heatley was supported by an assistant) tended to be big and discussion limited. None of this, of course, stopped a student from working. Perhaps it even encouraged some of them to use the library.

David Horn worked all right; a string of class medals bore witness to that. In 1922 he got a first. At this point Lodge invited him to tea, urged him to do research, promised him a job in a year or two either at Edinburgh or elsewhere. The young man had the Kirkpatrick Prize Scholarship (which still rewards the virtuous) and off he went with his £75 to master the resources of the B.M. and the P.R.O. Lodge also produced a subject – Charles Hanbury Williams, with an edition of his poetry.

A year later Horn was back in Edinburgh as an assistant in the History department. In those days the job of an assistant was precarious, normally lasting for three or four years. The stipend of £250 p.a. was not out of step with other British universities which at that time also often had assistant lecturers without security. In the event David Horn's promotion to lecturer came promptly enough in 1927. It went through not, however, under Lodge (who retired in 1925) but under his successor, Basil Williams.

Sir Charles Hanbury Williams and European Diplomacy was published in 1930.[3] It was to be followed by a number of other works, including the Camden volume, *British Diplomatic Representatives 1689–1789*, in 1932.

Year III. Political Science (including Elementary Politics), Economic History honours, Constitutional Law and History.

Year IV. Constitutional History honours, European History honours (1715–1815). The final examination consisted of Political Science, British History (55 B.C.–A.D. 1837, two papers), Constitutional History (three papers divided at 1399 and 1688), European History (1715–1815, two papers), Economic History (two papers).

[3] It was not Horn's first book. *A History of Europe 1871–1920* came out in 1927. In what follows I make no attempt at a proper bibliographical record, which is provided elsewhere in this volume.

While this research was being prosecuted, changes gradually came in the department. Williams (whose experience of academic work was confined to holding a chair at McGill from 1921 to 1925) was an admirer of tutorials, sitting in on some of those of his junior colleagues to ensure that they met his high standards. This offended some of them, but David Horn passed with flying colours with a discussion (in a first year tutorial) about King Alfred. Tutorial instruction was to be the main part of Horn's job for the next thirty years. (He reckoned that in the pre-war period he was teaching about a dozen hours a week through the year.) Williams also introduced European history as such. A new survey course of European history made its appearance, and Horn and Balfour-Melville jointly mounted an honours course in European history (1815–1914). In due course medieval history appeared; this did not affect Horn, despite his competence with Alfred. Medieval history was even represented by Williams's successor in the Chair, V. H. Galbraith. But then the war came and changes stopped. Horn, who had already for long been a director of studies, was loaded with fresh responsibilities (including teaching Air Force law and administration to cadets in the R.A.F.). In the last year of the war Galbraith was followed by B. H. Sumner. And with the peace Sumner was followed by Richard Pares and the heavy teaching commitments of the post-war bulge.

With his interest in eighteenth-century and English history, Pares represented something of a return to the Lodge tradition. But in all other respects his tenure of the Chair involved innovations. By this time, with the rapid turnover of professors, Horn and Balfour-Melville were the anchors of the department. As director of studies David Horn was the one man all students met, for multiplying choices and a growing department eroded earlier coherences. Horn was now given the chance to teach his main interest and his special subject, the Diplomatic Revolution, was steadily followed by a large number of final year students. The fresh concentration of his efforts on Georgian England and its foreign policy was to be reflected in his two substantial works: *The British Diplomatic Service 1689–1789* (1961) and *Great Britain and Europe in the Eighteenth Century* (1967).

Richard Pares went back to Oxford in 1954, at the very moment when the University had decided to divide the Chair into two – medieval and modern. David Horn was appointed to the modern chair. The ordinance creating the chair of Modern History was some months in moving through its due constitutional stages and during that interval he was—as his predecessors had been—Professor of History *simpliciter*. Lodge's pupil had Lodge's title. Lodge would have been very pleased.[4] The next fifteen years were to see even more radical changes in the department: more staff, more specialities, more subdivisions and greater variety of all kinds. In this prolonged upheaval David Horn collaborated and counselled wisely. One of the penalties of having been in an institution a long time is that it loads one with experiences often unwelcome to newcomers. It is all too easy to say, of some new proposal, 'We tried that out ten (or twenty) years ago, and it didn't work'. One of David Horn's nicest characteristics was that he did not do this. He was prevented, I believe, because of his disposition, with its inbuilt courtesy; he had an alarming propensity to think other people were as courteous as himself. His gentle nature led him to avoid pomposity and dogmatism. And so did his history. Despite that early flirtation with Chemistry, he was a historian to the marrow. Historians are relativists. By understanding the past they become understanding, or at any rate some of them do. Those of us who worked (as I did) with David Horn for a long time should, I suppose, have learned never to be astonished, as we sometimes were, by the extent of his generosity, his loyalty and his compassion.

In very recent years he acquired a new interest and purpose: the history of Edinburgh University. Again (like Chemistry being defeated by British History) he used to say it was all accidental. Is this another case of events dictating the obvious? The corner of the Old College, Robert Adam's building which began to go up in 1790 to replace the seventeenth-century ranges of the University, was the home of the History department until 1967. The stones and mortar of the old University clothed him for forty years. He was predestined to become its historian.

Horn's pupils are now to be numbered in thousands. They are doing all manner of jobs though I suppose the two biggest identifiable groups are civil servants and teachers. They are all over the world, and some (as will be evident from this volume) are in the world of learning. I have always had a suspicion that collections of essays dedicated to a scholar are usually inspired by his own institution, by the disciples on the door step, so to

[4] He called Horn 'one of the most brilliant of my honours students', in his essay on 'History in Scottish Universities', *University of Edinburgh Journal*, IV (1930–31), 107.

speak. This was not the case with the collection of essays which follows. The prime movers were Professor Ragnhild Hatton and Dr Matthew Anderson and we owe to their enterprise and energy a book which, like David Horn himself, is quite remarkably coherent, and which demonstrates the significant place he had attained among scholars of modern diplomatic history.

* * *

The account I had originally written was with the printer, along with the other contributions to this volume, when David Horn died, after a very short illness, on 7 August 1969. I have revised miserably into the past tense. His friends will remember him always and will wish me here to record their affectionate sympathy for David's widow and his two daughters.

2

JAMES N. M. MACLEAN

Montrose's Preparations for the Invasion of Scotland, and Royalist Missions to Sweden, 1649–1651

The Deeds of Montrose[1] is the only work which has attempted to give a full account of the last two years in the life of James Graham, Marquess of Montrose. Unfortunately it not only contains numerous errors of fact and interpretation, but also gives the impression that the failure of his last expedition was due to haphazard preparations. This is not true. In spite of many frustrations Montrose tried to carry through a planned invasion of Scotland. Indeed, in the years 1649 and 1650, he was probably the only leading royalist who came to terms with his exiled king's poverty, or had enough skill to raise the men, arms, food, ships, and above all, money, for an expedition of any sort. He needed a hard core of seasoned soldiers to stiffen the untrained troops he hoped to raise after landing in Scotland, and he planned to recruit this major force from the large number of mercenaries (mostly Scots) who had been discharged throughout Europe at the end of the Thirty Years War.[2] For arms, supplies, and money, he counted upon help from European rulers.

The most important of these proved to be Queen Christina of Sweden, not only because Gothenburg on the western seaboard of her country offered the best point for coordinating a landing in the Orkneys (where royalist sympathies were strong), but because envoys persuaded her to supply arms and ammunition through a Scottish merchant in Gothenburg

[1] George Wishart, *The Memoirs of James, Marquis of Montrose: 1639–1650*, ed. A. D. Murdoch and H. F. Morland Simpson (London, 1893) (commonly called *Deeds of Montrose*). Although some of the documents in this work provide valuable evidence, many have been transcribed inaccurately. Confusion is increased by the muddled use of Old and New Style dates. In this article all dates accord with the New Style calendar. Most have been fixed by direct evidence; a few have been determined by discovering the usage of correspondents.

[2] *Ibid.*, pp. 195 and 263.

called Johan Macklier, whose real name was John Maclean.[3] The help which Montrose eventually received in Sweden was, however, largely due to the foundations laid by the Earl of Brentford,[4] who received his instructions to negotiate with Christina on the eve of Charles I's execution from the latter's heir, Charles II, then at The Hague.

Brentford was ordered on 29 January 1649 to go to Sweden and to obtain from Christina 'foot and horse, armes of all kindes, and some good quantity of pouder', and to negotiate for 'the sending of some good quantity of corne into Ireland'.[5] He was also told to use the services of Sir William Bellenden,[6] the royalist resident in Stockholm. By 17 March Brentford was able to tell Charles II that he had 'a promise of arms and ammunition, which must not appear to be sent immediately from the Queen'. This set the tone of all future dealings with Christina. She was willing to help Charles, but discreetly. The United Netherlands and Denmark were about to conclude a treaty regulating trade through the Sound, which could hurt Swedish commerce. Christina had, therefore, no intention of turning republican England, with its powerful navy, from a potential ally into a resentful or obstructive neutral by openly siding with the royalists. Brentford told Charles that Christina's ministers thought that his best hope was 'to adhere to the Scots'.[7]

[3] Sir John Maclean *alias* Johan Macklier (*c.* 1599–1666); cr. 1st Adlad Macklier by Christina (1649), and 1st (English) Baronet of Dowart by Charles II (1650). He was the youngest son of Hector Maclean of Dowart, feudal baron of Dowart in Mull. A former naval officer, he settled in Gothenburg in 1629 as the partner of a fellow Scot known as Jacob Makler (i.e. James the Merchant), later Jacob Macklier, whose name he adopted. He held various political offices between 1632 and 1650. By 1635 he had his own shipyard, sail-making factory, and fleet of ships, and was acting as banker to the Swedish crown. By 1645 he was the richest merchant in Sweden, and an arms dealer on a grand scale. When he died he owned the estates of Gåsevadholm, Hageby, Hammerö, Särö, and Fröllinge. His youngest son, Baron David Maclean (1646–1708), was created a Friherre.

[4] Sir Patrick Ruthven (*c.* 1573–1651), later Lord Ruthven of Ettrick (1639), Earl of Forth (1642), and Earl of Brentford (1644). Joined Swedish army 1612; cr. Graf von Kirchberg and Major-General 1632; left Sweden and apptd. Muster-Master General of Scotland 1637; Governor of Edinburgh Castle 1639; Field Marshal 1642; Lord Chamberlain 1648; P.C. 1649.

[5] *Ruthven Correspondence*. ed. William D. Macray (London, 1868), pp. 97–9, from Bod. Lib., Rawlinson MSS. 148 fos. 58r–v.

[6] Sir William Bellenden (*c.* 1604–71), later (1661) Lord Bellenden of Broughton, Edinburgh.

[7] H.M.C., *Pepys MSS.*, ed. E. K. Purnell (London, 1911) p. 292.

Commissioners representing the Estates of Scotland and the General Assembly of the Kirk arrived at The Hague in March to offer Charles their full support, if he would accept the Solemn League and Covenant, which bound all its supporters to the exclusive establishment of the Presbyterian system. Charles's mother, Henrietta Maria, and her Catholic friends, were naturally opposed to the Covenanters' demand and supported the Marquess of Ormonde, the Lord Lieutenant of Ireland. Montrose, who detested the Marquess of Argyll, the most powerful Covenanter of all, was sure that Charles could frighten the Covenanters into abandoning their exclusive stand by invading Scotland with a truly royalist army. On this occasion Charles rejected the Covenanters' offer and gave Ormonde and Montrose the impression that he relied upon them for success. On 4 May he told Ormonde that he hoped to start for Ireland in a few days; that he had ordered Brentford to send Ormonde 1000 horsemen's arms, 900 pistols, and a quantity of powder; and that Brentford had already prevailed on several Swedish merchants to send ships laden with corn to Ireland, one of which would bring the arms.[8] As Charles had already promised to go to Scotland a few days earlier, and went to neither Ireland nor Scotland in 1649, he was guilty of duplicity; but his wish to support Ormonde was genuine. He had also endorsed Montrose's plans.

In March Charles had given Montrose the title of Lieutenant-Governor of Scotland.[9] In the same month Montrose had secured nearly £10,000 for his campaign from Corfitz Ulfeld, the Lord Chamberlain of Denmark, who was in The Hague negotiating the Sound Treaty.[10] In April Montrose was commissioned to treat with 'Northern Kings and States'. In May the king's secretary, Robert Long, gave Montrose a *general* commission from Charles 'to treat for foreign levies and supplies of all natures, and to transport and conduct them accordingly'; and a *special* commission to deal by 'letters and trusts' with the rulers of Denmark, Holstein, Brandenburg, Lüneburg, Brunswick, Oldenburg, Friesland, Hesse, and Saxony; with the towns of Hamburg, Emden, Lübeck, and 'the Swedish

[8] *Ibid.*, pp. 253 and xxix.

[9] *Deeds of Montrose*, p. 230, n. 10.

[10] *Ibid.*, p. 260, n. 46. This loan later caused Ulfeld great trouble with King Frederick of Denmark. Charles II denied the debt. Ulfeld was charged with embezzlement and imprisoned, but escaped to Sweden, where he vindicated himself by producing Montrose's receipts. See also *The Nicholas Papers*, ed. Sir George F. Warner (London, 1892) II, 73–6.

Council in Stettin'; and 'with those who command the Swedish forces in Low Germany and Holstein'. In the memoranda requesting these commissions, Montrose said that he wanted Sweden 'to be powerfully dealt with at this conjuncture', a point he stressed by sending a Lt. Col. Montgomery there immediately as his personal agent, with a royal pass from Long.[11]

Montrose also told Long to supply extra credentials to Major-General Johan Adam von Karphen, a Hessian serving as the principal royalist envoy to the German states, who was supported in his mission by Montrose's illegitimate half-brother, Sir Henry Graham.[12] At the end of May a tough but devious colonel named Sir John Cochrane,[13] who had served Charles I in Denmark, Poland, Courland, and Danzig, was confirmed as Charles II's ambassador to those places, and given the additional job of obtaining support from Hamburg. Von Karphen and Graham were fully covered by Montrose's commissions, and Cochrane was partly covered not only by his orders relating to Hamburg, but also by a letter which Charles sent on 3 June to King Frederick of Denmark 'accrediting the Marquis of Montrose, whom he had appointed commander-in-chief of all forces that can be raised'.[14] On 16 June Sir Patrick Drummond was commissioned to act as treasurer to Montrose. Two days later a Captain William Swan received a letter of introduction to the Duke of Saxony (a ruler covered by Montrose's commission) and special instructions to persuade the Emperor Ferdinand III to engage the German princes 'in aiding the king with supplies of men, arms, and money'.[15] Finally, on 6 July at Brussels, Charles invested Montrose with wide powers by appointing him 'Ambassador-Extraordinary to Foreign Princes'.[16]

The following day Charles and Montrose parted company. It was the

[11] H.M.C., *Pepys MSS.*, pp. 253, n. 1, 254, 257, 258.

[12] *Ibid.*, pp. 253–5. For Von Karphen's retrospective reports see *Charles II and Scotland in 1650*, ed. Samuel R. Gardiner (Edinburgh, 1894) pp. 92–4.

[13] Sir John Cochrane (*c.* 1604–*c.* 1657), elder brother of William Cochrane, 1st Earl of Dundonald, to whom he resigned his Scottish estates in 1642. He married Grace Butler, cousin of the Marquess of Ormonde, and had one daughter, Catherine, who married Colonel Jacob Maclean (1632–63), the eldest son of Sir John Maclean *alias* Johan Macklier. For Cochrane's commissions and reports see *Miscellany of the Scottish History Society* I (Edinburgh, 1893), 169–212.

[14] *Deeds of Montrose*, p. 250, n. 5.

[15] H.M.C., *Pepys MSS.*, pp. 278 and 288.

[16] *Deeds of Montrose*, p. 251, n. 13.

last time they saw each other. Charles went south to Paris, and Montrose went back to The Hague, where he found Brentford, who had just returned from Sweden. The last dispatch which Brentford had received from Long was probably that dated 2 May, which proposed that a Lt. Col. Dicks should be sent to Sweden to arrange for the shipment of arms to Ormonde in Ireland.[17] Dicks never made these arrangements; and the arms were still not available by the time Brentford reached The Hague in early July.[18] They were originally intended for Ormonde's sole use; but Montrose now wanted a voice in their allocation, and Secretary Long in Paris was asked to send new instructions[19] to Brentford, who continued to have charge of Swedish affairs. On 28 July Long drew up these instructions (confirmed as orders on 2 August[20]) which empowered Brentford to inform Macklier in Gothenburg that all the arms he collected were to be equally divided between Ormonde and Montrose.

So far, Montrose's plans had evolved quite smoothly. From August 1649 onwards, however, he began to meet setbacks. In early July, following a visit from Graham and Von Karphen, the Elector of Brandenburg had promised to lend about £2250 to Montrose, who tried to secure the money for immediate use by writing for it later the same month.[21] In early August Montrose received an apologetic letter from the Elector who, for undisclosed reasons, had changed his mind about the loan.[22] The lack of these promised funds undoubtedly delayed the departure for the Orkneys of Montrose's advance detachment under the Earl of Kinnoul, whose task during the winter of 1649–50 was to establish a strong base there for the major force, which Montrose hoped to have in position by the early spring of 1650. Without the Brandenburg money Montrose was forced to spend the whole of August 1649 in the Netherlands scraping together[23]

[17] H.M.C., *Pepys MSS.*, p. 302.

[18] *Ruthven Correspondence*, pp. 111–13.

[19] H.M.C., *Pepys MSS.*, p. 260.

[20] *Charles II and Scotland in 1650*, p. 125.

[21] *Deeds of Montrose*, p. 252 (and n. 19), and p. 506.

[22] *Ibid.*, pp. 252 and 507. By July Montrose had already distributed Ulfeld's loan, and was without money.

[23] Montrose obtained the money for paying Kinnoul's men, and the ship for transporting them, from Capt. John Griffith with the help of John Poliander van Kirckhoven, Baron van Heenvliet. Griffith tried to recover 800 guilders advanced by Heenvliet from Secretary Long on 17 August 1649. See H.M.C., *Pepys MSS.*, pp. 286, 304.

the basic needs for Kinnoul's men, instead of moving on at the beginning of that month to meet Cochrane in Hamburg. When Kinnoul and his 180 mercenaries sailed from Amsterdam at the end of August they went not, as hoped, in a first-class warship but (to quote John Gwynne, the ship's captain) in 'an old one, new vamp't, without a gun'.[24]

The problem of inadequate finance and delayed supplies was also worrying Brentford, who had now joined Charles in Paris. On 30 August he ordered Macklier to send Ormonde's share of the arms to Ireland immediately[25] and, if lack of money was delaying shipment, to draw upon Brentford's own small resources[26] in Sweden, or call upon Christina's aid through Lord Eythin[27] or Sir William Bellenden. By the time Macklier received the letter further delays were inevitable. Bellenden was in Stockholm but on the point of leaving for Paris, while Eythin, who lived near Stockholm, was away in Hamburg, probably waiting to see Montrose. No evidence has been found to prove that they met in Hamburg; but as Montrose eventually chose Eythin as the leader of his second invasion force (which was supposed to land in the Orkneys after the major force had established itself there), it is reasonable to assume that they began making their plans at this time. Eythin was certainly in Hamburg when Montrose arrived there in early September from Amsterdam, where he had left Colonel John Ogilvie as his personal agent.[28]

In Hamburg Montrose met Sir John Cochrane, who had been expecting him since 10 August and was impatient to proceed on his own mission to Courland and Poland.[29] Cochrane had been pestering the Hamburg Senate to recognize Charles as lawful king of England, and to reject the rival claim of a large number of resident English merchants, who wanted

[24] John Gwynne, *Memoirs*, ed. Sir Walter Scott (Edinburgh, 1822) pp. 83–5.

[25] *Ruthven Correspondence*, p. 113.

[26] In 1649 Brentford tried to obtain funds for the royalists by petitioning Christina and her cousin, the Pfalzgraf Carl Gustaf, for money they owed him for past services: R.A., Oxenstierna MSS. In a superficial account of these pleas, Brentford has been libelled as a greedy man: see Thomas Alfred (*alias* Ernst Ludwig) Fischer, *The Scots in Sweden*, ed. John Kirkpatrick (Edinburgh, 1907) pp. 116–17.

[27] Sir James King (1589–1652), later (1642) Lord Eythin, the son of David King of Warbester Hoy in the Orkneys. Joined Swedish army 1614. Retired as Lt. General 1637. His nephew, Colonel David Sinclair of Finnekumla, married (1651) Catherina (1631–1709), daughter of Sir John Maclean *alias* Johan Macklier.

[28] *Deeds of Montrose*, p. 270, n. 74.

[29] *Misc. Scot. Hist. Soc.* 1, 175; and *Charles II and Scotland in 1650*, p. 125.

recognition of the republican government in London. Although the senators had tried to remain neutral, Cochrane had managed to persuade them to acknowledge him as an accredited diplomat. He had then embarrassed the senators by organizing violent physical assaults on English republicans who (unknown to Cochrane until it was too late) were supported by leading citizens of Hamburg.[30] These crude tactics had not only undermined his diplomatic status, but also the cause he represented. Montrose, therefore, must have regarded Cochrane with mixed feelings. Cochrane had good prospects of raising ships and supplies from the Duke of Courland for the Scottish invasion; but, by releasing him for this vital mission, Montrose himself was obliged to linger in Hamburg to restore the relationships which Cochrane had soured. Indeed, he had no way of avoiding this responsibility, because Charles sent him a belated commission[31] to compose all differences with Hamburg, and to treat for a loan, half of which (if obtained) Montrose could keep for his own campaign. As soon as it became clear that the Senate were going to procrastinate, Montrose saved further delays by sending Colonel Sir William Johnstone, Cochrane's deputy in Hamburg, to solicit a loan from the Duke of Brunswick.[32] By this time Montrose's lines of communication were stretched beyond his full control. Charles was in Jersey, but part of his court was in Paris and another part in The Hague; all wasting time writing to each other or indulging in factional quarrels before deciding on any policy which affected Montrose, who, in spite of delays in Amsterdam and Hamburg, was moving further away from them all each month. Being in transit also meant that it was very difficult for Montrose to keep in touch with his agents in Europe and Scotland[33] or his detachment under

[30] *Misc. Scot. Hist. Soc.* I, 175–87.

[31] *Deeds of Montrose*, p. 259.

[32] *Ibid.*, p. 259. A letter Johnstone wrote on 24 December 1649, when he returned to Hamburg, was included in Sir Edward Nicholas's report on Montrose dated 30 January 1650: see *The Duke of Ormonde's Papers*, ed. Thomas Carte (London, 1739) I, 347. This contains several probable exaggerations, and cannot be wholly trusted. Nicholas said that while in Brunswick, Celle, and Hanover, Johnstone had received 'all sorts of contentment', which can be interpreted as vague promises of help and nothing more.

[33] Two were caught. William Orde was captured in Kirriemuir in April 1649. Colonel William Sibbald was taken prisoner at Musselburgh in November 1649, and executed in June 1650. See Sir James Balfour, *Historical Works* (Edinburgh, 1824–25) III, 397–8; and IV, 22.

Kinnoul. By the beginning of October, when he moved from Hamburg to Denmark, he had not heard from Kinnoul's detachment, which had only just arrived in the Orkneys and had been unexpectedly joined there by Captain John Hall of Leith, who had defected with his frigate and a cargo of arms belonging to Argyll and the Covenanters.[34] Nor did Montrose know that Bellenden had arrived in Paris, and had received orders concerning his future as the resident in Stockholm on 29 September,[35] the day when Brentford's overall responsibilities for Swedish affairs were probably assumed by Lord Hatton.[36]

In Paris, Henrietta Maria and her Catholic court at the Louvre, together with Lord Hatton and Sir Edward Hyde, all supporters of Ormonde or Montrose or both, were opposing Lord Jermyn (who advocated a treaty between Charles and the Covenanters) and his alleged allies Secretary Long and Sir William Bellenden.[37] This discord was aggravated by the gossip of time-servers such as the Earl of Seaforth, who spread the rumour, later to cause Montrose anxiety, that the loyal Brentford, who retired to The Hague in early October, was plotting with the English republicans.[38] It was also Seaforth who probably insinuated that Montrose intended to take Charles with him on the Scottish expedition. This rumour was firmly rejected by Sir Edward Hyde on 30 September,[39] when he informed Sir Edward Nicholas, the king's secretary in Jersey, that he had drafted (for Hatton's approval) a set of instructions for Captain Robert Meade,[40] the new envoy to Sweden.

News of Meade's appointment probably did not reach Montrose while he was in Copenhagen, where he spent the whole of October and early November recruiting soldiers and arranging audiences with the King of

34 *Ibid.*, IV, 32–3; and *Deeds of Montrose*, pp. 256 and 257, n. 37.

35 H.M.C., *Pepys MSS.*, p. 306.

36 Christopher Hatton (1605–70), later (1643) Lord Hatton of Kirby, son of Sir Charles Hatton of Clay Hill, Essex. The draft of his plenipotentiary powers is dated 1649 without day or month: B.M. Add. MSS. 37047, fo. 33. In *Deeds of Montrose*, p. 271, n. 79, a brief note wrongly identifies him as Lauderdale's brother, who was Charles Maitland, Lord Hatton.

37 *Nicholas Papers* I, 147 and 149.

38 *Ibid.*, I, 151; and *Deeds of Montrose*, p. 262, n. 54.

39 *State Papers collected by Edward, Earl of Clarendon* (Oxford, 1786) III, 6.

40 Robert Meade (1616–53), son of Robert Meade, stationer of Fleet Street, London. After graduating M.A. at Christ Church, Oxford, in 1641, he qualified M.D. in 1646.

Denmark, the Council of Nobles, and the Duke of Holstein.[41] He did, however, learn of Jermyn's scheme for a treaty with the Covenanters which, if concluded before the invasion of Scotland, could destroy his whole conception of the purpose of the expedition. Speed, and Charles's unqualified support for the invasion, were all-important. On 29 October Montrose warned Charles: 'Delays are the worst of all evils. What your Majesty shall please to do will be doubled by being done soon. In such affairs a refusal that sets us free to act is better than a promise that ruins us.'[42] A few days later, in early November, Montrose tried to undermine the growing belief in such a treaty by publishing his famous *Declaration* against the Covenanters.[43] Then, without wasting any more time on negotiations with the cautious Danes, he left Copenhagen. Two days later, on 12 November, he arrived in Gothenburg, his headquarters for marshalling the invasion forces.[44] He had already made it clear that nothing must be done to compromise Christina.[45] In fact, although he had ambassadorial status, he never tried to see her.[46] During his whole stay in Sweden Montrose lived discreetly as the private guest of Macklier.[47]

A thousand miles away in Jersey, Charles had been joined by Secretary Long, who had brought from Paris the draft of Meade's instructions, which were confirmed as orders on 21 November.[48] Meade left for Sweden the same day; but his journey entailed several stops *en route*, and took very much longer than his superior Hatton anticipated.[49] Apart from telling Meade to acquaint Christina with the terms of the treaty offered by the Covenanters, Charles's main order was as follows:

> You shall take Gothenburg in your way, where now remains a

[41] *Deeds of Montrose*, pp. 260 and 264 (and n. 61).

[42] *Ibid.*, p. 264.

[43] *Ibid.*, pp. 267–9; *Declaration* printed in full.

[44] *Ibid.*, pp. 273 and 510–11.

[45] *Ibid.*, p. 266; Montrose's letter to an unidentified friend.

[46] *Misc. Scot. Hist. Soc.* I, 215.

[47] *Deeds of Montrose*, pp. 276 and 512.

[48] B.M., Egerton MS. 2542, fos. 17–18v.

[49] *Nicholas Papers* I, 157. On 24 December 1649 Hatton told Nicholas that Meade had just left Paris, after being delayed there by Henrietta Maria. On 15 January 1650 Hatton again wrote to Nicholas to say that Meade had reached The Hague, where he had found Bellenden 'doeing all the mischief he can' (*ibid.*, p. 163). Hatton also said: '[I] have in money and bills already advanced Capt. Meade two hundred pounds'; and that was all Meade ever received to cover the expenses of his important mission.

considerable quantity of Arms Ammunition and Cannon, which by the care and order of Our right trusty and right wellbeloved Cousin and Councillor the Earl of Brentford have been conveyed and transported from several parts unto the said Port of Gothenburg for Our use, and are now remaining in the hands of John Macklier, a Scottish Merchant, who has disbursed several sums of money for the charge of bringing the said Arms Ammunition and Cannon to that place. And whereas We have formerly sent Our orders to the said John Macklier for the delivering of one half of the said Arms Ammunition and Cannon to the Marquess of Montrose or to such person or persons as he should appoint to receive the same for Our Service; and for the delivering of the other full half of the said Arms Ammunition and Cannon unto such person or persons as the Marquess of Ormonde, Our Lieutenant General of the Kingdom of Ireland, should send to receive the same for Our Service in that Kingdom. . . . It is therefore Our pleasure that you repair first to Gothenburg and there deliver Our Letters to the said John Macklier, with such others as shall be written to him upon the occasion by Our said Cousin the Earl of Brentford, and that you examine and settle the Accompts of all moneys due to the said John Macklier for his disbursements concerning the said Arms, and use your utmost endeavours to prevail with him to hire a ship. . . . But if you cannot prevail with the said John Macklier nor any other at Gothenburg to hire a ship to transport the said Arms into Ireland, you shall then advise with the Lord Eythin and Sir William Bellenden, how by the assistance of the Queen or otherwise, money may be procured to hire a ship and pay the charges to the said Macklier.[50]

If Charles's orders were quoted in full, it would be evident that he still rested his hopes on Ormonde, the Covenanters, and Montrose, in that order. A competent leader would have cut his losses in Ireland; dismissed any thought of a treaty with the Covenanters until Montrose's expedition had succeeded or failed; and given priority to Montrose by committing every available resource to the invasion of Scotland. There were not enough arms, supplies or money for one campaign, let alone two. Montrose needed all Ormonde's allocation, but could not appropriate it without Charles's permission.

[50] B.M., Egerton MSS. 2542, fos. 17r–v.

Montrose was, however, lucky in having Macklier to help him; although nobody has ever asked why this wealthy Scot, who had settled permanently in Sweden and had been ennobled by Christina, risked his money and ships when powerful rulers throughout Europe were avoiding involvement in the royalist cause. The main reason was that Macklier, in common with Montrose, loathed the Marquess of Argyll and wished to see him destroyed.[51] Montrose probably never knew Macklier's real identity; but that did not matter. Macklier was trusted by Christina and her ministers, by Brentford and Eythin, and by a network of merchants, agents, and shippers. Christina could not afford to admit that aliens were organizing a military operation in her land, and Montrose was determined not to embarrass her by blatant activity, or by trying to recruit any officer serving in Sweden itself (including those of Scottish origin).[52] Macklier was the unofficial intermediary between Christina and Montrose; and all the relevant authorities in Sweden seemed to know this except Peder Ribbing, the officious Provincial Governor in Gothenburg, who tried to draw official attention to Montrose until he was tactfully dealt with by Count Lennart Torstensson, the Governor-General of Western Sweden.[53] Ribbing's fussy reports provide most of the information about

[51] John Maclean *alias* Johan Macklier was the youngest brother of Sir Lachlan Maclean of Dowart (cr. 1st (Nova Scotia) Baronet of Morvaren by Charles I in 1631), who was the only Maclean feudal baron to inherit a family debt to Argyll. In 1645 the five consanguineous but independent Maclean feudal barons (Dowart, Lochbuie, Kingairloch, Ardgour, and Coll) joined Montrose's unsuccessful campaign against Argyll, which increased Argyll's determination to crush the Macleans, especially Maclean of Dowart. By 1649, when Sir Lachlan died and was succeeded by his young and impoverished son Sir Hector, the family debt stood at £60,000 Scots and was still unpaid. Argyll was now ready to demand the entire Dowart estates in settlement of his claim; and Sir Hector's best hope of remaining an independent laird rested on the aid he could get, directly or indirectly, from his uncle John in Gothenburg. Few people knew that John Macklier was a Maclean; and neither friend nor foe seemed to suspect him of having strong personal motives for helping the royalists. By supporting Montrose he chose an indirect way of fighting for his family against Argyll. Events proved that he should have suffocated his hatred of Argyll and used the money he spent on the royalists to pay off his family's debts. This direct action might have prevented the lawsuit which eventually allowed the Argyll family to seize the Dowart lands. See my forthcoming publication: *The Macleans of Sweden*.

[52] In *Deeds of Montrose*, p. 283, the significance of a letter from Colonel John Gordon, a Scot in the Swedish army, to Montrose is completely misinterpreted.

[53] *Deeds of Montrose*, p. 513.

Montrose's movements in Gothenburg.[54] Other evidence helps to clarify how many ships and arms Montrose actually employed.

He faced great problems. He had to coordinate, pay, feed, arm, and transport to the Orkneys at least 1000 mercenaries, who had been recruited far from Gothenburg; but he had no wish to congregate all these men in any port while they were in transit, as this might have alerted enemy spies or have placed too great a strain on local food supplies. None the less, what he wished to avoid actually happened. The first ships to join his force were the 16-gun frigate of the defector Captain John Hall, and a 10-gun crayer belonging to Captain John Love, a Covenanter of Kirkwall, which had been captured by Hall and placed under the command of Captain John Anstruther.[55] Hall had left the Orkneys for Denmark in November to tell Montrose that Kinnoul, the commander of the advance detachment, had died.[56] Arriving in Denmark after Montrose's departure from that country, he picked up 200 mercenaries and arrived with them and Anstruther's crayer in Gothenburg in early December.[57] Although Montrose undoubtedly welcomed the unexpected addition of two Scottish ships to his force, his pleasure must have been clouded by the news of Kinnoul's death, and by the unplanned arrival of 200 men from a country on bad terms with Sweden. Indeed, these events probably caused him to act.

On 7 December Macklier, whose own ships were at sea but expected back shortly,[58] hired a merchantman belonging to Captain Hans Michelson of Gothenburg, and loaded it with a few arms which he scraped together from an undisclosed source.[59] Five days later Ribbing noted that the two Scottish ships (Hall and Anstruther) were ready to leave.[60] On 15 December

[54] *Ibid.*, pp. 510–15, the letter of Ribbing, Torstensson, and Anckarhielm printed (with errors) in Swedish. The present writer has checked them against the originals in Riksarkivet.

[55] *Ibid.*, p. 294. The editors wrongly imply that Love's crayer returned to the Orkneys. For correct details see Balfour, *Historical Works*, IV, 36 and 41.

[56] *Deeds of Montrose*, pp. 256 and 276.

[57] *Ibid.*, p. 511.

[58] S.R.O., Montrose Muniments, G.D. 220/6/Misc.Acc./ (Temp.) Box 1. A list of ships wholly or partly owned by Macklier which were trading abroad on 9 December 1649.

[59] *Ibid.*, orders from Macklier to Michelson, dated 6 January 1650, showing days on which arms were loaded.

[60] *Deeds of Montrose*, p. 511.

Montrose himself confirmed (in a letter to Seaforth)[61] that he was on the point of sailing for the Orkneys; but somebody or something (and certainly not the weather at this juncture) changed his mind, and he and the ships stayed in Gothenburg. It was also on 15 December that Matthias Römer, the Dutch Commissary in Stockholm, told his superior: 'It is reported by letter from Gottenburg that another ship has arrived with soldiers from Stralsund, and that Montrose has a crayer lying there with people to send to his king.'[62] This implies that an earlier ship 'with soldiers from Stralsund' had already arrived in Gothenburg. A third ship, which had also probably started from Stralsund, sailed with five companies (about 200 men) under the command of Major David Guthrie on 14 December, and passed through the Sound to join Montrose.[63] It would seem, therefore, that the Duke of Holstein had kept a promise to let Montrose have three ships,[64] and that these had been hurried through the Sound before the treaty affecting that waterway came into operation on 1 January 1650. If each of the Straslund ships contained five companies, then 600 men arrived in Gothenburg in December in addition to the 200 men who came with Hall: a total of 800. Such a large number of aliens could not be tolerated on Swedish soil; and from what occurred later it is almost certain that the three Stralsund ships, and nearly all of the mercenaries, were sent to Marstrand at the mouth of the River Göta, which was inside Norway and under Danish rule.

On 26 December Admiral Mårten Thyssen-Anckarhielm, the Dutch-born commander of the Swedish navy in Gothenburg, reported that the two Scottish ships (Hall and Anstruther) and the hired Gothenburg merchantman (Michelson) had moved upstream to Billinge, and that the Swedish frigate *Herderinnan*, with two months' supplies for fifty men, had been sold to Montrose and would be handed over to Macklier at Billinge on the following day.[65] At the same time Macklier convinced Governor Ribbing that he had Christina's authority to take delivery of the long-awaited consignment of arms which he had purchased from the Swedish crown; and these were also handed over to him by Anckarhielm.[66] Before

[61] *Ibid.*, p. 274.
[62] *Misc. Scot. Hist. Soc.* I, 215.
[63] *The Duke of Ormonde's Papers* I, 347.
[64] *Deeds of Montrose*, pp. 262–3.
[65] *Ibid.*, p. 511.
[66] *Ibid.*, p. 512; and B.M., Egerton MS. 2542, fos. 19r–v.

the end of December the Danish Viceroy of Norway, Hannibal Sehested,[67] met one of Macklier's trading associates named Ivar Krabbe in Bohus, which, like Marstrand, was close to Gothenburg but inside Norway. These talks were immediately followed, according to Ribbing, by Krabbe visiting Gothenburg for a secret meeting with Montrose.[68] Once again promises made to Montrose in Denmark seem to have borne fruit; and through Sehested and Krabbe he was probably able to arrange food supplies for the mercenaries at Marstrand. On 1 January Ribbing reported that Lord Eythin[69] was expected in Gothenburg, probably to discuss the plans for the second invasion force. By the end of the week, most of Montrose's officers, including Sir Henry Graham, Sir William Johnstone, Captain William Swan, and the new Earl of Kinnoul, had arrived in Gothenburg, the first three having concluded their missions to various German states without success.

On 6 January Macklier finished loading Michelson's merchantman and the *Herderinnan* with Montrose's share of the arms; but the wind dropped and sailing became impossible.[70] On 14 January the weather improved, and Michelson with the arms, and Hall with 200 mercenaries (under the command of the new Earl of Kinnoul) and a crew made up of men captured in the crayer, left Billinge. At Marstrand they probably joined the three Stralsund ships; and together they all sailed in convoy for the Orkneys.[71] The *Herderinnan* (commanded by Captain Walter Strachan) and the crayer (with John Anstruther still in command) remained in Gothenburg, and so did Montrose.[72] Within a few days the temperature fell rapidly, and all shipping from Billinge to the mouth of the Göta was trapped in ice.[73]

[67] Hannibal Sehested later fell into disgrace with King Frederick of Denmark and was forced, like his fellow-countryman Corfitz Ulfeld, to seek asylum in Sweden: see *The Nicholas Papers* II, p. 239 and *passim*. The fact that Montrose was helped by two powerful Danes who fell from favour after his death may or may not be significant.

[68] *Deeds of Montrose*, pp. 512–13.

[69] *Ibid.*, p. 282, repeats a printer's error in *The Duke of Ormonde's Papers* I, 351 and gives Ruthven (i.e. Brentford) instead of Eythin for 'Rythin'.

[70] S.R.O., Montrose Muniments, G.D.220/6/Misc.Acc./(Temp.) Box 1.

[71] *Charles II and Scotland in 1650*, p. 10: this reprints a report in *A Brief Relation*, the English republican newspaper, from a letter sent by a spy in Bremen, whose reports were usually reliable.

[72] *Deeds of Montrose*, pp. 277, and 512–13.

[73] *Charles II and Scotland in 1650*, p. 5: this reprints a report in *A Brief Encounter*,

Severe weather conditions had also hampered Robert Meade, the long-awaited envoy. In a letter he sent Secretary Long on 13 February, the day he arrived in Gothenburg, he first explained all the reasons for his delays, and then said:

I met with *Sir William Bellenden* at the Hague and gave him your Letter, but he seemed not very well satisfied. . . . I met *the Earl of Brentford* in *Holland*—also gave him your Letters, but he expected *the King* should have been pleased to write to him, which I must confess I am sorry was not done. He wrote by me to the Merchant here [Macklier], who is, without doubt, a man most *zealous* in *the King's affairs* and seems not to me to be troubled so much *about the money which he has* disbursed. *About the arms:* as how to employ them best *for the King's Service.* To send them *from Gothenburg to the Marquess of Ormonde* I consider it almost impossible; for *ships*-men [seamen] of *Sweden are* generally very unskilful and no less fearful, especially of venturing for Ireland. *The Merchant* here [Macklier] *could* hardly persuade to get *Montrose's ship* manned, *though this employment* would be nothing in comparison *to that.* Insomuch [So much so], that he desires *Montrose* may have orders to send for them *to Scotland*, from whence *Montrose* himself tells me he will dispose of them as *His Majesty* shall think fit. He is now *in his ship* ready *for Scotland, awaiting the fine* wind. *He has been* aboard these five days. *His share of the arms is* sent before, and considered to be safely arrived. *He* with great impatience *lacks* a good wind himself. The charges upon *the arms* and other necessary disbursements for *the King's Service are about three thousand five hundred pounds. . . .*

I am confident *Sir John Cochrane* has given you a better account of his *business* than I am able to glean up by reports. *His Lady* is very active at Hamburg. I found most *Merchants* there will not refuse *Cochrane.* It would [be] very requisite [if] *the Merchant* here [Macklier] were encouraged in all ways, *for* he has behaved himself very nobly in the *King's business* and continues most *zealous in it.* I am advancing tomorrow towards *Stockholm*, but it will be ten days before I shall get there, by reason of the unseasonableness of the weather. I shall then report further orders from you concerning *the arms* which, I beseech you, may

---

from a spy in Stockholm, who garbled a story he had heard about Montrose's difficulties with the ice.

be despatched with all speed through *Sir Richard Browne* or *Sir William Boswell's* hands.[74]

Meade arrived in Stockholm[75] ten days after he sent this important letter, in which he explained why Macklier had been unable to send any arms to Ormonde although pressed to do so by Brentford since mid-1649. Firstly, they had not been released to him by the Swedish crown until late December; but secondly, and more important, he had not been able to persuade Swedish seamen to risk capture by the English republican navy on the voyage to Ireland. Michelson was the only Swedish captain involved in a royalist operation, but he had been hired for the less dangerous run to the Orkneys. The rest of the captains were Scots; and they were desperately short of seamen. Hall had manned his own frigate with the Scots he had captured in the crayer.[76] He had taken this chance so that he could leave his own loyal crew behind in Gothenburg to form skeleton complements for three ships expected from Courland, which Cochrane had requested from the Duke as transporters for the second invasion force under Eythin. This arrangement is referred to in a letter which Macklier sent on 23 February to Montrose on board his frigate *Herderinnan*, which had freed itself of the ice at Billinge and was lying off the mouth of the Göta, waiting for a favourable wind. Macklier wrote:

> ... The Stockholm's post is not come as yet. Receiving any further news before your Excellency's departure [I] shall not omit [to] give your Excellency notice thereof. William Davidson [the Duke of Courland's factor in Danzig] assures me that Colonel Ogilvie

[74] B.M. Add. MSS. 37047, fos. 58–9. (The words given in numeral code have been decyphered and shown in italics.) Sir Richard Browne was the royalist resident in Paris, and Sir William Boswell, who was dead before Meade reached Sweden, had been the royalist ambassador at The Hague.

[75] In Stockholm, on 25 February 1650, Meade gave Christina a Letter of Proposals from Charles. The Latin original is printed in full in *Deeds of Montrose*, pp. 509–10; and the English translation is printed in *Calendar of State Papers, Domestic: 1650*, p. 610. In clause 5 Christina was asked to relieve Macklier of all tax burdens on goods for the royalists.

[76] After Montrose's defeat Hall and Sir Henry Graham escaped from the Orkneys; but on reaching Norway the crew, who had resented their enforced service under Hall and Anstruther, mutinied. Hall and Graham were left in Norway, and the frigate was brought to Leith by Simon Vanderson of Pittenweem, who, on 11 June 1650, was awarded the ship and its contents as a prize of war. See Balfour, *Historical Works* IV, 32–3, 36 and 53.

[Montrose's agent in Amsterdam] will get most of Captain Hall's men, but it will cost him great charges for entertaining them until the ships be ready. So far [as] I can learn by Mr Davidson's letter, it will be the end of this month before the ships be clear. Herewith he recommends your Excellency into the protection of the omnipotent God. Remaining your Excellency's

Most humble servant,

JOHN MACKLIER

At Gothenburg the 13/23 February 1650

[Postscript] I send here Colonel Ogilvie's letter, together with the advises. We have had a hard storm here last night and [for a] while this midday. [? While] the wind is [? shifting] easterly [one] hopes in God it will continue to further your Excellency's voyage. The great God prosper and preserve your Excellency, granting your Excellency a safe arrival, which shall be the faithful prayer of your Excellency's most humble servant. I have received notice from Stockholm concerning petards, shot pieces and handgrenades. Expecting presently from your Excellency a happy arrival confirming all matters. Thereafter [I] shall regulate myself and use uttermost endeavour in performing all concern[ing] your Excellency's orders. It will be very requisite [if] your Excellency let[s] Captain Strachan [master of the *Herderinnan*] make trial for some good expert mariners for transporting the 3 ships as yet expected from the Duke of Courland, which I conjecture will be in the end of April before they come here, in which time [one] hopes there will ever pass frigates between [us] for notice of all affairs. I hope we shall have firemen [artillerymen] and what else your Excellency stands in need of, ready against that time; I receiving timely notice thereof for preparing.[77]

On this evidence it would seem that Hall's own men were sent to Amsterdam to await the delivery there of three Courland ships, which were expected to be clear of the Baltic ice by the end of February. In Amsterdam the Courland ships would be taken over by skeleton crews

[77] N.L.S., Wodrow MSS. vol. 67, fos. 172r–v. No alterations have been made, except to modernize spelling and extend abbreviations. Macklier scratched out the N.S. date 23 Febr. and substituted 13 to conform with Montrose's O.S. usage. The version of this letter in *Deeds of Montrose*, pp. 284–5, is so inaccurate that it is not worth consulting. I am grateful to Professor Gordon Donaldson for checking the version given here.

made up of Hall's men, and brought to Gothenburg or Marstrand, where extra seamen recruited by Captain Strachan would bring each of the ship's complements up to full strength. Macklier estimated that this would take until the end of April, when the ships were expected to arrive in Gothenburg having, in all probability, picked up in Amsterdam, Bremen, and other ports, the various detachments of mercenaries who had been enlisted for Eythin's second invasion force. Some of these mercenaries had probably been recruited by Montrose on his journey north between July and November 1649;[78] the rest had certainly been raised by Von Karphen as a Corps of High Germans and the King's German Guards.[79] By the end of April 1650, if all had gone well in Scotland, Macklier hoped to receive timely orders from Montrose to despatch Eythin's invasion force in the three Courland ships.

Montrose acted on Macklier's advice to use Strachan for recruiting seamen. On 28 February Ribbing reported that the *Herderinnan* had sailed for Marstrand without Montrose, who had returned briefly to Gothenburg and then travelled overland to Bergen in Norway.[80] This gave Strachan the chance to recruit extra seamen for the Courland ships at Marstrand before going on to Bergen to pick up Montrose and a small detachment of about fifty mercenaries recruited there by Colonel Thomas Gray.[81] From Bergen Montrose sailed in the *Herderinnan* to Kirkwall in the Orkneys, where he arrived at the end of March 1650. On 2 April a royal messenger named Henry May landed in Kirkwall.[82] The letter which Montrose had sent from Denmark on 29 October 1649 asking for the king's wholehearted support had produced results. Henry May had left Jersey on 22 January 1650, and it was he who brought Charles's reply of the same date. Charles was unequivocal: 'Proceed', he told Montrose,

[78] *Charles II and Scotland in 1650*, p. 9. On 12 February 1650 the republican spy in Bremen reported that a Colonel Taylor had sold, on Montrose's orders, a consignment of arms 'which were begged off the Dane in the Sound' for 3000 Riksdalers (£750), and had brought this money to Bremen to pay 10 Riksdalers to each of the mercenaries still waiting there for Montrose's orders. In short: there were about 300 mercenaries in Bremen waiting to go to Scotland. The suggestion that the mercenaries had been paid from the sale of arms sounds false.

[79] *Ibid.*, p. 93. By May 1650 the units raised by Von Karphen had been waiting for nearly a year on the Continent for orders to join Montrose in Scotland.

[80] *Ibid.*, pp. 35 and 42; and *Deeds of Montrose*, p. 515.

[81] *Ibid.*, pp. 493–4.

[82] *Charles II and Scotland in 1650*, pp. 42–3.

'in your business with your usual courage and alacrity; which I am sure will bring great advantage to my affairs, and much honour to yourself. I wish you all good success in it.'[83] Heartened by these long overdue assurances, Montrose thanked his king[84] and prepared for battle.

Estimates of how well Montrose was equipped for that fight have varied considerably. The major aim of Brentford and Meade's missions had been to secure Swedish arms for Ormonde and Montrose, and now, for the first time, it is possible to give the exact number of arms allocated to Montrose, and the quantities left in Macklier's hands in Gothenburg.[85]

[83] *Deeds of Montrose*, p. 279.

[84] *Charles II and Scotland in 1650*, pp. 42–3.

[85] Equivalent weights have been shown in square brackets. All other weights are those given in original documents. The standard weights used for mid-seventeenth-century cargoes were as follows:

1 Last = 2 Tons = 20 Barrels = 16 Ship Pounds (sh. lb.) = 320 Stone = 4000 Land Pounds.

Arms and Equipment	*Ordered by Brentford: for Ormonde**	*for Montrose†*	*Supplied to Macklier by Christina‡*	*Sent to the Orkneys in: Michelson's ship §*	*Montrose's frigate §*	*Quantities left with Macklier*
3-pounder cannon	6	6	12	8	4	–
3-pounder cannon-balls	600	600	1200	800	400	–
muskets:						
flintlock and matchlock	3000	2994	6000	1536	–	4464
musket-bullets	15 barrels	15 barrels	[?30] barrels	20 barrels	–	[?10] barrels
powder	3 lasts [60 brls]	3 lasts [60 brls]	5 lasts [100 brls]	[1–4/5 lasts] 36 brls	–	3–1/5 lasts [64 barrels]
match	15 sh. lb [300 st]	15 sh. lb [300 st]	8 lasts [2560 st]	20 sh. lb [400 st]	–	108 sh. lb [2160 stone]
bandoliers	1500	1500	8000	1040	–	6960
swords:						
cavalry	300	300	600	200	1	399
infantry	2000	2000	4000	2520	–	1480
horsemen's-armour	1000 sets	1000 sets	2000 sets	100 sets	–	1900 sets
pikes	2500	2500	5000	1510	–	3490
halberts and partizans	75	75	150	150	–	–
drums	25	24	50	24	–	26
pistols	900 pr	900 pr	1800 pr	45 pr	–	1755 pair
pistol-holsters‖	–	–	–	12	–	–
bullet-moulds‖	3	–	–	1	–	–

This analysis reveals that apart from taking all the available cannon, cannon-balls, and halberts, Montrose did not touch Ormonde's share of the arms; and, although he was short of equipment, he left a considerable proportion of his own share in Gothenburg, probably to ensure that the second invasion force under Eythin was basically equipped. Montrose rationed himself in vain. Ormonde never received his half share of the Swedish arms; and the second invasion force never sailed for the Orkneys.[86] On 28 February 1650 Macklier did his best to honour the remaining orders he had received from Charles through Meade by despatching four ships full of corn (but no arms) to Ormonde in Ireland and to other royalist groups in France and Portugal. These four ships, which Macklier wholly or partly owned, were the *King David* (24 guns, Capt. Jonas Lawson of Crail), *Unicorn* (12 guns, Capt. Robert Law of Anstruther Wester), *Mary* (12 guns, Capt. William Keir of Leith), and *Catherine* (unarmed, Capt. Walter Gibson of Queensferry); all commanded and manned by Scots. They were all captured by the English republican navy in the North Sea and confiscated as prizes of war.[87] This left Macklier with only two ships: the *Thistle* (10 guns, Capt. George Smith of Pittenweem), and *Anna* (12 guns, Capt. Carsten Erickson of Gothenburg). Smith was nearly captured when he took a cargo of arms to Fife in early 1651. Erickson, whose crew was Swedish, was never employed on a royalist mission. The only ship unaccounted for was the captured crayer, which was undoubtedly recaptured trying to get food supplies to Montrose in May 1650.[88]

---

* *Ruthven Correspondence*, p. 112. Brentford's order to Macklier: Ormonde's share of the arms, dated 30 August 1649.

† S.R.O., Montrose Muniments, G.D. 220/6/Misc. Acc./(Temp.) Box 1. Macklier's confirmation of an order from Brentford: Montrose's share of the arms, dated 9 December 1649.

‡ B.M., Egerton MS. 2542, fos. 19r–v. Particulars of all the Arms etc. supplied by Christina to Charles II through Macklier, n.d. (December 1649).

§ S.R.O., Montrose Muniments, G.D. 220/6/Misc. Acc./(Temp.) Box 1. Notice of all Arms etc. loaded by Macklier on Hans Michelson's ship and the frigate *Herderinnan* on the orders of Montrose, dated 6 January 1650 (with a note of the days when loading took place).

|| No pistol-holsters were ordered by Brentford, but Macklier supplied 12 to Montrose from an undisclosed source.

|| Three bullet-moulds were ordered for Ormonde and none for Montrose, but Macklier supplied one to Montrose from an undisclosed source.

[86] *Charles II and Scotland in 1650*, p. 49.

[87] R.A., Maclean eller Macklier MSS., Biographica series, M.1b. 'An Account of the Dammages and Losses of Sr. John Macklier', dated 26 August 1650. Printed (with numerous errors) in *The Scots in Sweden*, pp. 254–5.

[88] Balfour, *Historical Works* IV, 34.

The three Courland ships never left their home port in the Baltic. Just as all seemed to be going well, the Duke of Courland suddenly suspected Cochrane of sharp practice and refused to let his ships go to Amsterdam, where Ogilvie was supposed to be waiting to arrange their onward despatch to Gothenburg in the care of Hall's men. It later came to light that Cochrane and Ogilvie were in league to defraud the royalists of money and supplies which the former had obtained in Courland and Poland.[89] The mercenaries in Amsterdam and Bremen waiting for ships to take them first to Gothenburg and then on to Scotland under Eythin's command were never picked up. On 29 and 30 March 1650 Lord Eythin's commissions[90] as Montrose's second-in-command were issued by Charles, whose signature further endorsed his support of Montrose's campaign. By that time Charles knew that it was too late to halt the Scottish invasion, yet, without waiting for news of its outcome, he had already started to negotiate with the Covenanters.

The story of Montrose's last campaign has been given elsewhere.[91] It ended in his defeat at Carbisdale in Sutherland on 7 May, a week after Charles and the Covenanters signed the Treaty of Breda. Montrose escaped from the battlefield; but he was betrayed by Neil Macleod of Assynt and hanged in Edinburgh on 21 May.One writer has tried to vindicate Charles by publishing his order of 15 May, which instructed Montrose 'to lay down armes, leave cannon, armes, ammunition brought from Gottenburg, in Orkney. or deliver 'em to sherif of Cty—10,000 rixdollars [£2500] paid to his use in Sir Patr. Drummond's hands'.[92] Having committed Montrose to an invasion, it was insulting of Charles to reverse his orders of 22 January at such a late date. He must have known that there was not the remotest chance of his orders of 15 May reaching Montrose in time to help him. But Charles always hedged his bets. Even while he was contemplating a treaty with the Covenanters and making Montrose's expedition irrelevant, he thought of a way to secure the future loyalty of Macklier. On 13 April 1650, Charles created Macklier a baronet of

[89] *Montrose Redivivus* (London, 1652), II, 172; and *Misc. Scot. Hist. Soc.* I, 191, and 194–201.

[90] *Charles II and Scotland in 1650*, pp. 38–9.

[91] *Deeds of Montrose*, pp. 289–309 and 493–501.

[92] *Charles II and Scotland in 1650*, p. 126.

England, with the designation 'of Dowart'.[93] It was a typical Stuart incentive or reward, costing Charles nothing; but it flattered Macklier, for he used the title. By the time the warrant reached Sweden both Macklier and Meade knew that Montrose had failed. Indeed, Meade had already told Secretary Nicholas that there was nothing more he could do by staying in Sweden; and on 21 May he had reported his intention of leaving for Hamburg on his way back to the court.[94] Bellenden, who continued as resident in Stockholm, had done nothing to help Montrose, which tends to confirm Hatton and Meade's belief that he was an ally of Lord Jermyn, the Covenanters' friend. Argyll, it appeared, had won.

The summer of 1650 passed uneventfully for Macklier. At the end of August he compiled an account of his shipping losses with the help of his captains, Lawson, Keir, and Law, who, after a short period of captivity in England, had returned to Gothenburg. Macklier initially reckoned the value of his seized ships at £6000.[95] Later, after careful assessment, he amended the figure to £4649.[96] On 15 October the Scottish Committee of Estates ordered 'the armes belonging to his Maiestie that are at Bergen in Norruay, and Gottinberry in Sueden, to be sent for'.[97] This matter received further attention on 24 December in Perth, where Charles, who was regretting his deal with the Covenanters, drew up a letter to Macklier asking him 'to send hither the armes and ammunition belonging unto us in your hands'.[98] On 26 December David Wemyss, a merchant burgess of Dundee, was commissioned by Charles to take his letter to Gothenburg

[93] B.M. Add. MSS. 15856, fo. 85v; Wilhelm Berg, *Samlingar till Göteborgs historia* (Stockholm, 1882) I, 89, and supp., p. 48; G.L., Gothenburg Landsarkivet, Göteborgs Kristine Församling Kronologi för Kristine Församling: 1623–1723, p. 16; and *The Scots in Sweden*, p. 13.

[94] *Calendar of State Papers, Dom.: 1650*, pp. 104, 158, and 611; *Charles II and Scotland in 1650*, pp. 100–1; and *Nicholas Papers* I, 240.

[95] R.A., Maclean eller Macklier MSS., Biographica series M.1b.

[96] *Calendar of State Papers, Dom.: 1660–61*, p. 458.

[97] Balfour, *Historical Works* IV, 124. The arms at Bergen had nothing to do with Macklier. They had been ordered as early as 28 February 1649 by Cochrane from the Duke of Courland for delivery 'at Weymouth, Dartmouth, Exeter, and Falmouth, or other places not yet occupied by the Parliamentary troops.' See also *Misc. Scot. Hist. Soc.* I, 211.

[98] R.A., Maclean eller Macklier MSS., Biographica series M.1b, Charles II to Sir John Macklier, 24 December 1650.

and hand it to Macklier personally.[99] The arms referred to were, of course, those originally allocated to Ormonde which Macklier had never shipped. He now complied promptly by sending some of them to Fife in the care of Captain Alexander Cunningham, a merchant and former Provost of Crail. The consignment, consisting of 278 muskets, 4200 musket-balls, 70 carbines, 1000 swords, 800 pikes, 220 pair of pistols, 50 stone of match, 6 barrels of powder, and 8 drums, was worth £350.[100] They were nearly seized by the enemy; but Cunningham saved them by lying about their destination in an affidavit he swore at Anstruther on 27 January 1651.[101] On 31 January David Wemyss signed an obligation in Gothenburg on behalf of Charles. After listing the reasons for the king's inability to pay immediately, Wemyss promised Macklier a bond under the Great Seal of Scotland, which guaranteed repayment with interest at 8 per cent per annum of *all* the money disbursed by Macklier up to that date. Wemyss also undertook to send Macklier a penalty payment of 5000 Riksdalers (£1250) if the bond did not pass the Great Seal within six months.[102] The value of all these arms, including transport costs of £106, amounted to £4113,[103] which, added to the £350 for Cunningham's cargo, brought the total sum disbursed by Macklier for arms alone to £4463. With £4649 also due for shipping losses, Charles owed Macklier nearly £10,000 sterling. It might have been more. On 31 January Captain George Smith set out for Fife with a cargo; but he was intercepted and had to run for Gothenburg without delivering any arms. From Kinnaird on 24 February Charles sent another messenger, Captain Frederick Cooke, to press

[99] *Ibid.*, Obligation by David Wemyss, dated 30 January 1651. Incorrectly printed, with the date '30th June 1654' and other errors in *The Scots in Sweden*, pp. 251–3.

[100] *Ibid.*, Obligation by Charles II, dated 19 March 1651; and *A Collection of the State Papers of John Thurloe*, ed. Thomas Birch (London, 1752) I, 170.

[101] *Ibid.*, p. 171.

[102] R.A., Maclean eller Macklier MSS., Biographica series M.1b: Obligation by David Wemyss, dated 30 January 1651.

[103] *Ibid.*, 'An abregement of Sr. John89Mackliers Pretensions from his Gracious Maj:te of England' dated 30 June 1651. Macklier gave the value of the arms sent before 1651 (without transport costs) as £4007 or 16,030 Riksdalers. In the Whitelocke Papers at Longleat, XI, fos. 18–19, an anonymous spy in Stockholm reporting to his republican chief, Bulstrode Whitelocke, on 19 January 1650, said that Macklier had disbursed 'about 60,000 Crownes'. This report was reprinted almost verbatim in *A Brief Relation*, except the sum was changed to 'sixty thousand Rix dollars'; see *Charles II and Scotland in 1650*, p. 6. The spy exaggerated 16,000 Riksdalers (or Crowns) to 60,000; probably for propaganda purposes.

Macklier for assistance.[104] Back in Perth on 19 March Charles wrote again to Macklier to say that Cunningham had managed to get the arms through to Viscount Newburgh, a royalist general.[105] They were distributed to a small royalist army which had been mustered at Stirling. In that army, which was defeated at Inverkeithing on 20 July 1651, was a regiment commanded by Macklier's nephew, Sir Hector Maclean of Dowart, who was killed in the battle.[106] This seemed to mark the end of Macklier's interest in the royalist cause.

Charles, however, continued to ask for help. On 28 December 1652 he wrote to Macklier: 'We doe at this time desire you, that if any armes or ammunition doe yet remaine in your hands, wich hath heretofore belonged to us, that you cause the same to be delivered to our trusty and welbeloved servant liefetenant general Middleton.'[107] Macklier ignored this request. Firstly, he undoubtedly had no wish to help John Middleton, a turncoat general, who had helped to defeat Montrose and the Macleans in 1646. Secondly, Charles had made no attempt to honour Wemyss's pledge to pass a bond under the Great Seal, or to keep his promise to pay the £1250 penalty for failing to do so. Macklier was not prepared to sacrifice any more money or ships in order to subsidise the royalists. When Bulstrode Whitelocke, Cromwell's ambassador to Sweden, visited Gothenburg on 23 November 1653 he met Macklier and admitted that he respected him, although 'he had been of the King's party'.[108] The tense was the past. Later, on 15 July 1654, Bellenden wrote to Secretary Nicholas to enquire further about the possibility of Macklier supplying arms to Charles for General Middleton; but nothing came of the idea.[109]

Immediately after the Restoration in 1660 Macklier sent Charles a bill for £9112 at 8 per cent for ten years, together with copies of Charles's own letters guaranteeing repayment.[110] The matter was totally ignored.

[104] R.A., Maclean eller Macklier MSS., Biographica series M.1b: Charles II to Sir John Macklier, dated 24 February 1651.

[105] *Ibid.*, Charles II to Sir John Macklier, 19 March 1651.

[106] Alexander Maclean Sinclair, *The Clan Gillean* (Charlottetown, 1899) pp. 193–5.

[107] R.A., Maclean eller Macklier MSS., Biographica series M.1b. Charles II to Sir John Macklier, dated 28 Dec. 1652.

[108] Bulstrode Whitelocke, *A Journal of the Swedish Embassy in the years 1653 and 1654* (London, 1885) I, 159.

[109] *Nicholas Papers* II, 77.

[110] *Calendar of State Papers, Dom.: 1660–61*, p. 458.

When Sir John Maclean *alias* Johan Macklier, 1st baronet of Dowart and 1st Adlad Macklier, died in Gothenburg on 7 July 1666, Charles had still not honoured his written promises.[111] As late as 1725 one of Sir John's grandsons, Captain Carl Leonard Maclean, made a special journey to England to claim the money.[112] He was obviously an uninformed optimist. The Hanoverian succession had finally shattered all hope of anybody using a Stuart promise to obtain money from a British government. The debts were never repaid.

[111] Hugo Fröding, *Berättelser ur Göteborgs äldsta historia* (Gothenburg, 1908) p. 248.
[112] Wilhelm Berg, *Samlingar till Göteborgs historia* I, supp., 49.

3

ANDREW LOSSKY

Dutch Diplomacy and the Franco-Russian Trade Negotiations in 1681

The Russian files in the Archives of the Ministry of Foreign Affairs in Paris contain an interesting report with the heading 'Resident qui est a moscou[,] escrit le 4 Juillet 1681 receu le 20 aoust'.[1] This document has been published twice—first in the *Sbornik* of the Russian Imperial Historical Society, and the second time by A. Rambaud in the *Recueil des Instructions aux Ambassadeurs et Ministres de France.*[2] In the former publication the report is attributed to Colbert de Croissy, the French secretary of state for foreign affairs. However, the title given to it in the *Sbornik* ('Minister of Foreign Affairs de Croissi Colbert to the resident in Moscow') does not appear on the original document, the contents and language of which clearly indicate that neither Croissy nor any member of his staff in Paris could have been its author, and that it was drawn up in Russia. Therefore Rambaud was apparently justified in treating this document as a report of the French resident in Moscow to his government. The only drawback of this attribution is that all the other available evidence indicates that there was no French diplomatic representative in Moscow in the 1680s.

The author of the document in question says that he has paid a number of visits to 'Monsieur Knees [i.e. 'Prince'], one of the chief ministers of this

[1] Paris, Archives du Ministère des Affaires Etrangères, Correspondance Politique (hereafter cited as Paris, A.A.E., C.P.), Russie, vol. I, fo. 139.

[2] *Sbornik Imperatorskogo Russkogo Istoricheskogo Obshchestva*, XXXIV (St Petersburg, 1881) 399–401; France, Commission des archives diplomatiques au Ministère des Affaires Etrangères, *Recueil des Instructions données aux Ambassadeurs et Ministres de France* . . . (hereafter cited as *Recueil*), *Russie*, I (Paris, 1890) 74.

country' (whom Rambaud identifies as Prince Vasilii Vasilievich Golitsyn), and broached the subject of commercial relations and of the Russian tolls hampering the trade of foreign merchants. Moreover, he inquired about the treaty of commerce that the Tsar had concluded with the King of France. The Prince replied that the treaty dealt with the transit through Russia of silk bought by the French in Persia and with the establishment of maritime trade between Russia and France. However, the Prince went on, the more farsighted people in Russia were of the opinion that this treaty would be shortlived, since the main reasons for its conclusion no longer existed: the trade treaty had been designed to induce the King of France to help the Russians settle their disputes with Poland and Sweden. But now that the Russians had made peace with the Turks and the Tatars[3] they were strong enough to make the Poles and the Swedes agree to reasonable terms; moreover, the King of Sweden, being disgusted with Louis XIV's proceedings in the Duchy of Zweibrücken,[4] could no longer expect any considerable support from abroad. As a result of this new situation, the Tsar would lose all interest in the trade treaty with France; and, furthermore, the Russians and the French were so different in their 'humours and maxims' that an accord between them could not last, and thus the treaty with France would collapse of itself.

To solve the mystery of the authorship of this memorandum we must examine the dispatch of Baron Willem van Keller, the Dutch resident in Moscow, dated 4 July (O.S.) 1681 and received at The Hague on 20 August (N.S.) of the same year.[5] We shall then see that the document in question is a translation of a part of van Keller's dispatch just mentioned. Though quite literal for the most part, this translation contains some significant omissions and inaccuracies. For example, it fails to identify van Keller's interlocutor as Prince Iurii Dolgoruky.[6] It omits van Keller's long harangue against the Russian 'New Trade Statute' of 1667, and fails to

[3] Russia had concluded a twenty years' truce at Bakhchi-Sarai with the Turks and the Crimean Tatars in May 1681.

[4] The Duchy of Zweibrücken, a part of which was claimed by Charles XI of Sweden as his inheritance, had been adjudged to Louis XIV by the Chamber of Reunions of Metz in June 1680; see *Recueil, Suède* (Paris, 1885) p. 8.

[5] A.R.A., Staten Generaal (hereafter cited as A.R.A., St. Gen.), no. 6609.

[6] *Ibid.*: 'hebbe iterativelijck de visite gegeven aen den Heere Knëes, ofte Vorst Juriaen Dolgarouka (Dewelcke Een is van d'oudtste RijxRader, ende ten Hove hooch aengesien ende gë-ëert).'

mention Dolgoruky's promise to bring van Keller's views to the attention of Tsar Theodore. Van Keller's pointed question about 'the trade treaty, which Potemkin, the ambassador of his Tsarly Majesty, has concluded in Paris with his Royal Majesty of France' is presented as an innocuous general inquiry. It also passes over in silence Dolgoruky's reluctance to answer van Keller's question, his attempts to divert the conversation, and his assertion that 'his Tsarly Majesty's ambassadors usually raise more hopes and cause more expenses than they procure tangible results and profits for his Tsarly Majesty'. 'On n'auroit plus esgard sur led. Traitté de Commerce' is much stronger than the statement in the original that the Russians need no longer ask for French mediation. Van Keller's closing remark on his conversations with Dolgoruky is also omitted: 'The good subjects of your High Mightinesses know rather better [than the French] how to handle matters of this sort, and should, no doubt, be able to check this little overture [*lit.*: 'hook']; to which end . . . I shall apply my utmost endeavours.'

On 21 August (N.S.) 1681, one day after van Keller's dispatch had been received by the States General, Count d'Avaux, the French ambassador at The Hague, wrote to his king that he was enclosing 'a copy of the letter which the resident of the States at Moscow has written to his masters concerning the treaty of commerce made between your Majesty and the Grand Duke of Moscovy'.[7] No doubt this is the document that came to be filed in *Correspondance Politique, Russie*, vol. I. The speed with which some member of the Dutch governing circles at The Hague produced a cleverly garbled French version of van Keller's dispatch is remarkable.[8] He suppressed all evidence of the isolationist tendencies of the Russian statesman involved, he laid stress on the Russians' lack of interest in

[7] A.A.E., C.P., Hollande, vol. 127, fo. 373. On 28 August Louis acknowledged the receipt, on 25 August, of d'Avaux's dispatch with a copy of the letter 'of the resident of the States General in Moscow' (*ibid.*, vol. 129, fo. 124).

[8] Whoever produced this translation at The Hague was obviously well versed in Russian affairs. The most likely candidate is Coenraet van Klenck, the 'grand ambassador' to Russia in 1675–76, in whose suite van Keller had first arrived in Moscow; see van Keller's dispatches of 15 and 21 March 1681, The Hague, A.R.A., St. Gen., no. 6609, and below, p. 45, fn. 34; on van Klenck see the *Nieuw Nederlandsch Biografisch Woordenboek* X (Leiden, 1937) 469–70. Nicolaas Witsen and Jacob Boreel were also well qualified for this job. The Gemeentearchief in Amsterdam has a number of van Keller's letters to Witsen.

the French treaty, and he toned down the Dutch curiosity about the Franco-Russian trade talks. Obviously, the aim of this concoction was to dissuade the French from taking their trade negotiations with the Russians seriously.

Direct Franco-Russian trade would have undermined the Dutch mercantile hegemony in Russia and would have lessened the French navy's dependence on the Dutch carrying trade for its supply of naval stores. If drawn into Louis XIV's orbit Russia might even help to shore up the French 'eastern barrier' against the Habsburgs. It is therefore appropriate to ask whether the Franco-Russian negotiations in 1681 were seriously meant on both sides and whether they had any prospect of success. This problem is rather complex, and is bound up with the international political situation, with questions of religion, and with party strife at the court of Tsar Theodore. To solve it fully would require a thorough exploration in the Russian archives, as well as the use of certain French documents that do not seem to be readily available.[9]

In the late 1670s and early 1680s the international problem that seemed most pressing to the Russians was the renascent might of the Turks, who were pushing their designs to dominate the Ukraine. To cope with this danger it was necessary to cooperate with the Poles, who were equally menaced by the Turkish inroads. However, Russo-Polish relations were strained, in spite of the agreement reached in 1678 to prolong the Andrusovo Truce of 1667 for another term of thirteen years. With the aid of Louis XIV, John Sobieski had made peace with the Turks in 1676, and in 1677 he had entered into a secret agreement with Charles XI of Sweden for an eventual attack on Ducal Prussia.[10] Thus the Poles were in a strong position to bargain with the Russians: their price for a resumption of hostilities with the Turks included the cession of Smolensk, a yearly subsidy of 600,000 rubles, a strong Russian auxiliary corps placed under Sobieski's command, and the erection of a Roman Catholic church

[9] For example, I have not been able to find the French merchants' memoranda on Russian trade drawn up in 1681–82, which are mentioned in Louis XIV's letter to Theodore of 11 May 1681 and in La Piquetière's instructions in 1682 (*Recueil, Russie*, I, 78); cf. C. W. Cole, *Colbert and a Century of French Mercantilism* II (New York, 1939) 84; see also below, pp. 44, 46 and fns. 33, 35.

[10] W. Sobieski, *Der Kampf um die Ostsee* (Leipzig, 1933) pp. 169–71; G. Landberg, *S.U.P.H.* I: 3, *1648–1697* (Stockholm, 1952) pp. 193–4.

in Moscow.[11] Without losing a major war, no Russian government could have ceded Smolensk; nevertheless, Russo-Polish negotiations continued. The Russians preferred to negotiate with the Poles without intermediaries. But the Poles insisted, in February 1679, on convening a congress in which the Pope, the Holy Roman Emperor, the kings of France and England, and the Dutch Republic would be represented as mediators. After some resistance, the Russians agreed in principle to such a gathering; later they suggested that the King of Denmark be added to the list of mediators.[12] Since this congress never actually met, it is idle to speculate on the interesting appearance it would have presented. At the very least it would have had to cope with the procedural problem of multiple mediation.

It was natural that the Russians should have turned to the Holy Roman Emperor with an appeal to enter an anti-Turkish coalition and a request to help in bringing about a Polish-Russian rapprochement. For this purpose, Theodore's government decided, in March 1679, to send Boyar Ivan Vasilievich Buturlin and *Okolnichii* Ivan Ivanovich Chaadaev as ambassadors plenipotentiary to Vienna.[13] After lengthy debates, the imperial government gave its answer in August 1679: Leopold was willing to mediate between Russia and Poland at a conference to be held in June 1680; but he declined to take up arms against the Turks unless Sobieski and the Polish-Lithuanian Commonwealth were to join in the enterprise. The reason for this refusal, as explained by the imperial commissioners and by Bonvisi, the papal nuncio in Vienna, was that the peace recently concluded with Louis XIV was unstable, and that it would be foolhardy to start a war against the Turks while the leader of the pro-French party in Poland—John Sobieski—retained his freedom of action in Leopold's rear. If, on the other hand, Sobieski were induced to join in the war, this

[11] See M. Posselt, *Der General und Admiral Franz Lefort*, I (Frankfurt-am-Main, 1866) 285; see also *Pamiatniki diplomaticheskikh snoshenii drevnei Rossii s derzhavami inostrannymi* (hereafter cited as *Pam. dipl. snosh.*), V (St Petersburg, 1858) 1017–20.

[12] *Ibid.*, V, 589–91, 1161–4. Later the King of Sweden and the Elector of Brandenburg were also included among the prospective mediators. The list of suggested mediators varied somewhat in the next two years, but their number never fell below four.

[13] See the secret part of Buturlin's instructions, dated 20 March 1679, in *Pam. dipl. snosh.* V, 676–95; for the official report ('*stateinyi spisok*') of the ambassadors' negotiation see *ibid.*, V, 949–1159.

might cause the pro-French faction in the Commonwealth to wither away.[14]

Apparently Theodore's government was as unaware as Vienna of Sobieski's growing estrangement from Louis XIV. There is reason to believe that as late as 1679–82 Moscow continued to regard him as a puppet of the French king.[15] Hence the key to an alliance with him was to be sought at Versailles, and, in the spring of 1680, the Russians began to talk of sending Peter Ivanovich Potemkin at the head of a 'grand embassy' to Louis XIV. The ambassador designate seems to have relished the idea of revisiting France, where he had been well received in 1668 during a mission which, like the present scheme, had involved both Russo-Polish relations and Franco-Russian trade. To make the French king more interested in the mediation project, the Russians proposed to offer him certain commercial advantages: direct Franco-Russian trade could be established at Archangel, where French ships would bring French wines, which were in vogue in Russia, and either sell them for cash or exchange them for Russian goods needed in France.[16]

These proceedings did not fail to attract the attention of Baron van Keller, who was probably the best informed foreign diplomat in Russia: in the course of his sojourn in Moscow since 1675 he had acquired many friends in Russian governing circles and in the *Posolsky Prikaz*, the Foreign Office. Van Keller said he would keep a close watch on Russian designs in connection with French trade as 'a matter of concern to the subjects of your High Mightinesses who carry on trade here'.[17] Indeed, this was a

[14] *Ibid.*, v, 762–4, 1023–5, 1074–8, 1103, 1106–13. A contributing factor to imperial caution was the suspicion that the Russians were carrying on secret peace talks with the Turks and the Tatars. This suspicion was well founded: see S. M. Soloviev, *Istoriia Rossii* (6 vols, St Petersburg, *c.* 1900) III, 489 ff.

[15] See, for example, van Keller's dispatches of 8 February 1681, 4 April 1682, The Hague, A.R.A., St. Gen., no. 6609, and his secret dispatch, 3 January 1682, *ibid.*, no. 7301; cf. *Pam. dipl. snosh.*, v, 1154–8, and Soloviev, *Istoriia Rossii* III, 845. On Sobieski's quarrels with Louis XIV, which began in 1677, see *Recueil*, *Pologne* I, liii, 157 ff.

[16] Van Keller's dispatches of 6 and 27 April 1680, The Hague, A.R.A., St. Gen., no. 6609.

[17] *Ibid.* On van Keller's position in Russia see Posselt, *Lefort*, I, 188 ff. Whenever it is possible to compare van Keller's reports with other sources one is impressed by the accuracy of his information and by the speed with which he obtained it. However, in the late summer of 1680 he seems to have experienced some difficulties and delays in getting information on the Russo-Polish negotiations.

matter of some importance to the Dutch: as Jacques Savary, the renowned French commercial expert, had noted in 1675, the twenty-five or thirty ships that the Dutch sent yearly to Archangel were laden mainly with French goods, and sailed back with the bulk of their cargo consigned to France.[18]

During the summer and early autumn of 1680 the project of Potemkin's mission remained in abeyance. News of an Anglo-Spanish alliance seems to have made the Russians hesitate for a moment, and, more important, a grand embassy from Sobieski was expected in Moscow. The Polish ambassador, Count Tomicki, arrived at the end of August with a retinue of four hundred persons and had his first audience on 27 August (o.s.). A letter also came from Sobieski: he stressed the military preparations of the Turks for next spring and demanded that Theodore accept forthwith the Polish conditions for an alliance, which remained unaltered.[19] Naturally enough, Tomicki's sessions with the Russians proved rather stormy. On one point, however, the two parties agreed with difficulty: to reopen their peace conference at Andrusovo on 20/30 June 1681. The Russians lost no time in requesting Christian V of Denmark to mediate between them and the Poles;[20] probably they thought that they could count on more effective support from a prince with whom they had long entertained friendly relations.

While the negotiations with Tomicki proceeded from bad to worse, the project of Potemkin's mission to France was again taken up, and, on 14 September (o.s.) 1680, letters of credence were ready for Potemkin and Volkov, the embassy secretary. As a preparation for this embassy, a decree of 30 August 1680 gave French and German merchants the right to trade at Archangel.[21] On 28 September (o.s.) van Keller reported a

[18] J. Savary, *Le Parfait Négociant*, Part II, Bk. ii, ch. 7 (pp. 197–8 of the 1736 edition). Savary's chapters on northern trade are based on the reports drawn up in 1671 by Delagny and Pagès, two of the directors of the *Compagnie du Nord*, during their inspection trip in the North: see P. Charliat, *Colbert et la Compagnie de Commerce du Nord* (Paris, 1930), pp. 93–102, 122.

[19] Van Keller's dispatches, 3, 17, 31 August and 21 September 1680, The Hague, A.R.A., St. Gen., no. 6609; Posselt, *Lefort* I, 290–2.

[20] Theodore to Christian V, 30 August (o.s.) and Christian V to Theodore, 20 November (o.s.) 1680, D.R.A., Tyske Kancellis udenrigske Afdeling, Ausländisches Registrant, 1680–84, fos. 86–9.

[21] Theodore to Louis XIV, 14 September 1680, Paris, A.A.E., Corr. Pol., Russie, vol. 1, fos. 95–6; cf. *ibid.*, fos. 92–4; *Polnoe sobranie zakonov Rossiiskoi Imperii* II, no. 833.

complete breakdown in the Polish ambassador's negotiation, and a week later he wrote that Potemkin, with a retinue of eighty men, would soon leave for France via Riga and either Amsterdam or London; his mission, according to van Keller, was to ask the kings of France and England to mediate between Russia and Poland and to help in building an anti-Turkish coalition.[22]

Potemkin's embassy travelled through Amsterdam, where it was very well received, and arrived at Calais on 28 March (N.S.) 1681. On 20 April it reached St Denis on the outskirts of Paris. After the customary civilities, Colbert de Croissy was appointed to negotiate with Potemkin. The Russians held only one conference with him, on 8 May. Three days later they had their leave audience and received letters of recredence from Louis XIV; they received the royal presents on 16 May, and left Paris shortly thereafter.[23]

On 29 April/9 May 1681 the Russian negotiators drew up a memorandum on their meeting of 8 May and presented it to Colbert de Croissy. Most of this document was obviously intended as a draft of a commercial treaty with specific and detailed articles.[24] French merchants were to have free access to Archangel, each ship paying a toll of five golden ducats or ten thalers. No export duty was to be levied on goods paid for in specie. The import duty was to be the same as for other foreign merchants: five per cent for goods sold by weight, and four per cent for all other goods. However, a special tariff was set up for French and Spanish red and white wines, church wine, *eau de vie*, sugar and sweetmeats. The relative value of several currencies was also specified. The French government, in its answer dated 11 May 1681, promised to discuss the Russian proposal with the interested French merchants, after which an envoy would go to

[22] Van Keller's dispatch, 5 October (O.S.) 1680, The Hague, A.R.A., St. Gen., no. 6609.

[23] Paris, A.A.E., Corr. Pol., Russie, vol. 1, fos. 99, 107 ff; *Receuil, Russie*, 1, 70–2. Cf. Alexander Brückner, *Beiträge zur Kulturgeschichte Russlands im XVII Jahrhundert* (Leipzig, 1887) Pt. vi: 'Eine russische Gesandtschaft in Paris im Jahre 1681', pp. 169–87. Brückner's account is based on the report which Rinhuber (who had been employed by Croissy as translator) drew up largely from memory for the Elector of Saxony in 1681 (see below, pp. 42–3); hence the discrepancies between it and the documents in the A.A.E.

[24] A.A.E., C.P., Russie, vol. 1, fos. 130–3. The concluding sentence states: 'In quem finem Nos Tsareae Suae Majestatis Ablegati praesens pactum propriis manibus subscripsimus et sigillo firmavimus.'

Moscow to conclude a trade treaty on a permanent footing. In the meantime they accepted the Russian proposal and offered reciprocal treatment to Russian merchants in France, with the additional freedom to exercise their religion; similar freedom of religious worship was expected to be accorded to the French merchants in Russia.[25]

The theme of reciprocity of commercial rights had been prominent in Potemkin's mission to France in 1668, when both sides seem to have agreed to it in principle; however, the whole negotiation of 1668 proved to be abortive. In the Russian proposal of 1681 commercial reciprocity is mentioned only in the introduction to the memorandum of 9 May dealing with the earlier negotiation. This deliberate omission of the reciprocity claim provides indirect evidence that originally the Russian negotiation plan for 1681 had included a request for some other favour from Louis XIV. In its formative stages Potemkin's mission had obviously been connected with the desire for a rapprochement with Poland. Yet the remarkable feature of the ambassador's negotiation in Paris is that neither side appears to have brought up the subject of French mediation between Russia and Poland. We are forced to conclude that prior to his arrival in France Potemkin must have received fresh instructions from Moscow to concentrate on the commercial aspect of his negotiation only.

When did this alteration in Potemkin's mission occur? One is tempted to agree with Prince Dolgoruky that it was the Truce of Bakhchi-Sarai that had deprived Potemkin's mission of its political meaning. This interpretation may be correct in the long run, but it cannot explain the change in Potemkin's instructions. The Truce of Bakhchi-Sarai, concluded in May 1681, did in fact strengthen the Russian position vis-à-vis the Poles, and they could now revert to direct negotiations without intermediaries. These negotiations lasted until the conclusion of the Russo-Polish treaty of peace and alliance in 1686, when Russia acceded to the Holy League against the Turk. But the outcome of the Russo-Turkish-Crimean negotiations had remained uncertain at least until mid-March 1681, when news was received that the Sultan had ordered the Crimean Khan to suspend his raids into Russia. This first intimation that the truce talks were nearing success came too late for the Russian government to have had time to instruct Potemkin to change his tack in France. The decision to change the nature of Potemkin's mission must be placed earlier, some time

[25] Louis XIV to Theodore, 11 May 1681, *ibid.*, fos. 112–15; see below, n. 32.

between October 1680 and February 1681. Perhaps it was taken when the Russians had learned that Christian V of Denmark had definitely consented to be a mediator.[26]

The French government, for its part, had been mildly interested in Russo-Polish relations: if the Poles and the Russians could jointly assume a good defensive posture vis-à-vis the Turks, the latter might turn their energies on the Austrian Habsburgs. Thus, for some time, the French had been ready to work for a Russo-Polish rapprochement, and in June 1680, Marquis de Béthune, the French ambassador in Poland, was designated to act as a mediator at a Russo-Polish peace conference.[27] However, any grand design was conspicuously absent from French foreign policy in 1679–85. Its objectives were strictly limited: to make the north-eastern and eastern frontiers of France more secure by minor encroachments, known as 'reunions', on the lands of its neighbours. The secretary of state for foreign affairs, Colbert de Croissy, was an efficient and unscrupulous legalist, brutal in words and narrow in outlook. Quite unlike his predecessor, Pomponne, he seems to have entertained no notion of a 'system of Europe'. Nevertheless, Croissy could not fail to see that to pursue the reunions it was necessary to keep the Austrian Habsburgs occupied elsewhere, preferably in the East, and also to make sure that the quarrels between William III and the States Party, or 'Amsterdam Party', in the Dutch Republic would go on. To do this the French had to humour the States Party, which was especially sensitive to any threat to Dutch economic preponderance. Croissy's policy, therefore, was incompatible with the earlier Colbertian dream of rearing the prosperity of the French state on the ruins of Dutch commerce, especially of Dutch commerce in the North. A Franco-Russian trade treaty would have had a logical place within

[26] Theodore's letter of 30 August 1680 (see above, n. 20) seems to have arrived in Copenhagen between 13 and 20 November; according to van Keller, Christian's answer, of 20 November, arrived in Moscow in late January or early February (o.s.), but already in early January the Russians seemed certain that Christian would agree to mediate. See van Keller's dispatches, 10 January and 8 February (o.s.), 1681, The Hague, A.R.A., St. Gen., no. 6609.

[27] Draft of letter of Louis XIV to Tsar Alexis (*sic*), June 1680, A.A.E., C.P., Russie, vol. 1, fos. 90–1. This letter was published, with some mistakes, by Rambaud in *Recueil, Russie* 1, 66. It is not clear who had made the first move in the French mediation project; but Louis's letter says: 'Nous avons apris que nostre entremise seroit tres agreable a vostre Ma.^{té}.

Colbert's scheme; in the policy of his brother it would have led to untoward complications.

While the proceedings we have described were hanging fire, a new actor appeared on the stage in the person of Laurentius Rinhuber, a Saxon doctor and adventurer.[28] Since 1668 he had resided, off and on, in Moscow, where he practised medicine, taught in the German school, and wrote plays; he also served as secretary or interpreter to various embassies, both in Russia and in the West. Most of the diplomatic activity on the periphery of which he played minor roles had to do with the formation of a league of Christian states against the Turk. Rinhuber travelled widely in western and central Europe, where he posed as an expert on Russia; indeed, he seems to have been acquainted with most of the government figures in Moscow. But his writings are a bizarre mixture of factual information, rumour, occasional insights, wishful thinking, and sheer fantasy. Their main purpose is to stress the author's own importance.

Rinhuber was an ardent Catholic neophyte from early 1679 to the end of 1681, when he returned to the Lutheran fold. In 1679–80 he submitted two memoranda to Pope Innocent XI on the possibilities of drawing Russia into an anti-Turkish league—a theme near to Innocent's heart—and on the situation of the Catholics in Russia.[29] According to Rinhuber, the plight of the Catholics is aggravated by the fact that the Poles plead their cause. This invariably raises memories of Polish occupation and religious persecution in Russia during the 'Time of Troubles' early in the seventeenth century. If some other Catholic power would raise the issue, it might be possible to obtain for Catholics the same degree of toleration as that enjoyed by Lutherans and Calvinists. In his second memorandum to the Pope Rinhuber develops the idea that French diplomacy and French commerce would be the best vehicle to achieve this end.

Early in 1681 Rinhuber appeared in Paris and drew up a lengthy

[28] The best account of Rinhuber's life is in Paul Pierling, *Saxe et Moscou. Un médecin diplomate: Laurent Rinhuber de Reinufer* (Paris, 1893); see also his *La Russie et le Saint Siège* IV (Paris, 1907) 73 ff.; Laurent Rinhuber, *Relation du voyage en Russie fait en 1684* (Berlin, 1883); A. Brückner, *Beiträge zur Kulturgeschichte Russlands*, pp. 213–77.

[29] Pierling, *Saxe et Moscou*, pp. 60–70, 127–47. There is a copy of the first memorandum in A.A.E., C.P., Russie, vol. 1, fos. 78–85.

proposal to the French government.[30] In this document he points out that there exists a strong Francophile faction in Russian governing circles; the Russians are much impressed by the power of France and want to enjoy the support of Louis XIV. A minister of Tsar Theodore, whom he does not name, has written to Rinhuber recently, suggesting that he should visit the French court and let it be known that the Russians would gladly see a French ambassador in Moscow in order to negotiate on French political support and on Franco-Russian trade; both the government and the merchants, says this correspondent, are disappointed with the Dutch and the English and would rather deal with the French directly. Rinhuber further presents himself as a spokesman of the Roman Catholics residing in Russia, and raises the question of building a Catholic church in Moscow. In 1675–76 the Russians assured the Emperor's ambassador, Bottoni, that, though they had rejected a Polish request in this matter, it need not present a major difficulty if the Emperor reopened hostilities against the Turks. Surely the Russians would now readily grant a similar request from Louis XIV; this would please the Pope and be useful to all Christendom. Furthermore, the time is propitious for making new proposals to the Russians, since Tsar Theodore is very young, and opinions are divided in his Council.[31] Rinhuber also makes detailed suggestions on the type of goods that the French and Russians could exchange and stresses the possibility of obtaining articles from Persia, Central Asia and China through Archangel. In conclusion he begs that his memorandum be kept secret for fear of Russian reprisals against himself and other Catholics, and offers his services to the French government as a Russian expert, interpreter, or member of the future ambassador's staff in Moscow.

We do not know how far Rinhuber would have got with his proposals had not Potemkin's embassy shown up in France at the end of March. Potemkin had known Rinhuber for some time, and, during his stay in

[30] *Ibid.*, fos. 100–4. This document is dated January 1681, and its covering letter (fos. 105–106, published in Pierling, *Saxe et Moscou*, pp. 71–2) has the date 18 February 1681; it was received on 28 February. Rinhuber had been in France before, and had even met Louis XIV in 1678 (*ibid.*, pp. 55–6, 70).

[31] In most of his writings Rinhuber stresses the fact that the form of Russian government under Theodore is 'aristocratic' rather than 'monarcho-despotic', since decisions are taken not by a prime minister but 'ex senatus consulto bojarorum, id est consiliarorum et principum imperii' (memorandum to the Pope, 1679: Pierling, *Saxe et Moscou*, p. 132).

Paris, held him at arm's length. While Croissy employed Rinhuber as his interpreter, it could not have escaped his notice that the ambassador disavowed the self-appointed emissary of the Francophile faction in Russia. This, as well as Potemkin's reticence on French mediation between Poland and Russia, must have produced a strange impression on Croissy; it may have contributed to the general vagueness of the French reply to Potemkin on 11 May and to the long delay in sending the letter drafted on that date to Moscow. This delay was probably lengthened by the receipt of the garbled version of van Keller's dispatch of 4 July. The French letter finally had to be redrafted and readdressed to Tsars Ivan and Peter, who succeeded to Theodore in 1682.[32]

The initial delay in dispatching the answer to Potemkin's mission was perhaps also partly due to the desire of the French to see the results of their latest move in Moscow before committing themselves any further. For it seems that Rinhuber's earlier machinations in France had had some effect. Before submitting his long memorandum Rinhuber must have imparted his general ideas to some member of the French government: at least two of his ideas seem to have found an echo in the letter that Theodore received from Louis XIV about 20 March (N.S.) 1681.[33] In this letter Louis asks for free passage through Russia of the silk that certain French merchants had ordered from the Armenians, and also that the French merchants who would come to Russia be permitted to exercise the Catholic religion freely, on the same footing as the Lutherans and the Calvinists. Van Keller reports that the *gosti* (the Tsar's commercial councillors) and other advisers discussed this letter in several conferences. The first request raised no difficulty, provided the ordinary tolls were paid. But the second item caused some perplexity. According to van Keller, the Russians feared that, making use of the affinities between the Orthodox and the Catholic Churches, 'the cunning Jesuits, priests, and monks' might corrupt and convert some of the common folk to Romanism; the Russian

[32] Louis XIV to Theodore, 11 May 1681, Paris, A.A.E., C.P., Russie, vol. 1, fos. 112 ff. On fo. 112 there is a notation: 'Le Tsar Theodore mourut et l'on substitua a cette lettre une autre adressée a ses freres et successeurs Jean et Pierre.'

[33] I have not found this letter in the A.A.E. It may be in the Archives de la Marine (since it deals with maritime trade), or among Colbert's papers in the Bibliothèque Nationale. We know of its arrival in Moscow from van Keller's dispatch of 15 March (O.S.) 1681, The Hague, A.R.A., St. Gen., no. 6609.

court was therefore averse to the proposed measure 'as contrary to the fundamental laws of this nation'.[34]

Indeed, Rinhuber, for all his flights of imagination about specific facts, was right on one major issue: in the second half of the seventeenth century the Russian government was often a prey to doubt and faction, and its counsels were usually divided. There were four major parties in Russia at that time. The Old Believers, or radical conservatives, could not hope to gain control of the state, but their violent opposition to the established church and state could shake the Russian polity to its very foundations, as it did when they joined in the orgy of riots in 1682. Within the governing group there were at least three rival groups vying for power, which, for want of better terms, we can call the 'Latin', the 'Dutch' or 'German', and the 'Greek' factions. Each had a foreign policy programme of its own. The Latin party, more or less in power under Tsar Theodore, was inclined to an aristocratic form of government, classical education, an understanding with the Polish-Lithuanian Commonwealth, and a broad coalition of Christendom against the Turk. The Dutch, or German, party were men of technocratic tendencies who believed that all blessings flowed from the Dutch Republic. Their favourite ambition was to reclaim Ingria on the Baltic Sea, which the Swedes had wrested from Russia early in the seventeenth century—and with it an easy access to the United Provinces. The Greek party, with which the other two had to count, was strong in the Established Church. Though it was all for maintaining Patriarch Nikon's reforms in the Russian Church, it was scandalized by the alien ideologies paraded by the Latin and the Dutch factions. It might condone a war against the infidel, provided that this did not entail too close a cultural tie with the Catholics or Protestants. Small wonder then, that, when there was no clear and major threat from the Poles or the Turks, the Russian government was often indecisive, confused, and contradictory in its measures—until Peter the Great brought the programme of the Dutch party to triumph.

In the circumstances we have described, Baron van Keller and the

[34] *Ibid.* In a postscript to this letter van Keller goes on: 'I see clearly that people here are somewhat embarrassed by [the French overtures] and would not be displeased if they could be turned away in a decent manner, either through a wise and timely intervention of . . . Amsterdam merchants, or by some other appropriate means. I am addressing some proposals about this matter to Heer Conraedt van Klenck by the same post'.

Dutch government might have spared their pains: the Franco-Russian trade negotiations, like the Franco-Russian political negotiations, would have petered out even without their help.[35] But most Dutch diplomats, like Dutch merchants, believed in leaving nothing to chance.

[35] Some further abortive attempts at Franco-Russian political negotiations are discussed in my article 'La Piquetière's projected mission to Moscow in 1682 and the Swedish policy of Louis XIV', *Essays in Russian History: A collection dedicated to George Vernadsky*, ed. Alan P. Ferguson and Alfred Levin (Hamden, Conn., 1964).

4

HENRY L. SNYDER

The British Diplomatic Service during the Godolphin Ministry

After the Revolution of 1688 the negotiations consequent on the two long wars with Louis XIV, and the new diplomatic commitments introduced by first a Dutch and later a German sovereign, resulted in the establishment of a far larger number of permanent diplomatic missions abroad than England had ever maintained in the past.[1] Under the tutelage of William III, ministers at home and envoys abroad went through their apprenticeship, with policy and initiative mainly in the hands of the sovereign. On the king's death the English politicians were faced for the first time with the maintenance and direction of a major diplomatic system. Professor Horn, in his admirable study *The British Diplomatic Service*, has provided an excellent survey of its personnel problems during the eighteenth century. Because of the seminal importance of the period between 1689 and 1714, a study of the personnel situation in these formative years of the service is the basis for understanding the later development of the corps. The system of diplomatic representation under Queen Anne, during the Godolphin ministry (1702–10), provides part of this case study in the recruitment and manning of the service. From the appointments made during these years the problems and needs of the service and how they were accommodated to political and personal pressures operating in the government at London can be demonstrated.

The method of recruiting and supervision employed depended in large measure upon the abilities and initiative of the senior ministers. Although

[1] The principal authorities for the history of the diplomatic service in this period are Professor Horn's own *British Diplomatic Representatives 1689–1789* (London, 1932) and *The British Diplomatic Service 1689–1789* (Oxford, 1961); Phyllis S. Lachs, *The Diplomatic Corps under Charles II and James II* (New Brunswick, 1965); and Margery Lane, 'The diplomatic Service under William III', *Transactions of the Royal Historical Society*, 4th ser., x (1927) 87–109.

the Duke of Marlborough together with his friend Lord Godolphin soon established an ascendancy in Anne's councils, they had to share authority and patronage with the Tory chiefs at the beginning and the Whigs at the end of their ministry. Moreover, the formal designation of envoys was made and approved at the Cabinet Council. The Earl of Nottingham, appointed Southern Secretary soon after Anne's accession, had an important voice in diplomatic appointments. Like any secretary it was assumed that he had the right to recommend in his own province, a right he exercised, and his senior place in Tory circles reinforced his position.[2] As a consequence he was able to settle his friends and adherents in several diplomatic posts. The first rule he laid down, heartily accepted by his xenophobic colleagues, was that Englishmen were to be employed everywhere. No more would Dutchmen or other foreigners carry English credentials.[3] But the realities of the situation, the necessity to rely on trained men, the crisis caused by the rupture with France and Spain, left Nottingham little scope for action in his own department. The key posts, at The Hague and Vienna, were in the Northern department. Within a week of Anne's accession Marlborough was accredited to the States General and remained the main channel of communication between London and The Hague until the fall of the Godolphin ministry.[4] It was still essential to have a resident representative there, and since the current envoy, Alexander Stanhope, demonstrated a lamentable want of judgment, it was decided very early to replace him. The tortuous gyrations the ministry went through to accomplish this and the four years it required amply illustrate the complexities of diplomatic recruitment. Immediate recall was a needless insult to a man who had served with great faithfulness over many years. It was resolved to wait until the autumn of 1702 to send over his replacement, Edmund Poley, when Marlborough could be on

[2] Godolphin to Robert Harley, 27 [Dec. 1704], H.M.C., *Bath MSS.* I, 63 (misdated by editor as September); Chesterfield to Nottingham, 14 August 1703, *Letters of Philip, 2nd Earl of Chesterfield* (London, 1829) pp. 382–3.

[3] James Vernon to George Stepney, 13 March 1702, *Letters Illustrative of the Reign of William III* (henceforth cited as *Letters Illustrative*) ed. G. P. R. James III (London, 1841) 194; Marlborough to Nottingham, 18 May, 24 July 1702 (N.S.), *Letters and Dispatches of John Churchill, 1st Duke of Marlborough*, ed. Sir George Murray I (London, 1845) 3, 8.

[4] See *Correspondence of John Churchill, 1st Duke of Marlborough, and Anthonie Heinsius* (henceforth cited as *Marlborough-Heinsius Corres.*) ed. B. van t'Hoff (The Hague, 1951).

hand to 'inform him of the several tempers and interests of the people there'.[5] A further delay followed because a place had to be found for Stanhope in England as a reward for his services in lieu of a pension. The press for places from the Tories was so great that Godolphin gave up the thought of making Stanhope a Commissioner of the Customs and could find no other post for him. Then a new representative had to be sent to Hanover and Poley was given that assignment. The Hague was now offered to Godolphin's nephew, Sir Philip Meadows. In February 1704 Meadows went over to survey the job proposed for him but found it wanting. He returned to England leaving the Treasurer with a double problem, how to provide both for his relation and for Stanhope. Meanwhile the places of a Teller of the Exchequer, a Clerk of the Pipe Office, and a Comptroller of the Army Accounts were considered in turn for Stanhope, but all had to be used to satisfy more pressing political obligations at home.[6]

The nomination of Meadows suggests the customary source of envoys —relations and dependents of the ministers. Waiting in the wings with Meadows were Thomas Harley and George Grenville, cousin and friend respectively of Robert Harley, and they provided a further distraction for the harried Treasurer.[7] Stanhope's eventual replacement was George Stepney, whose diplomatic service extended back to the Revolution. The Lords of the Whig Junto, especially Stepney's school friend Lord Halifax, ensured that his needs would not be neglected. At Vienna since 1701 and uneasy in his post, Stepney pressed his suit for Stanhope's place with both Marlborough and Halifax. He wanted to remain in the service as long as

[5] Marlborough to Nottingham, 24 July 1702, *Letters of Marlborough* I, 8; to Godolphin, 30 June, 24 July, 4, 28 Sept. 1702, Blenheim MSS. A1–14, E2. All letters by Marlborough cited are New Style dates.

[6] Marlborough to Godolphin, 3 April, 2 July 1703, 4 June 1704; Godolphin to the Duchess of Marlborough, [27 July 1703], Blenheim MSS. A1–14, E20; Godolphin to Somerset, 1 August 1703, Boston Public Library; Sir William Simpson to John Methuen, 19 Sept., 3 Oct. 1704, MS.C163, nos. 27, 28, Kenneth Spencer Research Library, University of Kansas; Erasmus Lewis to Stepney, 17 Oct. 1704, *State Papers*, ed. J. M. Kemble (London, 1857) pp. 381–2.

[7] Godolphin tried to send Harley to Hanover to succeed Poley, but was forced to give way to a Whig, Emmanuel Scrope Howe. Harley apparently refused Switzerland and Granville a Northern court so they remained unprovided for until Robert Harley succeeded to the Treasury: Kemble, *loc. cit.*; Godolphin to Harley, [4 Dec. 1704], Longleat MSS., Portland miscellaneous volume, fos. 122–3; 30 September [1706], H.M.C., *Bath MSS.* I, 77 (misdated by editor as 1705).

the war lasted and thought an assignment at The Hague would guarantee him a share in the peace negotiations, by which he could expect to profit handsomely. As he was the most able diplomat in the service the Court approved of his request.[8]

The condition of Stepney at Vienna illustrates another facet of the personnel problems with which the ministry had to contend. The rigid social structure and etiquette of most European courts inevitably complicated diplomatic representation. The Imperial court at Vienna was notorious in this respect. As the Duke of Shrewsbury explained:

> I know by what the German Emb[assador] at Rome used to say to me there, that quality is a maine recommendation in the Court of Vienna, for when Mr Stepney was perfectly well with most of those ministers, an objection to him was his want of quality, which they thought the more just, because they had sent hither [Counts] Wratislaw and Gallas, both men of considerable figure, and as in Germany and most countries abroad people of any figures have generally titles; they cannot easily comprehend what a gentleman of a good family is, and are always asking, 'n'est il pas my Lord?'[9]

Stepney's sympathy for the insurgent Hungarian subjects of the Emperor made him still more repugnant to the Viennese. Therefore when the Emperor agreed to accept a joint mission from the Dutch and English to mediate between him and his errant subjects someone else had to be found.

Now if foreign posts were regularly sought after in England and candidates appeared numerous, few possessed all the desirable qualifications: experience; the confidence of the ministry; wealth to sustain the considerable expenses to be borne before hoped-for reimbursement;[10] and social rank to satisfy the court to which they would be accredited. Some men were attracted to the service because of the pleasure of living abroad; but most nominees agreed to serve only to put the ministry under an obligation to provide for them at home. This was the reason Sir Philip

[8] Stepney to Halifax, 26 Sept. 1704, B.M., Egerton MSS. 929, fo. 63; Marlborough to Godolphin, 9 May 1705, Blenheim MSS. A1–14.

[9] Shrewsbury to James Vernon, 23 Nov. 1706, B.M. Add. MSS. 40776, fo. 19.

[10] Or better not need it. Shrewsbury thought this to be the government's intention in the case of Vienna: 'I fancy [the ministry] wd gladly find some man of quality & a plentifull fortune for there to go spend his own estate to make a figure in that Court for the nation's honour.' To Vernon, 2 Dec. 1706, B.M. Add. MSS. 40776, fos. 21–2.

Meadows urged his son to accept a diplomatic post, for he reckoned that such duty had little other merit to recommend it. 'Foreign services may sometimes prove a good stirrup but never a good saddle.'[11] Diplomatic service was no sinecure; the hours were long, the pace demanding.[12] The uncertainty of reimbursement was a further deterrent. When Godolphin cleared the arrears due to English envoys in 1708 by issuing them tallies on tin that bore no interest and could not be sold, he compromised his own efforts to attract suitable men into the service.[13] Paul Methuen, as others, made payment of past arrears owing him a condition to accepting new employment abroad.[14] All these factors lay behind the Treasurer's difficulty in finding someone to undertake the mission to mediate between the Emperor and the Hungarians.

As early as December 1704 Godolphin had a candidate in mind for this mission, William, Lord Paget, who had been envoy to Vienna under both James II and William III. Paget appears to have entertained the offer but set certain conditions which were deemed unacceptable. Most likely he demanded promotion in the peerage before embarking on his mission, a request made by his son, Henry, in a similar situation a decade later. He refused to go when the Queen promised to grant the honour only after his mission was completed.[15] In March 1705 Charles, Viscount Townshend was invited to go, a compliment to the Whigs; but he also declined. Meanwhile the Dutch had made their choice and pressed the English to do the same, so that the mission could be dispatched.[16] The next candidate considered was George Montagu, nephew and heir of Halifax. The invitation was made through Halifax, a bow again to the Whigs, with the

[11] To Sir William Trumbull, 28 July 1703, H.M.C., *Downshire MSS.* I, 814.

[12] Paul Methuen to Simpson, 9 Feb. 1707 (N.S.), MS. E163, no. 133, Spencer Library.

[13] Lewis to Robert Harley, 21 Aug. 1708, H.M.C., *Portland MSS.* IV, 502; [?] to Harley, B.M. loan, 29/45 I5, undated but endorsed by Harley 'Rd from abroad Oct: 31: 1710'.

[14] MSS. C163, E163, Spencer Library, *passim*.

[15] For the offer to the elder Paget see Godolphin to Harley, [4], 27 [Dec. 1704], Longleat MSS., Portland misc. vol., fos. 21–2, 122–3; Lewis to Davenant, 6 February 1705, B.M. Add. MSS. 4743, fo. 24; Shrewsbury to Stepney, 7 March 1705, Kemble, *State Papers*, p. 434. For the offer to the younger Paget see Horn, *Diplomatic Service*, p. 90; George Murray to [Oxford?], 22 May 1714 (N.S.) B.M. loan, 29/45 I.

[16] Robert Harley to the Duke of Newcastle, 16 March 1705, H.M.C., *Portland MSS.* II, 189; Marlborough to Godolphin, 17 April 1705, Blenheim MSS. A1–37.

Queen's approval. Halifax agreed at first but then had second thoughts: Stepney was an old friend and he did not want to create any ill-feeling by having his nephew supersede him at Vienna. The ministry turned next to the inadequate Alexander Stanhope. At least he could be removed from The Hague, in this manner to make room for Stepney. But Stanhope added to the list of refusals. As a last resort Godolphin was prepared to send Paget's son, Henry.[17] The situation was becoming ludicrous. As Harley commented dryly, having prepared instructions for three different men, 'I wish a proper man were as ready as his instructions.'[18] Then news arrived on 11 May 1705 of the death of the Emperor. Custom demanded that a special envoy be sent to present condolences and congratulations to his successor. This was a much pleasanter sort of duty. The duration would be limited, the prestige far higher. Henry St John, the Secretary at War, was one who thought to enhance his reputation by applying for this diplomatic plum.[19]

Godolphin had other plans. A third time the Treasurer offered the Vienna mission to the Whigs and with the inducements recently added it was now accepted. The post went to Charles, Earl of Sunderland, son-in-law of Marlborough, a leader of the Whig Junto, and the man the Whigs were pressing hard for high office as the opening wedge in their campaign to breach the cabinet. Tradition has it that Godolphin himself suggested Sunderland's name for the post as a way of warding off demands to take the latter into the ministry. This is not so. Sunderland was proposed to the Treasurer by Halifax, whom Godolphin visited on 13 May in his search for an envoy. Our authority is Halifax himself, who relayed an account of their meeting to the Duchess of Marlborough two days later.

> He spoke to me of sending some man of quality to Vienna, in such a manner, as if he would have had us propose somebody to be employed in that compliment. I was not prepared to offer one, and that discourse fell. I have since thought that if there was a disposition to make Lord Sunderland Secretary [of State], the employing him in such an embassy, for three or four months, might properly introduce him into the

[17] Harley to Marlborough, 13 April; Marlborough to Godolphin, 4, 9 May 1705, Blenheim MSS. A1–25, A1–37; Godolphin to Harley, 3 June [1705], H.M.C., *Bath MSS.* I, 68–9.

[18] To Marlborough, 1 May 1705, Blenheim MSS. A1–25.

[19] St John to Harley, 15 May 1705, H.M.C., *Portland MSS.* IV, 180.

method of the business. The Queen would be better acquainted with him, and he would *suffer by degrees*. If the Emperor ever makes peace with the Hungarians it will be done at his first entrance on the government, and it would give great reputation to the English minister that was then employed. The mourning would make his equipage less expensive, the relation he has to your Grace would make the present more valuable, and extraordinary allowances on such occasions have been generally made. But I think nothing of this kind has any great weight. Your Grace can best determine whether such a short excursion would bring him quicker into the Secretary's Office, and I would form my judgment by that. The ramble would not be unpleasant (but for what he leaves) and the commission would be profitable if the Prize was certain. If your Grace approves of it, you know how best to manage it. My meaning is to serve Lord Sunderland, and the Public in making mention of it to your Grace.

The Duchess approved the project but left it to the Whigs to put Sunderland's name forward. Unable to contact Sunderland, Halifax obtained the approval of Lord Somers, the chief of the Whigs. When Halifax reported back to the Treasurer, Godolphin asked him to persuade Sunderland to accept. Halifax agreed to do so on the basis of conditions he had outlined to the Duchess. Once the Queen gave her assent Sunderland accepted the appointment, recognizing the advantages it provided for him.[20]

Sunderland's mission was of short duration and Stepney continued to hold his place as permanent representative at Vienna. Stepney's move was becoming ever more urgent since his relationship with the Imperialists had deteriorated to a point at which the Queen's business suffered, and Stanhope's weaknesses grew more apparent with every dispatch.[21] To complicate matters still further Thomas, Lord Raby, the English ambassador to the King of Prussia, had become *persona non grata* at Berlin. A vain, contentious man whom Marlborough came to despise, Raby had entered into an affair with the wife of the prime minister, the Count

[20] Halifax to the Duchess, 15, 22 May, Blenheim MSS. E36; the Duchess to the Duke of Montagu, 21 May [1705], H.M.C., *Buccleuch* (*Montagu House*) *MSS.* I, 354; Queen Anne to Godolphin, [23 May 1705], H.M.C., *Morrison MSS.*, p. 472. For the traditional view of Sunderland's appointment see Sir Winston Churchill, *Marlborough, His Life and Times* I (London, 1947) 965.

[21] Marlborough to Godolphin, 13 August 1705, *Blenheim MSS.* A1–37.

Wartemberg. The King, also reputed to be a contender for her favours, demanded Raby's recall early in 1706, stating 'he has no objection to Lord Raby but his being well with the Grand Chamberlain's wife . . . gives him a ridicule all over the Empire'.[22] He offered to recall his own minister to Queen Anne as a pretext for the recall of Raby. To complete this uneasy saga of the principal courts in the Northern department, Emanuel Scroope Howe, the then minister at Hanover, was also an embarrassment because of his wife's indiscreet remarks about the Electress, and his transfer was thought desirable. When it was proposed that Howe go to Berlin in place of Raby, Marlborough questioned the choice but later agreed. 'My objection to Howe was his want of dexterity for so tricking a cort [*sic*] as that of Prussia, but since you have no better I think you will do well to send him, for he certainly can never be easy nor do her Majesty any service where he is.'[23] The problem of staffing the corps is readily apparent when we see that four of the major envoys in the North had to be moved or retired.

A grand interchange of places was arranged to settle all these difficulties: Stanhope was to be retired to London; Stepney shifted to The Hague; Raby sent to Vienna; and Howe to Berlin. How easy it sounded. Stanhope had a stroke in 1706 and was not expected to live long; for this reason the Queen decided she could risk a pension on him.[24] The news of his illness unleashed a flood of applicants for his post; and Godolphin was anxious to fill the position speedily to stay the torrent.[25] Then, unaccountably, the

[22] *Ibid.*, 8 July 1706; Kemble, *State Papers*, note, pp. 473–4.

[23] Marlborough to Godolphin, 9 August 1706, Blenheim MSS. A1–37; The Elector of Hanover to Marlborough, 13 April 1706, *Original Papers*, ed. James MacPherson II (London, 1775) 37; Godolphin to Harley, [4 Dec. 1704], Longleat MSS., Portland misc. vol., fos. 122–3; Godolphin to Marlborough, 11, 22, 26 July; Marlborough to Godolphin, 29 July; to the Duchess, 9 Aug. 1706, Blenheim MSS. A1–36, A1–37, E3.

[24] Godolphin to Marlborough, 3, 14 May, 4 Aug. 1706; Marlborough to Godolphin, 7, 11 June, 19, 26 Aug., Blenheim MSS. A1–36, A1–37; Harley to Marlborough, 13 Aug., Longleat MSS., Portland vol. v, fos. 79–80.

[25] For example, Charles Davenant wanted his son Henry moved from Frankfort, John Pulteney his son Daniel from Copenhagen. As Pulteney had obtained the Danish post for his son through the Duchess of Marlborough he may have hoped that she would use her influence with the ministers on his behalf once more. See Davenant to Marlborough, 30 Aug, Spencer MSS., Althorp; to his son, 2 April, B.M. Add. MSS. 4291, fos. 72–3; John Pulteney to Godolphin, 29 Sept. 1706, H.M.C., *Portland MSS* IV, 333; Godolphin to Harley, 30 Sept. [1706], H.M.C., *Bath MSS.* I, 77.

King of Prussia changed his mind. Once insistent to have Raby removed, he was just as insistent now to have him remain.[26] Raby had laid down so many conditions to his accepting the post at Vienna that his transfer had been held up and the ministers were quite willing to let him remain at Berlin where the expense for the crown would not be so great.[27] Raby returned to Berlin (he was absent at Hanover and in Holland from June to October); Howe remained at Hanover; Stanhope retired to London; and Stepney went to The Hague. There remained the problem of Vienna. The candidates were again numerous, but all unsuitable on one ground or another. Sir Lambert Blackwell's offer to serve was politely declined. James Vernon, through the agency of Shrewsbury, urged the appointment of his son James, recently recalled from Copenhagen. Both Godolphin and Harley on separate occasions offered the post to Sir John Guise, Bt, an impecunious Whig MP. But he was not to have it. Godolphin was still looking for a place for his nephew Meadows, and Meadows at the prompting of Sir William Trumbull reluctantly agreed to go. He was to repent before a year was out but for the moment at least every post in the North had an occupant.[28]

The posts in the Southern department were less numerous. At the beginning of the reign only Portugal and some Italian states required

[26] Marlborough to Godolphin, 26 Sept.; Godolphin to Marlborough, 29 Oct., Blenheim MSS. A1–36, A1–37; Godolphin to Harley, 23 Oct., H.M.C., *Bath MSS.* I, 115; Sir Charles Hedges to Harley, [22] Oct., H.M.C., *Portland MSS.* IV, 339.

[27] He demanded to be appointed to the Privy Council, to have his expense allowance raised, to continue in his other appointments, and to be made a plenipotentiary as well as ambassador extraordinary. Although he returned to Berlin his demands did not cease. In 1707 he added a request to be made Earl of Strafford. The climax came early in 1710 when he expressed a desire to 'assist' in the peace negotiations. Marlborough's attitude was clear: 'that is impracticable to be done with a man of his temper. He must only be named in the comission as Lord Lexington was at the last peace, but neither assist nor signe', letter to Godolphin, 1 March, Blenheim MSS. B2–9. Also 15 May 1707, 2 July 1708, 10 Oct. 1709 and Godolphin to Marlborough, 26 May, 21 July 1708, 23 March 1710, Blenheim MSS. A1–37, A2–39, A2–36, B2–8; Marlborough to Harley, 26 Aug. 1706, H.M.C., *Bath MSS.* I, 94; Adam Cardonnel to Stepney, 28 Aug. 1706 (N.S.), *Epistolary Curiosities*, 2nd ser., ed. R. Warner (Bath, 1818) pp. 81–2.

[28] Shrewsbury to Vernon, 5 October, 2, 9 Nov. 1706, B.M. Add. MSS. 40776 fos. 11–15; Lewis to Harley, 31 Oct. 1706, H.M.C., *Portland MSS.* IV, 344; Meadows to Trumbull, 17 Aug. 1707 (N.S.), H.M.C., *Downshire MSS.* I, 850; *Memoirs of the Family of Guise*, ed. G. Davies (London, 1917) pp. 148–9; Godolphin to Harley, [12 Dec. 1706], B.M. loan, 29/64/7.

attention, though each presented its own problems. Portugal was the more important. The Maritime Powers badly needed the port of Lisbon for both military and commercial reasons. The King of Portugal, fearful of the power of France, had made his peace with Louis XIV and his grandson, the King of Spain, in 1701; and was bound to them by an alliance. Undaunted, the English dispatched a veteran diplomat to test the strength of the ties that bound King Pedro to the Bourbons. The man chosen was John Methuen, at that time Chancellor of Ireland. A lawyer by training, his previous diplomatic service, skill as a negotiator, and service on the Board of Trade made him eminently qualified. Methuen's objective was to bring Portugal into the Grand Alliance, which he ultimately achieved.[29] He returned to London in the spring of 1703 with a treaty nearly concluded, to defend his negotiations and obtain further instructions. There he ran into a great snag, for it became obvious that Nottingham did not favour him and may even have proposed his recall. There seems to have been a personal lack of sympathy between the two men, perhaps long-standing, which observers were later to interpret as Nottingham's disapproval of the commitments the treaty involved, both military and diplomatic, in Spain and Portugal. Because of Nottingham's patent enthusiasm for the Portugal alliance this version must be discounted and the ill-feeling attributed to more personal grounds. Besides being dilatory in preparing Methuen's instructions, Nottingham made difficulties about his rank. Methuen had served previously as envoy extraordinary but was now promoted to ambassador extraordinary. Nottingham, however, in drawing up the instructions left out the 'extraordinary' much to Methuen's chagrin. The ambassador turned therefore to the Duchess of Marlborough and pleaded for her intercession with Godolphin and the Queen. She was successful; and Methuen returned with his new dignity but remained supersensitive thereafter about the reaction of the English court to his activities.[30] He continued at his post with success, negotiating the famous trade treaty soon after his return. In May 1704 he suffered a stroke that paralsyed one side of his body. Though he gradually regained

[29] See A. Francis, *The Methuens and Portugal* (Cambridge, 1966) *passim*.

[30] Queen Anne to the Duchess, [?], 2, [9 July], [4 Aug. 1703]; Methuen to the Duchess, [*c.* 4 Aug.]; Marlborough to Godolphin, 2 Aug., Blenheim MSS.E18/9, E45, A1–14; Godolphin to Nottingham, 3, 4 Aug., B.M. Add. MSS. 29689, fos. 68–9, 76–7.

some use of his left limbs he never fully regained his health. But such was his desire to maintain his income and such the ministry's reliance upon him that he stayed at Lisbon until his death in July 1706.[31]

After Portugal the most important post was that of Savoy, where again the Allies hoped to lure a reluctant ally of Louis XIV into their camp. Here Nottingham had his say, and Richard Hill, a staunch Tory and friend of the Earl of Rochester, the leader of the High Church party, won the appointment. His experience as envoy at Brussels and a previous mission to Turin made the appointment seem suitable, although the Duumvirs, Marlborough and Godolphin, had misgivings. The Duke of Savoy was a notoriously untrustworthy ally who considered only his own interests, but he deemed these to be best served by supporting the Emperor and the Maritime Powers and chose accordingly. Once Nottingham was out of office Hill's dismissal was decided on by Godolphin, but the lack of a qualified replacement caused his stay at Turin to be extended until 1706.[32] Apart from some minor residents maintained at Genoa and Florence for commercial reasons, no other major diplomatic mission was sent to Italy except once to Venice. As in the case of Savoy the Allies were eager to draw the Venetians into a military alliance. It was planned to send Hill to Venice in 1704 but the successes of the French against the Duke of Savoy and his Imperial comrades-in-arms made this move inappropriate.[33] It was not until 1707 that the Earl of Manchester was finally sent on this mission. Matthew Prior, James Vernon Sr, Lord Dartmouth and Shrewsbury were all put forward at various times as candidates for this appointment. When Hill was finally recalled from Turin he tried to obtain the post for his secretary, John Chetwynd; but it went instead to Paul Methuen, whose father requested it for him 'to make him a master in the Italian which he

[31] Methuen to Simpson, MS. E163, Spencer Library, no. 27 ff; Godolphin to Marlborough, 26 July 1706, Blenheim MSS. A1–36.

[32] *Marlborough-Heinsius Corres.*, p. 91; Godolphin to Harley, 16 June 1703, H.M.C., *Portland MSS.* IV, 63–4; the same, 27 [Dec. 1704], H.M.C., *Bath MSS.* I, 63; Queen Anne to the Duchess of Marlborough, [*c.* 11 October 1703], *Letters and Diplomatic Instructions of Queen Anne*, ed. B. C. Brown (London, 1935) p. 127; Marlborough to Godolphin, 13 Aug. 1705, Blenheim MSS. A1–37; Simpson to Methuen, 4, 11 Dec. 1705, MS. C163, Spencer Library, nos. 88–90.

[33] Vernon to Shrewsbury, 15 Oct. 1703; *Letters Illustrative* III, 239; Harley to Marlborough, 8 Sept. 1704; Marlborough to Godolphin, 16 Sept. 1703, 23 Sept. 1706, Blenheim MSS. F2–16, A1–14, A1–37; Gilbert Burnet, *History of his own Time* V (Oxford, 1823) 140.

understands well already so it will much advantage him and give him a little of the Italian soft supplenes which he wants'.[34] He held the post only a few months because the death of his father caused his translation to Lisbon whereupon Chetwynd took his place at Turin.

Normally the major post in the Southern department was Spain. Owing to the assumption of the crown by Philip V England had no resident representative there until 1706. This omission was finally rectified when James Stanhope, son of Alexander, was accredited to Archduke Charles (or Charles III, King of Spain, as he was recognized by the Maritime Powers) at the beginning of the year. Because of his later eminence Stanhope's entrance into the diplomatic service deserves some notice here, for it illustrates well the accidents of fate and the importance of political influence for success in the service. Gifted in languages and knowledgeable in European affairs, he early obtained the support of the Duke of Somerset, a troublesome grandee of uncertain Whig principles who held a cabinet post more because of his social position than his usefulness or ability. Somerset prided himself on being a patron of promising young men. After failing to get Stanhope appointed to Turin in 1703 he tried hard to obtain him an appointment as envoy to Archduke Charles, who went to claim the Spanish crown in 1704. But Stanhope had to be satisfied with his commission as colonel of the eleventh foot, which was sent to Spain with the Archduke. Left behind at Lisbon because of illness, he gained the confidence of the invalid Methuen who sent him back to London with his dispatches. He spent the winter in the House of Commons, to which he had been elected from Somerset's borough of Cockermouth in 1702, though this did little to enhance his prospects. Godolphin even remarked 'I know nobody much inclined to favour Collonel Stanhope',[35] for Stanhope had made himself a nuisance by taking the part of the country Whigs in their attempt to pass a place bill through the Commons.

[34] Methuen to Simpson, 26 April 1706 (N.S.) MS. E163, Spencer Library, no. 107; Addison to Stepney, 6 Sept. 1705, *Letters of Joseph Addison*, ed. W. Graham (Oxford, 1941) p. 53.

[35] Godolphin to Harley, [4 Dec. 1704], Longleat MSS., Portland misc. vol., fos. 122–3; Nottingham to Alexander Stanhope, 1 June 1703, Finch-Hatton MSS. 277, Northamptonshire Record Office; Godolphin to Somerset, 1 Aug. 1703, Boston Public Library; Chesterfield to Nottingham and reply, 14 Aug. 1703, *Letters of Chesterfield*, pp. 382–4; Methuen to Simpson, 23 July 1704 (N.S.), MS. E163, Spencer Library, no. 31; A. F. B. Williams, *Stanhope* (Oxford, 1932) pp. 31–4; Marlborough to Godolphin, 19 July 1703, Blenheim MSS. A1–14.

His fortunes improved when he was left an annuity by the Earl of Huntington. Then Somerset obtained a promotion for him to brigadier, much to the astonishment of Stanhope's contemporaries, for 'his zeal in the house against places had given offence to ye court and made it doubtfull whether he should be turned out of the post he was in or preferred to a better'.[36] He returned to Spain to the army in 1705 and was present at the taking of Barcelona, but was back in London again for the next session of Parliament, when he was again suggested as minister to Turin. Undaunted, he once more joined the country Whigs and was one of the leaders of the effort to insert a place clause in the Regency Act of 1706. This gained him the support of another non-junto Whig duke, Newcastle, apart from Somerset. As they both held places in the cabinet fortune continued to smile upon Stanhope and he returned a third time to Spain, now finally with the long coveted credentials of envoy extraordinary to Archduke Charles as King of Spain.

The situation in Spain deteriorated after the successes of 1705. Peterborough, Stanhope, Galway and Rivers, all English generals with some diplomatic credentials, quarrelled between themselves, with the Spanish and Austrian advisers around the Archduke, and with the Portuguese, to such an extent that Godolphin considered recalling the lot by the middle of 1707 and vesting military and diplomatic authority in the hands of still another general on duty in Spain; Thomas Erle.[37] Peterborough and Rivers came home voluntarily but the question of diplomatic representation was still far from settled.

The year 1707 was one of great trial for the ministry on many accounts,[38] not least because of the problem of the diplomatic corps. Stepney, who had replaced Stanhope at The Hague, was fatally stricken with consumption and returned to England to die in the autumn. Meadows, who had gone to Vienna only after great hesitation, repented as soon as he arrived and immediately importuned his uncle, Godolphin, to recall him. Stanhope

[36] Simpson to Methuen, 27, 13 Feb. 1705, MS. C163, Spencer Library, nos. 54, 52.

[37] *Ibid.*, 4 Dec. 1705, 15 Jan., 30 April 1706, nos. 88–9, 94, 92; Anne to Godolphin, 4 June [1706], *Letters of Queen Anne*, p. 188; Addison to Stepney, 15, 19 Nov. 1706, *Letters of Addison*, pp. 59–61; Stanhope to Hedges, 15 Jan. 1707 (N.S.), H.M.C., *Downshire MSS.* I, 847; Godolphin to Sunderland, 20 Aug. 1707, Blenheim MSS. D2–18/9.

[38] See H. L. Snyder, 'Formulation of Foreign and Domestic Policy in the Reign of Queen Anne', *Historical Journal*, XI (1968) 144–60.

returned from Spain to look after his father's estate, leaving behind only one general officer, Galway, where at the beginning of the year there had been four; and Galway also sought his recall. Paul Methuen had no more taste for his post at Lisbon and his replacement at Turin, Chetwynd, petitioned to return. Only in the North was there some stability, but even there so many English representatives sought promotions or translations that the ministry had many uneasy moments. John Robinson, accredited to Charles XII of Sweden, asked leave to come home, but Godolphin questioned that he could 'be allowed, at present, to bee anywhere, but as near the King of Sweden, as his irregular motions will suffer him to be'.[39] Raby insisted on an earldom as the price for his remaining at Berlin, a demand which no one was prepared to grant. The situation was so depressing that Godolphin finally lamented to Marlborough, 'Mr Methuen is very pressing to come home, and wee have no great plenty of proper persons to send there, or, indeed, anywhere.'[40]

The hand of Marlborough now becomes clearer. His personal and professional interests in the conduct of the war combined to make him exert his influence. This was greatest in the Northern department, the area in which he conducted his military operations; and the successive secretaries, Hedges, Harley and Boyle, all deferred readily to his recommendations.[41] The Southern department was farther from his post and Sunderland, after his appointment in 1706, took a strong hand in the conduct of affairs; but even there Marlborough was consulted. The extent of his influence is illustrated most notably by the fact that most of the major diplomatic appointments in both departments after 1706 were in the hands of generals.

The most pressing situation was in the United Provinces because of its critical importance and the absence of any qualified representative after Stepney's enforced departure. There was as usual no dearth of candidates, though Harley disclaimed any competence to recommend and left the matter entirely to the discretion of Marlborough and Godolphin. Richard

[39] Godolphin to Marlborough, 19 Sept. 1707, Blenheim MSS A2–23.

[40] *Ibid.*, 12 Aug. 1707.

[41] Harley regularly refused to recommend in his own department, though years later he protested that he had not been permitted to do so. Harley to Marlborough, 16 Nov. 1706 in William Coxe, *Memoirs of John, Duke of Marlborough* II (London, 1818–19) 160; the same, 5, 16 Sept. 1707, Blenheim MSS. A2–24; autobiographical fragment of Oxford, B.M. loan, 29/36/5.

Hill had once offered to go and his name was handed about as Stepney's successor. Matthew Prior and the Earl of Berkeley made overtures. Sunderland, not so reticent as Harley, suggested Abraham Stanyan, the envoy to Switzerland. William Walsh, a Kit-Kat and gentleman of the horse to the queen, had the surprising blessing of Shrewsbury. Lord Raby and the recalcitrant Meadows were also considered and found wanting. James Stanhope was put forward, as usual, by Somerset; and Godolphin approved except that he was away in Spain.[42] Then Godolphin thought he had found the proper person: a man 'willing to bee commanded, . . . very capable of doing service in that station, since nobody has better inclinations, and he wants neither temper, discretion, capacity, or integrity. He wants indeed a little more youth and health.'[43] This paragon was James Vernon Sr, a secretary of state in the previous reign. The prize was awarded to none of these but to a general, William Cadogan, Quartermaster-General of the army. Marlborough had left him in Flanders temporarily to look after affairs in Stepney's absence. Godolphin agreed that he should stay on until Marlborough returned to England and a permanent representative could be selected. But Marlborough preferred his own trusted subaltern at this key spot and Cadogan remained accredited to both The Hague and Brussels until 1711.[44] The latter post was particularly crucial, for after Flanders was retaken from the French in 1706 it was ruled by an Anglo-Dutch condominium and Marlborough had pretensions to its government which he wanted to safeguard. The immediate consequence of Cadogan's appointment was that England was virtually without a senior representative at The Hague for two years. Marlborough and Cadogan were so occupied with affairs of the army in Flanders that they were in The Hague only for short visits. Even when Townshend was sent over to The Hague in 1709 Marlborough, wishing no interference in his special preserve, insisted he not be accredited to Flanders.

[42] Godolphin to Marlborough, 3 May 1706, 16 Aug., 19, 23 Sept. 1707; Prior to Marlborough, [Sept. 1707]; Shrewsbury to Marlborough, 22 Sept.; Somerset to Marlborough, 18 Sept., Blenheim MSS. A1–36, A2–23, A2–25; Narcissus Luttrell, *Brief Historical Relation* VI (Oxford, 1857) 213; Lewis to Harley, 7 Oct. 1707, H.M.C., *Portland MSS.* IV, 455.

[43] Godolphin to Marlborough, 28 Sept.; Marlborough to Godolphin, 23 Oct., Blenheim MSS. A2–23, A1–37.

[44] *Ibid.*; Marlborough to Godolphin, 5 May 1708, A2–39.

In Portugal and Spain the importunities and entreaties of both Methuen and Galway were answered. The former was recalled and the latter was retired from the battlefield to succeed Methuen as ambassador at Lisbon, where he remained reluctantly for another three years. Major-General Francis Palmes was selected to succeed Chetwynd at Turin, though Chetwynd changed his mind and asked to remain. As a consequence Palmes accompanied the Duke of Savoy to the field while Chetwynd remained at the capital.[45] In 1709 Palmes took Meadows's place at Vienna. The case of Spain is somewhat of a puzzle for historians. Stanhope was recalled in 1707 at his own request and spent yet another winter in the Commons. At the beginning of 1708 Henry Worsley, Whig MP from the Isle of Wight, was appointed to go and his credentials were prepared. Earl Rivers was to accompany him as commander of the English forces in Catalonia. Then, mysteriously, when all was in readiness, both appointments were withdrawn and Stanhope was sent instead in both capacities. The contemporary historian Alexander Cunningham attributed the change to Marlborough's jealousy of Rivers. Undoubtedly the influence of Somerset and Newcastle, who stood by the Duumvirs in February in the crisis over Harley's efforts to eject them, had some weight. It may have been the decisive factor, for Stanhope had been active with their supporters in the Commons on this occasion. Marlborough gave Charles III credit for his appointment, but the king probably acted at Stanhope's request, as he did for Stanhope's promotion in 1706.[46]

The last major post to be filled in this second round of appointments was Vienna; and that took the longest. In May 1708 the Earl of Berkeley was selected to succeed Meadows. A veteran diplomat of three previous reigns, he soon began to temporize and make new conditions. After procrastinating for nine months he finally decided not to go after all, pleading 'his old age and infirmities'. The real casualty was the man who expected to go as his secretary, Jonathan Swift. The course of English history and

[45] W. Greg to Michel de Chamillart, 30 Dec. 1707, H.M.C., *Portland MSS.* IV, 469; Chetwynd to Manchester, 14 Jan. 1708 (N.S.), H.M.C., *Manchester MSS.* p. 94b; Godolphin to Marlborough, 21 Sept. 1708, Blenheim MSS. A2–36.

[46] Luttrell, *op. cit.*, VI, 251; Addison to Manchester, 2, 23, 30 March 1708, *Letters of Addison*, pp. 97, 103–4, 106; Alexander Cunningham, *History of Great Britain* (London, 1788) II, 204–5. Godolphin to Marlborough, 5 June 1706, Blenheim MSS. A1–36; Marlborough to Moles, 17 April, to King Charles, 18 April, *Marlborough Despatches* III, 701–4.

literature might have been changed had his hopes been realized.[47] Eventually Palmes was sent to Vienna during the course of 1709 and the thankful Meadows returned home to be rewarded with the office of a Comptroller of the Army Accounts.

With Palmes's dispatch to Vienna the major appointments during the Godolphin ministry were virtually completed. Palmes's appointment also meant that every major post was filled with a military officer: The Hague, Brussels, Spain, Lisbon, and Vienna. Marlborough himself was accredited to several courts. Both Raby at Berlin and Howe at Hanover held colonelcies of regiments and the rank of lieutenant-general, though neither served in a military capacity during the war. Moreover another of Marlborough's commanders in the field, the second Earl of Stair, began an important diplomatic career when he was sent to the King of Poland after Poltava. The middle years of the ministry represent in fact the high water mark of Marlborough's diplomatic influence for it began to ebb in 1709, even before his friends were turned out of office. The Whig victory in the elections of 1708 and the appointment of Somers and Wharton to the cabinet in October of that year gave the Whigs a new authority in the Queen's councils. This was especially true in the delicate task of opening peace negotiations with France and treating with the Netherlands for a barrier.

An expectation of imminent peace negotiations was a feature of the scene from 1705 onwards; but it was not until 1709 that formal meetings took place between representatives of England and France. Stepney, as noted earlier, had hoped to place himself advantageously so that he could take part, but his early death robbed him of this opportunity. Raby was a vociferous claimant for a place at the peace table. Marlborough denied this to him and Harley later won Raby over by granting him this plum as well as the earldom he coveted. Marlborough had a right to expect to head the English team but, mindful of the impeachments which followed the Partition Treaties, he did not want the full responsibility. Halifax had a strong claim to participate because of his past experience in office and his

[47] Newdigate newsletter, 6 May 1708, Folger Shakespeare Library; Jael Boscawen to Anne Evelyn, 15 May, Evelyn MSS., Christ Church, Oxford; Luttrell, *op. cit.*, VI, 304, 320; Lewis to Harley, 29 May, 21 Aug. 1708, H.M.C., *Portland MSS.*, 491, 502. For Swift's hopes see his letters to Archbishop William King, 9 Nov. 1708, 6 Jan. 1709, and to Archdeacon Walls, 9 Nov. 1708, *Correspondence of Jonathan Swift*, ed. Harold Williams (Oxford, 1963–5) I, 105, 108, 118–19.

political importance. Moreover as he could not accept a great office of state without sacrificing his life-place as Auditor of the Exchequer, and he was denied the seat in the cabinet he hoped for, this prestigious diplomatic post had a special attraction for him. At the beginning of 1709 when the prospects for a conference were evident, Halifax asserted his claim through the Duchess of Marlborough. Somers endorsed both Halifax and Townshend, a Whig lord whose stock was high in party and ministerial circles. Townshend's appointment as a privy councillor in 1707 may have been made in anticipation of his employment in the peace negotiations for Marlborough had certainly led him to hope for such employment no later than the winter of 1706–7. The Earl of Manchester, Trumbull, Shrewsbury, Somerset, and Sunderland all seem to have been suggested and considered, but the claims of Halifax and Townshend were too strong to be ignored. Then Halifax declined to serve, apparently for fear of impeachment if the Tories returned to power. Marlborough had little use for Halifax, so that he welcomed his withdrawal and in the end Marlborough himself and Townshend were designated as plenipotentiaries.[48] The negotiations came to naught because the King of France refused to accept the preliminaries agreed to at The Hague; but Townshend stayed on at The Hague taking up the place left vacant since the death of Stepney. He proved an able minister, and popular with the Dutch, and remained until the Tories recalled him two years later.[49] His chief assignment was to negotiate a barrier treaty, one of the most controversial projects the Godolphin ministry undertook.

The influence of the Junto was not so apparent otherwise, for few changes were necessary during their remaining time in office. Hanover was the main post to be filled after the death of Howe in 1709 and a Junto

[48] Marlborough to Godolphin, 30 Dec. 1708 (for the former's promise to Townshend); Godolphin to Marlborough, 23 Dec. 1708, 3 Feb., 19 April, 31 May 1709; Marlborough to the Duchess, 4 February 1709; Halifax to Marlborough, 24 April 1709, Blenheim MSS, A2–39, A2–36, B1–22b, E4, B2–34; Raby to Oxford, 29 June 1711, H.M.C., *Portland MSS.* IX, 293; Marlborough to the Duchess, 25, 31 May 1709, *Correspondence of the Duchess of Marlborough*, 2nd edn I (London, 1838) 183, 185–6; Lady Hervey to John Hervey, 30 April 1709, *Letterbooks of John Hervey, 1st Earl of Bristol* I (Wells, 1894) 255; Onno Klopp, *Fall des Hauses Stuarts* (Vienna, 1875–89) XIII, 226–7.

[49] Earl Rivers to Harley, 12 Sept. 1710 (N.S.), John Drummond to Harley, 10 March 1711 (N.S.), H.M.C., *Portland MSS.* IV, 581, 663.

candidate, Edward Hopkins, designated for Hanover in 1701 and Sunderland's companion on his embassy to Vienna in 1705, was selected. Hopkins and his uncle, Thomas Hopkins, Sunderland's under-secretary, were both Kit-Kats, and close to the ministers. Hopkins had first been proposed for Vienna to succeed Meadows and it had been confidently expected that he would go. When Howe died, Sunderland proposed Hopkins to be sent instead to Hanover, to which Godolphin agreed. His departure was delayed until the spring, however, to permit him to attend to his duties as an M.P. The session did not end until 5 April 1710, and in the intervening time Dr John Robinson had impressed the government with the need for a minister at Stockholm, where England had been represented only by a commissary in charge of affairs since Robinson's departure for Poland in 1703. Godolphin now decided to send Hopkins to Stockholm instead of to Hanover; but a further unexplained delay ensued during which Robert Jackson, the commissary at Stockholm, was promoted to minister resident on 22 May. Hopkins lost his chance for either post when the dismissal of Sunderland in June and then of Godolphin in August put the initiative in the hands of the latter's successor, Harley. Jackson retained his post into the next reign and Harley obtained Hanover for James Cresset (and when he died suddenly for Earl Rivers) while Godolphin and his Whig colleagues were still in office. The appointment was recognized as a clear sign of Harley's new influence with the Queen.[50]

A special embassy that revealed the paucity of suitable candidates for diplomatic missions was that to the Tsar in 1709. The arrest of the Russian ambassador, Matveev, for debt in London in 1708 was a matter of great concern for the effect it might have on Anglo-Russian relations and the threat it posed of Russian intervention on the side of France in the war. The English government thought it necessary to send a special representative to the Tsar to deliver the Queen's apologies. Once again the ministry searched the ranks of the nobility for a suitable person because Charles

[50] Luttrell, VI, 507; Arthur Maynwaring to the Duchess of Marlborough, [29 Sept. 1709], Blenheim MSS. E28; Ralph Bridges to Trumbull, 31 Oct. 1709, H.M.C., *Downshire MSS.* I, 882; Somerset to Harley, 18 June, 26 July 1710, H.M.C., *Portland MSS.* IV, 491, 552; Henry Boyle to Marlborough, 28 March 1710, Blenheim MSS. B2–7; Marlborough to Boyle, 12 April 1710, *Marlborough Dispatches* IV, 718; the Duchess of Marlborough to Bishop Burnet, 29 June 1710. Bod. Lib. Add. MSS. A–191; Mary D. Harris, 'Memoirs of Edward Hopkins', *English Historical Review* XXXIV (1919) 491–504.

Whitworth, the English envoy at Moscow, lacked the desirable social standing. Godolphin had hopes of persuading the Marquess of Carmarthen, heir to the Duke of Leeds and an admiral, to undertake the mission. (Carmarthen had become acquainted with the Tsar when he visited England in 1697). But as was so often the case, Godolphin was disappointed. Finally, with no other alternative, the Queen recalled Whitworth, who retired just across the border from Muscovy to Poland and then returned to Moscow armed with new credentials as ambassador extraordinary. Befitting his new rank and the character of his mission, he made a public entry with grand ceremony and equipage that was described at great length in the contemporary prints to amuse and impress the curious.[51]

Ceremonial missions were infrequent and usually of little importance, but attracted noble candidates because of their prestige, short duration, and limited duties. More frequent short-term missions were those to accomplish some particular business. Many of the resident envoys abroad undertook this sort of assignment in addition to their regular responsibilities. Marlborough, for example, made frequent visits to the courts of central and northern Europe to obtain military assistance and ease frictions among the Allies. When the Dutch refused to attack the French army in Flanders in July 1705, the popular outcry of anger and humiliation prompted the ministry to send a minister of cabinet rank to remonstrate with the States General. The Duke of Newcastle, Lord Privy Seal, was first considered but was able to avoid the assignment which went instead to the Earl of Pembroke, Lord President of the Council. Credentials were prepared and Pembroke was on the point of going when Marlborough requested that his errand be stopped in order to avoid further inflaming Anglo-Dutch relations.[52] The selection of Pembroke was extraordinary, however. Except for the choice of Shrewsbury to represent the Queen at the formal resumption of diplomatic relations with France at the end of the war and Bolingbroke's trip to negotiate the peace, no other cabinet officer agreed to undertake a diplomatic assignment during the reign. Indeed,

[51] Boyle to Marlborough, 30 July 1708, Blenheim MSS. B1–1; Sunderland to Whitworth, 24 September 1708, B.M. Add. MSS. 37356, fo. 230; David Jones, *Compleat History of Europe* (London, 1698–1720) XV, 151–62.

[52] Harley to Newcastle, 6 Sept. 1705, H.M.C., *Portland MSS.* IV, 190; Newcastle to Harley, 10 Sept., *ibid.*, II, 243; Godolphin to Harley, 5 Sept. 1705, H.M.C., *Bath MSS.* I, 75.

only one other nobleman of high rank (generals excepted) undertook any mission other than a ceremonial one throughout the reign. This was the Earl of Manchester who was sent to Venice in 1707 and he did so solely to secure some greater preferment at home on his return.[53]

There was at least one occasion on which a person was sent abroad in order to be rid of him in England. This was the peripatetic Earl of Peterborough, who was a thorn in the side of several ministries. His escapades on the continent from 1704 to 1707 were sufficient to cause his recall; but the ministry regretted doing so on his arrival, for he caused a considerable stir in Parliament. After Harley succeeded to power Peterborough was proposed for several posts. Eventually he was given broad instructions that he used to while away the time on a progress through half the capitals of Europe. This was quite agreeable to the ministry and their royal mistress who remarked: 'I think he should be sent somewhere, for I fear if he comes home while the Parliament is sitting he will be very troublesome.'[54] Another example is that of John Molesworth, who was suggested for a diplomatic post in 1705 primarily to remove him from the Commons where his zeal for country measures, like that of the young Stanhope, was an embarrassment to the Junto. He had to wait until 1710 for his 'reward' when he was sent to the distinctly minor post at Florence, and by then we may assume the original impetus for his appointment no longer had force.[55] The Queen's comments on Peterborough and others show that she was no more a cipher in these matters than in other affairs of the government. To be sure, she generally left policy-making and its direction to her advisers; but she was regularly consulted, particularly in making appointments to offices. She shared the concern of sovereigns on the continent in regard to the social rank of diplomats, although she usually had to acquiesce in accrediting persons of inferior rank. As she herself expressed it: 'I always thought it very wrong to send people abroad of mean extraction.'[56]

The haphazard patronage system employed to recruit to diplomatic posts worked better than might be expected. For the very reason that the persons employed were almost invariably commoners of modest means,

[53] Edward to Abigail Harley, 15 Dec. 1708, H.M.C., *Portland MSS.* IV, 515.

[54] Anne to Oxford, 16 Nov. 1711, *Letters of Queen Anne*, p. 357.

[55] Simpson to Methuen, 27 March 1705, MS. C163, no. 56, Spencer Library.

[56] Anne to Oxford, 19 November 1711, *Letters of Queen Anne*, p. 358.

young men in need of an employment, they tended to be diligent and faithful in the performance of their duties and responsive to the directions of the ministry. The patronage system also operated at a secondary level because envoys going abroad normally had the right to nominate their secretaries and these men in turn, after serving a suitable period of apprenticeship, were often promoted to higher posts. What we can conclude is that through the process of selection described, an able experienced corps of diplomats was developed by England at the beginning of the eighteenth century; and the principal diplomatic posts during the following decades were filled by men recruited and trained during the Godolphin ministry under the guidance of Marlborough. The Whig supremacy which lasted through the reigns of the first two Georges confirmed these men in their places and the pattern of representation developed after the Revolution became regularized and was continued on a permanent basis. The diplomatic service of the eighteenth century and the pioneer cadre that staffed it were essentially the creation of William III, Anne and their ministers.[57]

[57] I am grateful to the Duke of Marlborough, the Duke of Portland, the Marquess of Bath, the Earl Spencer, the Trustees of the Evelyn Heirlooms, and to the archivists of the Northamptonshire Record Office, the Boston Public Library, and the Spencer Library for permission to use manuscripts in their possession.

5

RAGNHILD HATTON

John Drummond in the War of the Spanish Succession: Merchant turned Diplomatic Agent

John Drummond is known to historians interested in the last years of the reign of Queen Anne as a Scots merchant and banker settled in Amsterdam who became the correspondent of Robert Harley and Henry St John. Letters which he wrote to, or received from, these two statesmen, both before and after they became—respectively—Earl of Oxford and Viscount Bolingbroke,[1] have long been available in print. G. Parke's 1798 edition of Bolingbroke's correspondence[2] contains the many semi-official letters which the Secretary of State for the Northern department wrote to Drummond from the autumn of 1710 till he transferred to the Southern department in 1713; and Bolingbroke's praise (to the effect that Drummond was more valuable than any of Her Majesty's ministers abroad)[3] is usually quoted whenever Drummond's name is mentioned. In 1887 and 1889 two volumes of the Portland papers, published by the Historical Manuscripts Commission,[4] printed Drummond's letters to Oxford between 1710 and 1715 and also the few drafts or copies of Oxford's letters to Drummond which had survived. The editor of these volumes, J. J. Cartwright, thought Drummond's own letters 'long and often tedious',[5] but generations of historians have found in them valuable information on

[1] Robert Harley was created Earl of Mortimer and Oxford in May 1711; Henry St John was created Viscount Bolingbroke in July 1712.

[2] *Letter and Correspondence Public and Private of the Right Honourable Henry St John Lord Viscount Bolingbroke during the Time he was Secretary of State to Queen Anne*, ed. G. Parke, 4 vols. (London, 1789) hereafter cited as *Bolingbroke Correspondence*.

[3] *Bolingbroke Correspondence* I, 58, letter of 5 Jan. 1710/11 (o.s.).

[4] 15th Report, Appendix, Part IV: *The Manuscripts of His Grace the Duke of Portland*, ed. J. J. Cartwright, IV (London, 1897) and V (London, 1899), hereafter cited as H.M.C., *Portland Papers*.

[5] H.M.C., *Portland Papers* V, ii.

a variety of topics. As long ago as 1938 Winston Churchill made use of them in his biography of Marlborough to throw light on the efforts at reconciliation with Harley which the Duke made via Drummond late in 1710;[6] as recently as 1964 Dr J. G. Stork-Penning collated them with material from The Hague archives to illuminate Anglo-Dutch relations in 1711.[7] Historians concerned with the struggle for power in Whitehall, with the difficulties of financing the last years of the War of the Spanish Succession, and with the negotiations leading, first to the Anglo-French preliminary peace and, then, to the Peace of Utrecht, have all had recourse to the Drummond correspondence as printed by Parke and Cartwright.[8] A selection of letters to Drummond from a variety of writers was made by W. Fraser from the Stirling-Home-Drummond Moray papers at Blair Drummond and published for the Historical Manuscripts Commission in 1885.[9] These have been little used (I have never come across a reference to them) though they offer a fascinating letter of August 1711 from Marlborough in which the Duke empowers Drummond, on the eve of a visit to London with its 'opportunity of conversing frequently with the persons whose friendship and confidence it is so necessary for me to preserve and improve', to pledge the Duke's word to cooperate with those now in office.[10] They also give us several letters from Henry Watkins (Judge

[6] *Marlborough, His Life and Times*, hereafter cited as Churchill, *Marlborough*, IV (London, 1938) 342–3.

[7] J. G. Stork-Penning, 'Het gedrag van de staten 1711', *Bijdragen voor de Geschiedenis der Nederlanden*, hereafter cited as Stork-Penning, *Bijdragen*, XVIII (1963–4), 193–229, and in particular pp. 206 ff; cp. her use, but to a lesser extent, of the correspondence in *Het Grote Werk* (Groningen, 1958), her study of the peace negotiations of 1705–10. Note a brief summary of her conclusions in English in *Acta Historiae Neerlandica* II (Leiden, 1967) 107–41.

[8] See e.g. R. Geikie and I. Montgomery, *The Dutch Barrier 1705–1719* (Cambridge, 1930) pp. 198 ff; G. M. Trevelyan, *England Under Queen Anne*, III. *The Peace and the Protestant Succession* (London, 1934) *passim*, though note that Drummond's name is not used; A. J. Veenendaal, *Het Engels-Nederlands Condominium in de Zuidelijke Nederlanden tijdens de spaanse successieoorlog* (Utrecht, 1945) pp. 182 ff; D. Coombs, *The Conduct of the Dutch* (The Hague, 1958) *passim*; J. Carswell, *The South Sea Bubble* (London, 1960) pp. 41–63.

[9] 10th Report, Appendix I, pp. 81 ff. *Report on the Manuscripts of Charles Stirling-Home-Drummond Moray Esq. of Blair-Drummond, at Blair Drummond and Ardoch in the County of Perth*, ed. W. Fraser (London, 1885) hereafter cited as H.M.C., *Drummond Moray Papers*.

[10] H.M.C., *Drummond Moray Papers*, p. 141: Marlborough to Drummond, 13 Aug. 1711; cp. p. 144, the Marlborough to Drummond letter of 10 Nov. 1711, for the

Advocate in the army in the Low Countries and Drummond's chief link with Marlborough's headquarters while he was in England) not included among those sent on to Oxford and thus not published with the Portland Papers.[11]

Though the Drummond correspondence has proved such a mine of information, hardly anything has been known of the man himself. Cartwright, in his introduction to the relevant volumes of the Portland Papers, quoted from Drummond's own letters to the effect that he had lived among the Dutch since his very early years and that he was thirty-four years old in 1710.[12] This is the sum of knowledge, repeated by all historians (not always with due acknowledgement) who have quoted from the printed correspondence. A close study of Drummond's letters to Oxford provides further factual information, particularly on that financial disaster which Parke, editing Bolingbroke's offer of help of 2 May 1712, refers to somewhat mysteriously if decidedly sympathetically: 'The party in England and Holland who opposed the peace were so much displeased with Mr Drummond's exertions to provide it that they conspired to ruin him; and in the attempt were too successful.'[13] Similarly, one of the published entries relating to John Drummond in the Fraser selection solves the problem raised by his acting (and informed contemporaries addressing him) as 'Commissaire de S. M. La Reine de la Grande Bretagne' for the 1713–14 negotiations in respect of English trade to the Southern Netherlands, and his non-inclusion in any list of official English representatives: a copy of an undated petition of his to Queen Anne refers to instructions of 30 March 1713 received from Lord Viscount Bolingbroke to settle this trade, with further instructions of 23 August to proceed to Utrecht to

---

Duke's sending to London a letter to Oxford (the one printed by W. Coxe, *Memoirs of the Duke of Marlborough*, revised ed. by J. Wade, III (London, 1896) 263–4) with a copy for Drummond that he might be fully informed and make the best use of it in conversation with the Treasurer.

[11] Henry Watkins was formerly secretary to Bolingbroke and is the 'Dear Judge' of his correspondence. (It is worth noting that the Cadogan letter printed by Churchill, *Marlborough* IV, 509–10, as to an 'unknown contemporary' begins 'Dear Judge' and is certainly addressed to Watkins). For the link between Watkins and Drummond see e.g. H.M.C., *Portland Papers* IV, 61, Drummond's letter of 4 Aug. 1711.

[12] H.M.C., *Portland Papers* IV, xiii.

[13] *Bolingbroke Correspondence* I, 9, with letter of 2 May 1712 printed *ibid.*, II, 306.

negotiate with the French, and appeals for full powers and pay.[14] Such powers never reached him and he had to rest content with Bolingbroke's thanks: 'No matter who signed the provisional regulations, you made it.'[15]

No collating of the relevant material in print suffices, though clues may be picked up here and there in other published letters,[16] for a sketch of Drummond's career; and it is fortunate that archives have yielded rich returns in a search for material which would permit a surer assessment of the value of his reports during the War of the Spanish Succession.[17] First, a series of letters exchanged by Drummond and James Brydges, the Paye master General, between 1705 and 1713 have survived in the Stow-collection at the Huntington Library: indeed, this series is the most voluminous in the Brydges correspondence at Huntington.[18] Secondly,

[14] H.M.C., *Drummond Moray Papers*, p. 147. Drummond's official letters from the trade negotiations are, as W. Fraser pointed out, in the Public Record Office; and I am indebted to Professor D. B. Horn for their exact location in Treaty Papers (S.P. 103/6) where they are classified as 'trade negotiations'.

[15] *Bolingbroke Correspondence* III, 208: letter of 25 July 1713. The senior plenipotentiary at the Congress of Utrecht, John Robinson, Bishop of Bristol (later Bishop of London), scrupulously gave Drummond the correct title for his mission (see H.M.C., *Drummond Moray Papers*, p. 176, letter of 7 Jan. 1713/14) and thought it 'an injustice' that the junior plenipotentiary, Thomas Wentworth, Earl of Strafford, was not willing to let Drummond sign (H.M.C., *Portland Papers* V, 309: Drummond's letter of 4 Aug. 1713). In the absence of full powers Drummond confessed (*ibid.*, p. 323, letter of 1 Sept. 1713) that the French commissaries 'have made some scruples about my Commission'.

[16] Most are found in the letters of Dr William Stratford, canon of Christ Church, Oxford, to Edward Harley, printed in H.M.C., *Portland Papers* VII (London, 1901), ed. S. C. Lomas (though note that the tentative identification of the Dutch friend of the amusing Anglo-Dutch quote on p. 9 as Drummond cannot—alas—be sustained); a few are in the correspondence between Brydges and Harley, ed. by G. Davies, *Huntington Library Quarterly* I (1937–8) 457–72; in the letters from St John to Brydges 1706–12, ed. G. Davies and M. Tinling, *Huntington Library Bulletin* VIII (1935) 135–70; and in those from Brydges to St John for the same period, *ibid.*, IX, (1936) 119–66. Cp. C. H. Collins Baker and Muriel Baker, *The Life and Circumstances of James Brydges First Duke of Chandos as Patron of the Liberal Arts* (Oxford, 1949); they print (pp. 41–49) two letters from Brydges to Drummond of 22 and 28 Nov. 1706 (o.s.) and have valuable information on the personal friendship of the two men after 1714 (note, however, the confusion between John Drummond and Andrew Drummond, pp. 154–5, 179, 364 and 428).

[17] I wished to undertake such an assessment for my work in progress on Europe and the Spanish Succession: for Drummond's career after 1714, see my forthcoming article 'John Drummond of Quarrell'.

[18] For these see E. L. Harvey, 'Letters and Accounts of James Brydges 1705–1713', *Huntington Library Bulletin* I (1931) 123–47, who lists among Brydges's correspondents

the Portland loan deposit at the British Museum contains some scattered but important Drummond material and enables us to pinpoint the Drummond connection with Harley as having begun as early as 1704;[19] while odd letters in other British Museum collections throw light on the Anglo-Dutch negotiations with which he was entrusted in 1711 and 1712.[20] Thirdly, the Abercairny Manuscripts now deposited in the Scottish Record Office contain eighteen bundles of letters (from which Fraser made his selection) addressed to Drummond between 1682 and 1745, as well as other relevant material, and enable us to follow his career both before and after the War of the Spanish Succession.[21] Finally, the identification of two ledgers (covering 1697 to 1709) in Drummond's Branch, Royal Bank of Scotland, as being those of John Drummond from his trading days as a partner in the firm of Van der Heiden and Drummond,[22] and the kind permission to use these and other papers belonging to this Bank, have clarified his financial position throughout life.[23]

John Drummond was born in 1676, the third son of George Drummond of Blair, and Elisabeth, daughter of Sir Gilbert Ramsay, first Baronet. In 1682 his father sold his inherited estate and purchased (from James Drummond, fourth Earl of Perth, to whom he was chamberlain) the lands of Kincardine in Menteith to which he gave the name of Blair-Drummond.[24] According to John's own testimony he was fifteen years

---

Drummond, with 238 letters sent and 156 received. To these must be added letters to and from the firm of Van der Heiden and Drummond.

[19] I wish to thank Dr A. MacLachlan, of the University of Sydney, who first drew my attention to the fact that papers from Drummond to Harley could be traced back to 1704 in the Portland Loan Deposit. For permission to quote from this Deposit I am grateful to His Grace the Earl of Portland.

[20] Especially the letters addressed by Drummond to Buys in B.M. Add. MSS. 20983 and 20985.

[21] Inv. GD. 24 Section 1. I became aware of this collection from *A Guide to the Materials for Swedish Historical Research in Great Britain*, ed. B. Steckzén (Stockholm, 1958) pp. 221–3. (Note, however, that in this *Guide* John Drummond is confused with the Jacobite exile John Drummond, Earl of Melfort.)

[22] For my identification of these ledgers, see Hector Bolitho and Derek Peel, *The Drummonds of Charing Cross* (London, 1967) p. 22.

[23] I am grateful for permission from Drummond's Branch, The Royal Bank of Scotland, to quote from the Bank's ledgers, and for the courtesy of its manager, J. R. C. Cuthbertson, Esq.

[24] D. Malcolm, *A Genealogical Memoir of the Most noble and ancient House of Drummond* (Edinburgh, 1808) pp. 47–9; cp. H.M.C., *Drummond Moray Papers*, p. 82.

old when he came to the Dutch side of the water.[25] His search for a good Amsterdam merchant willing to take him on as an apprentice met with some difficulties which we learn about in a letter home by his eldest brother James, sent to sort matters out.[26] The merchant (given as Mr Serrurier) to whom John had been recommended was unable to take him on as he was on the point of closing shop—John arriving only 'a little time before he broke'. He then had recourse to Mr Henderson, a broker 'whose trade it is to find out merchants for young men', and a contract was duly drawn up with a Mr Spilman, of good standing both in business and church. The contract, however, was unfavourable in various ways: the boy was to be at a charge to have his laundry and mending done 'without doors'; he was—as the younger of two apprentices—to work 'indoors' only, without opportunities to go on the Change; the accounts for which he was responsible would be made up only every nine months which left him as short of practice in book-keeping as innocent of the world of business 'out of doors'. By threatening to take John away, the brother achieved a compromise: the cost of washing and mending was fixed at 12 guilders a year; the accounts would be done every fortnight; and an undertaking was given that when the senior apprentice left two years hence John would be permitted to learn the ways of the Change. James was not particularly satisfied, but felt John had no choice: if he ran away from Spilman he would not get a good reference and no other merchant would employ him. Spilman's business was solid and the letter concluded on the happier note that John would certainly make a livelihood and be a credit to his family.

> Though he is your son, my brother, I must say this much of him that I doubt if there be in Amsterdam any who have improved [so much] in so short a time. He goes about his business carefully and readily (serves his Countrymen to purpose when occasion offers yet neglects not his master's business). In short, he is beloved by Everybody, especially by forrainers . . .

This willingness to help others was to remain characteristic of him

[25] H.M.C., *Portland Papers* IV, 559; Drummond's letter of 19 Aug. 1710.

[26] Abercairny MSS. 471, letter from James Drummond, dated Leiden, after six days in Amsterdam on John's behalf, 19 June o.s. 1693, addressed to 'Laird of Blair Drummond in Mylness Square Edinburgh'.

throughout life, though after an illness in his mid-fifties he proved temporarily testy at the number of solicitations and commissions from Scotland his work as a Member of Parliament brought: a 'terrible and unreasonable drudge of many things without sense or reason'.[27] Equally characteristic was a concern to get ahead. He always remained conscious that he had started with little and made his own way gradually. In the Nine Years' War he was under age and could not profit from its trading opportunities, 'when', as he somewhat ruefully wrote to Harley at a later date, 'all the estates were got by that trade'.[28] But at the time the peace congress of Ryswick got under way, he came out of his apprenticeship and set up as a merchant in partnership with one Jan van der Heiden.[29] We know, from information which Drummond gave Brydges, that this partner—with the help of his family—initially provided the greater share of capital for the business;[30] but after Drummond's marriage to Agatha Van der Bent he was able to put first her dowry and later the major part of her inheritance (£8000 in all) into the firm.[31] Her background was that of prosperous mercantile circles. One of her prized possessions was that silver dish and ewer (engraved with the Brandenburg arms) which had been given to her as an infant by the Elector of Brandenburg for whose family her brother was agent at Amsterdam.[32] By 1710 Drummond's stake in Van der Heiden and Drummond had risen to £6000 and by the

[27] Abercairny MSS. 464(d), letter from London of 23 Nov. 1731 to his brother William Drummond of Grange.

[28] H.M.C., *Portland Papers* IV, 559, Drummond's letter of 19 Aug. 1710; cp. *ibid.*, V, 150, Drummond's letter of 18 March 1712.

[29] The Christian name of the partner is found in the ledger book at Drummond's Branch, The Royal Bank of Scotland. In the *Calendar of Treasury Books*, the Dutch partner's name is sometimes spelt Vanderheiden or (a case of misprint) Van der Leiden.

[30] The father (vide the ledger cited above) was Joris, who preferred to spell his name Van der Heyden, a form sometimes used by others also for the son. The Abercairny MSS. 464(a) has a letter from a Johannes van der Heyden, son of Joris.

[31] Malcolm, *House of Drummond*, p. 47, gives the wife's maiden name as Vander (clearly a slip); the correct name is given in letters to and from her in the Abercairny MSS. 464(a). For the death of two of his wife's 'near relations', see Portland Loan, 29/45x, vol. 70, Drummond's letter of 6 Feb. 1705; for the death of his mother-in-law on 25 July 1706, *ibid.*, letter of that date.

[32] Information about this gift is taken from Drummond's will, for a copy of which I am indebted to Dr E. Cruickshanks. H.M.C., *Drummond Moray Papers*, p. 140, prints a letter from Matthew Prior of 10 Sept. 1697, to a Vanderbent in connexion with a bill of exchange.

time the crash came in 1712 he was the dominant partner by virtue of investment and energy.[33]

In the early years the firm prospered. The partners specialized in fine materials (velvets, silks, oriental embroidered cloth, silver and gold braid are some of the merchandise listed in their first ledger) and in the fashionable coffee, tea and chocolate (which all figure prominently in the accounts). The Peace congress brought festivities and balls for the entertainment of diplomats and their families and there was a general revival of trade in luxury goods. Pleasure in being able to afford a splendid suit for himself is evidenced in the form of the entry of Drummond's payment for it in the firm's accounts. Among the names of early customers one notes the Swedish mediator at Ryswick, Baron Lillieroot, and other foreign dignitaries as well as many of the noble and regent families of the Dutch Republic. With the return of peace with France, Drummond began to develop also those connections in the wine trade which he managed to keep open during the War of the Spanish Succession. He bought wine for customers in England throughout the war, receiving skilled advice on how to get it through the Customs,[34] and sent presents of wine to friends and patrons. He discussed the merits and treatment (such as the fining down with egg whites) of the Cahors 'in fashion at ye Court', and of Tokays, Champagnes, and Burgundys, but he made no secret of preferring claret himself, being a 'good Scots Claret Man'.[35] He further obliged friends and acquaintances by buying on their behalf books, table linen, paintings, *objets d'art* and rare plants. His lifelong friendship with Brydges began in 1705 when Brydges visited the Netherlands and received Drummond's help in building up his picture collection and his library.[36]

[33] Brydges Papers, vol. 6, Drummond's letter of 30 May 1710, and vol. 7, letter of 25 March 1712; H.M.C., *Portland Papers* v, 160, Drummond's letter of 15 April 1712.

[34] Portland Loan 29/45x, vol. 70, Drummond's letter to Harley of 3 Nov. 1705.

[35] For discussions on wine and presents of wine see Brydges Papers, vol. 2, Drummond's letters of 28 April 1707; vol. 5, of 18 Oct. 1709; vol. 6 of 28 Jan. 1710; Portland Loan 29/45x, vol. 70, Drummond's letters of 26 Oct. and 31 Dec. 1706; B.M. Add. MSS. 28893, Drummond's letter to John Ellis of 18 Jan. 1707; H.M.C., *Portland Papers* v, 13, Drummond's letter of 30 June 1711.

[36] Portland Loan 29/45x, vol. 70, Drummond's letter of 3 Nov. 1705; Brydges Papers, vol. 1, Drummond's letter of 21 Nov. 1705; cp. *ibid.* letter of 1 Nov. 1709 and Baker, *Brydges*, pp. 44–5 and 73–8. For services to Harley, see Portland Loan 29/45x, vol. 70, Drummond's letter of 5 Nov. 1706; to Ellis, B.M. Add. MSS. 28893, fo. 228 (a); to St John, *Bolingbroke Correspondence* I, 207 and 279.

By this time Drummond had already made the acquaintance of Harley, whom he was to regard as his chief patron throughout Anne's reign, during a brief stay in London in the autumn of 1704 after a fairly prolonged visit to Scotland to see his relatives.[37] He was introduced to the Secretary of State for the Northern department by Dr William Stratford (chaplain to the Speaker of the House of Commons when Harley filled that office), praising Drummond as 'an old true friend' who might be 'of service' to Harley at a time when he was busy building up a network of correspondents.[38] Drummond immediately wrote a report (part of which has survived but without signature) on the workings of European wartime financial transactions;[39] and—on his return to Amsterdam—corresponded with Harley, transmitted letters from Harley's agents on the Continent to Whitehall and wrote newsletters and reports to the Under-Secretary John Ellis.[40] Harley for his part was instrumental in obtaining for Drummond the government agency for selling Cornish tin, the contract for which he held between 1704 and 1707.[41]

The profit which this agency brought (estimated by Drummond at £1000 a year)[42] was welcome, since the War of the Spanish Succession had hit Van der Heiden and Drummond, with their emphasis on luxury goods, hard. Rumours (which proved only too true) that Godolphin intended to transfer the contract to Sir Henry Furnese, even before Harley's removal from the Secretaryship in 1708, brought appeals from

[37] Portland Loan 29/45x, vol. 70, letter from Drummond of 25 Nov. 1704, thanking Harley 'for the great honour and many civilitys and friendships, you were pleased to bestow on me in England'; cp., H.M.C., *Portland Papers* v, 11, Drummond's letter of 26 June 1711, stressing that he has only spent 'three months these twenty-two years in Scotland'.

[38] *Ibid.*, VII, 161, Stratford's letter to Edward Harley of 2 Aug. 1713; cp. *ibid.*, 60, Stratford to Edward Harley, 24 Sept. 1711.

[39] Portland Loan 29/45x, vol. 70, with the date endorsed 22 Sept. 1704.

[40] *Ibid.*, for the surviving letters to Harley for the years 1704 to 1707. These letters Drummond (see his letter of 5 Dec. 1704) expected not to 'bee exposed in the Office, for my hand is knowne to severalls in both ye offices'. For transmission of letters see, e.g., H.M.C., *Portland Papers* IV, 298, John [Lebrun] Ogilvy's letter to [Robert Harley] of 9 May 1706.

[41] Portland Loan 29/45x, vol. 70, Drummond's letter of 6 Jan. 1705; cp. Add. MSS. 28916, Drummond's letter to Ellis of 20 Jan. 1705. For the contract see *Calendar of Treasury Books* IX to XII (London 1938–50), under Drummond's name. Much detailed information about the tin contracts in Portland Loan 29/38B.

[42] Baker, *Brydges*, p. 56.

Drummond for a prolongation of his own commission for at least one more year, when he hoped for 'a good peace and a free trade and then I can employ my time and money to better advantage'.[43] With the failure of his plea, he was drawn further into banking transactions. We know that he financed at least some of Harley's secret agents on the Continent as early as 1705.[44] Bigger opportunities for profit were, however, to be found within the Paymaster General's sphere, in the payment of English troops and foreign auxiliary forces in the Low Countries. Brydges had indeed promised Drummond in the late autumn of 1705 'some employment in the privilege of remitting money to the forces', and Drummond in his turn had begged Harley that the Paymaster General might, discreetly, be reminded of his promise; a stratagem which seems to have worked since at the end of December 1706 we find Drummond informing Harley of a fact he wants kept secret: 'I now and then write to Mr Brydges the Paymaster Generall about money affaires.'[45] The only banker's day-book which survives from his hand opens on 21 July 1709 and by this time he was styling himself a 'Banquier' rather than a merchant.[46]

These transactions brought him into closer professional contact with Brydges and he moved also to the fringes of that 'seamy side of Marlborough's wars' which Godfrey Davies has examined from the papers of the Paymaster General.[47] Drummond disapproved of Englishmen lining their pockets at the expense of the country or of allies if this was 'ruthlessly done' (and earned for that reason the nickname of 'Honest John'),[48] and may have not been fully informed of the way in which Brydges amassed

[43] B.M. Add. MSS. 28893, Drummond's letter to Ellis of 18 Jan. 1707.

[44] H.M.C., *Portland Papers* IV, 258, Ogilvie's letter of 23 Oct. 1705; Portland Loan 29/45X, vol. 70, Drummond's letter of 5 Feb. 1706.

[45] *Ibid.*, Drummond's letters of 3 Nov. 1705, and 31 Dec. 1706.

[46] Abercairny MSS. 480, a bound vellum book with entries from 26 July 1709 till 1 Sept. 1710, recording transactions in discounted bills. The spelling 'Banquier' is the one Drummond uses in a letter to Brydges, 15 July 1710: Brydges Papers, vol. 6.

[47] G. Davies, 'The seamy side of Marlborough's Wars', *Huntington Library Quarterly* XV (1951–2) 21–44, based on Cadogan's letters to Brydges; cp. Baker, *Brydges*, p. 47.

[48] Brydges Papers, vol. 3, Drummond's letter of 28 Nov. 1709, criticizing Cadogan for taking 'particular care of himself, whatever may become of others'; cp. H.M.C., *Portland Papers* V, 366, Drummond's letter of 10 Dec. 1713, condemning the methods used by Lawes at Brussels, adding that his own circumstances must become 'more desperate ere I take such methods to better them'. For Drummond's nickname see, e.g., *ibid.*, VII, 86, Stratford's letter to Edward Harley of 5 June 1714.

a fortune by private investments of public funds. But he must have guessed a good deal. Certainly he himself provided the Paymaster General with regular and detailed news of the progress, or otherwise, of peace negotiations which enabled Brydges to buy and sell stocks profitably;[49] and at a time when Brydges was alarmed at the thought of investigations Drummond stressed that all secret transactions on his side of the water were safe with him: he entered them in a separate book of which his partner had no knowledge. This book, which he always carried on his person, contained details also of moneys which Brydges had put him in the way of earning, mainly by helping him to acquire Bank stock 'under the current course'. By the spring of 1710 Drummond had put by £5000 in England, unknown to his partner, and planned, as soon as he had made sure of a regular income of £500 in annuities and provided himself with a capital of £6000 to £7000 for trading, to leave 'the good city' of Amsterdam and 'end my days' in Britain.[50]

Paradoxically enough it was Drummond's 'Dutchness' which in 1710 recommended him, along with his willingness to support financially the new ministry, to Harley and St John, Chancellor of the Exchequer and Secretary of State for the North respectively. Many Dutchmen thought him 'one of themselves' and assumed he had taken Dutch nationality;[51] both Harley and St John used phrases, in the early stages of the intense Drummond correspondence which followed their taking office in 1710, which show that they tended to look upon him as so long settled in the United Provinces as to be a Dutchman.[52] It was only gradually that they realized the distinction Drummond himself made ('I never was a burgher, only an inhabitant')[53] and appreciated his determination to remain 'a Queen's subject'.[54]

With the distrust which Harley and St John felt of the regular diplomatic representatives at The Hague—Townsend as ambassador and Dayrolle as resident, Whig nominees as far as the new ministry was concerned—they stood in particular need of new channels of communication.

[49] Brydges Papers, vols. 1–6, Drummond's letters, *passim*.

[50] *Ibid.*, vol. 6, Drummond's letter of 30 May 1710.

[51] H.M.C., *Portland Papers* v, 320, Drummond's letter of 18 Aug. 1713.

[52] *Ibid.*, IV, 624–5, Harley (draft) to Drummond, 7 Nov. 1710; *Bolingbroke Correspondence* I, 52, letter of 26 Dec. 1710.

[53] H.M.C. *Portland Papers*, v, 280, Drummond's letter of 25 April 1713.

[54] Brydges Papers, vol. 6, Drummond's letter of 30 May 1710.

Harley directed Drummond to correspond not only with himself but also with St John.[55] As well as carrying on all kinds of intelligence work for the Secretary via his French contacts (news from Saint-Germain,[56] reports of French naval preparations and the state of the French ports[57]), Drummond arranged a correspondence between St John and Willem Buys, the Pensionary of the States of Holland,[58] whom he knew well (and of whose character and opinions he had kept Harley informed since 1704).[59] At the same time he continued to give sound advice to Harley on how to secure public remittances, in whom to trust and of whom to be suspicious in the world of finance at home and abroad. He had good connections with bankers in England—with Sir Theodore Janssen, Sir John Lambert, Richard Hoare and Edward Gibbon; he had particular ties with the Dutch-born Matthew Decker (naturalized in 1702) and with Andrew Pels in Amsterdam. He himself became deeply committed in the credit struggle which ensued once the new ministry was established. A great many bills began to pass through Drummond and Van der Heiden, the reversal of the firm's name in English correspondence being indicative of Drummond's growing importance. Possibly too many, for as one of the more cautious Rotterdam bankers, Senserf, wrote to Brydges, admittedly with the wisdom of hindsight after the crash: 'They were rising, but out of their sphere.'[60]

There had throughout 1710 been anxious moments for Drummond in the counting house over exchanges fluctuating with the fortunes of war and rumours of government changes in England,[61] but these multiplied once he started backing the new ministry. By October 1710 he and his partner were committed to pay £100,000 before mid-March 1711 and he railed to Brydges at 'that damned villainous jesuitically fanatick resolution of the Governors and Directors of the Bank to discount no foreign

[55] H.M.C., *Portland Papers* IV, 651, Drummond's letter of 13 Jan. 1711.

[56] Brydges Papers, vol. 7, Drummond's letter of 24 Oct. 1710: *Bolingbroke Correspondence* I, 16, letter of 10 Nov. 1710.

[57] *Ibid.*, pp. 8, 11, 87, 106, 111: letters of 17 Oct. 1710 and 2, 6, 20 March 1710/11.

[58] *Ibid.*, where the opening letter of 13 Oct. 1710 is to Buys; cp. letters to Drummond of 13, 14 and 27 Oct. 1710.

[59] Portland Loan 29/45X, vol. 70, e.g. Drummond's letters of 6 Jan. and 11 May 1706.

[60] Brydges Papers, vol. 11. Senserf's letter of 31 May 1712.

[61] *Ibid.*, vol. 5, Drummond's letters of 25 March, 25 and 28 April 1710.

Bills except for Exchequer Bills', labelling the men responsible 'traitors to the country in the name of patriots'.[62] By July 1711 he seemed to have won through. Van der Heiden and Drummond was still short of money, but he could congratulate himself that he had helped to put the English credit, 'which stood on trial and some of us with it', on a better footing in the Republic than it had possessed since war broke out—a verdict which was gratefully endorsed in Whitehall.[63]

The struggle had been wearying, however, and this was no doubt one reason why he began to contemplate a less nerve-racking mode of making a living: banking was for richer men than he.[64] He had thrown out hints to Harley (Lord Treasurer and head of the government since May 1711 with the title of Earl of Mortimer and Oxford) that he might welcome some official employment from June 1711 onwards; and he was anxious to make use of the opportunity of a visit to London which he and his wife undertook in the autumn of 1711 to obtain 'some security for the future'.[65]

The purpose behind this visit was political. Heinsius, the Dutch Grand Pensionary, had, on the advice of the Earl of Albemarle (an old friend of Drummond's)[66] begun to use Drummond as a channel of communication with the new ministry in mid-December 1710. Drummond excitedly reported (in an unsigned letter) to Harley that Lord Albemarle had arranged that the Grand Pensionary should take 'information of English affairs from me quite unknown to the great man [i.e. Marlborough] and Townshend', and how this was to be managed. His Amsterdam home was thirty-six English miles from The Hague but this would not prevent him keeping in touch with Heinsius; by post-chaise he could cover the distance in six hours, 'so that on a moonlight night I make but one day and evening Journey'. 'I am', Drummond concluded with pardonable pride, 'always

[62] *Ibid.*, vol. 7, Drummond's letters of 24 Oct. 1710, 11 Jan. and 20 Feb. 1711, and H.M.C., *Portland Papers* IV, 617–8, Drummond's letter of 7 Nov. 1710. For the Bank's policy in relation to the new ministry, see Carswell, *The South Sea Bubble*, pp. 49 ff., and P. G. M. Dickson, *The Financial Revolution in England* (London, 1967) pp. 19, 26.

[63] For Drummond's opinion see Brydges Papers, vol. 8, letter of 21 July 1711; for that of Whitehall, see *The Wentworth Papers*, ed. J. J. Cartwright, II (London, 1883), 212, Peter Wentworth's letter of 25 Nov. 1711.

[64] H.M.C., *Portland Papers* V, 10–11, Drummond's letter of 26 June 1711.

[65] *Ibid.*, and p. 49, letter of 24 July 1711.

[66] For the Albemarles spending a Christmas vacation with the Drummonds, see Brydges Papers, vol. 6, Drummond's letter of 31 Dec. 1706.

to be admitted at the pentionarys at any hour.'[67] Heinsius's overtures were welcomed in Whitehall as they relieved Harley of fear that the Dutch leaders might, because of their attachment to the Whigs, attempt to topple the new ministry. From now on letters from Drummond to Harley with political 'secret' information were initialled J.D. while those with ordinary news were signed in full.[68] After Townshend's recall and Baron Raby's appointment to the States General in March 1711, this irascible diplomat took umbrage at Drummond's role in negotiations which he suspected rather than knew of in detail; and though St John tried to mollify him as best he could, Raby's dislike of Drummond (which was to affect the latter's career) was probably caused by rumours of the banker's secret access to the Grand Pensionary.[69] Drummond was by nature hospitable and gregarious. He and his wife had no children and enjoyed having people around them. At their home friends—such as the Albemarles—came to stay in an ever widening circle tied together by interest and sentiment. Even a marriage was arranged, between Henry Watkins's sister and Matthew Decker: 'A match of my making', Drummond confessed, 'which is the only one I ever meddled in.'[70] Officers drank to the success of impending campaigns of a convivial evening,[71] diplomats and notables in transit were entertained and helped on their way.[72] But once Drummond had become a go-between of Oxford and Heinsius he guarded his tongue. 'My friends rather found fault', he wrote in June 1711, 'that I was over quiet than talkative.'[73] He could not, however, forbear to hint in his letters to St John and Brydges that the London journey he was preparing for in the summer of 1711 was undertaken at the Grand Pensionary's request.

[67] Portland Loan 29/38[1] copy of an unsigned letter dated The Hague, 15 Dec. (the year and the writer can be deduced from the contents).

[68] See *Portland Papers* IV and V. A similar division, but into signed and unsigned letters, can be observed in the Portland Loan, 29/45X, vol. 70, letters.

[69] See *Bolingbroke Correspondence* I, 190–97, letter to Raby of 6 May 1711, in which St John tries to mollify the diplomat. Cp. Geikie and Montgomery, *op. cit.*, p. 212.

[70] H.M.C., *Portland Papers* V, 111, Drummond's letter of 25 Nov. [1710]. Note misplacement in series due to an incorrect endorsement by Harley.

[71] See, e.g., Brydges Papers, vol. 6, letter of 29 Nov. 1709.

[72] See, e.g., Portland Loan 29/38, Drummond's letter of 15 Dec. [1710] for Prince Eugène's visiting his house; and H.M.C., *Portland Papers* IV, 594, Drummond's letter of 23 Sept. 1711 for his entertaining Pitts, the governor of Madras.

[73] *Ibid.*, V, 8, Drummond's letter of 26 June 1711.

Heinsius, uneasy at the separate Anglo-French negotiations, of which he was well aware though insufficiently informed, had decided to send Drummond to London in the hope of securing, first, full and frank information of English intentions as to peace terms and, secondly, Dutch participation in the peace negotiations.[74] For this purpose he was willing to sacrifice Marlborough;[75] and Drummond himself—though he attempted to carry out the mission of reconciliation with which the Duke had entrusted him—soon became convinced that he could not be saved and salved his conscience by accepting the current cliché that the great man had ruined himself by following the bad advice of wife and son-in-law.[76] To Oxford Drummond now took care to stress his slight acquaintance with the Duke,[77] just as he later was to minimize his acquaintance with Prince Eugène (though he had been pleased enough in earlier days to report his admiration for 'the finest most generous oblidging great man that ever I saw, the easiest to live with',[78] and expand on their common interest in books and paintings: the Prince 'makes me a sort of favourite in his own little affairs')[79] once the Anglo-Austrian alliance broke down.[80]

In the political sense, seen from the Dutch point of view, Drummond's mission to London—which lasted from September 1711 till March 1712 (and then only came to an end because the concerns of Van der Heiden and Drummond demanded his return to Amsterdam)—was a failure, as was the mission by Buys (as envoy extraordinary) for which he prepared the ground and with whom he kept in close touch once the Dutchman

[74] The best treatment of Heinsius's policy in 1711 is in the article by J. Stork-Penning in *Bijdragen*, 1963–64 (noted above, p. 70, fn. 7), who shows one section of Geikie and Montgomery, *The Dutch Barrier, 1705–1719* to be seriously misleading.

[75] That Oxford and St John were informed by Drummond of this even before Drummond's mission to London is clear from H.M.C., *Portland Papers* v, 84, St John's letter of 4 Sept. 1711 to Oxford. Cp. *Bolingbroke Correspondence* I, 254 and 345.

[76] H.M.C., *Portland Papers*, IV, 655, Drummond's letter of 27 Jan. 1710/11; cp. *ibid.*, 594, 23 Sept. 1710 and 619, 11 Nov. 1710.

[77] This contrasts not only with the Duke of Marlborough's thanks for 'professions of friendship' (see H.M.C., *Drummond Moray Papers*, 141, 144, letters of 13 Aug. and 10 Nov. 1711), but also with Drummond's letters to Harley in earlier years (see Portland Loan, 29/45x, vol. 70, letters of 6 Jan. 1705, 11 May 1706 and 27 May 1707).

[78] Portland Loan 29/38, Drummond's letter of 15 Dec. [1710].

[79] H.M.C., *Portland Papers* v, 8, Drummond's letter of 26 June 1711.

[80] *Ibid.*, v, 367, Drummond's letter of 10 Dec. 1713.

arrived in London, where he stayed from the end of October to the end of December 1711. Drummond was indeed used, throughout the Anglo-French negotiations of this period, to calm Dutch unease and lull Dutch suspicions by his letters—'to be kept secret from all people'[81]—to Heinsius. He was not fully aware of the role he was made to play. He accepted the Oxford–St John argument that England ought to reap separate advantages from negotiating on English soil and tried to convince himself that the Dutch would have done the same had the tables been turned;[82] but his own suggestions and proposals as long as he was a free agent—that is before the crash of 1712—were of a kind which would tend to preserve the harmony of cooperation between the Maritime Powers.[83] But even in his brief period of relative importance—when he felt 'the utmost joy and gratitude' for the many civilities and kindnesses shown him at Whitehall,[84] and when he and his wife were received at Hampton Court and 'very much carrest' by Mrs Masham[85]—he failed to take an independent line in the political discussions he was permitted alone with Oxford and St John. He listened respectfully to their self-assured boast that England did not need the Dutch, nor anyone else, to make peace on her behalf ('England could and would make peace on its own and needed no Mediator') and was reduced to begging them to treat the Dutch well and grant them equivalents for those clauses of the Barrier Treaty of 1709 which the new ministry were not prepared to honour.[86]

This subservience can in part be explained by Drummond's anxiety to obtain private advantage. Brydges was willing, and even anxious (as investigations into financial irregularities still threatened), to replace his

[81] O. Weber, *Der Friede von Utrecht* (Gotha, 1891) p. 110: Weber was the first historian to discover, from his work in The Hague archives, Drummond's correspondence with Heinsius.

[82] H.M.C., *Portland Papers* v, 104, Drummond's letter (from London) of 22 Oct. 1711.

[83] *Ibid.*, pp. 103–5 for such suggestions; B.M. Add. MSS. 20985, Drummond's letter to Buys (from London) of 25 Jan. 1712; cp. R. M. Hatton, *Diplomatic Relations between Great Britain and the Dutch Republic, 1714–1721*, (London, 1950), Introduction, and in particular p. 15.

[84] H.M.C., *Portland Papers* VII, 60, Stratford's letter to Edward Harley, 24 Sept. 1711; cp. *ibid.*, v 145–6, Drummond's letter of 8 March 1712.

[85] *Wentworth Papers* II, 212, Peter Wentworth's letter of 24 Nov. 1711.

[86] B.M. Add. MSS. 20985, Drummond's letter to Buys of 25 Jan. 1712, reporting conversations (often verbatim).

two deputy paymasters in Brussels, Sweet and Cartwright, with a sole deputy, Drummond, on condition that he offered a security of £30,000.[87] Two-thirds of this sum was arranged immediately with the help of friends in the City, and Drummond expected to be able to raise the remainder from business associates.[88] Sweet had made himself unpopular in the army and he and Cartwright were not working well together;[89] but there is no doubt that Drummond coveted the deputy paymastership because it offered the right opportunity to accumulate profit on a big enough scale to speed up his plans to settle in England and trade on his own. He, as well as his friends and connections, regarded the matter as settled: 'Do you know', St John wrote to Watkins on 18 January 1711/12, 'Drummond is to succeed Sweet?'[90]

The Secretary of State cooperated with Brydges in pressing Drummond's suit from a sense of personal obligation towards the Drummonds who had, in their Amsterdam home, nursed young George St John, the Secretary's half-brother, through a dangerous illness in the first half of 1711.[91] It was the Secretary who vetted the Paymaster General's draft letter to Oxford of 11 February 1711/12, asking permission to dismiss Sweet and let him be succeeded by Drummond as sole deputy.[92] On 16 February official confirmation that 'the Lord Treasurer has no objection to your so appointing him' was returned.[93]

It was at this nice point, with the prize he wanted within his grasp, that the irony of fate caught up with Drummond. Before the end of the month he was urgently called to Amsterdam, ostensibly because of the serious illness of his partner, but in reality because of rumours that Van der

[87] Brydges Papers, vol. 11, Drummond's letter of 11 March 1711/12; cp. Baker. *Brydges*, p. 56.

[88] H.M.C., *Portland Papers* v, 150–1, Drummond's letter of 18 March 1712.

[89] See Brydges Papers, vol. 6, Sweet's letter of 2 May 1710, Cardonnel's of 8 May 1710 and Drummond's of 2 Sept. 1710 for friction in existing arrangements and *ibid.*, vol. 8, for Cardonnel's letter of 13 Sept. 1711 suggesting that one replacement might be made 'because of the bad intelligence between the two paymasters'.

[90] *Bolingbroke Correspondence* II, 161.

[91] *Ibid.*, I, 320–1, letter to Drummond of 20 Aug. 1711; also 339–41, letter of 28 Aug. 1711.

[92] Printed in *Huntington Library Quarterly* I (1937–8) 465; cp. Brydges to St John, 21 Jan. 1711/12, printed in *Huntington Library Bulletin* IX, (1936) 131–2.

[93] *Calendar of Treasury Books* XXVI (London, 1944) 156.

Heiden and Drummond were in trouble.[94] The partner recovered even before Drummond's arrival, but the financial difficulties which were to break the firm mounted day by day. 'Times are dangerous', Senserf wrote from Amsterdam.[95] 'People break daily and bring new hardships on us', Drummond intimated to Brydges on 8 April.[96] The firm was particularly affected by the crash of Francis Stratford,[97] but Drummond was naturally anxious to minimize his own precarious state in letters to the Paymaster General who had so recently emphasized his financial soundness as a prerequisite for the post of deputy paymaster in the Low Countries. To Oxford he was by contrast very outspoken because he needed his help—'secret and quick'—badly. As early as 18 March he appealed to the Treasurer to advance Sir John Lambert, Mr Hoare and Mr Gibbon the £100,000 shortly due from the Treasury for their own contracts: if this could be done they would in their turn be willing to lend him £30,000 for six months and he would be saved, otherwise he would 'in 25 days sink under the loss and discredit which Stratford and his house has so unmercifully brought on me'.[98]

There was little, however, that could be done for him. Oxford immediately arranged that £1200, which Drummond was owed on public business, should be repaid him;[99] but the Treasurer was unable to advance the large sum for Drummond's City friends which would have made it possible for him to weather the storm. Rumours of the firm's difficulties naturally made creditors call for their money. Senserf, who had 'some notice', was able to make certain of his £6000 and expressed—after the crash became public—rather smug sympathy for Brydges who had been unable (but probably also unwilling, even if he had been informed in time)

[94] Brydges Papers, vol. 11, Drummond's letter of 11 March 1711/12; see also H.M.C., *Portland Papers* v, 146, Drummond's letter of 8 March 1712, reporting his arrival at The Hague on 1 March and at Amsterdam on 8 March.

[95] Brydges Papers, vol. 11, Senserf's letter of 17 May 1712.

[96] *Ibid.*, Drummond's letter of 8 April 1712.

[97] H.M.C., *Portland Papers* v, 150, Drummond's letter of 18 March 1712 informing Oxford that he had advanced Stratford £7000. For Stratford's crash, see Carswell, *The South Sea Bubble*, p. 283.

[98] H.M.C., *Portland Papers* v, 149–51, Drummond's long letter of 18 March 1712.

[99] *Calendar of Treasury Books* XXVI 26 and 226: the sum was paid out of civil list with £37. 10s. in fees 'for special services relating to the war without account'.

to do so.[100] Drummond's own relations were not in a position to help 'at the moment'; while Jan van der Heiden's family, who had capital, regarded the bankruptcy as inevitable and decided to let matters take their course, keeping their capital to set their son up afresh later.[101]

Drummond's share in the firm was 'without reserve', so he was liable to lose all he possessed. He lived in 'perpetual terror . . . almost out of my wits', fearing that when the crash came his creditors might not permit his wife to keep even her personal possessions of furniture and plate. He grieved for his good name, that he would not be able 'to satisfy the world', and for his inability now to 'undertake that employment' which he so desired.[102] On 29 April he confessed the full extent of the calamity to Brydges, though he felt hardly 'capable of writing or speaking common sense', knowing that he had lost all 'that is valuable in life' and feeling desperately sorry for his wife whom he had repaid so poorly for the fortune she had brought him: 'shame and misery' had now ruined her health. He reckoned that his creditors would lose £20,000 even after all moneys due to the firm were handed over and he and his wife had sacrificed their house. He blamed bad management during his absence in London, his partner having—unbeknown to him—drawn £50,000 on the firm.[103] Drummond's inability to supervise the details of the business when in London may have had something to do with the crash of the firm; but Senserf's comment about 'ruin being at hand' when there is 'no order in the books' may have been directed at Drummond as well as his partner.[104]

By 10 May 'the fatal hour' had come,[105] and the firm was stopped owing payment for 100,000 guilders.[106] Drummond's creditors on the Dutch side (of whom Sweet was the one he could not satisfy) had agreed that his wife might keep her annuity of £160 and her personal possessions. If

[100] Brydges Papers, vol. 11, Senserf's letter of 31 May 1712.

[101] H.M.C., *Portland Papers* v, 159, Drummond's letter of 15 April 1712; 162, letter of 19 April 1712; 164, letter of 26 April 1712.

[102] The quotations are, in sequence, from Brydges Papers, vol. 11, letter of 8 April 1712; H.M.C., *Portland Papers* v, 159–64, letter of 15 April 1712; *ibid.*, 164, letter of 26 April 1712.

[103] Brydges Papers, vol. 11, Drummond's letter of 29 April 1712.

[104] *Ibid.*, Senserf's letter of 31 May 1712.

[105] *Ibid.*, Drummond's letter of 10 May 1712.

[106] H.M.C., *Portland Papers* v, 169, Drummond's letter of 10 May 1702.

he had sacrificed the annuity he might have paid them in full, but he could not bring himself to rob his wife of her sole remaining security, small though it was.[107] In England Mr Hoare and the East India Company were the main sufferers; [108] among his private friends Brydges, who lost £4700.[109] He met with a great deal of sympathy and understanding in England. St John assured him that his friends would not forget him and took care that his brother settled what he owed him, 'though the debt of gratitude he owes you can never be repaid'.[110] His wife—who made a trip to Amsterdam to pack her plate and personal belongings[111]—was as well received after the crash as before by the Earl of Oxford's family and by their friends and acquaintances.[112] But one man in the City turned against him in a way that Drummond feared would 'ruin me completely'.[113] The money which Drummond had put aside in England unknown to his partner was of the greatest importance after the Amsterdam crash: it would enable him to satisfy at least some of his English creditors and, he hoped, leave some capital to tide him over the difficult period of a new start. It was this sheet-anchor which Edward Gibbon threatened to cut by taking out an exeat against 'some effects' he pleaded the firm of Drummond and Van der Heiden had in London. His object was to recover part at least of the £10,000 owing to him; but if he succeeded the whole of the Drummond nest-egg would disappear. The Lord Treasurer gained time by referring Gibbon's request for investigation and Matthew Decker undertook delicate negotiations on Drummond's behalf, which by October 1712 resulted in an arrangement with the English creditors 'by which he [Drummond] is to pay them 30 per cent in two months time and 20 per cent in six months more—and to pay beside to Gibbon £2,500 out of Mrs Drummond's money now in Decker's hands'. Stratford conveyed this 'welcome news' to Edward Harley with obvious

[107] *Ibid.*, v, 282, Drummond's letter of 26 April 1713.

[108] *Ibid.*, v, 160, Drummond's letter of 15 April 1712; and 164, letter of 26 April 1712; 282, letter of 26 April 1713.

[109] Brydges Papers, vol. 11, Drummond's letter of 10 May 1712.

[110] *Bolingbroke Correspondence* II, 306, letter of 2 May 1712.

[111] H.M.C., *Portland Papers* v, 282, Drummond's letter of 26 April 1713, when seeing his wife off at Rotterdam.

[112] *Ibid.*, 165, Drummond's letter of 26 April 1712; *Bolingbroke Correspondence* II, 306, letter of 2 May 1712.

[113] H.M.C., *Portland Papers* v, 196, Drummond's letter of 12 July 1712.

relief: 'By this agreement, that honest unfortunate man will be at liberty again in eight months at farthest.'[114]

The problem of a future career remained. Drummond hoped, against near certainty of disappointment, for as long as he dared, that the deputy paymastership might yet materialize. 'Whether Mr Brydges will now send me my commission or not I must leave to his good opinion of me', he wrote to Oxford on 19 April.[115] The commission was made out on 22 April (o.s.), but it was Oxford himself who ordered that it was not to be sent till he gave specific instructions for its dispatch[116] and in June the deputy paymastership was given to Humphrey Walcott.[117] Lord Albemarle offered to make Drummond an officer in his regiment, but to join the 'carabineers' ('a trade I was never used to') seemed to Drummond's non-martial personality synonymous with death: 'the world would easily get rid of me'. While protesting that 'rather than be a burden to anyone for my subsistence or be blamed for detaining one farthing, I would undergo any hardship',[118] he declined the offer 'for his wife's sake'. Other Dutch friends, notably Buys and the banker Pels, proved equally kind but more useful in various ways; he was 'universally pitied, and many came to offer me assistance, believing my stop proceeded only from the general want of credit and scarcity of money'.[119] He felt bitter, however, towards the English traders and financiers in the Low Countries: they had spread rumours that he had been arrested in London on a charge of corresponding with 'James III' at Saint-Germain, and to the chagrined Drummond it looked as if they had 'whispered me out of my credit that they might rob me of my business'.[120] He would not like to remain, despised and

[114] *Ibid.*, VII, 96, Stratford's letter of 19 Oct. 1712; cp. Drummond's hope, *ibid.*, V, 170, letter of 10 May 1712, to pay 'at least ten shillings in the pound'. For Decker continuing to take care of Drummond's financial affairs in London see *Calendar of Treasury Books* XXVII (London, 1957) 313, entry of 18 Nov. 1713.

[115] H.M.C., *Portland Papers* V, 162.

[116] *Calendar of Treasury Books* XXVI, 251, letter of 22 April.

[117] G. Davies, *Huntington Library Quarterly* I (1937–8), 465, n. 34. For Walcott's arrival, see H.M.C., *Portland Papers* V, 195, Drummond's letter of 12 July 1712.

[118] *Ibid.*, pp. 175–6, Drummond's letter to Stratford of 27 May 1712.

[119] *Ibid.*, p. 152, Drummond's letters of 29 March 1712; p. 164, of 26 April 1712; pp. 169–70, of 10 May 1712; p. 282, of 26 April 1713.

[120] *Ibid.*, p. 152, Drummond's letter of 29 March 1712. The charge that Drummond was a Jacobite has died hard; see, e.g., John J. Murray, *George I, the Baltic and the Whig Split* (London, 1969), index. It probably arises from a [1705?] memorandum

humiliated, in the business community of Amsterdam. A growing tendency among Dutchmen to link his visit to England with the deterioration in Anglo-Dutch relations also made a move from the Republic at large seem desirable. He worried that blame was being attached to him for the split between the Maritime Powers and felt hurt at the charge that he had betrayed the Dutch. 'I have suffered much', he wrote to Buys in January 1713, apologizing for speaking freely ('ick moet myn haart eens wat lught geeven'), and proceeded to discuss at length the dilemma in which political circumstances had put him, deploring the 'bad times' which forced a 'good Englishman' to be judged a 'bad Hollander'. He defended himself ('some Dutch ministers', he charged, had too long remained 'the dupes of the Whigs') and took his stand with 'the courageous Oxford and his fresh counsels'. He would stay in the Republic till he had settled his affairs, but it was in England that he 'must once more attempt to seek my fortune'.[121]

Drummond trusted, as he wrote to Stratford, to the 'kindness and compassion' of his 'great friends' in England.[122] He appealed openly to Oxford for employment, however 'laborious', which would permit him to link his fate with that of the government.[123] But it was from Bolingbroke that rescue eventually came. 'I have not been unmindful of your interests', he wrote to Drummond on 14 March 1712/13. He had awaited an opportunity of acknowledging his personal obligations as well as those of the ministry for previous support and now sent a commission for Drummond to participate in the Utrecht negotiations in so far as they affected the English trade to the Southern Netherlands. At the same time, the Secretary outlined a scheme whereby he hoped, after the peace treaties were signed, to make Drummond consul at Ostend (in place of the 'bad' Loggan) and resident in Brussels (in place of Lawes, who 'can't be continued beyond the peace').[124] That Drummond grabbed at a chance to

by Ogilvie to Harley in H.M.C., *Portland Papers* IV, 277; it was denied by Drummond in a letter of 29 May 1711 to Oxford: *ibid.*, v, 692.

[121] B.M. Add. MSS. 20985, Drummond's letter to Buys from Amsterdam, 21 Jan. 1713.

[122] H.M.C., *Portland Papers* v, 175–6, Drummond's letter to Stratford of 27 May, 1712.

[123] *Ibid.*, 170, Drummond's letter of 10 May 1712.

[124] *Bolingbroke Correspondence* III, 516, letter of 14 March 1712/13. Cp. D. B. Horn, *The British Diplomatic Service, 1689–1789* (Oxford, 1961) pp. 149, 243.

re-establish himself is clear both from the way in which he hastened, by repeated letters, to express a politic assumption that Oxford had consented to, if not obtained for him, the suggested employment,[125] and in the way in which (shocking and grievous to his Dutch friends) he pressed the English case in the ensuing negotiations.

Drummond had been justifiably hurt at the accusations of his having worked against the United Provinces during his 1711–12 stay in London; but from March 1713 his determination to serve the English cause (and so secure also his own future) certainly made him use his intimate knowledge of Low Countries trade to the disadvantage of the Republic. The *règlement* which he achieved was anti-Dutch in spirit and the tone of his many letters to Oxford during the period of the negotiations is distinctly anti-Dutch. He clearly expected that his zeal and expertise would help obtain for him the post at Brussels, held by Lawes, which Bolingbroke had given him hopes of: to Oxford he gives broad hints of how grateful he would be for the chance to serve there as minister or resident.[126] Drummond's letters, the private ones to Oxford and Bolingbroke as well as the official letters to the latter as Secretary of State in 1713 and 1714, are very full and well-informed—even self-assured—on all political and commercial matters that came his way; but the private ones to Oxford are noticeably servile and humble whenever he touches upon his hopes of future employment.

His uncertainty was intensified on two counts. First, the Earl of Stratford (as Baron Raby was created late in 1711) proved inimical to the prospect of Lawes being replaced by Drummond, whom he disliked and mistrusted, and Drummond came to accept the impossibility of Bolingbroke putting his plan into effect. He wrote to the Secretary, declining the prospect of the residency at Brussels and the consulship at Ostend (as well as the one at Bruges which had also been mooted), but still had—as late as February

[125] H.M.C., *Portland Papers* v, 279, Drummond's letter of 25 April 1713 (referring also to an earlier letter on the same subject); 282, letter of 26 April 1713.

[126] *Ibid.*, v, 282, Drummond's letter of 26 April 1713; 302, of 11 July 1713; 310, of 4 Aug. 1713; 366, of 10 Dec. 1713; cp. P.R.O., S.P. 103/6, Drummond to Bromley, The Hague, 9 Jan. 1714. For specifically anti-Dutch letters, see H.M.C., *Portland Papers* v, 286, letter of 8 May 1713; 300–2, of 11 July 1713; 309–10, of 4 Aug. 1713 and H.M.C., *Drummond Moray Papers*, p. 146, the Earl of Strafford's letter to Drummond of 18 Oct. 1713; cp. S.P. 103/6, *passim*. For the work of the commission see Geikie and Montgomery, *op. cit.*, pp. 311–15.

1714—to remind Strafford that he had done so and was not plotting to undermine Lawes' position as the ambassador insisted. Characteristically he continued his attempts to remedy damage done by Lawes to English traders in the Low Countries to gain 'some reputation' for himself, and presumably still hoped that the wind might change in his own favour and against Strafford's 'favourite at Brussels'.[127] Secondly, the growing rivalry between his two political patrons at home perplexed him. It was vitally important for him to offend neither Bolingbroke nor Oxford. This was made somewhat easier by Bolingbroke's transference to the Southern Secretaryship in August 1713, permitting Drummond to tie closer to Oxford without disobliging Bolingbroke by too intermittent a correspondence. Bolingbroke's official parting words were meant to be reassuring: 'My Lord Treasurer is your friend'; he himself had seen to it that 'the Queen is so justly prepared in your favour that I make no doubt you will immediately have another payment than what the Court usually make, hope and promises'.[128] To Drummond, in his nervous state, they carried a hint of dismissal.

Rumours in the United Provinces of the Oxford–Bolingbroke split came, somewhat unexpectedly, to Drummond's rescue and made him an important figure once more in the eyes of Dutch statesmen. Heinsius in particular badly needed information and channels of contact with Whitehall at a time when Bolingbroke's connection with the Pretender was strongly rumoured on the Continent. The liabilities of the Republic, the chief foreign guarantor of the Protestant Succession of Great Britain, had to be considered, as well as the effects on the Republic of a successful Jacobite coup. Drummond—to his surprise—found himself well received by the Grand Pensionary and other Dutch high officials during his visits to The Hague in the early autumn of 1713.[129] Matthew Decker, who spent some time on the Dutch side of the water in August and September 1713, had instigated informal contacts between Oxford and Heinsius;[130] and Heinsius now took the line that Dutch sacrifices in commerce (some

[127] S.P. 103/6, Drummond to Secretary of State William Bromley, Rotterdam, 25 Feb. 1714. I am grateful to Professor John Rule of Ohio State University for bringing this letter to my attention.

[128] *Bolingbroke Correspondence* IV, 208–9, letter of 25 July 1713.

[129] H.M.C., *Portland Papers* V, 329, Drummond's letter of 22 Sept. 1713.

[130] *Ibid.*, 307–8, Decker's letter of 1 Aug. 1713; 316–18, of 18 Aug. 1713; cp. 318, Drummond's letter of 18 Aug. 1713.

of them brought on by Drummond) must be forgiven and forgotten in the interest of Anglo-Dutch cooperation to save the Protestant Succession.[131] He asked Drummond if he would be willing to undertake a new mission to London, of the same semi-official kind as that of 1711–12, to prepare for a more formal mission by Lord Albermarle to Oxford. Drummond, anxious to be employed, skilfully encouraged Heinsius and emphasized to Oxford the gain in reputation and position the Treasurer might secure if he, with the consent of the Queen and the connivance of Shrewsbury, restored Anglo-Dutch friendship, the bulwark of the Protestant Succession.[132] Oxford, who had approved of Drummond's work in 1713–14,[133] responded to Heinsius's rapprochement and by mid-April 1714 (o.s.) Drummond was in London.[134]

Oxford was well aware of the good use he could make of Drummond's mission in his struggle for retention of power, or at least equality of power, against Bolingbroke. He presented Drummond to the Queen;[135] and the letter of 21 April which Drummond penned on the damage done to Anglo-Dutch relations by the 'differences and animosities at Court', and by the Republic's fear of 'measures for bringing in the Pretender', is endorsed by Oxford: 'Read to her Majesty'.[136] Drummond's letter to Oxford's cousin, Thomas Harley (whom he knew quite well from having attended him in the Republic and for part of the way on his journey to Hanover),[137] reveals—if my reading of the cypher is correct—that he was well informed on the coming crisis between Bolingbroke and Oxford:

> At my arrival, I found 25 [Oxford] had been very ill treated by 27 [Bolingbroke] and his friends, both male and female, but 25 and the

[131] *Ibid.*, 338, Drummond's letter of 29 Sept. 1713; 354, of 1 Nov. 1713; 361–2, of 8 Dec. 1713.

[132] *Ibid.*, 355, Drummond's letter of 1 Nov. 1713; 362–3, of 8 Dec. 1713.

[133] *Ibid.*, VII, 161, Stratford to Edward Harley of 2 Aug. 1713.

[134] *Ibid.*, V, 434, Drummond's letter to Thomas Harley of 4 May 1714 (O.S.) from London, on his 'speedy passage 16 days ago'.

[135] *Ibid.*, 425, Drummond's letter of 21 April 1714 (O.S.)

[136] *Ibid.*, 425–7, with endorsement. For the latest treatment of Oxford and Bolingbroke's attitudes to the Pretender, see J. H. and Margaret Shennan, 'The Protestant Succession in English Politics', *William III and Louis XIV. Essays by and for Mark A. Thomson* (Liverpool, 1968) ed. Ragnhild Hatton and J. S. Bromley, pp. 252–70. Cp. G. Holmes, *Party Politics in the Age of Anne* (London, 1967) pp. 268, 279 ff.; and Elizabeth Hamilton, *Backstairs Dragon* (London, 1969) pp. 240 ff.

[137] H.M.C., *Portland Papers* V, 426, Drummond's letter of 21 April 1714 (o.s.)

females are very well, and 27 will be sacrificed unless he be able to justify himself, 33 [?] for that reason will remain where he is, 27 is charged with having great friendship and intimacy with 32 [the Pretender], and 25 takes no pains to justify him, neither can they live together without being esteemed equally affected to 32 and in prejudice to 29 [the Queen].[138]

Drummond had seen 27 on his arrival and had tried—though in vain—to see him again;[139] but it is clear that his hopes of preferment were now focused strongly on Oxford. Dr Stratford, well aware of the way in which Drummond's messages from The Hague had been used to boost —at least temporarily—Oxford's standing with the Queen and with Bolingbroke ('Honest John's coming over was very providential', we find him writing on 5 June 1714, 'he has done greater service at home than abroad'), pressed his case for a post;[140] but the 'good place in the Customs' which 25 had hoped to obtain for him had already been promised,[141] and William Ayerst (Strafford's chaplain) was nominated to the secretaryship at the English embassy at The Hague, where Drummond had recently, and with a modicum of success, tried to overcome Strafford's hostility.[142] Drummond's departure from London had originally been fixed for the end of May;[143] but he stayed on out of a need, both for his semi-official mission and his private affairs, to see the outcome of the struggle between the Treasurer and the Secretary of State. When Oxford's fall became known on 27 July, he was sincerely sorry for the disgrace of his patron and the minister who had moved him from the mercantile life to that of politics and diplomacy: 'I never knew the Court till your Lordship was at it, I never was acquainted with any of it but by your Lordship.'[144] Whereas most of Oxford's correspondents discreetly congratulated him on his *quietus*, Decker and Drummond expressed their 'grief for the

[138] *Ibid.*, 434–5. Drummond's letter of 4 May 1714 (o.s.)

[139] *Ibid.*, p. 434, adding: 'everybody else makes the same complaint'.

[140] *Ibid.*, VII, 186, Stratford to Edward Harley.

[141] *Ibid.*, V, 434, Drummond's letter to Thomas Harley of 4 May 1714 (o.s.)

[142] H.M.C., *Drummond Moray Papers*, 146, the Earl of Strafford to Drummond, 18 Oct. 1713, writing 'without reserve because of your professions of friendship'. For Ayerst's nomination see H.M.C., *Portland Papers* V, 450, Dr William Ayerst to Thomas Harley, 5 June 1714.

[143] *Ibid.*, 435, Drummond's letter to Thomas Harley of 4 May 1714 (o.s.)

[144] *Ibid.*, 282, Drummond's letter of 26 April 1713.

news . . . of your being out of that great employment which you have borne with so much reputation'. By this time, however, Drummond had to some extent managed to hedge his bets; and it is significant that it was Decker who signed the letter expressing their joint sentiments.[145] Drummond had never wished to break with Bolingbroke and self-interest dictated cooperation with the new head of the ministry. So did his mission from the Dutch side of the water. Bolingbroke for his part was perfectly willing and even anxious, once his own victory was assured, to make use of Drummond's continental connections: already on 28 July Drummond could tell an acquaintance that he was going to The Hague, 'in a day's time', to engage Lord Albemarle to negotiate with Hanover on behalf of Bolingbroke and his friends.[146] The Queen's death cheated Bolingbroke of the fruits of victory over his rival and made it, incidentally, impossible for him to be useful to Drummond.

Self-interest alone is not the only clue to Drummond's behaviour in the spring and summer of 1714; nor does his concern to carry out his Dutch mission, whoever won the contest for power in Whitehall, fully explain his trying to keep on good terms with Bolingbroke as well as Oxford. It is typical of him that when his two former patrons had become equally discredited after the accession of George I, he remained in touch with both and tried to play the role of a conciliator. With scandal and impeachment threatening the two fallen statesmen, it was Drummond who wrote on Bolingbroke's behalf to Oxford,[147] pleading that they must make a common stand and support each other; and it was at his house that a meeting (which proved fruitless) between Oxford's son, Lord Harley, and Bolingbroke took place.[148] At this time Drummond himself had begun to rise in the world once more with the help of his friend Brydges, but that is another story. His moment of real glory, in spite of that rise, had fallen in the period here discussed: in 1710 and 1711, when paragraphs of his letters had been read by St John to the Queen of England, when he had felt the pleasure of being in the know and at the centre of affairs; again in 1714, when he had been buoyed by hopes of reconciling

[145] *Ibid.*, 476, Decker to Oxford, 27 July 1714.

[146] James Macpherson, *Original Papers* II (London, 1775) 533, 'Stuart Papers, Anecdotes of L.L.'

[147] H.M.C., *Portland Papers* v, 508, Drummond's letter, Saturday [March 1714/15].

[148] *Ibid.*, 509, Drummond to Lord Harley, Sunday [March 1714/15].

not only Bolingbroke and Oxford but also the Maritime Powers, and when he was presented to the Queen. His role in the War of the Spanish Succession in so far as Anglo-Dutch relations were concerned was a less significant one and a less straightforward one than he himself imagined; but in the very critical situation for the new English ministry of 1710 he had played a vital role in rallying political and financial support behind it on both sides of the Channel. Oxford and Bolingbroke never forgot this. Harley was profuse in his thanks in November 1710;[149] St John—once the crisis was past—succinctly acknowledged Drummond's services in affairs of state 'at a time when the situation of them was extremely nice'.[150]

[149] *Ibid.*, IV, 623, Robert Harley (draft) to Drummond, 7 Nov. 1710.

[150] *Bolingbroke Correspondence* III, 516, letter of 14 March 1712/13. Cp. his comment to Raby, *ibid.*, I, 86, of 6 March 1710/11: 'We have, on this side, very great obligations to him [Drummond].'

6

JOHN C. RULE

France and the Preliminaries to the Gertruydenberg Conference, September 1709 to March 1710

Following France's formal rejection of the Preliminaries of The Hague in June 1709, the French foreign minister, Colbert de Torcy, renewed his correspondence with Anthonie Heinsius, the Grand Pensionary of the province of Holland in the Dutch Republic. The French minister hoped to obtain from these continued conversations with the Allies a modification of the harsh terms of the Preliminaries; his hopes, however, were dashed by Heinsius's evasiveness, by the Duke of Marlborough's scepticism, and by Austrian intransigence. In early September 1709 the stalemate in the negotiations was rudely broken by a mighty clash of arms near the village of Malplaquet, in which 80,000 French troops were pitted against a superior allied force of 110,000 men.[1]

A letter from one of the French field commanders, Marshal de Boufflers, relayed to the ministers at Versailles the shocking news that Marshal de Villars had been severely wounded during the battle. In a separate missive to the French foreign minister, Colbert de Torcy, Boufflers assured him that Villars was not dead and that the French had withdrawn, in relatively good order, to new defensive lines.[2] As it turned out, the French lost some 14,000 men to the allied 24,000.[3] The bloody engagement at Malplaquet,

[1] For Malplaquet see M. Sautai, *La bataille de Malplaquet d'après la correspondence du duc de Maine à l'armée de Flandre* (Paris, 1904); a more recent account in Ivor F. Burton, *The Captain-General, The Career of John Churchill, Duke of Marlborough, from 1702 to 1711* (London, 1968) pp. 150–5. Burton's description of Marlborough's rôle in the preliminaries to and the negotiations of the Gertruydenberg Conference, 1709–10, (*ibid.*, 159 ff.) is misleading, Marlborough playing a more active and a more hostile rôle in these negotiations than suggested.

[2] B.N., Fonds fr[ancais], Nouvelles Acquisitions, 3288, fos. 317 r–v, Boufflers to Louis XIV, 11 Sept. 1709, Quesnoy; *ibid.*, fos. 321 r–v, Boufflers to Louis XIV, 13 Sept. 1709, Quesnoy.

[3] B.N., Fonds fr., Nouv. Acq. 3288 fos. 206 r–v, Nicolas Voysin to Marshal

as Torcy later reported, 'raised the courage of the [French] nation rather than weakened it'. Among the Allies the Dutch who had sacrificed 'over 30 of their (best) battalions' were particularly disheartened by the battle.[4]

Colbert de Torcy seized on the Dutch discontent to press for renewed peace talks.[5] A few weeks after the battle of Malplaquet he wrote to his confidant in The Hague, Herman Petkum, 'that his Master [Louis XIV] is very sincere . . . with his desire to see Mons. Petkum at Paris . . .'. The British ambassador, Lord Townshend, observed that 'I doubt not but Mons. Torcy may have been informed that in some of the [Dutch] Provinces the inclination to a peace runs very high of late.'

In the months that followed Malplaquet, the Dutch peace parties did indeed press the government to reopen negotiations with France. The Grand Pensionary Heinsius deferred an answer to Torcy's request as long as he dared; then, in early November, he frankly admitted to Prince Eugène and to Lord Townshend that the French proposal for the sending of Petkum to Paris 'had been so far favoured by great numbers in the Government . . .' that it would be difficult to ignore. On Heinsius's advice, Prince Eugène and Townshend agreed, though reluctantly, to Petkum's mission.[6]

Meanwhile, in the months before Petkum arrived at Versailles, the French ministers had completed a tentative realignment of political factions that had been in the making since June 1709. At that time Louis XIV had disgraced his war minister, Michel Chamillart, and had enlarged his *conseil d'en haut* by appointing to membership the controller-general Nicolas Desmaretz and the new war minister Daniel-François Voysin. Desmaretz, a nephew of Jean-Baptiste Colbert, owed his preferment to

---

Bezons, 13 Sept. 1709, Versailles. Voysin speaks of the 'bataille sanglante.'; also, *ibid.*, fos. 212 r–v, Voysin to Bezons, 23 Sept. 1709. For contemporary British reaction to the battle of Malplaquet, see B.M. Add. MSS. 9107, fos. 19r–20r; B.M. Add. MSS. 38498, fos. 73v–74r, Lord Townshend to Secretary Boyle, 13 Sept. 1709, The Hague.

[4] B.M. Add. MSS. 15876, fo. 273r, Dayrolle to Boyle, 17 Sept. 1709, The Hague; also *ibid.*, fo. 273v, Dayrolle to Boyle, 20 Sept. 1709, The Hague.

[5] H.M.C., *House of Lords MSS* IX (London, 1952) 289, Townshend to Sunderland, 15 Oct. 1709, The Hague.

[6] *Ibid.*, 291, Marlborough and Townshend to Sunderland, 8 Nov. 1709, The Hague; P.R.O., S.P. 84/233, part 1, fos. 308v–338v, contains the letters of Townshend to Boyle from 18 Oct. to 8 Nov. 1710.

his long service in the controller-general's office and to his unrivalled personal acquaintance with the chief financiers of the realm; Voysin, a 'creature' of Madame de Maintenon, was a cautious, conscientious civil servant, whose loyalty to the king and to the state was unquestioned. On joining the council both men sought political allies among the older ministers. Voysin tended to side with the war party, whose titular leader was the king's son, Monseigneur, but whose chief spokesman was the Chancellor, Louis Phélypeaux, comte de Pontchartrain, who was supported by his son, Jérôme Phélypeaux, comte de Pontchartrain, secretary of state for the marine. Opposition to the war party sprang from the *dévots*, the devout party, headed by the Duc de Beauvilliers, by his cousin the Duc de Chevreuse, and by the king's grandson, the Duke of Burgundy. The *dévots* were in disfavour with the king due in part to the role that Burgundy had played in the disastrous battle of Oudenarde (1708) and in part to the correspondence the *dévots* maintained with the Archbishop-Duke of Cambrai, Fénelon. The third faction, which represented the *via media* in French politics, was headed by the foreign minister, Colbert de Torcy, and supported by Nicolas Desmaretz. This faction, which sought a negotiated peace short of unconditional surrender, found its chief ally in the king himself.[7]

It was to Torcy that the king turned after the battle of Malplaquet for a reappraisal of French policy. The foreign minister had many diverse strands of diplomacy to weave into an articulated whole. What considerations did he weigh as he gave advice to the king and his council in the troubled winter months of 1709–10?

Two immediate military events gave Torcy courage to hope for a compromise peace. The first was the battle of Malplaquet, in which, as Horatio Walpole wrote to Secretary Boyle from The Hague, 'France . . . imprudently believes she was victorious . . . and will have sufficient time to talk following the end of the campaign'.[8] Modern critics tend to support the French view; as David Chandler reports: 'The most lasting

[7] For a study of factions in the last years of Louis XIV's reign, see John C. Rule, 'King and Minister: Louis XIV and Colbert de Torcy', in *William III and Louis XIV: Essays 1680–1720 by and for Mark A. Thomson*, ed. Ragnhild Hatton and J. S. Bromley (Liverpool, 1968) pp. 213–36; A. Baudrillart, 'Madame de Maintenon: son rôle politique', *Revue des Questions Historiques* xxv (1890), particularly 111–13.

[8] S.P. 84/233, part 1, fo. 258r, H. Walpole to Boyle, 8 Oct. 1709, The Hague.

effects [of Malplaquet] . . . were to rally French national morale and damage Marlborough's reputation in England.'[9]

Torcy was also heartened by another, slightly earlier, military confrontation in which French troops frustrated an allied invasion of the province of Alsace. On 27 August 1709, in the valley of the Rhine, Marshal d'Harcourt had routed an allied force headed by Count Mercy. The Duke of Marlborough in writing to Baron Somers in late September 1709 was quick to divine the significance of this brief but brisk encounter: 'Your Lordship', he observed, 'has been informed of what has passed between the Pensioner [Heinsius] and M. de Torcy since the negotiations were broken off at The Hague [in June 1709], and of the contents of the last letter the French minister wrote to Petkum, which we can attribute to nothing but the effect of Comte Merci's misfortune.'[10] In a note to Count Mercy, Marlborough referred to the 'malheur qui vous est arrivé en Alsace'.[11]

The French military establishment, as Torcy himself admitted, was still desperately weak; but not so weak as the allied commanders made out; nor so weak that the French could not twice within two months halt a direct invasion of the northern heartland—*le coeur*—of France.

Following Count Mercy's misadventure on the Rhine, Torcy sent his personal *courrier de cabinet*, with trumpeter, to the Duke of Marlborough's camp, carrying a message from Louis XIV requesting the release of Marshal Tallard from his English prison.[12] It would appear that Torcy had little interest in Tallard's release, but, in reality, sought some hint of a shift in allied policy. Marlborough did not rise to the bait and in late October, following the battle of Malplaquet, Torcy turned his thoughts to what may be termed 'the Scottish diversion'.

The term 'Scottish diversion' refers to the several Jacobite attempts to invade Scotland during the War of the Spanish Succession, one of which had occurred in the late autumn of 1708 and had failed because of a conflict over command between the war minister, Chamillart, and the secretary of the marine, Jérome de Pontchartrain. With Chamillart's removal

[9] *A Traveller's Guide to the Battlefields of Europe*, ed. David Chandler, 2 vols. (London, 1965) I, 13–14.

[10] *The Letters and Dispatches of John Churchill, First Duke of Marlborough, from 1702 to 1712*, ed. Sir George Murray, IV (London, 1845), 609.

[11] *Ibid.*, 660.

[12] *Ibid.*, 623–4.

from office in 1709, Torcy's hopes for a successful Scottish diversion rose. Such an invasion, Torcy confided to his *Journal*, would give 'une nouvelle face aux affaires'.[13] Torcy's espousal of the Jacobite cause was seconded by Marshal Villars, the hero of Malplaquet, who assured the foreign minister that 'il lui [Madame de Maintenon] avait parlé très-longtemps de l'entreprise d'Écosse comme du seul événement qui pouvait donner moyen de faire la campagne prochaine'.[14] At Torcy's and Villars's urgings, the king himself agreed 'à la proposition tant de fois rebattue de faire passer le Roi d'Angleterre en Écosse, il avait enfin resolu d'en tenter l'entreprise comme seule qui pouvait changer la face des affaires'.[15]

To organize the expedition the king appointed as military commander Marshal d'Éstrées; but the number of troops the king could free for such a Scottish venture were far fewer than the 8,000 to 10,000 men requested by the Pretender James III.[16] To hasten Franco-Jacobite designs, Torcy visited the English court at Saint-Germain-en-Laye several times during the late autumn of 1709, where he conferred with James, with the queen-mother, Beatrice Eleanor d'Este, and with the Jacobite secretary of state, Lord Middleton.[17] But sincere as Torcy's support of the Jacobite cause was, he admitted to the king in January 1710 that the Scottish diversion would probably not create 'une nouvelle face aux affaires', largely because the Jacobite leaders were hopelessly inept: the Marshal-Duke of Berwick was over-confident; the Pretender was well meaning but weak; Lord Middleton was disaffected; even Torcy's own agent, Nathaniel Hooke, asserted that the expedition might meet defeat.[18] Louis XIV, who had never looked upon the project with favour, added his own caveats, dwelling on 'des périls de la navigation dans la Manche de Saint-Georges, impracticable aux escadres et d'ailleurs peu connue, des embarras infinis qui auraient suivi une descente faite en pays ennemi, sans port assuré, sans

[13] *Journal Inédit de Jean-Baptiste Colbert, Marquis de Torcy, pendant les années 1709, 1710 et 1711*, ed. Frédéric Masson (Paris, 1884) p. 63. See also Archives Nationales, K.1351, No. 76, for Torcy's 'Mémoire touchant une entreprise à faire sur l'Écosse'; cp. *ibid.*, No. 77.

[14] Torcy, *Journal*, p. 64.

[15] *Ibid.*, p. 66.

[16] *Ibid.*, p. 55.

[17] See George Hilton Jones, *Charles Middleton: The Life and Times of a Restoration Politician* (Chicago, 1967), particularly pp. 278–90.

[18] Torcy, *Journal*, pp. 93, 95, 107, 119–20.

places et peut-être sans intelligences'.[19] To cap the king's own words, Desmaretz revealed that his office could not guarantee the monies needed. Reluctantly, then, at the end of January Torcy shelved the schemes for a Scottish diversion; but he did not abandon James III, and throughout the negotiations at Gertruydenberg Torcy urged the Jacobite cause.

A happier, if less spectacular, diplomatic manœuvre than the Scottish diversion was the role Torcy played in the consolidation of the Franco-Bavarian alliance.[20] The Elector of Bavaria, Max Emmanuel, a proud and independent prince of the Empire, was, like James III, a ruler in exile and a client of the French court. Like James, Max elicited the sympathy and support of Louis XIV and his council. Though dedicated to the restoration of the Wittelsbachs to their electoral thrones, Torcy found Max haughty and humourless and preferred to negotiate with the Bavarians through the more congenial offices of Ferdinand-Augustin de Solar, comte de Monasterol,[21] the Elector's plenipotentiary to France and a personal friend of Torcy's. It was with some dismay, then, that Torcy learned in early November of the Elector's intention to visit the French court. Happily for Franco-Bavarian relations, Max Emmanuel's sojourn at Versailles and Marly proved a major diplomatic success, which was in large measure due to the solicitude shown him by Louis XIV and his foreign minister.[22] While at court Max urged the French to reinforce their army of the Rhine, which, following Marshal d'Harcourt's defeat of Count Mercy's expeditionary force, seemed a reasonable suggestion. Times indeed looked ripe for an invasion of southern Germany, and Torcy's friend, the French minister to the Swiss cantons, Comte de Luc, seconded Max's advice.[23] Again, however, as with the Scottish expedition, the heavy military expenses of the army of Flanders overrode any other consideration. But if troops were not forthcoming, diplomatic reassurances were. In the meeting of the *conseil d'en haut* on 24 November Louis declared that the situation of 'les deux Électeurs [Max and his brother, Joseph Clemens of Cologne]

[19] *Ibid.*, pp. 128–9.

[20] For a study of Max Emmanuel's statecraft at this time see August Rosenlehner, 'Zur Restitutionspolitik Kurfürst Max Emanuels von Bayern', *Forschungen zur Geschichte Bayerns* X–XI (1901–03) 200 ff.

[21] Torcy, *Journal*, pp. 4–5, footnote 2.

[22] *Ibid.*, pp. 22 ff.

[23] *Ibid.*, p. 39.

était trés-injurieux et pouvait les exclure à jamais de leurs États'.[24] On 29 December king and council again assured Max Emmanuel of France's good will and Torcy further elaborated the theme of Franco-Bavarian solidarity by including in his Memorandum to the Allies of 2 January 1710 the demand that 'the Electors of Cologne and Bavaria shall be restored to their states and dignities'.[25] This statement served as a major refrain in French foreign policy from 1710 until the Franco-Imperial settlement in 1714.

In the same month that the renewal of the Bourbon-Wittlesbach *entente cordiale* was discussed in the *conseil d'en haut*, Torcy received encouraging news of the Great Northern War. On 7 November, M. Shum, one of the King of Denmark's agents in Paris, delivered a letter to the foreign minister which indicated that the Danes were once more preparing for war with Sweden.[26] Later letters from the secretary to the French embassy in Copenhagen confirmed M. Shum's disclosure. 'Les affaires du Nord', Torcy noted in his *Journal*, 's'enflammaient et le feu en serait utile à la France si elle ne se pressait pas de conclure la paix.'[27] The theme of the Great Northern War persisted in Torcy's correspondence and in his dealings with the allied agent Herman Petkum, who reported to the Dutch Pensionary Heinsius early in December that '[France's] chief dependence is upon the disturbances of the North which they think will be difficult for the Allies to prevent being carried into the Empire'.[28] The idea that the War of the Spanish Succession and the Great Northern War might merge so encouraged Torcy that he spoke to the council of detaching Prussia from the Grand Alliance, of seeking the mediation of the King of Denmark, Tsar Peter of Russia, and King Augustus of Poland at a general peace congress, and lastly, of pressing the Turks to attack Russia. Apropos of this last scheme the Duke of Marlborough noted in a letter to Heinsius 'that the French court is buoyed up with the hopes that something abroad may happen to their advantage . . . particularly in the rupture between the Czar and the Turks'.[29]

[24] *Ibid.*, p. 38.

[25] H.M.C., *Fourteenth Report, Round MSS* (London, 1895) p. 345.

[26] Torcy, *Journal*, p. 9.

[27] *Ibid.*, p. 34.

[28] H.M.C., *House of Lords MSS* IX, 293; see also S.P.84/233, part 2, fo. 404, Townshend to Boyle, 10 Dec. 1709, The Hague.

[29] *The Correspondence 1701–1711 of John Churchill, First Duke of Marlborough and*

Like the courts of Copenhagen, Berlin, and Constantinople, the court of Savoy at Turin furnished France with a fertile field for intrigue. To a meeting of the council of 8 December, Torcy read a letter from Isidor de Azevedo, marquis de Monteleone, the Spanish envoy to Genoa, in which the Spaniard reported that Victor-Amadeus II of Savoy had hinted that he was much interested in learning of revised peace terms.[30] The price of a Savoyard defection, Monteleone continued, was the cession of Mont-Dauphin, the forts of Barreaux and Briançon, with the Briançonnais. When Torcy had finished reading Monteleone's letter, the Duc de Beauvilliers exclaimed 'qu'il serait dangereux d'entamer une négociation avec le duc de Savoie . . . que ce prince artificieux ne voulait pas traiter sincèrement'.[31] On this occasion, it would seem, Beauvilliers's dislike of Victor-Amadeus overruled his usual plea for a peace at any cost. Torcy countered Beauvilliers's objections by urging that France treat with Savoy on general terms, letting Turin know that France would insist on retaining Strasbourg and the fortifications in Alsace. 'Le duc de Savoie', Torcy noted, 'ne manquait ni par l'esprit ni par les lumières';[32] if Savoy could be detached from the Grand Alliance, the French might open the back door to peace, as they had done in 1696.

Amid the pell-mell of diplomatic intrigues, rumours of peace and clandestine negotiations, the foreign minister did not lose sight of the major avenue to the peace table, the Dutch. At Torcy's urgent request Heinsius allowed Herman Petkum to carry allied demands to Paris. On 19 November 1709 Petkum arrived at the Hôtel de Torcy, on the rue Vivienne. The next day, agent and minister travelled by coach to Versailles, where Petkum reported that the Dutch 'souhaitèrent la paix, mais sans être maîtres de la faire conclure'. The British and the Austrians, he stressed, stood firm on the demands adumbrated in the Preliminaries of The Hague. The Allies, however, offered France two concessions: first, they were willing to 'retrancher de cet article le terme de "cédée" en

---

Anthonie Heinsius, Grand Pensionary of Holland, ed. B. Van t'Hoff (The Hague, 1951) pp. 480–1. See also, for the political background, R M. Hatton, *Charles XII of Sweden* (New York, 1969) pp. 327 ff., especially p. 331.

[30] Torcy, *Journal*, pp. 57–60.

[31] *Ibid.*, p. 58.

[32] *Ibid.*, p. 59.

parlant de la monarchie d'Espagne'; and, second, to extend the length of time of the truce from two months to three.[33]

During Petkum's mission the *conseil d'en haut* met on 20, 24, and 27 November to consider what reply Colbert de Torcy should tender the Allies. These sessions evoked heated debate: would Archduke Charles rule Spain by the same right as Charles II? And if he did, would his claims extend to the old Burgundian lands, to the Franche-Comté, Artois, and French Flanders? After weighing the legal claims and the military strength of Archduke Charles and Philip V, and after discussing the impracticability of enforcing Articles 4 and 37 of the Preliminaries of The Hague, the ministers rejected Petkum's proposals for a compromise.[34]

In the meantime Torcy employed his diplomatic arts to persuade Petkum of France's inability to carry out the provisions of the Preliminaries.[35] During their first extended conversation, which occurred in the gardens at Marly,[36] Torcy introduced the Allies' emissary to Abbé Melchior de Polignac, who had recently returned from a tour of duty as auditor to the Rota in Rome and was to become in the next few years one of France's most important ambassadors-on-mission. Polignac,[37] a great friend and

[33] *Ibid.*, p. 30.

[34] B.M. Add. MSS. 15876, fo. 282v, Dayrolle to Boyle, 12 Nov. 1709, The Hague. There are four important extant accounts of the Petkum mission: one is preserved among the Round Papers and printed in H.M.C., *Round MSS*, pp. 341–3; another is in the Gertruydenberg papers of Lord Townshend, published in H.M.C., *House of Lords MSS* IX, 291–3; the third is printed in Torcy's *Journal*, pp. 25–47 (Torcy's *Memoirs* are strangely silent on the period between The Hague and Gertruydenberg Conferences; Torcy's *Journal*, not to be confused with his *Mémoires*, begins 6 Nov. 1709, and ends 29 May 1711); the fourth account, in A.R.A., Archief Heinsius 1431, is in the form of four letters from Petkum to Heinsius, marked secret and dated 17, 22, and two of 29 Nov. 1709. See also, *ibid.*, Petkum to Heinsius 22 Nov. 1709, Versailles; Torcy, *Journal*, p. 37. At the council meeting of 25 Nov. the ministers discussed whether to negotiate with the Elector of Brandenburg (as the French still termed the King of Prussia), who had recently made peace overtures to France. Though France could not offer Prussia a large subsidy in return for leaving the war, attempts were made through a Brigadier Grumbkow ('Kromkow') to keep in touch with Berlin: see Torcy, *Journal*, pp. 32–3, 39–40. A. Legrelle devotes several pages to the French flirtations with Prussia in the autumn of 1709; see *La Diplomatie française et la Succession d'Espagne* IV (Ghent, 1892) 519–34.

[35] H.M.C., *House of Lords MSS* IX, 292.

[36] Torcy, *Journal*, pp. 32–40.

[37] For Polignac's career, see *Recueil, Hollande* II, ed. Louis André and Émile Bourgeois (Paris, 1923) p. 225, and fn. 2; Torcy, *Journal*, p. 33, fn. 1. See also S.P.84/233, part 2, fos. 369r–370r, Townshend to Boyle, 26 Nov. 1709, The Hague.

'creature' of Torcy, lent his voice to the foreign minister's counsels of moderation.[38] In a rehearsed conversation Torcy reviewed for Polignac's benefit—but more for Petkum's—the French grievances against the 37th article of the Preliminaries. The foreign minister emphasized that to make Louis XIV force his grandson to abdicate was 'against honour, against humanity, and against nature'.[39] Then, at a prearranged moment, Polignac turned to Petkum saying, 'hard as the preliminaries were, his Majesty would sign them, if he could thus secure peace for France, but that [unfortunately], by parting with fortresses, abandoning [a] kingdom, dismantling Dunkirk, he was only to gain a truce for two or three months'.[40]

Petkum replied that France had come to this sorry state because of 'such small respect for treaties',[41] particularly the treaties of partition. Polignac retorted, saying that the blame for France's disgrace was due to 'the unbridled ambition and dangerous principles of a haughty minister, (meaning Louvois)'. Petkum scoffed at the invocation of Louvois's ghost and laid the blame on more corporeal sources, pointing out that Louvois had long been dead at the time of the Partition Treaties. Torcy, 'seeing that . . . [Petkum] had nothing more to say . . . took [him] home'.[42]

Despite Petkum's reluctance to listen to the blandishments of Torcy and his colleagues, he was introduced by Torcy to Nicolas Desmaretz the very evening of the day that he had met Abbé Polignac. Desmaretz, who was controller-general, discoursed at length on the poor state of affairs into which the French army had fallen under his predecessor Chamillart. Desmaretz ended his observations with the remark 'that the affaires were now in much better Condition, and Necessary funds [thanks to contributions and to new taxes] in a great Measure [were] settled for the next Campaign'.[43] He also reminded Petkum of the dangers to the Allies inherent in what appeared to be an ever-expanding Northern War.

[38] H.M.C., *Round MSS.*, p. 342; Torcy, *Journal*, 33.

[39] A.R.A., Archief Heinsius 1431, Petkum to Heinsius, 22 Nov. 1709.

[40] H.M.C., *Round MSS.*, p. 342, also H.M.C., *House of Lords MSS.* IX, 293.

[41] *Ibid.*, see also S.P.84/233, part 2, fo. 369v, Townshend to Boyle, 26 Nov. 1709, The Hague.

[42] H.M.C., *Round MSS.*, p. 343.

[43] H.M.C., *House of Lords MSS.* IX, 293; Torcy, *Journal*, p. 38; S.P.84/233, part 2, fos. 403r–404v, Townshend to Boyle, 10 Dec. 1709, The Hague; another version of Desmaretz's conversation may be found in A.R.A., Archief Heinsius 1431, Petkum to Heinsius, 22 Nov. 1709, Versailles.

Petkum, who was too shrewd an observer of French diplomatic manœuvres to be taken in by the French game of hide and seek, called the French bluff by threatening to leave at once for The Hague.

Torcy, not wanting to lose the opportunity for opening a new peace conference, suggested to the king that Petkum should carry back to Heinsius a proposal to treat on the substance only of the Preliminaries. To this suggestion Louis and his council agreed, observing that the 1709 military campaign had ended and that the three months in which the armies were in winter quarters would probably be sufficient time in which to work out an expedient for Article 37. Louis also instructed his foreign minister to inform Petkum that France would by 1 January 1710 appoint plenipotentiaries to meet with the Allies.[44]

When Petkum returned to The Hague late in the evening of 7 December he submitted the French proposals to a conference of hostile Anglo-Dutch ministers. Both Townshend and Heinsius felt certain that the deputies for foreign affairs and the States General would reject the French overtures. They were not mistaken. The States General attacked France's sincerity and called for a renewal of the allied war effort.[45] Townshend's letter of 17 December glowed with personal satisfaction at the opposition to

[44] Torcy, *Journal*, pp. 41–2; S.P.84/233, part 2, fo. 380r, Townshend to Boyle, 3 Dec. 1709, The Hague.

[45] For the months of December 1709 and January and February 1710, I have drawn from the following sources: The English side; Townshend's draft letters, the Bodleian Library, MS. Eng. hist. d. 148, and Secretary Boyle's replies, *ibid.*, d. 147; their final drafts are to be found in S.P.84/233, parts 1 and 2. Photostats of the Sunderland Privy Council Minutes were kindly lent me by Professor J. H. Plumb of Christ's College, Cambridge; the James Dayrolle reports to Secretary Boyle are in B.M. Add. MSS. 15876. In many cases Dayrolle's secret reports are the most illuminating accounts from the English side. For the French, we have a long narrative account in B.M., Egerton MSS. 865; in the Archives Nationales K.1338, No. 30, is found 'Memoire sur les negotiations de Gertruydenberg'; see also in Archives des Affaires Etrangères, C.P. Hollande, vols. 229, 230, and 231. Vol. 230 of the C.P. Angleterre contains 450 pages, many of them secret reports from Abbé Gaultier; the B.N., Fonds fr., Nouv. Acq. 6135, contains the Harcourt and Blécourt reports from Spain; and the Algemeen Rijksarchief, Archief Heinsius 1489A, contains Huxelles's and Polignac's notes to Heinsius. For the Dutch side, we have Buys's correspondence in Archief Heinsius 1493 and 1583; Van der Dussen's letters are in the Archief Heinsius 1502 and 2230; Archief Heinsius 1553 contains Torcy's message to Heinsius, 24 January 1710. Dr J. G. Stork-Penning's *Het Grote Werk: Vredesonderhandelingen Gedurende De Spaanse Successie-Oorlog 1705–1710* (Groningen, 1958) is of great importance for the Dutch side of the negotiations leading to Gertruydenberg, see especially pp. 353–76.

France based on what he termed 'authentically to be the Sense of the whole [Dutch] Nation'.[46] But it could hardly be termed 'the Sense of the whole Nation'. In fact Dutch unity showed alarming signs of weakness. The province of Utrecht vigorously agitated for accepting the French peace proposals.[47] Utrecht's lead was followed by Gelderland and, it was rumoured, by Zeeland and Friesland too. Heinsius, genuinely upset, blamed not only Utrecht and Gelderland for the turn of events but the Amsterdam political factions as well. Willem Buys, that city's Pensionary, might, as Dayrolle reported to Whitehall, very well have promoted 'the Deputation from Utrecht . . . by means of a brother in Law he has in that government'.[48] Certainly it was well known that Buys strongly favoured accepting a French delegation. His motives are clear: first of all, he wished to keep the Dutch in firm control of the peace negotiations; and, secondly, he and his Amsterdam associates, though not members of the peace party, favoured treating with France because they feared England's apparent desire for naval bases in the Mediterranean and in the West Indies. In early January these fears were reinforced when it was learned that England was negotiating an agreement with the Archduke Charles for a naval base on Minorca. Buys blustered, saying that any 'signal proof of Her Majesty's affection for the States' had been but a chimera, and that England desired to continue the war so that she might gain mercantile supremacy at the expense of the Dutch.[49]

It was no coincidence that in early January a new French offer to negotiate a peace arrived in The Hague at the precise moment that news of the Minorca affair reached Amsterdam.[50] Torcy, it now appears, forwarded to François Mollo and his associates of the Amsterdam peace party the intercepted English letters telling of General Stanhope's overtures

[46] H.M.C., *House of Lords MSS.* IX, 294, Townshend to Boyle, 17 Dec. 1709, The Hague.

[47] B.M. Add. MSS. 15876, fo. 283v, Dayrolle to Boyle, 28 Jan. 1710, The Hague; also *ibid.*, Dayrolle to Boyle, 21 Jan. 1710, The Hague.

[48] *Ibid.*, fo. 283v, Dayrolle to Boyle, 28 Jan. 1710, The Hague.

[49] See C.P. Hollande, vol. 222, fos. 5r–v, Petkum to Torcy, 2 Jan. 1710 [Amsterdam]; *ibid.*, fos. 47r–v, Petkum to Torcy, 17 Jan. 1710, Amsterdam; *ibid.*, fos. 49r–v, Torcy to Petkum, 23 Jan. 1710, Versailles; see also Torcy, *Journal*, pp. 71–2.

[50] Torcy, *Journal*, p. 72; see also *Marlborough-Heinsius Correspondence*, pp. 480–1, Marlborough to Heinsius, 31 Jan. 1710, Windsor Lodge, in which Marlborough tries to calm Heinsius's fears about Minorca. Cp. Stork-Penning, *Het Grote Werk*, pp. 367–74.

to Archduke Charles.[51] The whole tenor of French diplomatic manuœvres dismayed Lord Townshend. In a letter to Secretary Boyle he revealed his uneasiness: Louis XIV, he said,

> will not sign the Preliminaries, but . . . he will give Assurances of his Agreeing at a Treaty of Peace to the Substance of all that is contained in them excepting the 4th and 37th Articles. . . . And as to the Monarchy of Spain he will oblige himself to no more than not to assist the Duke of Anjou either directly or indirectly, offering [instead] to putt four Towns in Flanders of his own Naming into the hands of the Allies as a Security for his observing an Exact Neutrality in relation to Spain, but not to deliver them up till the General Treaty of Peace is signed.[52]

If Townshend had but known what scenes of disorder marked the meetings of the *conseil d'en haut* at Versailles during the months of January and February 1710, he would not have been so uneasy. The ministers were divided and their master, Louis XIV, as Torcy recorded in his *Journal*, 'fut agitée'.[53] On the issue of the peace terms the ministers wrangled among themselves; they sought out new allies among their colleagues; they criticized the conduct of the war; they at once admonished Philip V's advisers and praised Philip's courage; they attacked the perfidy of Victor-Amadeus of Savoy but hastened to treat with him; they applauded Max Emmanuel of Bavaria and the Pretender, James III, then failed to offer them money or supplies. In a word, their conduct of affairs smacked of paradox, of uncertainty, and of drift.

To add to the confusion in the higher circles of the French government, Louis XIV himself seems to have suffered one of his frequent *crises de conscience politique* during the early months of 1710. The *crise* began with a stinging attack on the Duc de Beauvilliers, upon whom, Madame de Maintenon said, 'tout le démérite retombait' for the failure of France to

[51] Torcy, *Journal*, pp. 72–3.

[52] H.M.C., *House of Lords MSS.* IX, 298–9, Townshend to Boyle, 10 Jan. 1710, The Hague.

[53] See Torcy, *Journal*, pp. 28–147, for period from 20 Nov. 1709 to early March, 1710, which gives a vivid impression of the king and his ministers. Torcy's style in the *Journal* is far less finished than in his *Mémoires* of the same period, but it brings an immediacy and a candour that are sometimes missing from his more formal writings. Torcy is usually the master of the understatement; therefore, the greater the shock when we find him—as we do—describing in unguarded terms his quarrels with Louis XIV; see particularly, pp. 68–9 and pp. 124–5.

make peace. But as Torcy sagely observed: Beauvilliers's chief failing was 'd'avoir osé dire au Roi des choses très-desagréables'.[54] Subsequent to the attack on Beauvilliers, the king quarrelled with Desmaretz, to whom he then, in a moment of contrition, apologized, saying that Desmaretz 'devait le considérer comme une marque d'amitié de la part de Sa Majesté' that Louis could speak to him in harsh terms and could then reassure him 'de la satisfaction entière qu'Elle avait de ses services'.[55]

In January it was Torcy's turn. During a meeting with Louis XIV, the foreign minister found that his suggestion that he delay sending an answer to Petkum was 'très-mal reçue' by the king.

> Le Roi traita de vision et presque de sottise l'imagination qu'on avait de penser qu'un jour de plus ou de moins fît quelque chose dans une négociation de cette nature. [Then] . . . le Roi me fît l'honneur de me dire qu'il admirait que je fusse aussi pressant, moi qui étais le plus lent de tous les hommes dans mes négociations.

Torcy defended himself, replying with some warmth that 'je ne compris pas la raison de ce reproche et comment je le méritais, ne retardant jamais l'exécution de ses ordres et les prévenant souvent; mais comme les maîtres ne croient jamais avoir tort, je me tus et tâchai de mettre à profit cette mortification jointe à tant d'autres'.[56]

Amidst such bickering it is little wonder that Torcy expressed a weariness of affairs of state and a pessimism over the conduct of the war. 'L'état des affaires était deplorable. L'argent manquait absolument. Le crédit était perdu. Les troupes ne se rétablisseaient . . . nuls magasins, nuls moyens d'en faire.'[57] Above all, the council 'fut agitée'.

Torcy, however, but a few days before his confrontation with Louis, had sent to the Allies an offer of peace that included assurances of 'exact neutrality' and the promise of 'cautionary towns'. In essence the French merely reiterated their objections to the May 1709 Preliminaries, but with an added—and very important—provision: they would observe an 'Exact Neutrality in relation to Spain' to be ensured by handing over to the Allies four cautionary towns in Flanders.[58]

[54] *Ibid.*, p. 70.
[55] *Ibid.*, p. 75.
[56] *Ibid.*, p. 125.
[57] *Ibid.*, p. 135.
[58] H.M.C., *Round MSS.*, pp. 344–5.

The exact neutrality of the French vis-à-vis their Spanish ally is a very important question and one that needs further comment. Torcy asserts in his *Mémoires* that Louis 'had withdrawn all his troops from Spain'.[59] In addition, during the preceding August the French had promised to stop any Frenchman from going as a private citizen to take service under Philip V.[60] Such gestures, however, did not impress Townshend or Heinsius. Archival records indicate that Louis may have withdrawn eleven squadrons of cavalry and eleven to twelve battalions of infantry; but, in all likelihood, he allowed the bulk of the infantry to remain under Philip's command.[61]

Louis did, however, exhort his grandson to greater independence; the king even went so far as to suggest that the Princess des Ursins be dismissed.[62] Philip's reaction to his grandfather's suggestions was openly hostile. As President Rouillé reported to Petkum: 'The present attitude of Spain towards us should convince you that she will pay no attention to the advice, still less to the orders of France.'[63]

This strain in relations between Versailles and Madrid, though real, did not constitute a severance of relations. The French, aware of Philip's pride of family and of his political ambitions, employed their diplomatic agents to secure for him compensation in Italy for what appeared to be the inevitable loss of Spain. The search for 'compensation' led to the question of partitioning the Italian peninsula between the Austrian Habsburgs and the Spanish Bourbons. Louis thus demanded at the Gertruydenberg conference of 1710 that either Naples and Sicily, or Sardinia and Sicily, or Sardinia, Naples, and the Tuscan ports be granted to Philip.[64] In fact Torcy wrote to Petkum as early as January that 'a Partition might be the most likely Method to remove these difficultys which obstruct the

[59] Torcy, *Memoirs* II, 6. The quotation is from the English translation (vol. II, London, 1757).

[60] H.M.C., *House of Lords MSS.* IX, xiv.

[61] B.N., Fonds fr., Nouv. Acq. 3288, fos. 93r–v, Voysin to Marshal Bezons, 23 June 1709; *ibid.*, fos. 85r–v, Duke of Noailles to Voysin, 17 June 1709, Perpignan; *ibid.*, fos. 107r–v, Louis XIV to Bezons, 26 June 1709; for the increase in number of battalions to twenty-five, see *ibid.*, fos. 120r–123r, Louis XIV to Bezons, 3 July 1709, Versailles; *ibid.*, 138r–v, Bezons to Philip V, 12 July 1709, Lerida; *ibid.*, fos. 138r–v, Bezons to the Duke of Noailles, 14 July 1709, Lerida.

[62] *Ibid.*, fos. 107r–v, Louis XIV to Bezons, 26 June 1709.

[63] H.M.C., *Round MSS.*, p. 348.

[64] *Recueil, Hollande* II, 253.

Peace'.[65] There can be no doubt that this theme of partition was uppermost in French thinking throughout the Gertruydenberg conference. And it was the French insistence on a partition, balanced by allied intransigence in the matter,[66] that finally created a stalemate which was to be broken only by the formation of a new English ministry.

Following the January Proposals, Torcy dispatched a *courrier du cabinet*, who arrived in The Hague on 3 February bringing a letter that announced Louis XIV's readiness to send at once two ministers to The Hague. The persons 'pitched upon'[67] as plenipotentiaries were the Abbé Polignac[68] and Marshal d'Huxelles,[69] a delicate balancing of an experienced diplomat with a crusty, old-line military man.

The French courier patiently waited for a reply from the Allies. As the days passed the Dutch became increasingly impatient. On 11 February, after the courier had been in The Hague for eight days, Dayrolle peevishly observed that 'the Courrier du Cabinett [is] . . . still . . . walking and talking and examining how matters are disposed'.[70] It was even rumoured that Polignac and d'Huxelles had already left Paris on their way to the Netherlands.[71] At this point Heinsius precipitated a crisis by insisting that an answer had to be returned. Townshend acquiesced; on 13 February the French courier departed with a letter that requested Torcy to send a delegation which would treat only the question of the 37th article.[72]

Torcy made haste to reply. 'The King commands me', he wrote, 'to allow the existing 37th Article to be adjusted.' As Townshend sadly observed: 'All [were] of opinion that the Answer was such that the passports could not be refused.'[73]

In Paris Marshal d'Huxelles and Abbé Polignac prepared to depart for

[65] H.M.C., *House of Lords MSS.* IX, 299, Townshend to Boyle, 15 Jan. 1710, The Hague.

[66] Bodleian Library, MS. Eng. Hist. d. 148, fol. 24v, Townshend to Boyle, 17 Jan. 1710, The Hague.

[67] H.M.C., *House of Lords MSS.* IX, 303, Townshend to Boyle, 4 Feb. 1710.

[68] *Recueil, Hollande* II, 225 and fn. 2; Louis André, *Louis XIV et l'Europe* (Paris, 1950), pp. 329, 362.

[69] *Recueil, Hollande* II, 225 and fn. 1.

[70] B.M. Add. MSS. 15876, fo. 285v, Dayrolle to Boyle, 11 Feb. 1710, The Hague.

[71] *Ibid.*, also C.P. Hollande, vol. 222, fos. 61r–v, Torcy to Petkum, 29 Jan. 1710.

[72] H.M.C., *House of Lords MSS.* IX, 304, 'A Monsieur le Marquis de Torcy' 13 Feb. 1710.

[73] *Ibid.*, 305, Townshend to Boyle, 21 Feb. 1710, The Hague.

Moerdyke,[74] the small town picked by the Dutch for the first meetings. When they left, the plenipotentiaries received explicit instructions from Louis XIV and Torcy: first of all they must secure, if at all possible, a partition of the Spanish inheritance.[75] Reports from French informants in the United Provinces, including those of Petkum[76] and Mollo,[77] indicated that the Dutch might accept such a partition in view of the hostility towards England and English policy created by the Minorca issue.[78] In fact, Petkum boldly asserted that 'if France be then content with the Kingdom of Sicily or an equivalent, peace will be made'.[79]

The French instructions also hinted at the English domestic crisis. The Abbé Gaultier, Torcy's secret agent in London, repeatedly and gleefully referred in his letters to the quarrel between Queen Anne and Sarah, Duchess of Marlborough.[80] And as early as mid-February Gaultier reported that the Duke of Shrewsbury and the Queen's new favourite, Abigail Masham, 'govern absolutely'.[81] Torcy added these bits of information from London to the formal instructions.

The French ambassadors, following their final conference with the French foreign minister, left Paris for the north on 5 March,[82] just one year to the day after Rouillé had departed on a similar mission to the Dutch Republic. Having passed safely through Valenciennes,[83] Mons, Brussels, and Antwerp,[84] Polignac and d'Huxelles arrived in Moerdyke on 9 March. Moerdyke was located on an island, isolated alike from the physical world of the United Provinces and the diplomatic world of The Hague. From the Dutch and English points of view, it would have proved an admirable place for peace talks.[85] But the French recognized at once

[74] *Recueil, Hollande* II, 244, fn. 1; also C.P. Hollande, vol. 222, fo. 146, Torcy to Petkum, 27 Feb. 1710.

[75] *Recueil, Hollande* II, 253.

[76] H.M.C., *Round MSS.*, p. 347, Petkum to Torcy, 17 Jan. 1710, Amsterdam.

[77] Torcy, *Journal*, p. 72, fn. 2: 'Mollo . . . homme d'intrigue et de capacité'.

[78] *Recueil, Hollande* II, 243 and fn. 1; *ibid.*, 253.

[79] H.M.C., *Round MSS.*, p. 347, Petkum to Torcy, 17 Jan. 1710, Amsterdam.

[80] C.P., Angleterre, vol. 230, fos. 65r–v, Gaultier to Torcy, 28 Jan. 1710 (o.s.), London; *ibid.*, fos. 69r–v, Gaultier to Torcy, 11 Feb. 1710 (o.s.), London.

[81] *Ibid.*, fos. 70r–v, Gaultier to Torcy, 13 Feb. 1710 (o.s.), London.

[82] B.M. Add. MSS. 15876, fo. 289r, Dayrolle to Boyle, 7 March 1710, The Hague.

[83] C.P., Hollande, vol. 223, fo. 25r, Polignac to Torcy, 7 March 1710, Valenciennes.

[84] *Ibid.*, fo. 26r, Huxelles to Torcy, 8 March 1710, Antwerp.

[85] S.P.84/234, fos. 1r–2r, Townshend to Boyle, 4 March 1710, The Hague; and *ibid.*, fos. 5r–7v, Townshend to Boyle, 7 March 1710, The Hague.

that their complete isolation would lead to the same diplomatic *cul de sac* Rouillé had faced a year before. So, after a short preliminary conference, the French ambassadors asked Buys and Van der Dussen, that they be allowed to move on to Gertruydenberg.[86] Their request was granted and the Gertruydenberg Conference had begun.

Thus, as the conference began, we can see that Louis XIV, Colbert de Torcy, and their colleagues on the *conseil d'en haut*, had arrived at their decision to send the French plenipotentiaries only after weary months of bickering, debate, and dissension. Some signs indicated that France was recovering her military and diplomatic initiative: among the harbingers of hope was the fierce struggle put up by the French troops at Malplaquet; the defeat of Count Mercy's forces on the Rhine, the possible defection of Savoy, or Denmark, or even the United Provinces from the Grand Alliance; the promise of a future Jacobite invasion of Scotland—if not in early 1710, perhaps later in the year; and a strengthened *entente cordiale* with Bavaria. Nevertheless, France still suffered from both a severe economic crisis and a crisis of leadership: the Treasury sought desperately to subsist on short-term loans; the departments of the army and the marine quarrelled with one another and with their own commanders; the ablest marshal of France, Villars, lay sick abed at Versailles; and, above all, the king's high council could not agree on a concerted policy as regards peace or war. At one moment the Duc of Beauvilliers lectured his colleagues on the necessity for peace at any price; the next, he defended the honour of the house of Bourbon. Voysin assured Petkum that France was better able to face the Allies than she had been in 1708 and 1709; then he failed to support the expeditions against Scotland, or an invasion of the Germanies; yet, at the same moment that Torcy claimed that French troops were being withdrawn from Spain, Voysin left the major part of the French infantry there under Philip V's command. Desmaretz too had taken a warlike stance when talking to Petkum; but in his private conversations with the king he was most pessimistic about raising money for the war. Of all the ministers Colbert de Torcy suffered the gravest doubts about the future of France; and of all the ministers Torcy seemed to vacillate the most in the crucial months preceding the Gertruydenberg Conference. At one moment he seems elated at the idea of the Scottish

[86] C.P., Hollande, vol. 223, fo.50r, Huxelles and Polignac to Torcy, 10 March 1710, Gertruydenberg; see also B.M. Add. MSS. 37209, fos. 131r–v.

diversion, or of the possibility of detaching Savoy from the Grand Alliance, or of sowing dissension among the Dutch and their allies; yet in the next moment, he appears to suffer a *crise*: he admits the Scottish invasion was a poor idea; he notes in his *Journal* that Savoy and its duke are certainly not to be trusted; he confides to the Bavarian elector that France has no money with which to pay his pension, let alone equip an army for the Rhine.

These paradoxes in the ideas and actions of the French ministers can be explained, I think, by the growing irritability and possible senility of the king; by the inability of any one of the factions to cope with the dynastic problem of what was to become of Philip V if he were to be denied *by treaty* his right to the Spanish inheritance; and, lastly, by the months of readjustment that it took, after Chamillart's fall, for the ministers to realign their factions and to realize that each—Torcy, Desmaretz, Voysin—was *primus* in his own department.

The plenipotentiaries at Gertruydenberg mirrored the dilemmas of the king and his council. As the ministers in the months of March to July 1710 vacillated between a policy of partition of the Spanish empire and one of complete surrender, so did they. Only when the memory of Chamillart, of the Preliminaries of The Hague, of the dreadful year 1709 began to fade; only when the ministry began to unite under the leadership of Torcy and Desmaretz, only when the English began to treat in earnest with France, did the crisis of leadership begin to abate.

7

G. C. GIBBS

Laying Treaties before Parliament in the Eighteenth Century

In recent years historians have drawn attention to the distinctions made by contemporaries between absolutism and despotism in the Europe of the *ancien régime*.[1] Absolute monarchies, it is clear, though absolute, were not unlimited in the powers which they theoretically possessed over their subjects, even where those powers concerned the conduct of foreign policy,[2] and were certainly much more limited in their capacity to enforce those powers than historians have sometimes assumed.[3] Whether or not

[1] F. Hartung, and R. Mousnier, 'Quelques problèmes concernant la monarchie absolue', *Relazioni del X Congresso Internazionale di Scienze Storiche; IV, Storia moderna* (Florence, 1957) pp. 3–55. For a recent stimulating contribution, see E. H. Kossman, 'Typologie der Monarchieen van het Ancien Régime', in *De Monarchie* (Amsterdam, 1966) pp. 59–74.

[2] I am referring here to the restrictions imposed in French fundamental law upon the right of succession and upon the alienability of the royal domain, for which see G. Zeller, *Les Institutions de la France au XVIe siècle* (Paris, 1948) pp. 82–4. The French law of succession became an urgent question in Anglo-French and Anglo-Spanish relations in 1712 when an alarming series of deaths in the French royal family left in the main line of succession only the sickly infant Louis, afterwards Louis XV, between Philip V and the French throne. Bolingbroke's insistence that Philip renounce his claim to the French throne brought from Torcy the rejoinder that according to French fundamental law no renunciation of the crown by the rightful heir could be valid. (See G. M. Trevelyan, *England under Queen Anne:* III, *The Peace and the Protestant Succession* (London, 1934) pp. 213–14.) The renunciation, which was confirmed by the French Parlements and the Spanish Cortes, generated an enormous amount of discussion in the diplomatic correspondence at the time. Alienability was also a problem, though a very minor one, in Anglo-Spanish relations at the time. Lexington, the British ambassador at Madrid, made some abortive attempts to persuade Philip V to confirm the cessions of Sicily, Minorca and Gibraltar in the Cortes. See B.M. Add. MSS. 46547, Lexington to Dartmouth, 31 Oct. and 21 Nov. 1712.

[3] See P. Goubert, *Louis XIV et vingt millions de Français* (Paris, 1966) p. 229. For a recent case study in the limits of French absolutism under Louis XIV, see Eugene L.

English monarchy before 1640 conforms to the European absolutist model is a question which may be left to students of Tudor and early Stuart monarchy.[4] For students concerned with comparative constitutional history in the eighteenth century the question does not exist, or does not exist in the same terms.[5] Monarchy in England since 1689 was clearly limited and its history came to diverge sharply from that of other European monarchies. For this reason, indeed, precisely because in England the powers of the crown were otherwise so limited, it seemed sometimes a bit of an oddity—for example, to European political writers like de Lolme and Vattel[6]—that, in regard to the making of foreign policy, its powers should have remained theoretically absolute and unlimited. Yet, in strict constitutional law, such was indubitably the position, and has remained the position.

Blackstone, for example, in his classic account of the laws and constitution of England in the eighteenth century, ascribed to the crown a degree of authority and freedom in the making of foreign policy against which the most strenuous defenders of early Stuart monarchy would not have cavilled. According to Blackstone, foreign policy, by its very nature, could not be conducted by popular assemblies, but belonged, and ought to belong, to the crown, in which had been vested the sole prerogative to make war and peace and to conclude all treaties. Moreover, he asserted, once made such decisions were to be regarded as binding upon the whole community. The only constitutional check, indeed, which Blackstone recognized upon the abuse of this 'plenitude of authority', was that provided, *ex post facto*, by parliamentary impeachment of those ministers who, from criminal motives, had advised policies subsequently held by

Asher, *The Resistance to the Maritime Classes. The Survival of Feudalism in the France of Colbert* (Berkeley and Los Angeles, 1960) *passim*.

[4] See the valuable discussion in J. P. Cooper, 'Differences between English and Continental Governments in the early seventeenth century' in *Britain and the Netherlands. Papers delivered to the Oxford-Netherlands Historical Conference 1959*, ed. J. S. Bromley and E. H. Kossmann (London, 1960) pp. 62–90.

[5] Kossmann, *op. cit.*, p. 72. Professor Kossmann contrasts the limited power of French absolute monarchy with the unlimited power of the king-in-parliament 'in the late seventeenth century and in the first decades of the eighteenth century'. The contrast is more valid for a later period. In the period of which Professor Kossmann speaks the power of parliament was thought of as limited.

[6] J. L. de Lolme, *The Constitution of England* (London, 1777) p. 72; E. de Vattel, *The Law of Nations* (London, 1760) I, Book iii, p. 2.

parliament to derogate from the honour and interest of the nation.[7]

And Blackstone was not alone in these views. The doctrine that the making of foreign policy rested in the crown alone, without the participation of parliament, was a commonplace of eighteenth-century accounts and utterances on the English constitution. It was in the first place endorsed by other contemporary students of the English constitution.[8] It was also accepted as the starting point in discussions of the current problems of English foreign policy conducted in the pamphlets of the age, even where the writers of such pamphlets were concerned to criticize the continued validity of the doctrine and to suggest departures from its strictness.[9] Not surprisingly, ministers responsible for explaining and defending foreign policy in parliament embraced the doctrine wholeheartedly and proclaimed its virtues with arguments which, it seems, have changed little over the centuries.[10] More significantly, even members of parliament critical of the way in which foreign policy was being conducted did not dispute the crown's right to conduct it.[11] Here, indeed, was a doctrine which transcended party differences, an orthodoxy proclaimed throughout the eighteenth century by the overwhelming body of Members, irrespective of whether they were in office or out of it, in government or opposed to it.

Moreover, it followed from this doctrine that, strictly speaking, whatever part was played in the conduct of foreign policy by parliament was a

[7] Sir William Blackstone, *Commentaries on the Laws of England*, 5th edn. (Oxford, 1773) I, 252–3, 257–8.

[8] G. Jacob, *Lex Constitutionis: or the Gentleman's Law* (London, 1719) p. 71.

[9] *Reasons Why the Approaching Treaty of Peace should be debated in Parliament; As a Method most Expedient and Constitutional* (London, 1760) p. 10.

[10] For the comments of ministers in support of the view, see William Cobbett, *The Parliamentary History of England* (London, 1806–20) X, 588, 611–12, 664, 690, 833, 900, 975–6, 992, 997; XII, 1169–70; XIV, 598, 694, 1185; XXIII, 396. For the unchanging character of the arguments advanced, compare T. Brown, *1673. The Great Question Resolved. Whether a King of England can make Wars or Alliances without notifying it before to his two Houses of Parliament*, in *Miscellania Aulica: or a Collection of State-Treaties never before published* (London, 1702); John Locke, *Second Treatise on Civil Government*, sec. 156; Robert Walpole in 1738 (Cobbett, X, 690); and John Bright in 1858, as quoted in V. Cromwell, 'The Private Member of the House of Commons and Foreign Policy in the Nineteenth Century', *Liber Memorialis Sir Maurice Powicke. Studies presented to the International Commission for the History of Representative and Parliamentary Institutions* XXVII (Dublin, 1963) p. 199.

[11] See Cobbett, VII, 328; X, 623; *Journals of the House of Lords* (hereafter abbreviated *J.H.L.*) XXI, 606.

result of royal grace, issued, in the contemporary phrase, from condescension. Condescension, it is true, was hardly an accurate word to describe what in practice had rarely been voluntary and had never been prompted by mere politeness. Nevertheless the word exactly conveyed the relationship which existed in theory between crown and parliament in matters of foreign policy. But, as is well known, the appearance belied the reality.[12] In practice, the crown's prerogative in foreign affairs was seriously limited, in the first place, and most obviously and profoundly, by parliament's function as the provider of supply and as the sole source of legislation. In consequence, the crown was obliged in certain circumstances to lay certain treaties before parliament. It is the object of this essay to establish, from a study of the treaties laid before parliament, principally in the reigns of Anne and George I, which treaties required, and were thought to require, communication to parliament; to illustrate from the procedures and formulae customarily adopted in laying treaties before parliament something of the ritualistic care with which, even in practice, both crown and parliament sought to preserve the letter of the strict constitutional position in regard to the conduct of foreign policy; and, finally, to argue that in laying treaties before parliament, as in the conduct of foreign policy generally, the crown was influenced not only by parliament's taxative and legislative powers, but also—less obviously though none the less profoundly—by the ancient view of parliament as a deliberative body, 'the supreme council of the kingdom', with which the crown was expected to consult and to advise on all important matters of state.

The circumstances governing the laying of treaties before parliament in the eighteenth century were succinctly defined in 1755 by Lord Chancellor Hardwicke. 'The King,' he said, 'is not obliged by our constitution to ask either the consent or the approbation of parliament to any treaty he makes, nor even to communicate it to parliament, unless it requires a grant or an act of parliament, and even then he is obliged to communicate the treaty only when he applies for the grant or the act thereby required.'[13] The definition was precise enough in certain respects and it firmly preserved the strict constitutional position that such constitutional limitations as were admitted to exist affected not the crown's prerogative to make foreign

[12] D. B. Horn, *Great Britain and Europe in the Eighteenth Century* (Oxford, 1967) pp. 17–21.

[13] Cobbett, xv, 652.

policy, but its power to execute policy. According to Hardwicke's definition of the position, therefore, treaties attended with expense (to use an eighteenth-century phrase), which included not only subsidy treaties and treaties with a money clause but also treaties containing military commitments whose execution required a grant of supply, had to be laid before parliament at a certain point, but only if they were to be financed at the public expense, and even then only when the supply was actually required.

This rule did not bind the crown to lay before parliament all treaties attended by expense; if the crown could support such treaties out of its own private purse then the rule need not apply. It may be argued that this was to make a distinction without a difference and is merely another specimen to add to the museum of English eighteenth-century constitutional anachronisms. Certainly war had long since ceased to be a business which could be financed effectively out of the monarch's private purse. The point, and its constitutional implications, were put trenchantly by William Pulteney in 1739:

> In former times, Sir, when our kings made war, they did it at their own expense, they went to the field at the head of their own tenants: if any advantage was gained, it was enjoyed by the nation; and if any loss was sustained, it was sustained by the sovereign. It was then but reasonable to indulge the monarch in this prerogative, because he could only exercise it at his own expense. But our sovereigns now make war at the expense of the nation, and hazard not their own revenues but the fortunes, interests, and commerce of their subjects; and therefore, Sir, it would seem but reasonable that the people should be allowed to judge a little for themselves: that our kings hearken to their voice, especially when it is universal.[14]

Nevertheless, it was still possible, to a limited extent, for the crown to finance war out of its own purse, and, when it did, it appears to have stuck to the rules. Anne, for instance, by virtue of the so-called 'Queen's Donative', donated £100,000 out of the civil list for war purposes, and part of this was used to finance foreign subsidies.[15] Thus in June 1703 the queen supported out of the civil list a subsidy to the Circle of Swabia and in the royal speech from the throne opening parliament on 9 November

[14] *Ibid.*, x, 858.

[15] *Calendar of Treasury Books* XVIII (London, 1936), ed. W. A. Shaw, ix.

1703 (o.s.) duly drew attention to the crown's public-spiritedness, doubtless with the aim of inspiring the Commons to greater dispatch and generosity in the provision of supplies.[16] Moreover, when on 19 November (o.s.) the Commons, in response to an address, received, and referred to the Committee of Supply, such subsidy arrangements as had not been previously laid before them, that relating to the Circle of Swabia was not amongst the treaties and papers laid.[17]

The incident is a minor one, but it does illustrate the precise point Hardwicke was making, that treaties involving a money grant only required to be laid before parliament if a parliamentary grant was required. This was the essential point, and if the crown could meet its financial commitment in a treaty without having to come to parliament for a grant, then it would not need to lay the treaty on that account. Moreover, even where the monetary obligation in a treaty was met not out of the civil list, but out of a grant of supply, the crown might still not need to lay the treaty before parliament if the grant had taken the form of a vote of credit. George I's reign provides an illustration of this.

In December 1717 British ministers brought to a successful conclusion their negotiations with the Emperor Charles VI for the addition of a separate article to the treaty of Westminster, signed in May of the previous year, pledging the emperor not to give refuge in his German lands, or in the Austrian Netherlands, to the Pretender or his adherents. In return Britain promised to pay the sum of £130,000 as a final settlement of the arrears of subsidy outstanding to the emperor since the war of the Spanish Succession.[18] Since neither party to the arrangement wanted to appear as having bribed or received a bribe from the other, it was agreed to keep the monetary transaction secret, 'not to be disclosed or made publick by any means, unless the necessity of the king's affairs should oblige him to acquaint his parliament how the money has been disposed of'.[19] But in

[16] *Ibid.*, 313; *Journals of the House of Commons* (hereafter abbreviated *J.H.C.*) XIV, 210–11.

[17] *J.H.C.* XIV, 214–15.

[18] R. Hatton, *Diplomatic Relations between Great Britain and the Dutch Republic* (London, 1950), p. 163.

[19] Sunderland to Stanyan, 10 July (o.s.) 1717, P.R.O., S.P.104/42. For a good account of the negotiations, with the text of the treaty and its separate and secret article relating to the Pretender, see A. F. Pribram, *Oesterreichische Staatsverträge: England* I, 338–43, 347–8.

case that happened—'the better to save appearances',[20]—the secret article relating to the Pretender bore the date of 1 September 1717.[21] Payment of the arrears was duly made at the beginning of January 1718.[22] In the event, although the treaty was communicated to the House of Lords in February 1718 and to both houses of parliament in November 1718, the separate and secret article relating to the payment of the arrears of subsidy was not disclosed.[23] The money in fact had been paid out of a sum made available by parliament to the crown in 1717 to concert measures with foreign princes against the king of Sweden,[24] the residue of which, indeed, was used subsequently to pay subsidies to the crown of Sweden;[25] nor, despite repeated efforts, did parliament ever discover how the money granted in 1717 had been spent.[26]

However, in the overwhelming majority of cases, treaties attended with expense clearly could not avoid being laid before parliament in the last resort, and were in fact laid before parliament when a grant was required. Whether they were laid before parliament on the initiative of the crown—and expense, it was argued, was the only reason the crown could have for laying any treaty before either house of parliament before it was called for by the house[27]—or upon the addresses of either house varied according to circumstances and convenience. Where laid at the initiative of the crown, however, it was not always the case that such treaties were laid simultaneously or proximately before both houses. Anne did not discriminate between the two houses: whenever treaties were laid upon the initiative of the crown in her reign, they were laid simultaneously or nearly simultaneously before both houses of parliament.[28] Practice, however, varied in the reigns of George I and George II: the treaty of alliance with Sweden of March 1720, which had promised a subsidy to Sweden, was laid before

[20] Stanyan to Sunderland, 17 December 1717, S.P.80/35.

[21] Pribram, I, 338–43, 347–8.

[22] *Calendar of Treasury Books* XXXII, Part I (London, 1962), cvi; Part II (London, 1957), 122.

[23] *J.H.C.* XIX, 4; *J.H.L.* XXI, 7. For the treaties as laid before parliament, see House of Lords Records Office, *House of Lords MSS.*, 1718 (373), 11 November.

[24] *Calendar of Treasury Books* XXXII, Part I, cvi; Part II, 122.

[25] Townshend to Poyntz, 8/18 July 1725, S.P.43/6.

[26] *J.H.C.* XIX, 357 (6 May o.s. 1720); XX, 638 (24 March o.s. 1725).

[27] Cobbett, IX, 659.

[28] *J.H.L.* XVII, 102, 377–8, 635; *J.H.C.* XIII, 851; XIV, 289, 501.

both houses simultaneously in June 1721;[29] the subsidy convention with the landgrave of Hesse-Cassel of March 1726, however, was laid before the Commons upon the initiative of the crown in February 1727, the month when payment was due, but it was not laid before the Lords until March 1730, and then upon the address of the house.[30] Nor did discrimination on this occasion provoke criticism. Discrimination, however, or the prospect of discrimination, did arouse criticism in 1735. The king's speech opening parliament in January 1735 had included, in that section of the speech customarily addressed to the Commons alone, reference to the fact that since the treaty with Denmark (of December 1734) was attended with expense, it would in due course be laid before the house.[31] It was pointed out, however, quite correctly, in the Lords' debate on the speech,[32] that although grants of money were made first in the Commons, no grant could be effected without the consent of the Lords, and that to distinguish, therefore, between the two houses in the matter of the laying of the treaty was invidious. The point was taken and the Lords duly received the treaty without making an address, but ten days after it had been laid before the Commons,[33] perhaps to make the point that although the Commons were not entitled to exclusive communication of the treaty, they were, as the initiators of supply, entitled to its first communication.

Hardwicke, in defining those treaties which required communication to parliament, had referred not only to treaties requiring a grant for their execution, but also to treaties requiring an act of parliament for their execution. It was not always clear in the eighteenth century, indeed it was sometimes a matter of dispute, which treaties required parliamentary legislation. Commercial treaties clearly came within the category, though only where these involved the imposition or alteration of domestic tariffs: other commercial treaties might be laid, but at the discretion of the crown, and usually upon the addresses of either house. It was sometimes argued

[29] *J.H.C.* XIX, 592–3 (16 June o.s. 1721); *J.H.L.* XXI, 546 (20 June 1721 o.s.).

[30] *J.H.C.* XX, 729–30; *J.H.L.* XXIII, 512, 514. Another subsidy treaty, that between Great Britain and the United Provinces of October 1715, relating to the provision of Dutch troops for service against the Jacobites, was laid before the Commons of 28 Jan. 1716 o.s. (*J.H.C.* XVIII, 353–4), upon the initiative of the crown, but was not laid before the Lords.

[31] *J.H.L.* XXIV, 440.

[32] Cobbett, IX, 667–8.

[33] *J.H.L.* XXIV, 475.

that treaties of cession in certain circumstances required parliamentary legislation or some sort of parliamentary sanction.

The most fully reported discussion of this problem in the eighteenth century—and one to which Professor Horn has recently drawn our attention—occurred during the debates of February 1783 on the Shelburne peace preliminaries with America.[34] The problem then was admittedly an unprecedented one—the dismemberment of the empire—and it seemed to some at the time an extraordinary extension of the royal prerogative to allow that the crown could 'grant away five parts out of six of the dominions of the crown'.[35] The Marquis of Carmarthen, for one, felt baffled at the implications of such a doctrine: 'If such be the inherent prerogative of the crown it goes to this, that the King, for the sake of making peace, may transfer the seat of empire to any other part of his dominions, Ireland, for instance, and may make over this island to France or Spain or to the Pope.'[36] In the event, the question of the constitutionality of such unfettered royal prerogative was sidestepped, for it was resolved by the Commons that the independence of the United States had been acknowledged, not by virtue of the royal prerogative but by virtue of the powers vested in the crown by an act of the previous session enabling the king to conclude a peace or truce with the American colonies notwithstanding 'any Law, Act or Acts of Parliament, Matter or Thing to the contrary'.[37] This left open the question whether in other circumstances the crown could have ceded the American colonies or other territories without the consent of parliament and there were some who argued that under certain circumstances it could not. They argued that the crown could not surrender in a peace treaty without the sanction of parliament any territories, other than those acquired during the war which such a peace treaty was intended to terminate, and that no prerogative power existed in the crown to cede in any treaty, without the sanction of parliament, 'any part of the dominions of the crown in the possession of subjects under the allegiance and at the peace of the king'.[38] The argument came principally from the lawyers in parliament and was supported, indeed, by

[34] Cobbett, XXIII, 378–9, 381, 396, 430–2, 484–5, 514–19; Horn, pp. 19–20.

[35] J. Debrett, *The Parliamentary Register or History of the Proceedings and Debates of the House of Commons* IX (1783), 214.

[36] Cobbett, XXIII, 378.

[37] *Ibid.*, XXIII, 519–20. For the act, see 22 Geo. III cap. 46.

[38] *Ibid.*, XXIII, 430, 484, 515, 516.

three former attorney-generals, one of whom, Loughborough, subsequently became lord chancellor.[39] It was based in part on quotations from Burlamaqui and Vattel, writers on the law of nations.[40] This gave Thurlow, the lord chancellor at the time, an opportunity to scoff at 'the lucubrations and fancies of foreign writers and Swiss authors', and to defy those who advanced foreign notions to furnish 'proof from the records and authorities of the state, or at least the common opinion and consent of men'.[41] The scoffing, at Burlamaqui's expense at least, was overdone; Blackstone had held him in sufficient esteem in his *Laws* to appropriate almost verbatim a passage from a translation of Burlamaqui's treatise on Natural Law.[42] And whether or not proof existed sufficient to satisfy Thurlow, from the only authorities he was prepared to admit, the arguments advanced in 1783 were certainly not novel to an English parliament. They had been advanced earlier in the century in connection with the proposed retrocession of Gibraltar to Spain in the 1720s.

It may be recalled in this connection that Stanhope in 1718 and 1720 had held out hopes to Spain of the return of Gibraltar, under certain conditions, and that George I himself in a royal letter to Philip V in June 1721 had been prevailed upon to promise to settle the question at some unspecified future moment with the consent of parliament.[43] It may be readily conceded that if the sanction of parliament was a necessity, it was in the first place, and above all, a political necessity. Such was the attachment cherished for the fortress by parliament and public opinion by 1720 that no minister would have dared risk possible impeachment by agreeing

[39] The former attorney-generals were Mansfield, James Wallace, and Loughborough. Of other speakers who spoke in the same sense, John Lee was a former solicitor-general, who subsequently became attorney-general, and Sir Adam Fergusson was a barrister. For particulars, see Sir Lewis Namier and John Brooke, *The History of Parliament. The House of Commons 1754–1790* (London, 1964), II and III (Members).

[40] Cobbett, XXIII, 378. The quotations, given in a speech by Carmarthen, are from J. J. Burlamaqui, *The Principles of Natural and Politic Law* (London, 1763) II, 215–16, and Vattel, I, Book iii, 117. The Earl of Coventry was another speaker who referred to the law of nations, drawing attention to the distinctions made in respect of alienation between patrimonial and usufructuary kingdoms.

[41] Cobbett, XXIII, 431.

[42] J. W. Gough, *Fundamental Law in English Constitutional History* (Oxford, 1955) p. 190, fn. 5.

[43] Stetson Conn, *Gibraltar in British Diplomacy in the Eighteenth Century* (New Haven, 1942) pp. 31, 36, 56–60, 65–8.

to return Gibraltar without getting the consent of parliament. Ministers, it was argued in an anonymous pamphlet written in 1730 and prompted by rumours of a secret article in the treaty of Seville promising the restitution of Gibraltar within six years, were the stewards of the kingdom, and if knowingly and willingly they dismembered any part of the lands, inheritance, possessions or acquisitions of the kingdom, they could be held criminally to account.[44] Nor was the threat of impeachment merely part of the hyperbole of hostile pamphleteers. In January 1727 a number of members of the House of Lords had joined in a protest in which they had described the promise to return Gibraltar as an action 'highly criminal in those who advised it'.[45] The precise point at issue was put quite categorically by Townshend, writing as Secretary of State in June 1725 to William Stanhope, then ambassador extraordinary to the Court of Madrid. He opined: 'By our laws and constitution the Crown cannot yield to any foreign power whatsoever any part of his dominions without the consent of parliament, and that Gibraltar being yielded to Great Britain by the treaty of Utrecht is as much annexed to the Crown as Ireland or any part of England.'[46]

It may be justifiably riposted that English ministers were always apt to consider parliament as a rampart behind which they could shield themselves from hostile diplomatic assaults, and from which they could launch diplomatic assaults of their own; and that even in countries where inalienability was part of the fundamental law of the kingdom it had often been used as a weapon to defend or extend royal power or a royal bargaining position in negotiations with other powers.[47] Yet the advancement of the notion that alienation of lands annexed to the crown required

[44] 'A Londres le 6 Juillet 1730, Lettres à un membre du Parlement touchant l'Article Secret, conclu et ratifié par le Traité de Séville au sujet de Gibraltar et de l'Ile de Minorque', in D. Gomez Molleda, *Gibraltar. Una contienda diplomática en el reinado de Felipe V* (Madrid, 1953) p. 342.

[45] *J.H.L.* XXIII, 17.

[46] Townshend to William Stanhope, 28 June/9 July 1725: B.M. Add. MSS. 32743, fos. 505–8. Townshend apparently made the same point in conversation with Pozzobueno, the Spanish minister in London, in August 1725 (see Gomez Molleda, p. 127).

[47] Zeller, p. 84; J. Hitier, *La doctrine de l'absolutisme* (Paris, 1903) pp. 103–23 (a critical interpretation of Louis XIV's exploitation of fundamental law); Marcel David, *La Souveraineté et les limites juridiques du pouvoir monarchique du IXe au XVe siècle* (Paris, 1954) pp. 225–35. I should like to thank Dr Michael Wilks for bringing this last work to my attention.

parliament's consent was not confined to British ministers negotiating with France and Spain. The notion was also canvassed publicly on a number of occasions in connection with Gibraltar during, before, and after the 1720s, by ministers, members of parliament, and others, both in parliament, and outside parliament in pamphlets. Early in 1720 ministers had proposed a motion for a bill leaving to the king the power of disposing of Gibraltar—which lent colour to the view that otherwise he did not possess the power—only to withdraw it for fear of provoking a contrary bill, which it was suggested would have had the support of Macclesfield, the lord chancellor, and which would have prohibited its alienation 'for ever'.[48] Here again it is true that British ministers were concerned above all to impress upon the French and Spanish courts the impossibility of doing anything about Gibraltar; and that was certainly the way the incident struck a French observer of the English parliamentary scene at the time.[49] It is also the case, however, that the incident took place in the shadow of Thomas Gordon's influential pamphlet, *Considerations upon the Approaching Peace and upon the Importance of Gibraltar to the British Empire*,[50] which had asserted, amongst other things, that Gibraltar could

[48] W. Coxe, *Memoirs of the Kings of Spain of the House of Bourbon* (London, 1815) III, 12–13; and the same author's *Memoirs of the Life and Administration of Sir Robert Walpole, Earl of Orford* (London, 1798) I, 307, 310; II, 183–4; Conn, pp. 42–3. Rumours of other efforts in parliament to move for annexation by act of parliament, or by a vote of the Commons, occurred in 1727 and 1728. See Conn, p. 104, and *The Parliamentary Diary of Sir Edward Knatchbull*, ed. A. N. Newman (Royal Historical Society, Camden 3rd ser., XCIV) p. 62. Professor Conn draws his account of the debate of January 1720 from Chammorel, the French secretary in London, and comments (p. 291) that there is no published record of the debate. There is in fact an extract from the debate, apparently the same as that provided by Chammorel, in the contemporary French periodical, *La Clef du Cabinet* XXII (1720) 230–1. The same extract also occurs in a dispatch of the Dutch resident in London at the time; see B.M. Add. MSS. 17677 KKK(3) (Dutch transcripts) fos. 398–9, L'Hermitage, 6 Feb. 1720.

[49] P. Bliard, 'La question de Gibraltar au temps du Régent d'après les correspondances officielles 1720–1', *Revue des questions historiques* LVII (1895), 203. It was also the way Spanish ministers viewed the incident; see Conn, p. 50.

[50] Thomas Gordon, *Considerations upon the Approaching Peace and upon the Importance of Gibraltar to the British Empire, being the Second Part of the Independent Whig*, 2nd edn (London, 1720), p. 16. For other references in pamphlets on Gibraltar to the notion that annexation to the crown was an impediment to cession, and that in such circumstances only an act of parliament could achieve cession, see *Gibraltar a Bulwark of Great Britain* (London, 1725), p. 55; and *Reasons for giving up Gibraltar* (London, 1749), pp. 14–15, 74.

not be ceded but by act of parliament. Nor did this notion come out of the void in 1720, or in 1719 when the point had also been argued by an opposition M.P.[51] The same arguments, and the same remedies against cession, had been previously canvassed by parliament at the time of the sale of Dunkirk to France in 1662,[52] during Clarendon's impeachment in 1667 (for, amongst other things, 'having advised and effected the sale of Dunkirk . . . being Part of his Majesty's Dominions'),[53] and again at the time of the sale of Tangier in 1679.[54] On all three occasions it had been agreed that if the territories in question were in fact annexed to the crown then they could not be alienated without the consent of parliament. The essential question was whether in fact they had been annexed, and it was agreed that a parliamentary bill of incorporation would settle the matter once and for all. It was, indeed, to the sale of Dunkirk that the Marquis of Carmarthen had specifically referred in 1783 and the words he used, and which have been quoted above, were a clear echo of what had been said in the Commons in 1667.[55] And the arguments had not been new in 1667, but were rooted in the medieval notion of the inalienability of sovereignty.[56] Rather than introducing a further refinement in 1783,[57] therefore, lawyers were refurbishing a notion

[51] B.M. Add. MSS. 17677 KKK(3), fo. 45, L'Hermitage, 3 February 1719. For a similar report, see W. Michael, *Englische Geschichte im Achtzehnten Jahrhundert* II, (Berlin-Leipzig, 1920), Appendix 5: Destouches to Dubois, 1 February 1719.

[52] *State Papers Venetian* XXXII (*1659–1661*), ed. B. Hinds (London, 1931) 198, 200, 212, 221; *ibid.*, XXXIII (*1661–1664*) ed. B. Hinds (London, 1932), 130, 179, 194; L. Lemaire, *Le Rachat de Dunkerque par Louis XIV* (*1662*) *Documents inédits* (Dunkirk, 1924) pp. 18, 62, 116–17; *J.H.C.* VIII, 163; *J.H.L.* XI, 167, 183, 185, 189, 204; *State Trials* VI, 339.

[53] Anchitel Grey, *Debates of the House of Commons 1667–94* (London, 1769) I, 33–4; *The Diary of John Milward. September 1666 to May 1668*, ed. Caroline Robbins (Cambridge, 1938) pp. 123–5; *J.H.C.* IX, 16.

[54] Grey, VII, 97–101. In regard to Tangier it was argued that, being part of the king's patrimony—brought to him in his wife's dowry—it was alienable. See *ibid.*, I, 33–4.

[55] Compare Cobbett, XXIII, 379 with Grey, I, 33.

[56] P. N. Riesenberg, *Inalienability of Sovereignty in Mediaeval Political Thought* (New York, 1956) esp. pp. 98–105, 132, 133.

[57] Horn, p. 19. In a subsequent paper, Professor Horn has noted the earlier appearance of the notion in connection with Gibraltar. See D. B. Horn, 'The machinery for the conduct of British foreign policy in the eighteenth century', *Journal of the Society of Archivists* III, no. 5 (April, 1967) 239.

with which English parliamentarians had long been familiar.[58]

How far, it may now be asked, did the practice of the crown in the early eighteenth century support Hardwicke's dictum concerning the laying of treaties before parliament? In Anne's reign, with one notable exception, the only treaties laid before both houses of parliament upon the initiative of the crown were those which, according to Hardwicke, it was positively required to lay before parliament; namely, treaties attended with expense, either subsidy treaties or treaties of alliance, where and when these required a grant of supply, and the Methuen commercial treaty of December 1703, which involved a change in domestic tariffs. Further, all these treaties were laid either simultaneously or nearly simultaneously before both houses.[59] All other treaties laid before parliament during her reign—save the exception noted below—and including, for example, the other Methuen treaties with Portugal of July 1703 and the Barrier treaties with the Dutch of 1709 and 1713, were laid before parliament only in response to addresses from the houses.[60] The exception was the treaties of Utrecht with France and Spain, laid before the two houses of parliament on 9 May 1713 (o.s.).[61] Of the three treaties then laid, only the treaty of commerce with France, which involved an alteration in British tariffs, strictly speaking required communication to parliament. Both crown and parliament, however, acknowledged and indeed underlined the unprecedented character of the crown's condescension on this occasion. The crown prefaced its submission of the treaties with a statement drawing attention to 'the undoubted prerogative of the crown to make peace and war', and stressed that in communicating the treaties, 'on this extraordinary

[58] There has been a good deal of discussion since, and it still continues. McNair found the strict legal position somewhat unsettled, but added that as a matter of practice, 'now amounting probably to a binding constitutional convention', treaties involving the cession of British territory were submitted for the approval of parliament, whose approval took the form of a statute (Arnold D. McNair, 'When do British treaties involve legislation?', *The British Year Book of International Law* (1928), pp. 59–63; *ibid.*, *The Law of Treaties. British Practice and Opinions* (New York; Oxford, 1938), pp. 24–28). The turning point in practice would seem to have been the cession of Heligoland by parliament in 1890, a procedure which Anson strongly condemned at the time as unnecessary. Holdsworth holds to the view that in law the crown's power of making treaties of cession is unlimited (W. Holdsworth, 'The treaty-making power of the Crown', *Law Quarterly Review* LVIII (1924), 175–83).

[59] *J.H.C.* XIII, 851; XIV, 289, 501; *J.H.L.* XVII, 102, 377–8, 635.

[60] *J.H.C.* XIV, 215; XVII, 50–1, 379; *J.H.L.* XVII, 162; XIX, 547, 557.

[61] *J.H.C.* XVII, 319; *J.H.L.* XIX, 534.

occasion', it was acting freely, deliberately, and solely upon its own initiative.[62] And, for their part, both Lords and Commons were careful to tender thanks to the crown for its 'extraordinary condescension' in communicating the terms upon which a general peace had been made.[63] The episode, therefore, although a good example, as has been commonly noted, of the extent to which in practice foreign policy during Anne's reign had become a parliamentary foreign policy, declared and sanctioned in parliament,[64] is also a good illustration of the tenacity with which during her reign the crown clung to the letter of its theoretical position. Furthermore, all the treaties laid during Anne's reign had been previously ratified before their communication to parliament, with the solitary exception of the 1713 treaty of peace and friendship with Spain, the only exception as far as I know to what was certainly eighteenth-century orthodoxy.[65]

Nor did the reign of George I see any diminution in the crown's concern to preserve its formal constitutional rights in this field, though it did at times discriminate between the two houses in regard to the laying of subsidy treaties in a way Anne had not done. Only six treaties were laid before parliament that had not been previously called for by either house, and all can be construed as falling within the rules formulated by Hardwicke. They were: a subsidy treaty for the use of Dutch troops during the Jacobite invasion signed in December 1715 and laid before the Commons in January 1716, when it was immediately referred to the Committee of Supply; the treaties of Westminster of May 1716 and of Quadruple

[62] *J.H.C.* XVII, 319; *J.H.L.* XIX, 534. The Commons, it is true, had made an address on 11 April O.S. for the communication of the treaties 'in due time', (*J.H.C.* XVII, 282); but the Queen in her message of 9 May O.S. went out of her way to make it clear that in communicating the treaties she was not responding to the address, but was carrying out a previously determined resolution.

[63] *J.H.C.* XVII, 258–9; *J.H.L.* XIX, 474.

[64] Mark A. Thomson, 'Parliament and foreign policy, 1689–1714', in *William III and Louis XIV. Essays 1680–1720 by and for Mark A. Thomson*, ed. Ragnhild Hatton and J. S. Bromley (Liverpool, 1968) pp. 130–9; Horn, 'The machinery for the conduct of British foreign policy', p. 238.

[65] *J.H.C.* XVII, 319. I have come across only two demands by members of parliament in the debates of the period 1714 to 1763 for the communication of treaties to parliament before ratification: by Sir William Wyndham in 1739 and by Lord Chesterfield in 1743. On the latter occasion, Hardwicke replied that to concede the demand would be 'almost to annihilate the power of the crown' (Cobbett, X, 858; XII, 1145, 1169–70).

Alliance of July 1718 laid before both houses in November 1718, at the moment of execution, which set out military commitments that could only be fulfilled at the public expense and which pledged the country to the achievement of certain territorial rearrangements in Europe that it was clear could only be fulfilled by war; the treaty of alliance with Sweden of March 1720, concluded during a parliamentary session but not laid before the two houses until June of the following session, and then laid, as the crown's message conveying the treaty to the Commons explained, because a subsidy had been promised to Sweden which now required payment; the alliance of Hanover of September 1725, laid before the two houses in February 1726, which was intended to meet the threat of a European war and which set out certain military commitments which required for their execution public supply; and a subsidy convention with the landgrave of Hesse-Cassel, of March 1726 which was laid before the Commons alone in February of the following year, when a payment of subsidy became due.[66]

Other treaties, it is true, were regularly laid before parliament in the reigns of Anne and George I, but only upon the addresses of one or other of the houses of parliament, and sometimes a considerable time after they had been ratified and become public knowledge. Nor, such was the deference with which parliament normally regarded the crown's prerogative in foreign affairs, did failure to communicate a treaty usually provoke criticism on that account alone. A good illustration of the crown's freedom and parliament's forbearance is provided by the circumstances attending the laying before parliament of the treaty of Triple Alliance of January 1717, with France and the United Provinces, one of the major treaties of George I's reign. This was laid before the house of Lords for the first time in June 1717 upon the address of the house and was laid before the house of Commons for the first time in its entirety in February 1730 during the Commons investigation into reports of renewed French fortifications at Dunkirk, and then only upon the address of the house.[67] In a more exact sense than has been realized, therefore, the Triple Alliance of 1717 witnessed to what has been described as 'the long survival of the tradition that foreign policy was a mystery of state with which parliament

[66] *J.H.C.* XVIII, 353–4; XIX, 4, 592–3; XX, 567, 729–30; *J.H.L.* XXI, 7, 546; XXII, 590.

[67] *J.H.L.* XX, 513; *J.H.C.* XXI, 449–51. Article 5 of the treaty was laid before the Commons upon the address of the house on 24 April 1723 O.S. (*J.H.C.* XX, 197).

had no right to meddle and about which parliament had almost as little right to be informed'.[68] In another sense, however, it bore witness to the presence and the influence of parliament upon the formulation of foreign policy. Although the treaty was not communicated to parliament immediately, its main provisos, relating to the removal of French fortifications at Dunkirk and the nearby port of Mardyk, and the removal of the Pretender from French soil, were announced to parliament in the king's speech opening parliament on 20 February 1717 (o.s.), as soon as possible after the treaty had been concluded, and were in any case available in newspapers of the day.[69] More important, the main provisions of the treaty represented the achievement of objectives which parliament had more than once previously declared to be desirable.[70] To imply, therefore, that in presenting parliament with a definitive treaty the crown was necessarily presenting parliament with a *fait accompli* is sometimes to overlook the process of consultation and advice which had preceded it.[71]

Some degree of consultation and advice, indeed, was regarded not only as inevitable but as desirable. It was generally acknowledged that the crown should inform and consult parliament about the major decisions of foreign policy—even that in some sense it had a duty to do so,[72] especially where such decisions had been reached while parliament was sitting[73]—and

[68] Horn, *Great Britain and Europe*, p. 383.

[69] *J.H.C.* XVIII, 473–4. For references to the newspapers, see G. C. Gibbs, 'Newspapers, parliament and foreign policy in the age of Stanhope and Walpole', *Mélanges offerts à G. Jacquemyns* (Brussels, 1968) p. 308, fn. 62.

[70] *J.H.C.* XVIII, 22; *J.H.L.* XVIII, 654; XX, 32.

[71] Horn, *Great Britain and Europe*, p. 19.

[72] Cobbett, X, 611–12, 858; XII, 1134, 1169–70.

[73] Thomson, p. 132; Charles Davenant, *Essays upon I. The Ballance of Power, II. The Right of making War, Peace and Alliance, III. Universal Monarchy* (London, 1701), p. 158. (I am indebted to the late Professor Horn for drawing this work to my attention.) Sir Humphrey Mackworth, *A Vindication of the Rights of the Commons of England* (1701) in *Lord Somers Tracts* XI (London, 1814), 294; Cobbett, XIV, 386, 394–5. For the most part, however, the problem did not arise. In the first half of the eighteenth century at least—I have checked up to 1763—the overwhelming majority of important treaties was concluded during the parliamentary recess, including the treaty of Grand Alliance of 1701, the Methuen treaties of 1703, the Barrier treaties of 1709 and 1713, the treaties of Utrecht with France and Spain 1712 and 1713, the Triple Alliance of 1717, the Quadruple Alliance of 1718, the alliance of Hanover 1725, the Preliminaries of Paris 1727, the treaty of Seville 1729, the treaty of Vienna (alliance) of 1731, treaty of alliance between Britain and Denmark 1734, treaty of commerce with Russia 1734, Convention with Spain 1738, Convention of the Pardo 1739,

that for its part parliament had the right to offer advice and ask for information on such matters. Both the crown's duty and parliament's right, it was argued, proceeded from parliament's historic function as the supreme council of the kingdom.[74] English parliaments, said Lord Chesterfield on one occasion, were not just 'agents to raise the supplies'.[75] Not surprisingly in an age that sought to represent revolution as restoration and that made considerable contributions to English medieval scholarship, some time was spent by contemporaries in diligent searches through medieval records in order to establish that the revival in the eighteenth century of what was at the time described as a partnership with the prerogative was a happy return to an older and wiser tradition, which, it was argued, had been interrupted and corrupted by Tudor and Stuart monarchs, who had 'no longer considered parliaments as Channels for Instruction, but as Mines for Wealth; Ministers did not dive there for Advice but dig for Ore'.[76]

It was one thing to acknowledge the existence of such a partnership, quite another to define in detail the respective rôles of crown and parliament in it, and yet another to act consistently in accordance with any such definition. There was first of all the difficulty of agreeing on what was meant by consultation and advice. Definitions differed, and depended in the first place on who was making them. As defined by ministers, for example, consultation by the crown often amounted to little more than asking parliament to approve a *fait accompli*, while advice was held to

---

Treaty of Aix-la-Chapelle 1748, Preliminaries of Paris 1762. The pattern is striking and can scarcely have been an accident. One can see practical reasons why ministers under pressure of parliamentary business should have preferred the more leisurely negotiating afforded by the circumstances of the parliamentary recess which, in any case, was the time when the king customarily visited his German electorate with ministers and conducted foreign negotiations. There may be more to it, however, and perhaps the practice was in some degree an acknowledgement of the strength of opinion attached to the notion that important commitments should not be made during a parliamentary session without informing parliament.

[74] Cobbett, x, 611–12; xii, 1134–5.

[75] Cobbett, xii, 1135.

[76] *Reasons Why the Approaching Treaty of Peace should be debated in Parliament* (London, 1760) p. 29. References to a 'partnership' are to be found in Cobbett, x, 900, 979–80. Attempts to establish this historically are to be found in *Reasons Why . . .* pp. 22–9; Davenant, 136–200; William Petyt, *Miscellania Parliamentaria, with an appendix containing several instances wherein the Kings of England have consulted and advised with their parliaments* (1680) in *Miscellania Aulica* (London, 1702).

mean that parliament should only speak when it was spoken to.[77] To some members of parliament such attitudes were regarded as constituting contempt of parliament; their own definition of consultation meant participation in the making of decisions, and advice meant speaking out, and with effect, whenever parliament judged it fit to speak out.[78] But to the crown, of course, this might appear, or might be represented, as an encroachment upon its prerogative.[79]

Moreover, even when an apparently precise measure of agreement existed on what constituted proper behaviour, pressure of events might reveal its essential imprecision. For example, it was generally agreed that parliament should not enquire into negotiations still incomplete—'upon the anvil'.[80] But what did this mean? According to Horatio Walpole, speaking in his capacity as principal government spokesman on foreign affairs in the Commons in the 1730s, it meant preserving secrecy for negotiations 'while they continued in the shape of negotiations', until a treaty or a peace had been concluded or until the crown was about to declare war and had completed its military preparations.[81] This was restrictive enough, tantamount to presenting parliament with virtually irreversible decisions; but other ministers sometimes added a further restriction embracing peace preliminaries, even after they had been ratified, on the grounds that the royal prerogative had not been exercised until a definitive peace had been made.[82] This raised further problems; what was therefore a definitive treaty? when was a negotiation completed?

Relations with Spain in the 1730s, likened in 1738 to an hereditary suit in Chancery,[83] illustrate some of the difficulties of definition, difficulties vividly if extravagantly expressed by Sir William Wyndham in 1739 in the following words—

> I shall only trouble the House with a word or two more, with regard to the indecency of our addressing for papers that relate to a negociation not yet finished. This is an argument, that I own has had of late great

[77] Cobbett, x, 590, 611–12; xiv, 598; xv, 652.

[78] *Ibid.*, x, 631; xii, 1134–5, 1166.

[79] *Ibid.*, x, 588, 664–5, 707; xiv, 598.

[80] *Ibid.*, x, 584–5, 604, 611–12, 614, 1002, 1004.

[81] *Ibid.*, x, 611–12.

[82] Horn, 'The machinery for the conduct of foreign policy', pp. 238–9.

[83] Cobbett, x, 658.

weight with this House; and I do believe that formerly it was not very usual to address for such papers. But I must at the same time observe, that formerly our negociations were quite of a different kind from what they seem now. Our forefathers acted with resolution; they acted with prudence; they did not suffer themselves to be deceived by the outward protestations, or undermined by the secret treachery of their enemies; therefore the first notice which the public commonly had of a negociation, was by its being notified to the parliament that it was concluded: so that it was almost impossible for them to call for any papers relating to a negociation, that was depending. But we, Sir, have got into a new method of treaty-making; we are always negotiating, but we never conclude. We have been negociating with Spain these twenty years, without making one definitive treaty, that has not been broken before the parliament could have an opportunity of calling for any papers relating to it. For the breach that followed (such was our policy) always gave rise to new negociations, which were set on foot before the next meeting of parliament; then, Sir, when we called for papers relating to the former negociation, we were told that these papers related to the negociation in dependence, and that therefore they were very unfit to be communicated to the House; his Majesty would take it amiss; and the Spaniards would be displeased. This, Sir, I take to be the very case now. The treaty of Seville, though called a definitive treaty, was indeed as properly a preliminary treaty as the Convention; for the most material points, that then created the difference betwixt us, were left to the decision of our commissaries, in the same manner as they are now left to plenipotentiaries. The stipulations in the treaty of Seville, being either violated or not fulfilled by the Spaniards, gave rise to a new negociation, which produced the Convention; and the Convention itself is but a preliminary to a negociation, which negociation may continue heaven knows how long. Thus, Sir, it is evident, that, in the hon. gentleman's sense of the words, this House has not been able for these ten years past, to call for any papers relating to Spain, that might not be said to regard a negociation not yet concluded.[84]

In the case of relations with Spain, indeed, it seemed necessary to introduce a new rule; namely, that if a negotiation continued beyond a certain

[84] *Ibid.*, x, 989–90.

point—continued too long upon the anvil—that in itself might be a good reason for parliamentary enquiry.[85]

The construction that was placed upon consultation and advice, therefore, varied to some extent according to the circumstances and judgment of the moment. Yet, in the long run, the ambiguities and imprecisions of partnership, and its changing character in practice, counted for less than the fact that it was admitted to exist, and did exist. Although, as has been noted, the crown was obliged, strictly speaking, to lay before parliament only certain treaties and in certain circumstances, and in practice, during the reigns of Anne and George I, generally laid before parliament upon its own initiative only such treaties as it was positively obliged to bring before parliament, it sometimes did much more than that. George II, for example, began his reign by laying before both houses of parliament on his own initiative and at the earliest possible moment after their ratification, two treaties—the Preliminaries of Paris of May 1727 and the convention of the Pardo, of March 1728, for the execution of the preliminaries which, strictly speaking, he was not obliged to lay before parliament.[86] It was a measure, of course, of the crown's anxiety to appease an increasingly impatient parliament that it chose to do so. More significantly, the crown's difficulties on this occasion were, in large part, of its own creating, and indeed sprang directly from the consequences of parliament's partnership with the royal prerogative. At the time of the presentation of the alliance of Hanover to parliament in 1726 ministers of the crown, and others acting at their behest or in their support, had devoted considerable efforts to demonstrating its necessity and also to demonstrating both the necessity and the advantages of a war against the allies of Vienna. These efforts had been successful and the alliance of Hanover had been approved by large parliamentary majorities.[87] Subsequently these efforts proved to have been too successful. Having brought parliament to accept the idea of war, the crown then committed itself to a negotiated settlement of European problems, whose delays, frustrations, and expense caused parliament to view the prospect of war with less apprehension than the prospect of continuing uncertainty. Thus ministers found themselves

[85] *Ibid.*, x, 594.

[86] *J.H.C.* XXI, 48, 83; *J.H.L.* XXIII, 183, 213.

[87] G. C. Gibbs, 'Britain and the alliance of Hanover, April 1725–February 1726', *English Historical Review* LXXIII (1958), 274–86.

obliged to restrain parliament from actions which their own arguments had convinced it might be both necessary and advantageous. Laying before parliament the two above-mentioned treaties was part of the proof parliament required that the crown had retrieved, or was about to retrieve, the diplomatic situation.

Admittedly the pressures with which the crown had to contend in 1728 were unusually strong, but parliament was always there, if not always hurrying near. Thus, although it was agreed that foreign policy 'lay in His Majesty's breast', it was also agreed that no prudent king would act in literal accordance with that view.[88] As has been shown, the legal fiction was carefully and ritually observed by both crown and parliament. Nor was this simply a masquerade. The crown was bound to take the initiative in foreign affairs, and, in general, parliament was ready both to concede the initiative to the crown and to accept that initiative where it could be shown to be consistent with what parliament held to be the national interest. The provisos, however, were important, and in accepting the need to obtain parliament's backing for its foreign policy, the crown accepted the need to do much more than the constitution strictly required —which was simply the communication to parliament at a certain point of certain decisions. It was in fact obliged, if foreign policy was to be conducted effectively, to engage in a continuous dialogue with parliament, a development which a contemporary, possessed of that characteristic eighteenth-century determination to invest with a sense of immemorial antiquity any constitutional innovation, once welcomed as 'reviving this ancient and constitutional Custom of advising with Parliament'.[89]

[88] Cobbett, x, 858, 900.

[89] *Reasons Why . . .*, p. 33.

8

GUIDO QUAZZA

Italy's role in the European Problems of the First Half of the Eighteenth Century

During the first half of the eighteenth century, the vicissitudes of the Italian problem, in the general political framework of Europe, acquire a momentum which may be described not only as greater, but often as more chaotic and contradictory, than that of the seventeenth century. After a settlement that had remained almost intact in all essentials for about a hundred and fifty years, the political map of Italy was to be rearranged several times in the course of half a century. The Italian political balance, already an important continental question in the past, now becomes the central pivot of European equilibrium. The political and diplomatic relations between Italy and Europe are, therefore, an unavoidable point of departure for any research into the history of Italy during this period. A study of this kind requires, as a connecting link, some general conception of 'the Italian balance' on the part of European statesmen, a balance conceived as an indivisible political problem, to be faced as a whole and not merely in its component parts.

Apart from this unity as seen from without, it has so far been impossible to discover that awareness of common interests and ideals which, by constituting a deeper bond between groups and classes in the peninsula as a whole, would make it possible to write a proper history of Italy during this period. The politico-social tendencies and enterprises within the individual Italian states do not converge into a single stream, capable of unifying their varied and contrasting attitudes and of conferring upon them, even if only embryonically, that order which was destined to evolve towards the end of the century, when the aspirations of the *Risorgimento* began to take shape.

In spite of the claims or illusions of some historians (in Italy, particularly

Ettore Rota),[1] one must therefore give up the attempt to trace, before 1748, a progress shared by the whole of Italy towards a more satisfactory relationship between economic and social structures on the one hand and political and moral life on the other. From within the small provincial and regional 'nations' there emerges no endeavour of a general nature. Practically everything new, enterprising and progressive that rises above the dull preservation of the past comes, on the contrary, from the pressure of Europe, a pressure exercised even through political and territorial changes, which are thus a factor contributing to progress. This influence of Europe is also evident not only in the internal political action of governments and social groups, but also in the ethical and civil inspiration of those writers who succeed in commanding the attention of the whole country.

Being therefore an object rather than a subject of history, and such a multiform and composite reality, the Italian problem in the period between 1700 and 1748 must be studied, first of all, as the most controversial theme in the general political struggle of Europe; secondly, as a pointer to growing political and social tensions within the old régimes of the various Italian states; and finally, as a term of reference, through the more representative spokesmen, indicative of a mounting crisis in social consciousness.

What problems and what prospects are presented by Italian history in the first half of the eighteenth century?

In an abundant volume of historical research, this half-century has been discussed by two opposing groups of interpreters: those who, following the traditional viewpoint of the Italian *Risorgimento*, regard it as part of the age of 'foreign ascendancy',[2] and those who, in a period of nationalist and Fascist dictatorship, have preferred to consider it as the antecedent of the Italian *Risorgimento* and therefore the first stage in the rebirth of the 'fatherland'.[3]

It seems impossible, in a dispassionate view of the case, to maintain unreservedly either of these theses. The second must be rejected almost entirely, while the first should be qualified by laying greater stress on the

[1] *Origini del Risorgimento* (2 vols., Milan, 1938).

[2] A typical example was E. Callegari, *Preponderanze straniere* (Milan, n.d. [1895]).

[3] Rota, whom I have already quoted, had been preceded by A. Solmi, 'Le prime origini del Risorgimento', in *Politica*, 1925, and by G. Volpe, 'Principî di Risorgimento nel '700 italiano', *Rivista storica italiana* LIII (1936).

signs and urges in this period which reveal a mounting crisis in the old order.

That the Italian problem lies at the centre of European politics between 1701 and 1713 cannot be doubted; because we find that the recurring theme behind all wars, negotiations, and diplomatic manoeuvres is the struggle to gain possession of the Spanish heritage in Italy. And even between 1713 and 1738, the struggle for the succession in the duchies of Parma and Tuscany retains for Italy an important place in the general system of European states.

During the whole of this period, the policy and action of the Habsburgs was determined by economic motives, by personal and dynastic preoccupations, and by reasons of prestige and political ascendency. This is shown both in the attempts to gain control of former Italian domains of the Spanish kings and in the stubborn defence of the Austrian hegemony officially recognized in 1713 and 1714. Spain, after a vain attempt to hold on to her Italian territories, was urged by overriding personal and family factors, coupled with the natural economic and political needs of the state, to pursue Cardinal Alberoni's plan for a reconquest of Italy. The Italian peninsula was also an important, and at one point essential, pawn in the game of France; even if, precisely at this time, she was increasingly swayed by overseas ambitions and beginning to consider the possibility of a new Rhineland policy in place of her traditional one, of which D'Argenson's federal plan was a new and ingenious version. This traditional policy of France had demanded unremitting opposition to the Habsburgs, until recently an anti-Spanish and now mainly an anti-Austrian diplomacy, to be carried out above all in Italy. For Britain, the Italian problem presented itself simply as an instrument of defence, to be handled shrewdly, against continental hegemonies and eventual rivals to her Atlantic sea-power. In this attitude, Britain's future Mediterranean and Eastern policy was already foreshadowed. And she already contemplated, as a settlement favourable to her own interests, a new balance in the Italian peninsula based on three main factors: the House of Savoy, the Bourbon-Farnese dynasty, and Austria.

Having recognized this keen and vital interest of the four main European powers in the Italian problem, and therefore the close relationship between Italy and Europe, we should however take care not to overestimate the changes that occurred between 1700 and 1748 in the Italian situation, and refrain from regarding them as radical innovations or the prelude to the new conception of the Italian order which arose in the nineteenth century.

The feverish political and diplomatic events of the period do not, in fact, reveal any decisive change in the general opinion of leading statesmen on the Italian situation. There was still no emergent view of Italy as an organic whole, instead of an ensemble of balancing parts; and there was still no real attempt to reshape the map of the peninsula in a way which could lead to its unification, or to a genuine federation of states.

With the enthronement of Charles of Bourbon in the South and of his brother Philip at Parma, and by the assignment of Tuscany to a prince of Austria-Lorraine, there was indeed partial recognition of the principle that direct foreign rule should be discarded or reduced through the introduction of independent dynasties of foreign origin established in Italy. But the bonds between these new princes and Spain and Austria remained too close for the conclusion to be drawn that a radical change had taken place in the European view of the Italian situation. It was only a partial simplification of the old order, a new distribution of spheres of influence, and not a recognition of any advance towards real Italian independence.

A cool examination of the facts shows the principle mentioned above to have been something of an expedient, adopted as a lesser evil, to conciliate the many complicated interests upset by a long series of wars. Each government accepted it for its own ends. Austria tolerated it as the price for retaining most of her ascendancy and as a lien on the future of the Italian peninsula, now strictly controlled both in the North and in the South. France saw in it a means of limiting the dominion of the Habsburgs, and a bargaining counter to be used in promoting an agreement with Austria and Spain, in view of France's desire to acquire Lorraine and achieve her ambitions on the Rhine. As for Spain, she had no thought of a freer Italy, but only of a return, a *revanche* after the defeat of 1713: in other words, she evaluated the new situation in Italy solely in relation to her own power, and even in 1748 endeavoured to avoid too trenchant an acceptance of the principle that the Spanish courts in Italy should be regarded as distinct from the one in Madrid. Meanwhile, Britain made good use of the new autonomy of the Kingdom of the Two Sicilies to ease the way towards a more enterprising commercial policy, thus depriving the emperor of important maritime advantages and exercising a more direct and effective pressure in the Mediterranean.[4]

The Italian problem did become less important in the European scene after the third treaty of Vienna in 1738, which confirmed Fleury's victory over Walpole, France's *revanche* against Britain after the setbacks of 1713 and 1731. With the assignment of Lorraine to France, the Rhine became the centre of gravity of the continental struggle for power. But not many months later, even Fleury's victory, gained through the free use of the Italian instrument, proved less lasting and decisive than it had appeared to be after the sensational rapprochement between France and Austria in 1735. If the Balkan peace treaty between Russia and Turkey, signed at Belgrade on 18 September 1739, seemed through Cardinal Fleury's mediation to have widened the area of regained equilibrium, the beginning on 19 October of the same year of a war between Britain and Spain revealed how precarious this equilibrium was, since it had been achieved without taking into account the situation in and around the Atlantic.

The endeavour to load the scales of the balance with purely European politico-territorial weights was shown to be delusive. The revival of Spanish maritime power endangered Britain's privileges in her trade with America, and Britain's attempt to defend these privileges by embroiling continental states in the dispute soon introduced a new and decisive element into the situation: the ambitions of Prussia. Italy, without doubt, was still to be important in the struggle for the Austrian succession, but the main axis of the situation was shifting to Germany; and the area of ambitions for which compensatory advantages had to be found was soon extended to the whole Atlantic colonial system. In the new settlement that eventually emerged from the peace of Aix-la-Chapelle on 18 October 1748 the Italian problem found a solution that lasted for nearly fifty years, while the German, Baltic, Balkan, and Atlantic sectors were to remain perpetual bones of contention between the Great Powers.

The perfection of the general balance that had been devised was, therefore, impaired immediately after the downgrading of the Italian balance

[4] For a discussion of the views of French, British, German and Spanish historians, see G. Quazza, *Il problema italiano e l'equilibrio europeo, 1720–1738* (Turin, 1965); and for a general picture of the situation see his 'La politica dell'equilibrio nel secolo XVIII', in *Nuove Questioni di Storia moderna* (Milan, 1963).

from a primary to a secondary problem in international relations. Prussian pressures and Russian ambitions from within, the Anglo-Spanish war and the Anglo-French race to secure colonial empires from without, were now pushing Europe towards a new stage of development. From the Seven Years' War to the partition of Poland, from the clash between Britain and America to the coalitions against the French revolution, the endeavour to reach an equilibrium was to become ever more difficult, because (as Rousseau lucidly foresaw) the problem of a new relationship, not only between kings, but also between kings and their subjects, was to be presented with ever increasing urgency.

Although no longer of primary importance in European politics, the Italian balance did make some progress in the first half of the eighteenth century, and this fact has led some of our historians, too eager to show that the process of emancipation from foreign control was older and more venerable than many had believed, to speak of an initial movement at that time towards Italy's nineteenth-century unification. This view cannot be accepted. Regarded *per se*, the settlement of 1748 might have led in quite another direction, *viz*, towards a better balanced order of power relations in Italy between European states, and therefore to one more stable and more difficult to change. One had to wait until the experiences of the Napoleonic period for Europe to see any concrete possibility of solving the Italian problem otherwise than by the traditional pattern of balancing powers, and this possibility arose more through social and ideological factors than from political or territorial ones.

If the thesis that the origin of the *Risorgimento* is to be ascribed to political and territorial changes in the first half of the eighteenth century is not convincing in the light of Europe's view of the Italian problem, it is even less so when one comes to examine the foreign policy of the various Italian states.

The activities, for instance, of the Roman Curia are seen to be devoid of any new ideas, indeed of any coherent plan: they merely pursue, without enjoying their former prestige, the old conservative policy, confining themselves to vague plans for an Italian league or Platonic peace proposals, which come to nothing in the general indifference of the various courts. The popes no longer carry any weight in European politics and, when they do succeed in acting to some purpose, it is only in small local matters such as the ownership of Comacchio or of Castro and Ronciglione, or in problems closely concerned with ecclesiastical jurisdiction in other states.

Nor is it possible to qualify the generally acknowledged decadence of Venice, now neutral, constrained and resigned to neutrality, and increasingly hemmed in between pressure from Austria, disguised as offers of protection, and danger from the Turk. The capture of Alberoni and the various Corsican revolts are sufficient evidence of the hollowness of any claim to real autonomy on the part of Genoa, whose international influence had long been exercised only through the business ability of her patrician merchants, an ability unobtrusively at work in the whole of Europe and particularly in Spain.

The long drawnout demise of the Medici power in Tuscany is not marked by any bursts of energy, and the subsequent Habsburg-Lorraine regency emerges as a clear victory for foreign influences, in this case Austrian, and cannot be regarded as a positive step towards a more national policy. In Southern Italy, even after a return to autonomous rule, there were only a few cautious attempts at an independent policy, since the Bourbon kingdom remained almost entirely subservient to Madrid until 1747–48. And the end of the Farnese period in the duchy of Parma and Piacenza resulted in its being handed over first of all to the Austrian Empire, and then in 1748, with the advent of Don Philip, brother of the Bourbon king, in its reduction to the status of a pawn of the Southern kingdom.

The only positive achievement during this period, from an international point of view, was the consolidation of the Piedmontese state of the House of Savoy. Its expansion towards the river Ticino, the acquisition of Sicily and then Sardinia together with the enhanced status of a kingdom, were all signs of increasing power and prestige. But although the traditional aim of acquiring the duchy of Milan became less feasible as the strong neighbouring power of Austria took over from the weaker and more remote power of Spain, the progress of Piedmont was certainly due more to changes in Europe than to the steady growth of a government free of the limitations imposed by the ups and downs in the fortunes of Habsburgs and Bourbons. Proof of this came later when, soon after the middle of the century, the agreement between Versailles and Vienna halted any further expansion of the Piedmontese kingdom. So even here it is no longer possible to maintain the thesis championed by some earlier historians of a 'national' and 'patriotic' policy on the part of the House of Savoy. The dominant feature of its policy was, in fact, merely the old will to conquest and aggrandizement. Its proclaimed aspiration towards the 'freedom of Italy' continued to cloak concrete material aims: a device which certainly afforded proof of Savoy's realism, but disproved the existence of a more mature national consciousness. One cannot perceive in the actual course of events any profound difference in quality between the conception of Italian freedom elaborated in the seventeenth century and that adopted by Piedmont between 1700 and 1748. The cautious, piecemeal accumulation of political and territorial gains was still the only policy consistently followed by the House of Savoy.[5]

There was not, therefore, any real progress towards a pre-Risorgimento awareness of the need for national autonomy, but rather a step forward in the direction of closer contacts with Europe by setting up in Italy foreign dynasties more favourable to reform, such as the Habsburgs, the Lorrainese, and the Bourbons. This is the true measure of the advantages accruing, in the first half of the eighteenth century, from the changed nexus between 'the Italian balance' and European politics, and what really counts when we come to evaluate the significance of that period in the formation of modern Italy, which involved the development of a new relationship between the state and society.

The installing of monarchs more inclined to reform was the most positive result of the political and governmental changes in the first fifty years of the eighteenth century; but it reached maturity mainly after the peace treaty of Aix-la-Chapelle. If we consider the economic and social conditions, the relations between monarchs and the various social classes, the emergence of new forces in existing economic structures, we still cannot discover before 1748 any conclusive evidence of a meeting between *ideas* of reform and *forces*, either in monarchs or in their subjects, capable of translating them into concrete governmental action.

[5] For a full account of the politics of the various Italian states in the general framework of European politics between 1720 and 1738, see Quazza's *Il problema italiano e l'equilibrio*, already mentioned, which gives an ample bibliography of works in different languages, with an appendix on specific aspects of Spanish, Austrian, French and British policy. For the period 1740–48, see also C. Baudi di Vesme, *La politica mediterranea inglese nelle relazioni degli inviati italiani a Londra durante la cosiddetta 'guerra di successione d'Austria', 1741–48* (Turin, 1952).

In the kingdom of Naples and Sicily, and in the Papal States, there persisted, amidst the old conflict between town and country, an agricultural economic structure with an extremely low level of production, and one incapable of improvement since it was hamstrung both by the under-cultivated *latifundia* of the large landowners and by the minuscule 'handkerchiefs' of land of the small peasant proprietors. Except in a few districts of the Romagna legations, the land was made to produce only for a limited market, and in order to provide the Sicilian baron, the southern feudal landlord, the 'black' aristocrat,[6] the land speculator, and various parvenus, with a freely disposable income to be spent in the larger towns on a life of luxury and social prestige. The entire ancient system of feudal offices and privileges continued to impede any incentive to the development of production; and even the new prosperity of long-term tenants, wealthy farmers, dealers and shepherds, grown rich on speculation in grain and other commodities, failed to improve the sweated labour conditions of the farm labourers.

The town was the place where the revenues were spent; and it was dominated by the nobility, the prelates, and the trafficking bourgeoisie. The urban populace did benefit in some degree by the old victualling laws, but these benefits were subject to the approval of the holders of power and were, after all, conferred to the detriment of the peasants, whose products were subjected to deliberately lowered prices and obstacles or limitations to their distribution.

One does, nevertheless, discern in Naples and in Sicily a certain progress following the transition from Spanish to Austrian rule, and even more after the attainment of independence, since the Bourbon monarchy, in its desire for centralization and control, fought hard to limit aristocratic privileges and resumed with increased vigour the struggle with the Church over jurisdictional rights. But this did not involve the adoption of an economic policy of expansion in production and trade. One should not exaggerate the importance of the urge to reform among the so-called 'Giannonian set'.[7] These lawyers and thinkers never really succeeded in becoming an effective influence on public administration and economy,

[6] The 'black' aristocracy was the section of the Italian nobility that supported the temporal power of the Pope. (Trans.)

[7] The followers of Pietro Giannone (1676–1748), a well-known jurist and historian, author of the *Istoria civile del Regno di Napoli*. (Trans.)

or even on the schools of their day. They lacked the aid and stimulus of an upper class and bourgeoisie capable of taking economic initiatives; hence the will of the monarch remained too preponderant. These jurists were, in short, little more than advocates who interpreted the rights of the monarchy.[8]

Although somewhat more varied, the general picture of conditions in the Papal States did not show any substantial deviation from southern stagnation. Indeed the Papal government, carried out, particularly in internal affairs, by an aristocracy of prelates, could not by its very nature provide even the corrective of monarchic despotism against the tyranny of the ruling class. There was, therefore, no trace of a real and consistent opposition to feudal privilege, and no intellectual class showing signs of a modern outlook, even if only on a juridical plane. The prephysiocratic voice of Leone Pascoli was a lonely one, and only in the free port of Ancona and in the Romagne were there merchants and contractors for the collection of the excise and other public services who aimed at greater freedom for their economic enterprises. But even these were inclined towards a purely personal use of their capital gains.[9]

Genoa, Venice and Lucca had their own peculiar characteristics as aristocratic republics, in which a traditional oligarchic predominance was not subject to limitations imposed by the power of a dynasty. In these absolute kingdoms of the nobility, only ecclesiastical privileges were

[8] Besides the earlier but still important works of M. Schipa, *Il regno di Napoli al tempo di Carlo di Borbone* (2 vols., Milan-Rome-Naples, 1923); of H. Benedikt, *Das Königreich Neapel unter Kaiser Karl VI* (Vienna-Leipzig, 1927); and of E. Pontieri, *Il tramonto del baronaggio siciliano* (Florence, 1943), see L. Marini, *Pietro Giannone e il giannonismo a Napoli nel '700. Lo svolgimento della coscienza politica del ceto intellettuale del regno* (Bari, 1950). See also the same author's 'Il Mezzogiorno d'Italia di fronte a Vienna e a Roma (1707–1734)', in the *Annuario Istituto Storia Mod. Cont.*, 1953. Further details will be found in R. Ajello's *Il problema della riforma giudiziaria e legislativa nel regno di Napoli durante la prima metá del secolo XVIII*, I, *La vita giudiziaria* (Naples, 1961). F. Venturi's 'Il movimento riformatore degli illuministi meridionali', *Rivista storica italiana* LXXIV (1962) is also worthy of note.

[9] Among many studies in this field the most important are: L. Dal Pane, *Lo Stato pontificio e il movimento riformatore del Settecento* (Milan, 1959) and the following works by A. Caracciolo: *Ricerche sul mercante italiano del Settecento. Francesco Trionfi capitalista e magnate d'Ancona* (Milan, 1962); *Fortunato Cervelli, ferrarese neofita, e la politica commerciale dell'Impero* (Milan, 1962); *Le port-franc d'Ancône. Croissance et impasse d'un milieu marchand au XVIIIe siècle* (Paris, 1965).

fought against; and except in Venice, where the Sarpi[10] tradition was still strong, not always vigorously and consistently. The old sturdy progressiveness of the nobility, which lay in their commercial or financial enterprise, had now been reduced to a curb on all change, a stubborn determination to hold on to what they possessed. The numerical decline of the ruling caste, and its weakening through internal divisions between eldest and younger sons, were accompanied by the search for the safest investment of capital, almost exclusive of other uses, in great landed estates and luxurious palaces crowded with costly furniture, fittings, and pictures. Moreover the former substantial profits from maritime trade had disappeared, since Venice had been reduced to the rank of a minor port, and Genoa had been superseded by Leghorn. As for the relations between Venice and its territory on the mainland, the hope of a federal state capable of overcoming the deep cleavage between town and country was more and more frustrated by the steady growth of an aristocratic city-state, in which the Venetian *Serenissima* deprived its dependent mainland towns of their autonomy. In Genoa the former advantage enjoyed by its magnates of acting as bankers to Spain had sadly declined; and in Lucca the commercial and financial oligarchy had been reduced to a small clique, which retained its high incomes only through an oppressive tax and victualling system. But, unlike conditions in the first group of states we have mentioned, we do find in Venice, even before 1748, a number of minor corrective influences. The friction between the nobility of Venice itself and the leading families on the mainland of Venetia, the appearance in some of the lesser towns of a few industrial enterprises and of middle-class groups engaged in local trade, artisan manufacture, and free professional activities, an increase in the peasant population, a certain awareness among writers of the new economic developments in Europe, and a lively artistic and literary output: all these things could not be regarded as an adequate prelude, in the Venetian republic, to a period of full-blooded reform; but they did testify to a greater degree of vitality than can be discerned in Southern Italy and in the Papal States. In Genoa

[10] Paolo Sarpi (1552–1623), a famous Venetian theologian and historian, who led an effective resistance by the Venetian republic against papal encroachment on its temporal sovereignty. He was the author of the *Istoria del concilio tridentino*, a history of the Council of Trent (1545–1563) in which he strongly criticized its decisions. (Trans.)

the same could be said of the unrest among the cadets of the nobility, and of the early, tentative emergence of a small middle class engaged in commerce, artisan crafts, and the professions.[11]

The states which we have not yet examined certainly do show clearer signs of a less backward condition, but not even in these do we find a new orientation in the relations between the state and society.

In Piedmont, the contrast between town and country was less marked than in the rest of Italy; and the preponderant ownership of land on the part of the nobility and clergy, although very strong, was less exclusive than in Lombardy and Tuscany. There was a more even distribution of produce between the various provinces, and this meant less disparity between the incomes of the farmers. Social inequalities seemed to be less marked. These features did, however, tend to blunt the urge towards fundamental social changes. At the same time the scarcity of capital in the hands of the middle classes slowed down the investment of money in land and the emergence of large scale tenants. The undeniable revival of manufacturing enterprises was not sufficient to form a group of industrialists numerous and solid enough to wish for substantial changes in general economic policy. And the absence of a really autonomous Piedmontese culture deprived the monarchy of nearly all cultural interests and incentives; so we find that the indefatigable iron will to reform of the first king of Savoy, Victor Amadeus II, and the reorganizing diligence of his son, Charles Emmanuel III, were able to operate in almost complete freedom and make the fullest use of existing energies, particularly those of lawyers and bureaucrats, concentrating them on their plans for buttressing the monarchy. They thus erected a strong barrier against any future attempts at intervention by new and independent influences, a system both incapable of progressing from within and of feeling any impulses from without.[12]

[11] For Venice, see D. Beltrami, 'La crisi della marina mercantile veneziana e i provvedimenti del 1736 per fronteggiarla', *Rivista internazionale Scienze sociali*, 1942; and his other study of 'La composizione economica e professionale della popolazione di Venezia nei secoli XVII e XVIII', *Giornale degli economisti e Annali dell'economia*, 1951. On Genoa, see G. Giacchero, *Storia economica del Settecento genovese* (Genoa, 1951); and L. Bulferetti and C. Costantini, *Industria e commercio in Liguria nell'età del Risorgimento, 1700–1861* (Milan, 1966).

[12] See G. Quazza, *Le riforme in Piemonte nella prima metà del Settecento* (2 vols, Modena, 1957); and for the economics of Piedmont G. Prato, *La vita economica in*

The duchies of Parma and of Modena were dominated by the heavy-handed authority of the local dynasties, to which both the nobility and the clergy submitted without demur, having long been deprived of any independent initiative. However, the general picture of conditions in these duchies was better than that of some of the states already mentioned, since they possessed an urban bourgeoisie, centred around the courts, of considerable literary and scientific vitality, or engaged in luxury arts and crafts, in lucrative tax-levying contracts, and in the spinning and weaving of silk. Moreover on some of the large landed estates there were already tenants of a type which at a later date, and particularly in Lombardy, developed the character and ambitions of the modern entrepreneur.

Lombardy itself was still far from having recovered, even economically, from its decline in the seventeenth century. In a region with an agrarian economy, and with an agriculture unchanged in its methods, the ownership of two-thirds of the land, together with all the ancient feudal and victualling privileges, was reserved for the nobility and clergy, who also enjoyed an almost complete monopoly of the corn trade, of the high profits from the paddy-fields, and of ancient revenues derived from the irrigation system. The fiscal system was weighted entirely in their favour: although they owned three-fourths of the duchy's wealth, they paid less than a third of the taxes. Sharecroppers, wage-earners, small proprietors, and artisans were so overshadowed by this oligarchic predominance that they could hardly become an active or influential element in the population. There can be no doubt, however, that more than elsewhere in Italy one could see signs in the duchy of Milan of the advent of a capable business class, the forerunner of the middle class of the nineteenth century. If most of the profiteering taxfarmers and moneylenders tended to identify themselves with the privileged classes, other farmers of revenues, bankers, merchants and notaries in the towns, and some small peasant proprietors or long-lease tenants, attracted by the steady rise in corn prices, showed themselves, with the consent of the more liberal-minded noblemen, ready

Piemonte a mezzo il secolo XVIII (Turin, 1908) and S. Pugliese, *Due secoli di vita agricola. Produzione e valore dei terreni. Contratti agrari, salari e prezzi nel Vercellese nei secoli XVIII e XIX* (Turin, 1908). On the social aspects there is S. J. Woolf's 'Studi sulla nobiltà piemontese nell'epoca dell'assolutismo', published in the *Memorie dell' Accademia delle Scienze di Torino*, S. IV, n. 5, 1963.

to invest money in the leasing of large estates. Some of these people were already aiming at higher profits through increased production. This resulted in greater tension between them and their workers, but also in a less marked contrast between town and country, and in the growth of conditions less favourable to those with a vested interest in the urban victualling régime that weighed so heavily on the country. The broad European policy of the Viennese rulers was already rather favourable to this change; although the administrative machine remained a firmly aristocratic monopoly, and Lombard culture still showed no signs of independent strength. Here also, the important influences came from outside. Maria Theresa and Joseph II acquired their enlightenment from Europe, and not through any prompting from below by the people of Lombardy; and initially the process of reform was to be started largely through the advice of counsellors outside Italy or from other parts of Italy, such as the Genoese Beltrame Cristiani and the Tuscan Pompeo Neri.[13]

Even before the age of reform, Tuscany was certainly the richest nursery of intellectual administrators capable of applying their cultural qualifications to the daily business of government. While the 'Giannonian set' in Naples, already mentioned, devoted themselves mainly to a juridical analysis of the rights of the state in relation to the Church and feudal privilege, Tuscan culture delved into technical and scientific questions and conducted historico-juridical and economico-administrative researches in a non-metaphysical spirit. All this was achieved through a fruitful collaboration between university teachers, civil servants, and lawyers. Tuscan culture lay much closer to political realities than its counterparts in other regions of Italy, and as early as 1738 was responsible for the promulgation of a decree regulating 'the trade in grain in the Maremma of Siena'. Such an achievement was still a long way from the later enthusiasm and organization of Grand Duke Leopold, but one can already discern here the symptoms of a 'political realism' prompted by an economic and social situation that was beginning to change.[14]

[13] The most important works of reference are: S. Pugliese, *Condizioni economiche e finanziarie della Lombardia nella prima metà del secolo XVIII* (Turin, 1924); F. Valsecchi, *L'assolutismo illuminato in Austria e in Lombardia* (Bologna, 1931–34); M. Romani, *L'agricoltura in Lombardia dal periodo delle Riforme al 1859* (Milan, 1957).

[14] In this field the following studies of A. Anzilotti are still important: 'L'economia

It was undoubtedly true that the domination of Florence, and of the towns generally, over the countryside continued to be oppressive. The political and administrative bodies were monopolies of the prince and of the oligarchic nobility, who wielded in the towns the power derived from their economic ascendancy as owners of most of the land. Since they also controlled the various public offices, they believed in the traditional policy of privilege, without giving much thought to increases in production. Sharecropping contracts, which were very common in the Tuscan countryside, gave the landed proprietors no incentive to improve production, because they brought in good revenues without any need to cater for a market rather than for local consumption: a local feature which slowed down the pace of Tuscan agriculture in comparison with the potentially more dynamic growth of its Lombard counterpart.

Within this mainly static system there were, however, certain interests on the move: those of the *mezzaioli* or middlemen. They were generally town dwellers who took advantage of the difficulties encountered by small proprietors or tenants, using this opportunity to acquire for themselves independent properties or take over large tenancies. These middlemen were, for the most part, merchants and moneylenders; and they were inclined to be more openminded in their management of landed property, since they aimed not only at improving its cultivation, but also at breaking down restrictive victualling regulations and gaining the right to export. And here we must also mention certain Leghorn merchants, who were then engaged in quite an active trade with foreign countries. Compared with Lombardy, Tuscany was lacking in industrial activity, and therefore its entrepreneurs were less enterprising: but this poorer initiative was counterbalanced by a more widespread understanding of the need for change. Hence the cooperation between intellectual culture, the civil service, and the requirements of the economic and social situation was made easier, even if it was characterized by such a high degree of

---

toscana e l'origine del movimento riformatore del secolo XVIII', *Archivio storico italiano Anno LXXIII*, vol. II (1915); 'Il tramonto dello Stato cittadino', in *Movimenti e contrasti per l'unità italiana* (Bari, 1930); *Le riforme in Toscana nella seconda metà del secolo XVIII* (Bari, 1930). For later developments see F. Diaz, *Francesco Maria Gianni. Dalla burocrazia alla politica sotto Pietro Leopoldo di Toscana* (Milan-Naples, 1966); also A. Wandruszka, *Leopold II. Erzherzog von Österreich, Grossherzog von Toskana, König von Ungarn und Böhmen, Römischer Kaiser* (2 vols.; Vienna-Munich, 1963–64).

'moderation' that its future development was not capable of achievements as progressive as those of Lombardy.

In conclusion, the ethical and civil lines of thought, which in the various Italian states had not yet been able to conclude a full and fruitful marriage with existing political and economic forces, showed even in themselves, in their very formulations, a lack of political vigour, an incomplete 'commitment' to action. There had not been, as yet, any spiritual blending with the more progressive parts of Europe: the illuministic urge still lay in the future. The followers of Giannone in the south were still too tied to their legalistic positions; the Tuscan administrators, although technically able, were still a long way from the daring spirit of the second half of the nineteenth century; Bandini and Pascoli were interesting but still uncertain supporters of aspirations towards a partially free economy; the Piedmontese lawyer-bureaucrats were earnest men, but too conformist and insensitive to culture. All these people were more the partial and not fully conscious liquidators of an old order than the builders of a new one. They opened the way to reforming movements more in a negative and indirect manner than through positive and direct action.[15]

Nor did the highest contemporary representatives of the Italian spirit, Vico and Muratori, or the liveliest exponents of the Arcadian[16] literary movement, show any real capacity to free themselves from the prevalent humdrum conservatism, to convert their strictures on the old principle of the paramount interests of the state into coherent action on behalf of new ideas, in the name of common welfare and general happiness. One still feels in them the need to reopen the dialogue between Europe and Italy, which had been interrupted to some extent by the Counter-Reformation; there had indeed ripened in their minds a crisis in the old expressions of Italian civil consciousness; but their desire to change in some way the relationship between the sovereign and his subjects was not translated into action. They were still too accustomed to wait for a thrust

[15] Among the many works on Italian political thought during this period the most recent are: S. Bertelli, *Erudizione e storia in L. A. Muratori* (Naples, 1960); B. Vigezzi, *Pietro Giannone riformatore e storico* (Milan, 1961); N. Badaloni, *Introduzione a G. B. Vico* (Milan, 1961).

[16] The Arcadia Academy, founded in Rome in 1690, became the arbiter of Italian literary taste and style during the eighteenth century. The Academy championed the return to a more simple style of writing, a reaction against the turgid affectations of the Italian seventeenth century. (Trans.)

from above. The Italian of the Arcadian period was not yet the Italian envisaged by Giuseppe Parini.[17]

[17] Giuseppe Parini (1729–99), one of the greatest Italian poets of the eighteenth century, noted for his upright character and lofty ideals. His main work was *Il Giorno*, but the reference here is to his writings in general and in particular to *L'Educazione*, a didactic poem on the education of the young. (Trans.)

9

DIETRICH GERHARD

Regionalism and Corporate Order as a Basic Theme of European History[1]

To one who has lived half a lifetime in the still essentially unstructured and mobile society of the American Middle West, to one who has moreover struggled for years to understand Russian history, which for centuries was determined by geographical space and migration, internal stratification and external limitation show themselves to be significant components of European life—at least they are components which have not been given due attention by historians concerned with the forces of evolution and change.

Dominated by the genetic principle, historians have in most European countries often made a special point of tracing the origins of the forces determining their own existence to find the origins of our own state system, of the modern rationalized, centrally structured state, the beginnings of constitutional democracy, the first budding of power politics, of overseas trade and also, in connection with this, the rise of particular strata such as the bourgeoisie and bureaucracy.

You will certainly agree that in view of this emphasis on the prehistory of our own times, the longlived forces, which have been able to assert themselves against the onslaught of the modern world, ought to be properly evaluated. For centuries, right up to the great turning point of the Industrial and French Revolutions, these forces not only played a big part but acted also as determining factors. It was no mere *vis inertiae* which

[1] A number of questions closely related to my theme have deliberately been omitted, such as that of the 'Land', which has been much discussed in Germany in connection with Otto Brunner's *Land und Herrschaft* (3rd edn, Brünn, 1943); cf. in France the terminological research of Dupont-Ferrier in the *Revue Historique* CLX–CLXI (1929); and also the population problem and the questions of economic and technical development.

enabled the regional counterforces to the centralist and expansive tendency of the seventeenth- and eighteenth-century absolutist monarchies to resist on so broad a front.[2]

Natural geographical community feeling and the consciousness of particular craft and class traditions reaching back far into the medieval past have persisted even into the twentieth century, and appear to the foreigner as witnesses from a world long past in the midst of the ever more exclusive demands of the modern egalitarian and technological society. I need only remind you that in Germany today the feeling for the 'homeland' means something to the refugees from the East, that the class and cultural traditions of family background matter to those who are uprooted, that the longing for stability and time for reflection is not absent even among those who are thrown defenceless into the merciless ratrace of life. Such inherited 'patterns' may give them strength or may increase their difficulties. It is manifest that these old European forces are still operative despite the stresses and disintegration of the twentieth century.

How different in this respect is the old Europe from the spacious society of the two rival world powers. In them, the individual becomes a small part of the huge all-directing upsurge in the pioneer effort of his nation —in the one, by voluntarily following his own inclination and the incentives of the free economy, in the other more firmly directed or indeed compelled by the state. The pride of belonging to such a huge power leaves, for the majority, room for only vestiges of local patriotism.

You will no doubt agree with me also if I make a distinction between Europe on the one hand, and on the other those strivings of our time orientated primarily towards the present and the future, represented in different forms in both the world powers. For where, for all the trends towards modernity, have the forces of conservatism and the consciousness of the importance of local and estates tradition persisted more firmly than in Switzerland, that microcosm of Europe?

[2] In this sense Werner Kaegi evaluated the regionalism of the seventeenth and eighteenth centuries as a 'powerful, generally retarding, factor' inside the great monarchies (*Historische Meditationen*, Zweite Folge, Zurich, 1946, p. 75). For the mid-seventeenth century see R. B. Merriman's analysis in *Six Contemporaneous Revolutions* (Oxford, 1938).

But, you may retort, is this a historical subject? Can it still be the task of the historian to trace throughout the centuries the continuing effect of those forces of the social orders—aristocracy and peasantry, civic life and guilds, lawyers and bureaucrats, clergy and scholars—and their strong link with regional peculiarities? True, the degree of concentration with which the historian can and must endow his presentation of a particular epoch, if he wishes to reawaken the past to the fulness of life, can be achieved only if he distils from the course of centuries that which is lasting in the flux of time, the constancy of certain institutions and organizations and of the human societies pertaining to them. And so I must ask you this evening to let me venture on to the frontiers, if you like, of history and the sociology of culture—that is, if you will credit me with the genuine endeavour to remain true to the task of the historian of discovering that which is unique, in this case unique in the conservation of structures and their basic ethos from the High Middle Ages down to the beginning of modern society, i.e. down to the threshold of the nineteenth century or even well into that century.

Let us begin with a very simple statement. Anyone working in the field of the history of European society and institutions knows that for these areas a division between the medieval and the modern era is even less practicable than, say, in political history or the history of ideas. What since Tocqueville and Taine has entered the historian's vocabulary under the name of the *ancien régime* embraces social and legal institutions which, having crystallized in the Early and High Middle Ages, have ever since been able to assert themselves in the face of new forces.

The history of every town bears witness to the fact that the changeover from a corporative system to the complete equality of citizens took place only after the French Revolution; and that civic law was preserved through the centuries, often in considerable detail. Furthermore, it is true of many European towns that from the late Middle Ages, in some cases as early as from the thirteenth century, even their external appearance changed only little by the creation of suburbs, and even this to any appreciable extent only in the eighteenth century.[3] The enlargement of a town, the dismantling of the walls, has thus often been a phenomenon

[3] Cf. for the outward expansion of towns, F. L. Ganshof, *Étude sur le développement des villes entre Loire et Rhin au moyen âge* (Paris-Brussels, 1943) with striking quotations from literary sources, and R. Crozet, *Villes d'entre Loire et Gironde* (Poitiers, 1949).

of the nineteenth century. There are still people alive who remember these symbolic events from their own childhood.

For we know that this was indeed a symbolic event, a process parallel to all those other 'emancipations' which have characterized the course of European history since the transition from the eighteenth to the nineteenth century—the advent of an albeit relatively restricted freedom to practise any trade, the emancipation of the Jews, the liberation of the peasants, to mention only a few of the most important—and all this heralded by the collapse of the world of social orders and regional privileges, for which the night of 4 August 1789 gave the signal. Since then the most profound thinkers of Europe have recognized this change, and have from time to time tried to interpret to their contemporaries the fact that Europe is living under the sign of 'Revolution'. No historian has done this with greater insistence than Alexis de Tocqueville who, as a young man, shocked by the July Revolution of 1830, went to America to find out how the new world of equality—his own fate and that of subsequent generations—was taking shape.[4]

If in contrast to this modern world of equality the earlier centuries of European history appear for all their changes as a unit, a unit in which the fundamental structures of social orders and regionalism were hardly touched and nowhere destroyed, then a few words about international relations—if you like, about foreign policy—may not be out of place. For an incorrect assessment of territorial changes would block the way to a true understanding of our problem.

Let us recall that for centuries political methods showed a degree of moderation in the integration of territories which came to an end only with the conquests of the French Revolution. Only then did conquest and annexation lead to a radical attempt at social and constitutional reorganization.[5] From the fourteenth to the eighteenth century, however, during which time the idea of the territorially united state established itself firmly, cessions and unions did not take place with any idea of

[4] Tocqueville originally thought of giving the second part of his book the title: *De l'Égalité en Amérique*. For the German attitude to the Revolution during the nineteenth century cf. Th. Schieder in *Histor. Zeitschr.* CLXX (1950).

[5] At the same time, in association with the new idea of the sovereignty of the people, the first plebiscites appear: these are significant of the radically altered character of territorial annexations.

regional individuality being submerged in that of a larger unit.[6] In cases of conquest a sense of justice and the limitation of the political instruments of power worked together, if not to guarantee completely the constitution and legal system of the conquered territory, then at least in allowing them to persist to a large degree. And dynastic unions were—I do not need to discuss this in detail—unions of territories far removed from the modern notion of the federal state and the sovereignty of the nation as a whole. Therefore the repercussions within an area of a change in sovereignty were only very limited.

A glance at the development of Russia and the United States may again help us to see more clearly what was peculiar to European conditions up to the end of the eighteenth century.

Only in the border regions, primarily on the European side, did Russian expansion *not* lead to incorporation in the empire. The case of Finland in the nineteenth century is well known; and already a hundred years earlier Peter the Great, having conquered the Baltic provinces, promised to preserve their old constitutions. But these exceptions are just as uncharacteristic for the general course of the development of Russia as the separate provision for the Don Basin or the privileges granted at times to the Ukraine. Rather, the whole course of expansion from the days of the Moscow tsars, i.e. from the fifteenth century, followed the path of ruthless integration. In a short while the separate administration of the former member principalities disappeared, and direction from the centre through the organs of Moscow became the sole means of government during the following centuries.[7] Doubtless this was a process of reciprocal action: regional society in town and county had not yet developed and become legally consolidated in local groups to the degree found in Western civilization; conversely, the centre was not hindered by those limitations on the supreme power which everywhere determined the constitutions

[6] Still less is this the case for the earlier centuries of the Middle Ages with their ties of feudal law. According to the definition of H. Mitteis, *Lehnrecht und Staatsgewalt* (Weimar, 1933) p. 588, in the Middle Ages to cede a territory was to cede the *homagia* of the vassals inhabiting it.

[7] For the absorption of the *Udel* principalities and for the organization of the territories taken from the Tatars on the middle and lower Volga up to the end of the sixteenth century, see the second volume of V. O. Klyuchevskii's *History of Russia*, trans. C. J. Hogarth (London, Dent, 4 vols, 1911–31). The process is followed throughout the sixteenth century in A. Eck's *Le Moyen âge russe* (Brussels, 1933).

of the West—the combined effect of Church, feudal system and the tradition of law. One should not forget in this connection another constituent factor: the mobile frontier, the fact that Russian expansion into empty or only thinly populated areas meant not just conquest but the migration of settlers. For centuries, therefore, Russian society was much less consolidated and less rooted in the soil of a particular region than was that of Europe.

American expansion occurred at a different moment of history, under quite different auspices, in the post-eighteenth-century period, under the banner of individualism and free association. But here too we meet the movement of settlers, the temptation of pushing into easily conquered spaces in the hope of a lasting consolidation of unending horizons. Here also, and even more strongly than in Russia, internal migration, taking place over many generations, proved decisive for the structure of society as a whole. Since its establishment this federation was no mere union dedicated to the preservation of ancient liberties and to mutual support against centralist despotism and repression from outside, like the union of the Netherlands two centuries before. It very early became a state with an active objective in the penetration and political unification of the whole expanse of North America.[8] The geographical situation, and the conscious will with which the objective was pursued, did at last bring about (despite the frightful crisis of the Civil War) the conformist national society which overlies, or rather permeates, the constitutionally protected life of the member states. The historical moment was not the least decisive factor in this: union and expansion took place at a moment of history when the forces of modern economy and technology were visibly pushing towards large-scale organization and producing ever new changes in the external conditions of life.[9]

[8] The fundamental step was the issuing of the Northwest Ordinance of July 1787, in which the conditions for the creation of states from these new settlements were set out. At the same time, in Article 4 of the Federal Constitution provision was made for the acceptance of new states as equal members of the Union. In contrast to old federal unions like the Netherlands and Switzerland, a new type of colonial federation, which later decisively influenced the development even of the British Dominions, was thus created.

[9] Characteristic of this was the constantly renewed attempt to harmonize unity and freedom—with the emphasis on unity, typical of the modern state, though not of the older federations—which found its characteristic expression as early as 1830, more than a generation before the Civil War, in the toasts of Calhoun and Andrew Jackson.

If we trace back these fundamentals of conquest, expansion and territorial unions in the case of today's two world powers, it becomes clear that the corresponding processes in the European states have been far less dynamic. We recognize that here, even inside the territorial state, autonomous communities have been able to preserve their basic identity through centuries. But how do we assess the importance in the life of the individual of regional and social structures which have remained constant beneath conquests and territorial changes? How far can we trace these back in their basic features? And how far do they persist into our own times in Europe today?

Let us omit the last question from consideration (it is more suitable for the exchange of ideas in private conversation), and instead allow me to put forward some points of view important to the treatment of the other two sets of problems. I shall concentrate less on the question of the origins of corporate order and regionalism and more on the question of their significance. Comparisons may occasionally serve to bring out the specific features of the European structure as a unique phenomenon of history.

A few words first on the problem of when such a structure originated. When one is concerned with analysis of structure, one should in any case not be dominated by the genetic approach. To me it seems—but I make the point with due caution—that from the eleventh and twelfth centuries onwards there occurred a consolidation, a condensation—if you like a crystallization[10]—in western institutions and western society. From that time on certain common features stand out. The feudal knights, the towns, the guilds, then the universities and the trained magistrates, take on the forms henceforward significant for European culture. Intellectual movements spreading over the whole of Western Europe, the experience acquired in common enterprises to which the growing nations were exposed in varying degree, are easy to trace—above all the importance of Church reform, the Crusades, the elaboration of Canon Law, in association with the intellectual movement which has also been called

[10] I hope by using this definition to stress that this is not a question of a 'Kontinuitätsproblem' but of the final symbiosis characteristic of Western culture. By settling for so relatively late a starting point, I, like G. Tellenbach in his 'Die Bedeutung des Reformpapstums für die Einigung des Abendlandes', *Studi Gregoriani* II (1947)—and for similar reasons—move away from C. Dawson, *The Making of Europe* (London, 1932) and also from O. Halecki, *The Limits and Divisions of European History* (London, 1950), although I accept the geographical boundaries he adopts.

'the Renaissance of the twelfth century'.[11] Let us put aside this, in our context rather inadequate, concept of Renaissance, and limit ourselves to emphasizing three facts.

From the beginning of the second millennium, Europe has been spared invasion. European peoples have been able to develop their common structure without having their work destroyed by outsiders and invaders or having to incorporate foreign parts into the structure. What this means can be measured by considering the mass onslaughts to which India, and to a lesser extent Russia, were exposed in the same centuries.[12]

At the same time—and who can say which was cause and which was effect?—cultural and social relationships increased in density and stability, not least because of the development of town life. The transition from migrant commerce to the settled commerce of the merchant guilds—recent research on the history of towns in north-west Europe shows this to be one of the most significant factors in the growth of town life[13]—is only one very obvious sign of the increasingly settled state of the population. The clearer separation of knight and peasant, the growing limitation of the peasants' right to bear arms, as well as the whole development of bourgeois culture—in short, the sharper accentuation of differences between social orders in their way of life[14]—point in the same direction of a society in growth, surer of the security of its own foundations. Where a movement of settlers from Europe occurs—as in the East German colonization or the Spanish *reconquista*—the distinct corporate forms now peculiar to Europe were carried into the new territories and gave from the start a firm framework to the social structure. I need only remind you

[11] C. H. Haskins, *The Renaissance of the Twelfth Century* (Cambridge, Mass., 1927).

[12] Marc Bloch, *La Société féodale* (Paris, 1939–40) I, 94, points especially to Japan for comparison.

[13] In addition to Pirenne and Ganshof see all the works of H. Planitz, in *Zeitschr. der Savigny Stiftung für Rechtsgeschichte*, German Abt., LX, LXIII, LXIV (1940–44) and the important comments of E. Ennen, *Vierteljschr. für Sozial- und Wirtschaftsgeschichte* XXXVIII (1949–51), Heft i. Planitz's last essay, 'Zur Geschichte des städtischen Meliorats', *Zeitschrift für Rechtsgeschichte* LXVII (1950), shows that from the beginning municipal constitutions and stratification into social orders existed side by side.

[14] Marc Bloch, *Les Caractères originaux de l'histoire rurale française* (Oslo, 1931) p. 109, points out that in the twelfth century the old 'lignes verticales' with their personal ties were replaced by 'couches horizontales'; cf. also M. Bloch, *La Société féodale* II, 12 ff.

that close to the frontier of Europe, in the Baltic lands, the corporate order took a specific and striking form.

And finally: the twelfth and thirteenth centuries were called by Marc Bloch the 'second age of feudalism'—meaning the age in which the earlier, more fluid, relationships within society entered a stage of consolidation.[15] Philosophy and law played a decisive part in this development; under their influence the legal forms basic to the structure of social orders and of estates were defined to a degree which the remote world of Russia has always found strange. Relative peace abroad and increasingly settled life at home created the conditions in which the richly structured forms of a stratified society could develop.

Older traditions, Roman, Germanic or Slavonic, merged—and anyone who has worked on the comparative social history of Europe will know how far-reaching are their divergencies. In West Mediterranean lands there was a strong classical tradition, most clearly seen in the slighter differentiation between town and country and in the urbanization of the aristocracy.[16] In the almost townless European East (especially in Hungary, Bohemia and Poland), where the full development of the feudal system had not been experienced and where the autocracy of old guilds, blood brotherhoods and knight corporations persisted, the aristocratic structure of the regions was given an especially firm framework—a process which Otto Hintze has analysed.[17] But beyond all the differences in tradition and structure the fact remains that, in spite of all variations in the mixture, certain common features of the social structure of European countries have maintained themselves for centuries on end—features that never impressed themselves in Russia and which quickly disappeared in America.

Since the High Middle Ages this social-political order had found expression in local or regional corporative systems—more or less strong—but we must not forget that it was born of a deeper ethos which carried it along, an ethos which we can describe as common to Europe. It has a

[15] This is one of the main ideas of his book on the *société féodale*: cf. especially I, 185 ff; II, 35 ff.

[16] Cf. F. Steinbach, *Rheinische Vierteljahrsblätter*, 1948 and 1949. Though I cannot accept his idea that the 'estates' concept is solely derived from North European peasant-warrior culture.

[17] Vol. I of the *Gesammelte Abhandlungen* (1941), his Academy lecture on 'Staatenbildung und Kommunalverwaltung'.

double root: the Germanic sense of law and the government of the Church of Rome.

Belief in fundamental law was decisive for the medieval mind, as witness the inclination to find an eternal natural-law content in statute law, the consciousness of right taking precedence over might and, finally, the idea of the inviolability and permanence of law.[18] The last two concepts in particular lie at the centre of medieval law: the idea of privilege. Along with the concept of privilege—as Tellenbach has shown—went the concept of honour, status and, above all *libertas*;[19] concepts which in their manifold variations determine the position of the individual in the social order. Privilege fulfils for the individual as well as for the corporation the function which in the modern world, since the American and the French Revolutions—and only since then—has been taken by the fundamental concept of equality before the law, of equal citizenship, of the rights of man and of the citizen.[20]

Closely allied to privilege is the concept of corporatism and estates, for the political orders—regional diets, imperial diets, parliaments—campaigned under this banner in their fight against the absolute power of the state.

The Church influenced the social structure of Europe in at least four ways. Or to put it in other words: the structure grew out of the Church or at least was consolidated by her. In one sense—the formal one if you wish—the consequences of Church organization and Church law on the political estates were immense because of the example of the Church's own organization and legal system after the great Church conflicts of the eleventh and twelfth centuries, when she developed a centralized, hierarchical organization unknown to the Eastern Church.[21] No learned

[18] Cf. F. Kern, *Gottesgnadentum und Widerstandsrecht im früheren Mittelalter* (Leipzig, 1914) and 'Uber die mittelalterliche Anschauung vom Recht', *Historische Zeitschrift* cxv (1916).

[19] G. Tellenbach, *Libertas, Kirche und Weltordnung im Zeitalter des Investiturstreites* (Stuttgart, 1936).

[20] For German discussion of Russian legal concepts, see W. Philipp, *Ivan Peresvetov und seine Schriften zur Erneuerung des Moskauer Reiches* (Berlin, 1935); V. Leontoviysch, *Die Rechtsumwälzung unter Iwan dem Schrecklichen* (Stuttgart, 1949); F. Tezner, *Technik und Geist des ständisch-monarchischen Staatsrechts* (Leipzig, 1901); and A. H. Loebl, *Der Sieg des Fürstenrechts* (Leipzig, 1916).

[21] Cf. O. Hintze, 'Weltgeschichtliche Bedingungen der Repräsentativverfassung', in *Histor. Zeitschr.* CXLIII (1930–31), republished in *Gesammelte Abhandlungen* I (Leipzig, 1941). For the influence of canon law on the concept of representation, see G. Post, '*Plena potestas* and consent in medieval assemblies', *Traditio* I (1943).

evidence is needed to realize the indirect contribution to the consolidation of the political estates made by the fight of the Church against kings and emperors. It is obvious that the alliance of Church and aristocracy worked to the advantage of the freedom of both, quite opposite to the case of Russia where the Church never effected a similar alliance against the budding autocracy.

But over and above this political effect, ecclesiastical thought twice strongly underpinned consciousness of corporate order—or perhaps alone made it possible. Firstly, by the basic concept of stratification and hierarchical order which, emanating from the Church, influenced the standing of secular estates.[22] Secondly, however, and this is today seen as its most decisive effect—as it goes to the very roots of human attitudes—by its consciousness of the limits and imperfections of human endeavour. From the Church came the apportionment of man's place in God's system, and man's attempt to fill it (Luther giving this conviction a new form in his thinking on vocation); and from it developed limits to the arbitrary will of the rulers. In the modern secularized world only totalitarian democracy has completely freed itself from such limitation.

The social orders and estates which grew up in Europe under such stimuli had many facets. The political estates, as the whole juridical consolidation into political groups—for example, through the system of town government—are only one aspect of the whole problem, and we ought not to limit our study to this one point.[23]

In political history it may be correct to speak of a transition in the fourteenth century from the feudal system to the 'estates system', for only after this time did the political estates confront the ruler, often as partners with equal rights, mostly brought together by the princes themselves for concerted action and organized into chambers and *curias*. And yet, even politically, the curtailment of the central power derived by no means only from the assemblies of the political estates. We know that in France a stronger institution created originally by the crown, the courts of law

[22] W. Schwer, *Stand und Ständeordnung im Weltbild des Mittelalters* (Paderborn, 1934).

[23] This thought seems to me to be basic to the works of E. Lousse, the main protagonist today of the school which stresses the importance of corporate order; cf. *La Société d'ancien régime. Organisation et représentation corporatives* I (Paris, 1943). Cf. also F. Olivier-Martin, *L'Organisation corporative de la France d'ancien régime* (Paris, 1938).

(the *parlements*), took over this role. All the many intermediate powers—the regional self-governments, the towns, the lords of the manor—acted as successful opponents to the slow progress of the power of the Crown. They all protected regional interests, selfish to be sure, and in the towns they congealed in the seventeenth and eighteenth centuries into nepotism; but with their passive resistance and ubiquitous competition with the power of the crown, they preserved a profusion of regional centres of activity. One should not forget the role played in France, right into the eighteenth century, by the judiciary as organized in local corporations, sometimes of wider than regional importance, and acting like the *parlements* in focusing the intellectual and social powers of the region. And where, as in the small German states, the princes filled this position, they were surrounded and limited by aristocratic society with its privileges, as for instance its claim to occupy special seats reserved for the nobility in government offices or the law courts. Regional and corporative influence has always been exerted over the bureaucracy (the institution with which the princes opposed the political consolidation of the estates brought about by themselves), so as not to allow it to become an exclusive tool of sovereign will and state necessity. In the German lands, where the development of the princely bureaucracy proceeded much more resolutely than in the West, this resistance found its clearest expression throughout two centuries in the fight to fill public offices with 'natives'—the *Indigenat* or, as it was called in Austria, the *Inkolat*. In Austria until the Theresian reforms of the eighteenth century, it was not possible in the case of quite a number of offices to say whether they should be designated as filled by the princes or by the Estates.[24]

In England the influence of the gentry on the whole of county society, and the central significance of the country town socially dominated by them, is noticeable right up to the days of the first impact of the Industrial Revolution.[25] The crown and the big political 'interests' of the aristocracy

[24] F. v. Rechbach, *Observationes ad stylum curiae Graecensis* (1719) Preface. How the lack of executive organs of princely government right through the seventeenth century could lead to the successful sabotage of princely decrees is shown most strikingly by A. Kern, *Ein Kampf ums Recht. Grundherren und Weinbauern in der Steiermark im 16 und 17 Jahrhundert* (Graz, 1941).

[25] Cf. in particular, L. B. Namier, *The Structure of Politics at the Accession of George III* (London, 1929), and amongst the many works of recent years: D. Mathew, *The Social Structure in Caroline England* (Oxford, 1948); for the later seventeenth century

of the court, despite their well developed system of patronage, again and again had to come to terms with the gentry. The professional bureaucracy was achieved only with the reform of the civil service, after the middle of the nineteenth century.

It was in France that the reaction of the corporative and regional idea against national centralization, as embodied in the powers of the crown, was most clearly in evidence. France, too, is the best example of the fact that even where there was no active Diet or Estates through which the political influence of the social and corporative forces of the *ancien régime* could work, the social orders were yet able to assert themselves, even under absolutism. What one may call the modern 'feudalizing of offices' established itself firmly in the venality of offices.[26] Such purchasing of office was not absent in other countries either—in the seventeenth and eighteenth centuries it crept into many German states and there are parallels outside France to the inheritance of offices, in the form of 'expectances' and 'adjunctions'.[27] In fact the *esprit de corps* characteristic of the eighteenth-century French *noblesse de robe* is found elsewhere only in municipal and estates oligarchies, such as those in Württemberg,[28] and not where bureaucracy had been encouraged by the prince.

France thus illustrates clearly how institutions created by the central power might become so to speak regionalized in a social sense. Long before the *noblesse de robe* was trying to close its ranks, even when it was still prepared to assimilate newcomers, it had developed a strong professional *esprit de corps*—Montaigne called it the fourth Estate—and it had its own way of keeping at arm's length unwelcome competitors for an

---

as well as for an earlier period, J. E. Neale, *The Elizabethan House of Commons* (London, Cape, 1949).

[26] M. Göhring, *Die Ämterkauflichkeit im ancien régime* (Berlin, 1938); R. Mousnier, *La Vénalité des offices sous Henri IV et Louis XIII* (Rouen, 1946).

[27] Cf. for Bavaria, E. Rosenthal, *Geschichte des Gerichtswesens und der Verwaltungsorganisation Bayerns* II (Wurzburg, 1906) 88 ff; and G. Ferchl, 'Bayrische Behörden und Beamte 1550–1804', in *Oberbayerische Archiv* LXIII (1908–12) and LXIV (1925); for offices obtained *titulo oneroso* in Prussia by payments to the Recruiting Chest (*Rekrutenkasse*) see O. Hintze, 'Behördenorganisation und allgemeine Verwaltung in Preussen um 1740', in *Acta Borussica* VI, i (1901). Mousnier *op. cit.*, p. 624 shows the situation in Spain and Venice to have been similar to that of France.

[28] E. Hölzle, *Das alte Recht und die Revolution* (Munich-Berlin, 1931), pp. 27 ff. See also O. Hintze, *Acta Borussica, loc cit.*, p. 207, for a comparison between Prussian and French legal traditions.

office. The members of the Paris *parlement* in the early seventeenth century, for example, refused one of its former professors a post as judge —specially created for him by the king—on the grounds of his poor performance in a complicated examination.[29] Such corporate action created a regional bulwark, as Mousnier's research into the *parlement* of Rouen during the early seventeenth century has demonstrated. Roupnel's work on the Dijon region under Louis XIV shows more clearly still how the *parlement* of Dijon was able to absorb the aspiring, prosperous elements of the district who were almost always enabled to combine office and property.[30]

I have dwelt rather longer on the example of the French aristocracy of office holders because it clearly illustrates that the problem of professional corporate feeling goes much further than the question of political estates consciousness and the development of regional corporate assemblies. Certainly the social historian should not regard the development of a state with assemblies of estates as the inevitable next step from the older feudal constitution.

The corporate order state is older than the estates state. From the twelfth and thirteenth centuries, the main lines of these social orders are distinguishable. However much these are rooted in the common European soil, however little the concepts of chivalry, of scholarship, of the honour of the craft are tied to particular places and in theory to any particular national territory, every social order is rooted first and foremost in its locality and its region.[31] In Europe's now firmly settled society, the social

[29] Mousnier, *loc cit.*, p. 187.

[30] G. Roupnel, *La Ville et la campagne au 17e siècle: étude sur la population du pays dijonnais* (Paris, 1922). It is true that the Paris *parlement* continued to absorb members of the provincial *noblesse de robe*, vide the list of 1706 published by Göhring, *op. cit.*, pp. 347 ff. But the provincial *parlements* generally recruited their higher officials (even if they did not possess a formal right to do so, as e.g. Normandy did) from the regional *noblesse de robe*—except in times of crisis when the crown forced a president on them. See, for example, for Bordeaux, A. Communay, *Le Parlement de Bordeaux. Notes biographiques sur ses principaux officiers* (1866).

[31] This difference from the modern concept of corporatism is rightly stressed by W. Schwer, *Stand und Ständeordnung im Weltbild des Mittelalters*, pp. 31 ff. The significance of the local religious brotherhoods for the development of the craft guilds has been elaborated by one of the leading economic historians of the Pirenne school: G. Espinas, *Les Origines du droit d'association dans les villes de l'Artois et de la Flandre française jusqu'au début du 14e siècle* (Lille, 1941–42); cf. also E. Coornaert, *Les Corporations en France avant 1789* (Paris, 1941).

orders—with their feeling for structure and privilege—contributed greatly to the development of regional community feeling of the estates kind and to municipal pride. It mattered little whether corporate bodies were by law able to determine exclusively their own membership—as could be done through the regional registers of nobility, by the frequent cases of co-option to the municipal magistrature, and via the rights of admission to the judiciary and the craft guilds. On the contrary, it is well known how often such rights led to exclusiveness and fossilization. What is important is that the corporate group, the estate, was able to inspire new members with its specific tradition and so to assimilate them. The stability which existed side by side with freedom—which seems to me to be a cardinal feature of the European order—was a stability guaranteed not least by the corporate structure. Not only the form, not only the privileges and restrictions, which were bound up with the honour of the group, but also the spirit of social orders—and with this the stratification of society—preserved itself, even if, as was the case in many groups, an almost complete change of blood took place in the course of several generations.[32]

Let me try, at least sketchily, to identify the common traits of European social orders and estates. The comparison with other civilizations may prove helpful, notably a comparison with Russia as distinctly non-European, but also that with American civilization which, having originated from Europe, has in this very respect turned its back most decisively on

[32] Ennoblement through the buying of estates of offices, through financial transactions with the crown or other services to the prince, and the many opportunities which occurred for such services in times of political strife—as, for example, in the period of the Counter-Reformation—have been demonstrated in many works and especially in family histories. Of the socio-historical studies of recent years there may be mentioned: O. Brunner, 'Bürgertum und Adel in Nieder-und Oberösterreich', *Anzeiger der österreichischen Akademie der Wissenschaften*, 1949, No. 2; P. Feuchère, 'La noblesse du nord de la France', *Annales, E.S.C.* VI (1951); cp. also the examples from the thirteenth to the seventeenth centuries given by M. Bloch, *op. cit.*, pp. 129 f., 142 f. Particularly striking, and easy to trace, is the recruitment of the Swedish nobility after its firm corporative organization in the *Riddarhus* during Gustavus Adolphus's reign; see Pontus Fahlbeck, *Sveriges Adel* I (Lund, 1898) and the studies (which only came to my notice after this lecture had gone to press) by S. Carlsson, *Ståndssamhälle oc Ståndspersoner 1700–1865* (Lund, 1949) and *Svensk Ståndscirkulation 1680–1950* (Uppsala, 1950). On the question of the real assimilation of new families and the importance in this respect of the possession of land, see for south-west Germany in the late eighteenth century K. S. Bader, 'Zur Lage und Haltung des schwäbischen Adels am Ende des alters Reiches', *Zeitschrift für Württembergische Landesgeschichte* V (1941).

her and has thus, as Tocqueville noted, become the prototype of our modern society of social equality.

European society of these centuries is equally far removed from the ossification of the Indian caste system and from the lack of structure of the modern world which no longer recognizes social orders, only recognizing classes. A closed caste-type system developed in European society only at a much later stage—as for example in the case of the aristocracy in Denmark or in the German territories in the sixteenth and seventeenth centuries, or in France and Sweden in the later part of the *ancien régime*—and it was never complete. The rule is a steady rise in social rank, mostly in the course of several generations. It is a well-known fact that in seventeenth- and eighteenth-century England it was possible to gain easy entry into the gentry through the acquisition of land or by marriage, and in the space of three generations to forge ahead to a peerage, perhaps by way of a seat in the Commons. But even in countries where the barriers were more rigidly fixed there are parallels to the English system. In seventeenth-century France it needed only three generations of the nobleman's way of life in order to be recognized as a noble.[33] And at the same time in the Austrian territories wealth and patronage could, without much difficulty, overcome the theoretical barriers in the way of acceptance into the nobility.[34]

On the other hand, the feeling of difference between the social orders and between their respective ways of life remained all the more firmly rooted, in spite of the opportunities for advancement. Even in conflicts between the estates the basic structure was not called into question. As

[33] Cf. E. Esmonin, *La Taille en Normandie au temps de Colbert* (Paris, 1913) pp. 292 ff. For the sixteenth century the most recent synthesis is in G. Zeller, *Les Institutions de la France au 16e siècle* (Paris, 1948), and R. Doucet, *Les Institutions de la France au 16e siècle* (Paris, 1948).

[34] Even the regional registers of nobility and of estates did not provide a complete safeguard against the encroachment of new nobility; see S. Luschin von Ebengreuth, *Österreichische Reichsgeschichte* (Bamberg, 1896) pp. 496 ff., and F. Martin, 'Hauptzuge der niederösterreichischen Adelsgeschichte', *Deutches Archiv für Landes-und Volksforschung* IV (1940). The right to decide who should belong to the landed nobility was obtained, after great struggles with the Estates, by the prince during the time of the Counter-Reformation; see the nearly identical declarations by Karl von Steiermark in 1586 (in A. Mell, *Grundriss der Verfassungs-und Verwaltungsgeschichte des Landes Steiermark*, (Graz, 1929) p. 309) and by Maximilian of Bavaria in 1604 (in E. Rosenthal, *Geschichte des Gerichtswesens und der Verwaltungsorganisations Bayerns* (Wurzburg, 1906) II, 35).

Hans Freyer has put it, the estates 'stand on their hereditary rights, seeking to exploit, to consolidate and to enlarge them'. He has therefore rightly described conflicts between the estates as conflicts over the revision of social frontiers and the granting of privileges: 'The dictum that Society consists of different and differing parts is at bottom never questioned.'[35]

Let us compare this not only with the modern principle of class conflict—the 'ôte-toi que je m'y mette'—but also with the structure of modern American society.[36] The principle of keeping up with the Joneses will be familiar to you; and since there are theoretically no barriers between the different Joneses, there existed in people's minds from an early date not only a sense of complete egalitarianism, but also, at any rate since the early nineteenth century, the impulse to strive for rapid advancement in *one* generation. And in the course of our own century the development of a capitalist economy in the virgin soil of America has in large measure

[35] H. Freyer, *Soziologie als Wirklichkeitswissenschaft* (1930), pp. 276 ff. In the literature on estate and class note especially Max Weber, 'Wirtschaft und Gesellschaft', *Grundriss der Sozialökonomik*, 2nd edn. III, (1925). Pontus Fahlbeck writes, within the framework of his theory of the upward and downward movements of culture, on the development from estate to class in antiquity in *Die Klassen und die Gesellschaft* (Jena, 1922) and in the modern period in *Stand och Klasser* (1922). It is well known that in the period of social orders and estates—though differentiations remained strong—frequent and bitter struggles took place for the decisive influence on politics and economic policy. The latest attack on the 'école corporative' (of Lousse and his school, cf. p. 165, fn. 23 above) comes from J. Dhondt (in *Annales*, 1950, pp. 289 ff.) and is based on the records of the dynamic and aggressive estates of Flanders. Dhondt attacks the 'idyllic' attitude which sees static social orders and remains blind to the reality of struggles between estates. By the very title of his article (' "Ordres" ou "Puissances": l'exemple des États de Flandres'), however, Dhondt reveals his own tendency to regard Estates constitutionalism as no more than the arena for economic-political struggles.

[36] American sociology has, in the twenty-three years since it was founded by R. L. Lynd and H. M. Lynd's book, *Middletown* (London, 1929) analysed the growing stratification of American society in a steady stream of new investigations based on ever more refined research and questionnaire techniques. It also demonstrates an increasing rigidity in American society during the twentieth century; the old avenues for rising in the world have become blocked and a class structure has become noticeable. Simultaneously it has traced a growing differentiation in the patterns of daily living. The character of American society has not, however, become so changed that—as in a society of orders and estates—we can discover any fundamental conception of different functions of the different orders within society. On the contrary, the main aim of American education is still to prepare the individual for a harmonious fitting into a society of equals. Cf. the remarks of Freyer, *op. cit.*, pp. 265 f. against Max Weber.

turned this possibility into reality. A basic condition for such change was the removal of the barriers between social orders or classes. This was effected more easily and more radically here than anywhere in old Europe —largely because such barriers had been present only to a very limited extent from the very beginning of the settlement of the continent.

Since Frederick Jackson Turner the frontier mentality and the pioneering spirit have rightly been recognized as prime causes for the early development towards egalitarian democracy.[37] The American is tolerant, but also conscious of his own worth: 'He thinks everyone as good as his neighbour and himself a little better', as a Mid-western phrase has it. And Vernon L. Parrington tells of an incident in the early eighteenth century in upper Massachusetts for which it would be difficult to find a parallel even in Swiss democracy: a governor got out of his coach and asked some woodcutters to move their cart out of the way; he was told to get out of the way himself—they were as good as he was.[38]

Already about this time we see the beginning of the disintegration of corporative ties, in so far as they existed in the United States. It is visible in the transition from the village to the isolated farm, in the complete occupational freedom.[39] In that country of immigration and internal migration there was no cause to be tied to the soil—even in the form of feudal land laws[40]—or to a particular occupation. The immigrant himself, coming from a society whose structure was already crumbling, was only

[37] The best introduction to Turner and the researches to which he gave impetus is the volume (published in 1949) in the Amherst College series 'Problems in American Civilization', entitled *The Turner Thesis concerning the Role of the Frontier in American History*. The Turner controversy has naturally been much concerned with the rôle of the moving frontier as an economic-social 'security-vent' throughout the nineteenth century. But recent work on the early part of that century has shown that the frontier was not the only decisive factor in the political and social democratization of America: see A. M. Schlesinger, *The Age of Jackson* (Boston-London, 1945).

[38] V. L. Parrington, *Main Currents in American Thought* (New York, 1927) I, 126.

[39] For the dissolution of the village in New England after the late seventeenth century, and for the influence on this process of land speculation, see R. H. Akagi *The Town Proprietors of the New England Colonies* (Philadelphia, 1924); and also R. A. Billington, *Westward Expansion* (New York, 1949) particularly pp. 71 ff., and 93 ff. and the bibliography given there. For intimations of the few and unsuccessful attempts to organize the crafts into guilds in the seventeenth century or to regulate them through urban regulations, see C. Bridenbaugh, *The Colonial Craftsman* (New York-London, 1950), and *Cities in the Wilderness* (New York, 1938).

[40] Their last remnants—the entail and quitrent—disappear with the American revolution.

too glad to rid himself of these fetters. The revivalist movement,[41] the Revolution and the influence of the frontier in the spiritual sphere as well as the material one, undermined the older European traditions. With the dissolution of the state Church, and the advent of non-denominational schooling[42] at the end of the eighteenth century, the old theological and humanistic studies and mere book-learning were swept aside. There was progressively less room for them in the new society, orientated as it was towards the immediate tasks of the here and now.

It was a uniform society, industrious, informed, preoccupied with the immediate opening up and organization of the vast areas falling to its lot. When de Tocqueville travelled around this new world in 1831 he noted particularly that the same spirit, the same will, but also the same degree of education, existed on the edge of the virgin forests as in the coastal towns. It is surprising how far Americans at that time had already moved away from the old society of Europe, from its high degree of regional differentiation and its corporate tradition of society and estates the remnants of which, unscathed by two world wars, they, to their astonishment, still find in the Europe of today.

On the other hand, America vigorously cultivated those institutions and attitudes of the medieval tradition which could protect an increasingly egalitarian modern society from the misuse of power, growing ever more dangerous: the right to individual liberty and its protection, the safeguarding of the constitution through the courts, and above all the basic

[41] This led already by mid-eighteenth century to defeat for the principle of the closed geographic parish and thus, helped by the arrival of new sects and church communities through immigration, to that division and multiplicity characteristic of American church life. It should also be remembered that for the emotionally starved frontier population proper, without much theological education, the wandering preacher of the evangelical movement, the 'circuit rider', tended to replace the European type of clergyman.

[42] Even during the English period some colonies, notably Pennsylvania, had no state church; while in others immigration and evangelicalism had already undermined the foundations of the state church. The breakthrough in this development came in the revolutionary period with the complete separation of state and church in the Virginia Statute of Religious Liberty of 1786: the influence of all these factors on education can be traced in the progress and victory of the 'common school' in mid-19th cent. In the sphere of higher education this is paralleled by the advance of the utilitarian tendencies of the Enlightenment. The fundamental principle expressed as the goal of education by the Philips Andover Academy in 1778 is characteristic: 'to learn them the great end and real business of living'.

democratic right of corporative association—free and tied to no geographical or social boundaries.[43]

Compared with Russia, the distinctive traits of the old European order stand out even more markedly. For here we are not, as in the United States, faced with a process of development from a common native soil but, at any rate since the fourteenth and fifteenth centuries, with the emergence of traits totally different from those of the European structure of society. In an effort to explain these differences, attention has rightly been drawn to Byzantine influences and also to Tatar ones. But internal migration—the ever-advancing frontier—and the vast open spaces have no doubt here also contributed to the fact that nothing like the European structure of society emerged. In order to understand this aright, let us briefly examine the chief individual components of this structure.

At the highest level the contrast is clear: in Russia the development of autocracy, in Europe that of monarchy to whose limitations, even in the heyday of absolutism, writers, notably Montesquieu, drew attention. Montesquieu did no more than follow in the footsteps of the first exponent of the idea of sovereignty. One hundred and seventy years earlier Bodin, for all his condemnation of the unchecked monopoly of intermediary powers, declared corporative bodies to be as natural and necessary as family and state. And he had added: 'Remove the corporations and the communes, and you ruin the state and change it into a barbarous tyranny.'[44] Benda in his *Trahison des clercs* has rightly drawn attention to the fact that historians have overestimated the power of the absolute

[43] The inheritance from England, a heritage closely related to that of European tradition in general, was the basis on which new gains were built, as can be seen in the American history of self-government, of parties, of the press, and of social associations. Conversely, in Germany in the postwar period, much attention has been focused on the fact that in the modern period the feeling for social community has been pushed into the background by the tradition of power in the hands of the state and the ruling authorities. The old European counterforces to authoritarian centralization and lust for power have here been transplanted into the modern life of state and society less successfully than in many other western countries. H. Heffter, in his *Die deutsche Selbstverwaltung im 19. Jahrhundert* (Stuttgart, 1950), has stressed the central significance of the scope and limitations of such counterforces in Germany in the nineteenth century.

[44] In Book 3, ch. 7, of *Six livres de la République* (the quotation, translated from the French, is from the end of the chapter on 'Des corps et collèges, états et communautés').

monarchy and has stressed how important it is to emphasize anew the ancient function of the king as guardian of justice.[45]

It is especially difficult to find in Russia any true parallel for the limitations placed upon European monarchy by the feudal system. The Boyar Duma at the centre of the Muscovite state may recall the *curia regis* of the West or the Council of the Realm of the Scandinavian countries; but its influence steadily declined. Other features characteristic of European feudalism are completely absent, such as for instance the concepts of grace and fealty or of knightly honour.[46] And not until Catherine II's charter of 1785 was corporal punishment abolished for the Russian aristocracy.

It was not merely that ever since the fifteenth century, when a definitive relationship between land ownership and service emerged—such as for example property held in fief in place of the earlier freedom of movement—allegiance to the tsar became a one-sided and unrestricted obligation. More important still, perhaps in this connection, is the fact that there emerged in Russia neither a chain of vassals as in European feudalism, nor indeed any lasting aristocratic corporations.[47] We need only refer to the importance for nineteenth-century Styria of the laws relating to the *ministeriales* in the development of the unity of the region, or to the fact that the early eleventh- and twelfth-century formulation of these laws went hand in hand with a simultaneous elaboration of municipal laws,[48]

[45] J. Benda, *La Trahison des clercs* (Paris, 1927) p. 278.

[46] These concepts of unbroken common European tradition penetrated also into the borderlands of Europe, into Scandinavia for example, where no feudal system based on landholdings ever developed fully. Cf. K. E. Löfquist, *Om riddarväsen och frälse i Nordisk Medeltid* (1935) and A. E. Christensen, *Kongemagt og Aristokrati* (1945).

[47] Just these eastern borderlands of Europe, Hungary and Poland, which were only indirectly influenced by feudalism, developed such noble associations which became the real kernel of self-government and of the political estates system. Cf. for Hungary, apart from Hintze (*loc cit.*, p. 163, fn. 17 above) the works by G. Bonis known to me only through a review in the *Revue historique de droit français* of 1951; for Poland and feudalism see the contributions by Z. Wojciechowski in *ibid.* for the years 1936 and 1937, and the same author's *Das Ritterrecht in Polen* (Berlin, 1936) and his 'L'état Polonais au Moyen-Âge', in *Histoire des institutions* (Paris, 1949); also the articles by H. F. Schmid in *Zeitschrift für Rechtsgeschichte*, Germ. Abt. LIII (1933) 459 ff. and the same author's comparison in *Jahrbücher für Kultur und Geschichte der Slaven*, N.F., II (1926), of the remnants of the *volost* organization in Russia with corresponding institutions in other Slavonic countries, an organization, however, which he is able to show really alive only in the later sixteenth century.

[48] Besides the school of Pirenne and the emphasis on the growing importance of overseas trade for Germany, especially by Rörig, recent urban histories demonstrate

in order to realize the fundamental difference between Russia and Europe.

Do not let us forget in this connection the moving frontier, the fact that the Russian aristocracy apparently changed its domicile more frequently than its European counterpart, and this not only in the violent, revolutionary days of Ivan the Terrible. It is clear why it was less tied to a particular region and, apart from the old Boyars, also less class-conscious than the European aristocracy.[49] As late as the eighteenth century the opportunities for advancement were greater than in Europe; in the unlimited possibilities, in the speed with which the Russian aristocracy developed, Russia is reminiscent rather of nineteenth-century America than of contemporary Europe.

Recently one of the most imaginative scholars in the field of European feudalism, Otto Brunner, tried (basing his conclusions in part on the results of research carried out by Werner Conze for Lithuania) to analyse the characteristic features of European aristocracy in its relation to the villein, the serf, and to contrast it also with that of Russia.[50] His formulations deserve mention; they not only round off the picture but bring us up against questions of great significance for the distinction between social orders, regions, and settled communities—questions which in our epoch of predominantly nomadic trends deserve particular attention. The point at issue is nothing more nor less than whether a particular form of settled community—the medieval peasantry using the plough to farm land under their lord—was the precondition without which the wider

---

the links between urban constitutionalism and the world of feudalism: see C. Petit-Dutaillis, *Les Communes Françaises* (Paris, 1947) pp. 107 ff.; and C. Joset, *Les Villes au pays de Luxembourg* (Brussels-Louvain, 1940). In the field of social history we find a parallel discussion on the rise of the patriciate; see the controversy between Lestocquoy and Espinas in *Annales* I (1946) in France, and the works of F. von Klocke in Germany, especially *Patriziat und Stadtadel im alten Soest* (1927).

[49] For the use of forced migration see G. Rhode's contribution in the *Festgabe H. Aubin* (1951). According to him the ranking of the *mestnichestvo* did not spring from a regional order of estates but was based on strict genealogical criteria. It can be seen as an attempt to secure a certain privilege for the old families in the face of the unspecified and opportunist aspects of the service duties demanded by the government. The introduction of the *chin* in the later seventeenth century prepares the way for the complete bureaucratization of the nobility under Peter the Great.

[50] O. Brunner, 'Europäisches Bauerntum', *Geseschichte in Wissenschaft und Unterricht* II (1951); W. Conze, *Agrarverfassung und Bevölkerung in Litauen und Weissrussland*, I: *Die Hufenverfassung im ehemaligen Grossfürstentum Litauen* (1940).

European corporate and regional orders could not have evolved.

So much is clear, that well into the nineteenth century the Russian peasant differed fundamentally from the European one. This was due, for one thing, to his primitive agricultural techniques, so much so that he still appeared to Schulze-Gaevernitz, towards the end of the century, as a nomad who had but recently settled.[51] Closely connected with this is also the fact that there was in Russia in these centuries a complete absence of fixed manorial regulations. Not until state legislation on agriculture began in the early nineteenth century was any attempt made to change this state of affairs. And the more closely knit the Russian village may have been as a working (and suffering) community, the more easily, in its totality as well as in its individual components, could it be transplanted and was in fact transplanted: in the first instance, during the era of serfdom, through the owner (aristocracy or state); later, after the reforms of Alexander II and during the time of industrialization, by decision of the Commune itself.

Another contributory reason why urban and civil life of the European type did not develop in Russia is the lack of stratification of the vast lands of Muscovy. The basic features of European feudalism were indeed lacking: there was nothing corresponding to the inextricably intermingled bonds of seignorial and corporative rights.[52] Only in the Russian border areas could, and did, municipalities develop which correspond to the autonomous character and the richly stratified structure of the European city; but there are no town guilds to be found in Russia; there was no urban structure to which they might have belonged. Where we find anything resembling the guild, it is a version of the collective working community of the village. Peter the Great made strenuous, but in the end unsuccessful, efforts to introduce municipal institutions on the European pattern, but

[51] G. von Schulze-Gävernitz, *Volkwirtschaftliche Studien aus Russland* (Leipzig, 1899) p. 416.

[52] N. P. Pavlov-Silvanskii, *Feodalism v drevnei Rossii* (St Petersburg, 1907), stressed the Russian parallels with European feudalism. The problem has been discussed, and a mainly negative conclusion reached, by G. Vernadsky, 'Feudalism in Russia', *Bulletin of the International Committee of Historical Sciences* x (1938). Soviet historical writing, especially the works of B. D. Grekov and the studies influenced by him, has —so far as I know—limited itself to examination of the economic dependence of the subject peasants: this has been traced back to the Kiev period and characterized, according to Marxist terminology, as feudalism; cf. also P. J. Lyashchenko, *History of the National Economy of Russia* (English transl. 1949).

how artificial were the groupings within the towns which he created for the purpose!

And finally one last point: if the Russian town, the Russian village, the Russian nobility had no constitution in the European sense; if we cannot speak of a Russian patriciate or of a Russian system of dignitaries and titles, nor indeed of the Russian Middle Ages, then this has something to do with the fact that the Eastern Church was otherworldly. From it there sprang no philosophers in a scholastic sense, and no lawyers. The Slavophils saw in Western rationalism, as it took shape in ecclesiastical constitutions, ecclesiastical law and theological analysis, the original sin of the West, the apostasy from true Christianity. In the Kiev period Russia showed the clearest parallels to European vassaldom and to European serfdom. After that, however, came the parting of the ways. What Marc Bloch calls the second age of European feudalism—the legal definitions of relationships, the clearly articulated system of gradation linked to regional separateness and a settled way of life—all this Russia never experienced. Nor is it an accident that the growth of universities and of a legal profession began only very late under the influence of Europe, in the course of the nineteenth century.

Is it necessary to emphasize here that scholars, lawyers and universities were an integral part of that European order of which I have tried to speak to you?

You will rightly regard my exposition of the nature of the European corporate system and European regionalism as sketchy; you will also ask if it is legitimate to depict such traits, with all their change and flux, as lasting, as constant. For after all, from the late Middle Ages onwards the forces of modern life which were to dominate the nineteenth and twentieth centuries were clearly and increasingly gaining ground. These new forces were the modern state and, closely bound up with it, modern national consciousness; mobile capital which, outside the guilds or from within them, was already tending strongly in the direction of economic freedom; and—influenced by such freedom but determined even more strongly by the intellectual movement away from the corporative—the modern, bourgeois if you like, individualistic spirit which in the end refused to recognize any social structure organized in terms of orders or estates.

Let me reply to such objections in a twofold way. First, with the possibly naïve comment that as we are usually so much concerned with the prehistory of our own times, might we not give some attention to the past for its own sake? Only when 'today' and 'the day before yesterday' are taken together can 'yesterday' be seen in the correct perspective. This is a somewhat frivolous conclusion, but one which nevertheless contains a grain of truth. But on a more serious plane it must be said that we surely tend to underestimate the effect and range of the old European forces persisting until the French Revolution.

It may be admitted that the symbolic bath which the Upper Austrian Estates in 1452 prepared for the young Duke Ladislas in order to wash away the evil effects of his Styrian education[53] has no parallel even in the 1750s. Men had also by then outgrown the picturesque formalist language of the Middle Ages. But in Basque Guipúzcoa at the end of the eighteenth century the governor appointed by Madrid was never allowed to reside more than one year in any one town, to guard against the hated central power becoming too firmly entrenched.[54] This may be a particularly remote region; but it is true, for example, of the whole of the Prussian monarchy that as late as the middle of the eighteenth century there was, according to the findings of Otto Hintze, no distinction made between border disputes between different Prussian regions on the one hand and those with other states of the Empire, or even with foreign powers: according to the old tradition anything outside a particular region was 'abroad'.[55] And when in France at the time of Jacobin rule, lists were drawn up to establish who were foreigners, *étrangers*, in an attempt to combat the danger of foreign agitators, these included in many *départements* the names of all those not born in the province.

Thus under the cover of centralization and national consciousness the old attachment to the region still persisted. Who can adequately judge how strongly this contributed to the popular uprisings against the Napoleonic régime, say in Spain or in the Tyrol? Similarly, up to the collapse of the corporative order of society the influence of orders and estates on the individual remained strong.

[53] A. Hoffmann, 'Die oberösterreichischen Landstände und Landtage im alter Zeit', *Verfassung und Verwaltung des Landes Oberösterreich* (1937) p. 30.

[54] G. Desdevises du Dézert, 'La société espagnole au 18e siècle', 2nd edn., *Revue Hispanique* XIV (1925) 245.

[55] *Acta Borussica* VI, i, 81.

One could envisage an analysis of the early eighteenth century which tried to assess how limited the unifying force of the absolutist state still was in many respects:[56] how, for instance, in the legal system of many states the differing degrees of competence of individual courts were preserved in accordance with the different social orders; how strong also in the legal mind was the opposition to the standardization of the law; how in the Prussian administration, not yet separated from the law, the authority of the lord of the manor became restricted only with the growth of the military jurisdiction over conscripts; how for long in Austria the raising of recruits was still the business of the estates; how firmly everywhere in the machinery of the state the assessing and levying of direct taxes on the lowest level lay in the hands of local groups;[57] how necessary it is in the assessment of mercantilism to distinguish between objective and achievement—just as in the earlier centuries of our modern era as a whole the economic policy of the state had often aimed at a balance between the interests of the separate estates, rather than at a new economic dynamism which could transform the whole area.[58]

Would not France furnish a good example of how frequently historians have succumbed, in their interpretation of domestic history, to the temptation to lay too much stress upon a conscious development towards

[56] This attitude is strongly marked in Penfield Roberts, *The Quest for Security* (New York-London 1947), the volume in the series ed. by W. Langer 'The Rise of Modern Europe' dealing with the first part of the eighteenth century.

[57] This, including the many types of joint liability which persisted into the eighteenth century, cannot, in my opinion, be explained only by the continuing weakness of the state apparatus, as Strayer does for the Middle Ages in J. R. Strayer and C. H. Taylor, *Studies in Early French Taxation* (Cambridge, Mass., 1939) 21 f. To me they are signs of the continuing importance of the intermediate powers and of the corporative consciousness. Cf. J. Villain, 'Du caractère collectif de la taille royale', *Revue Historique de droit français* (1947), and the same author's 'L'abolition de la solidité', *ibid.*, 1950.

[58] The role of mercantilism as a unifying force has been strongly emphasized by E. Heckscher, *Mercantilism* (London, 1935). But E. Coornaert has shown in exemplary fashion in his study of Antwerp, how the traditional forces still managed to keep a decisive measure of influence even at the focal point of capitalist economic life in the early modern period: 'La genèse du système capitaliste: grand capitalisme et economie traditionelle à Anvers au 16e siècle', *Annales d'histoire économique et sociale* VIII (1936); and in his 'L'État et les villes à la fin du moyen âge. La politique d'Anvers', *Revue Historique*, CCVII (1952).

the modern era? From the wars of religion through the Fronde and the Regency down to the opposition of the *parlements* during the late *ancien régime*, they find a clear line of resistance to centralization and absolute power, resistance which proved partially successful.

Should these last remarks strike you as just a little dogmatic, perhaps I may refer you to a, if you like, naïve, but nevertheless characteristic and symbolic contemporary eighteenth-century reaction to the impact of the 'modern world'. In a travel diary of 1785,[59] Ludwig Meyer von Knonau, a native of Zurich, remarks: 'When we set foot on Austrian territory near Hornussen, beyond the Bözberg, we noticed with a kind of shudder the numbering of the houses; this seemed to us symbolic of the hand of the ruler stretching out inexorably over the property of the private citizen.' This numbering system, introduced as part of Joseph II's measures for military conscription,[60] seems quite natural to us today. Engraved as these numbers are on neat little plates, which often give also the name of the street, they even strike American visitors to Austria as a pleasant and gracious remnant of bygone days—as so many other remnants of that none too effectual era of Josephinism.

The rulers have since disappeared. The pressures of the modern state, tending strongly towards totalitarianism, remain constant, as do those of our no less exacting modern society tending strongly towards conformity. In view of this, it may at any rate be permissible to emphasize the fact that regional consciousness and corporate organization were constituent elements of the old Europe—not, indeed, in order forcibly to resuscitate or artificially preserve them, but in order not to lose sight of the extent to

[59] R. Feller, 'Von der alten Eidgenossenschaft', *Schweizerische Akademiereden*, ed. F. Strich (1945) p. 458.

[60] See the quotation from Luschin von Ebengreuth in F. Popelka, *Geschichte der Stadt Graz* I (Graz, 1928) 504; for house numbering in France at this time, see A. Babeau, *La ville sous l'ancien régime*, 2nd edn., II, (Paris, 1884) 122 f. Similarly, Camille Julian in his *Histoire de Bordeaux* (Bordeaux, 1895) p. 551, has drawn attention to the fact that it is only in the eighteenth century that the old custom of locally given street names for functional purposes, permitting change when necessary, gave way to the new custom of naming streets after persons, and above all, after patrons. This is another sign that the process of social continuity which we have traced in this paper, lasted from the Middle Ages right down to the revolutionary emergence of modern times in the eighteenth century. From the new custom it is only a step to those frequent changes of names motivated by changing political circumstances which in some places impose a great deal of work on the researcher interested in topography.

which diversity and permanence, in whatever manifestations, constitute the foundations of all civilization.

Editorial Note. The text of this lecture, entitled *Regionalismus und Ständisches Wesen als ein Grundthema Europäischer Geschichte*, given before the Historical and Antiquarian Society at Basel on 14 January 1952, was printed in *Historische Zeitschrift* CLXXIV (1952) 307–37. A few footnotes (nos. 20, 23, 28 and 30) have been abbreviated for reasons of space. 'Ständisches Wesen' is notoriously difficult to translate: the editors have in agreement with the author rendered it as 'corporate order', reserving 'estates' to the political assemblies of estates. The editors regret that it has not been possible to add references to books and articles on the subject published later than 1952.

10

M. S. ANDERSON

Eighteenth-Century Theories of the Balance of Power

'There is not, I believe, any doctrine in the law of nations, of more certain truth, of greater and more general importance to the prosperity of civil society, or that mankind has learnt at a dearer rate, than this of the balance of power', wrote an English pamphleteer in 1720.[1] Many of his contemporaries would have agreed with him. By the time these words were written the concept of international stability achieved through the workings of a system of conflicting or potentially conflicting forces had become securely established in the political thinking of Europe, and perhaps most of all of Great Britain. Its triumph can be seen as typical of an age in which religious rivalries had largely lost the power to influence the policies of governments and in which nationalism, over much of the continent, was still a negligible force, an age one of whose leading statesmen, Prince Kaunitz, could boast of his 'arithmetical methods' in diplomacy.[2]

Nevertheless the balance of power was still, as it was always to remain, a cloudy and indefinite concept. In England the pamphlet controversies stimulated at the beginning of the century by Louis XIV's acceptance of the will of Charles II of Spain, and still more by the bitter debates of 1710–13 about the peace terms to be imposed on France, had finally established the idea of such a balance. But its scope was not yet confined to international affairs. The phrase 'balance of power' was still frequently applied, at least in England, to the internal politics of states as well as to international relations; to many writers in the early eighteenth century it still suggested theories of a 'mixed constitution' and of the equilibrium of

[1] *Two Essays on the Balance of Europe* (London, 1720), in *A Collection of Scarce and Valuable Tracts* (London, 1809–15) XIII, 770.

[2] P. R. Rohden, *Die klassische Diplomatie von Kaunitz bis Metternich* (Leipzig, 1939) p. 4.

political forces which was alleged to make such a constitution viable.[3] In the states of continental Europe, however, most of which had a very different political structure, the phrase was seldom if at all used in this sense; and even in England it is rare after the 1720s to find it except in a foreign policy context. By the middle of the century it was widely agreed by pamphleteers and historians everywhere that a balance of power between the states of Europe had existed for several generations, perhaps (this was the most widely held view) since the French invasions of Italy at the end of the fifteenth century, perhaps from some later date. It had also become part of the conventional wisdom that this balance, once properly established, safeguarded the peace of Europe and the freedom and even the existence of its smaller states. Its maintenance should therefore be the aim of all wise and constructive statesmanship. It is well known that the Anglo-Spanish treaty signed at Utrecht in July 1713 explicitly declared as one of its major objectives the securing of peace in Europe through the balance of power, the first occasion on which any international agreement had done so;[4] and similar avowals can be found in several treaties of the eighteenth and early nineteenth centuries.[5] By the 1740s in England the idea of the international balance was familiar and everyday enough to be used as a vehicle for political satire.[6]

Yet it still remained a vague and imprecise one. Very often it was no more than a phrase used to inhibit thought. Frequently appealed to, it was

[3] See for example *A Discourse of the Contests and Dissensions between the Nobles and the Commons in Athens and Rome* (London, 1701), reprinted in *A Collection of State Tracts* (London, 1705–06) III, 210–29. *Two Essays on the Balance of Europe, loc. cit.* p. 774, speaks of 'a balance of power between prince and people', and Swift frequently uses the phrase without any reference to international affairs.

[4] Article II of the treaty gave its purpose as 'ad firmandam stabilendamque pacem ac tranquillitatem christiani orbis, justo potentiae equilibrio': J. Dumont, *Corps universel diplomatique du droit des gens* (The Hague, 1726-31) VIII, pt. 1, 393.

[5] The French guarantee of the Pragmatic Sanction in 1735 by the treaty of Vienna claimed to have as its object the preservation of the European balance: G. von Koch and F. Schoell, *Histoire abrégé des traités de paix* (Brussels, 1837–38) II, 258. The different treaties of alliance signed at Töplitz in September-October 1813 by Austria, Prussia, Russia and Britain gave as one of their explicit aims the restoration of the balance of power in Europe, as did the Austro-Neapolitan one of 11 January 1814: G. F. de Martens, *Nouveau Receuil de Traités* I (Göttingen, 1817) 596, 600, 607, 660.

[6] *Europe's Catechism* (London, 1741) is a parody of the Anglican catechism in which Europe is told by the catechist to 'walk in the Commandments of the Ballance of Power' and in which the ten 'Maxims of the Ballance of Power', an obvious parody of the Ten Commandments, are quoted (pp. 5–8).

seldom analysed in real depth or formulated with genuine rigour. Writers tended to shy away from the questions it raised and the difficulties it involved. It was widely agreed, for example, that there were certain areas of Europe within each of which a localized balance of power operated, and that these regional balances were essential elements of the European one. A pamphleteer in 1743 spoke of 'all the several Ballances, by which the Tranquillity of the Powers of Europe is maintain'd in its several Quarters'; and another a few years earlier had proclaimed that 'To fix the Balance of Power in Europe, attention must be paid to the inferior Balances elsewhere'.[7] One of these regional balances in particular—that in the Baltic—received throughout the century much anxious attention from British commentators, largely for commercial reasons. To it there had been added, by the middle decades of the century, two others—that in Germany, which now depended on an equilibrium between the power of the Habsburgs and that of the new state of Brandenburg-Prussia; and that in Italy, where it was argued that a Habsburg-Bourbon balance must be maintained and sometimes urged that the kingdom of Sardinia should be strengthened as its main safeguard.[8] Yet there was little attempt to show with any exactitude what rôle these 'particular' or 'inferior' balances played within the European one. A connection between the two was, rightly, assumed; but hardly any effort was made to analyse or even to illustrate it.

Moreover no agreed solution was found to the most difficult problem inherent in all balance of power theories: that of estimating with any accuracy the relative strength of different states at a given moment. Theories of this kind by their nature tended to be quantitative, or at least to contain a very large element of quantitative thinking. They envisaged power as something which could be not merely recognized but also measured with some precision. In principle it was therefore possible at any point in time to know whether one state or group of states was stronger or weaker than its rivals. Yet what should be the measure of the power of a

[7] *Observations on the Conduct of Great Britain in respect to Foreign Affairs* (London, 1743) p. 14; J. Campbell [?], *Memoirs of the Duke de Ripperda* (London, 1740) Appendix p. 357.

[8] For a brief but typical statement of these ideas in a successful reference book of the period see J. Campbell, *The Present State of Europe* (6th edn., London, 1761) pp. 26–7: the first edition was published in 1750.

state? In the first year of the century Charles Davenant pointed out the obvious truth that all calculations of this kind contained a large subjective element. 'Opinion is the principal Support of Power', he wrote, 'and States are seldom any longer Strong or Wise, than while they are thought so by their Neighbours; for all great Things subsist more by Fame, than any real Strength.'[9] Ministers in France, against which balance of power arguments had so often been used as a weapon, also tended on occasion to dismiss calculations of this kind as 'une chose de pure opinion'.[10] In the same vein a French writer argued that the balance was 'fort estimatif', that it 'reside beaucoup dans l'opinion des hommes', and that it was 'une matière où tout, pour ainsi dire, est opinion sujette par elle-même à variation'.[11] But this line of thought, however justified, was not one which appealed to most pamphleteers or politicians. Inevitably the simple and visible criteria of territory and population tended to dominate discussions of this question. There was indeed a tendency during the second half of the century to give increasing weight to the wealth of a state, to the quality of its government,[12] and to some extent also to its strategic position. A state could be more effectively controlled by its ruler, it was sometimes argued, and its resources more effectively mobilized and concentrated, if its territories were not extremely large.[13] Baron von Bielfeld, in one of the most systematic of eighteenth-century treatments of the problem of power-measurement, divided the states of Europe into four classes in terms of their ability to wage war: firstly Britain and France, which could make war by themselves, without the help of allies; secondly Austria, Russia, Prussia and Spain, which though formidable needed allies and outside financial support, especially in case of a long war; thirdly states such as Portugal, Sweden, and the Dutch Republic, which could

[9] 'An essay upon the balance of power', in *Essays* (London, 1701) p. 31.

[10] *Receuil, Autriche* (Paris, 1884) p. 310. (Instructions to the Marquis d'Hautefort, 1750).

[11] A. Pecquet, *L'Esprit des maximes politiques* (Paris, 1757) pp. 107–8, 112.

[12] The most forcible statement of this point of view is perhaps J. H. G. von Justi, *Die Chimäre des Gleichgewichts von Europa* (Altona, 1758) pp. 39, 56–8.

[13] A good example of this, from the pen of one of the major statesmen of the later eighteenth century, is Ewald Friedrich, Count von Hertzberg, 'Reflexions sur la force des états et sur leur puissance relative et proportionelle,' in *Huit dissertations* (Berlin, 1787–91) pp. 87–104. It should however be remembered that in it Hertzberg is thinking very much of Prussia and indulging in a good deal of conventional adulation of Frederick II.

act only as the auxiliaries of greater ones; and finally the negligible small states of Germany and Italy.[14] Most discussion of the problem of power-measurement was carried on, however, at a low level of analysis. Writers who attempted to treat it usually started from assumptions which favoured the case they were putting forward or the policy which their employers were advocating.

More fundamentally, the writers of the period failed to solve or even to face the problem of reconciling the concept of a balance, of something static or changing only slowly, with the incessant fluctuation and movement which made up the reality of international relations. It was quite possible to dismiss the balance of power out of hand as a phantom since, as Sorel put it a century later, 'Pour subsister, il implique l'immobilité, c'est-à-dire l'impossible'.[15] Some eighteenth-century writers on international affairs, though they were markedly in a minority, did in fact argue along these lines. The construction of a lasting balance of power, one contended,

> is like the Notion of Levelling among private Persons, it is first impossible to be done. And if it were done, if all the Riches of the World were equally Divided among all the Men in it, it would not Continue so until the Clock struck next, for some would be Stronger than others and Rob them, or Craftier and Cheat them. And there would be Confederacies of Thieves, Men void of Justice and Honour, who would combine to Oppress the Innocent, and make their Power the only Rule of Law and Equity. And thus it is among Nations, it is impossible to bring them to an equal Ballance of Power or Riches. And if it were done, if all the Nations of the Earth were reduced to an equal Ballance even of a Grain Weight, then a Grain on any Side would cast the Ballance. And this Ten Thousand Accidents every Day would produce, a prosperous Voyage on one Side, and Unfortunate on another; a Wiser or a Weaker Administration in one Government than another, would turn the Ballance vastly, So that We must Ballance the Wisdom, the Industry, and the Courage of Men, as well as their Honesty and Conscience; and likewise secure Providence not to favour one more

[14] Baron J. F. von Bielfeld, *Institutions politiques* (The Hague, 1760) II, 84–5.
[15] *L'Europe et la Révolution française*, 3rd edn (Paris, 1912) I, 34.

than another, if we would fix the Peace of the World upon this Project of Ballancing.[16]

The argument that the unpredictability of human affairs made a stable balance of power a futile dream was one to which the eighteenth century found no convincing answer. The writers of the period met the awkward problems which it raised by for the most part ignoring their existence. Friedrich von Gentz, one of the subtlest of writers on the subject, saw the difficulty and to some extent got round it by abandoning the traditional idea of a more or less rigid and stable balance.

> It perhaps [he wrote] would have been with more propriety called a system of *counterpoise*. For perhaps the highest of its results is not so much a perfect *equipoise* as a constant alternate vacillation in the scales of the balance, which, from the application of *counter-weights*, is prevented from ever passing certain limits.[17]

But this was too summary a dismissal of an important difficulty.

Even if the argument that a lasting equilibrium of power was impossible were overcome or wished out of existence there were still difficult problems facing any effort to probe the nature of the balance. Above all a writer on the subject, if his effort at analysis were genuine, had to find an answer to a question which was fundamentally important and yet seldom clearly formulated. It was generally agreed that the balance of power arose from the inherent aggressiveness of states and their rulers, from the fact that, as Frederick II put it, 'Le principe permanent des princes est de s'aggrandir autant que leur pouvoir le leur permet.'[18] The existence of a 'universal sense of this ambitious depravity in man, and of the value of whatever conduces to preserve a balance'[19] was common ground to most commentators. But just how did a state of balance, protecting the weak, arise from this morass of 'ambitious depravity'? Was the balance of power something which emerged naturally and inevitably within a system

[16] *Natural Reflections upon the Present Debates about Peace and War* (London, 1712) pp. 61–2; a similar argument, equally forcibly expressed, can be found in *A Project for Establishing the General Peace of Europe, by a more Equal Partition than has hitherto been proposed* (London, 1712) p. 5; and in Justi, pp. 67–70.

[17] *Fragments upon the Balance of Power in Europe* (London, 1806) p. 63 n.

[18] 'Considérations sur l'état présent du corps politique de l'Europe', (1738), in *Oeuvres de Frédéric le Grand* (Berlin, 1846–56) VIII, 15.

[19] *Two Essays on the Balance of Europe*, *loc. cit.*, 771.

of competing states once that system had reached a certain level of maturity? Was it therefore more or less independent of human foresight and volition, in some sense a natural phenomenon? Did the compulsions of the struggle for power affect states rather in the way that gravitation was now known to affect bodies in the physical world? Or was the balance rather something which *ought* to exist, something to be striven for by man and not achieved without his striving, therefore an aspiration and an ideal? Was the term 'balance of power' purely descriptive and morally neutral, or was it normative?

One current of thought regarded the balance as merely an observed fact of political life. It therefore tended, at least by implication, to play down or reject outright the belief that it expressed a moral ideal. Perhaps the most striking example of this view of the balance as a self-regulating and self-perpetuating mechanism was that given by Rousseau in his adaptation of the peace project published almost half a century earlier by the Abbé de Saint-Pierre.

> But whether we pay attention thereto or not [he wrote], this equipoise subsists without the interposition of a second person, and wants no foreign effort for its preservation; and when an alteration is made on one side, it immediately re-establishes itself on the other: so that if those princes, who are accused of aspiring to universal monarchy, have really aspired thereto, they have manifested more ambition than genius, for in what manner can they have imagined to themselves that project, without perceiving the ridicule thereof in the first moment? . . . In fine, not one amongst them being able to possess resources which the others cannot acquire, resistance at length becomes equal to the effort, and time soon re-establishes the rapid accidents of fortune, if not for each particular prince, at least for the general system.[20]

Almost simultaneously a British pamphleteer asserted that

> What gravity or attraction, we are told, is to the system of the universe, that the ballance of power is to Europe: a thing we cannot just point out to ocular inspection, and see or handle; but which is as real in its existence, and as sensible in its effects, as the weight is in scales.[21]

[20] J.-J. Rousseau, *A Project for Perpetual Peace* (London, 1761) pp. 12–13.

[21] *Occasional Reflections on the Importance of the War in America, and the Reasonableness of supporting the King of Prussia* (London, 1758) p. 58.

A few years earlier Frederick II had compared international relations to the workings of a watch,[22] while Kaunitz, his greatest rival, also thought of the balance of power as functioning to some extent automatically.[23] Four decades later Henry Brougham developed a more explicit comparison between the theory of the balance and that of gravitation. He went on logically to argue that international relations could be reduced to a science based on general principles, since they were little affected by personal and fortuitous factors.[24]

These, however, were minority views. Most writers thought of the balance in terms of something which *ought* to exist, something deliberately constructed by man and to be consciously fostered and safeguarded by him. So great and orthodox a moralist as Fénelon argued, in a memorandum drawn up in the early years of the century for the education of the Duc de Bourgogne, that rulers had not merely a right but a duty to resist the excessive growth of the power of any one of them.[25] A generation later the most famous international lawyer of the age, himself a practising diplomat, Éméric de Vattel, based the concept of a balance of power on the absolute right of the smaller states to safeguard their independence against the threats posed by their greater neighbours, and to combine for this purpose. In this he merely followed a current of ideas already well established; and his view was later echoed by another great lawyer, Martens.[26] In this way the balance became an aspect of the varied current of thought and feeling which centred on the idea of natural rights: one result may have been an increasing tendency to regard as morally justified any war which, whatever its immediate origins, could be presented as one in defence of the balance of power.[27] If the balance were a natural and overriding good, it followed that lesser goods, however desirable in

[22] *Oeuvres* VII, 3; Political Testament of 1752 in G. B. Volz ed., *Politische Correspondenz Friedrichs des Grossen: Ergänzungsband* (Berlin, 1920) p. 48.

[23] Rohden, p. 5.

[24] 'The Balance of Power', in *Works* (London-Glasgow, 1855–61) VIII, 11–12, 18–28. This essay, first published in the *Edinburgh Review*, was written in January 1803.

[25] 'Supplement à l'Examen de Conscience', in *Oeuvres de Fénelon* (Paris, 1820–30) XXII, 307–8.

[26] E. de Vattel, *Le Droit des gens, ou principes de la loi naturelle* (Leyden, 1758) II, 296–7; G. F. de Martens, *Précis du droit des gens moderne de l'Europe*, 2nd edn. (Göttingen, 1801) p. 190. (The first edition is of 1788.)

[27] E. Kaeber, *Die Idee des europäischen Gleichgewichts in der publizistischen Literatur von 16 bis zur Mitte des 18 Jahrhunderts* (Berlin, 1907) pp. 144–6.

themselves, must be sacrificed if necessary for its preservation. A ruler might well, for example, be justified in breaking his word if this were necessary to maintain it.[28] Just as the individual could be forced to sacrifice some of his personal wealth for the good of the community of which he was a member, so a ruler might justifiably be asked to give up territory, even territory to which he had every legal right, for the good of the European state system as a whole. One influential writer argued that 'les Maîtres les plus légitimes doivent quelquefois renoncer à leurs droits, pour procurer le maintien de l'équilibre'.[29] Another, in 1743, argued more specifically that the Habsburg lands must remain undivided in order to preserve the European balance, and that 'il s'agit ici de L'INTÉRÊT PUBLIC de toute l'Europe auquel, suivant toutes les Lois de la Nature et des gens, doit être sacrifié L'INTÉRÊT PARTICULIER de quelque État ou Potentat que ce soit'. Therefore even if the rulers of France, Spain or Bavaria had valid rights to parts of these lands, these must be disregarded in the interest of the general welfare of Europe.[30]

However, before the age of the French Revolution no writer of significance was willing to advocate interference in the internal affairs of a state merely in order to prevent its becoming stronger through better administration or a more sophisticated economic life. Such developments could obviously make it as great a threat to the balance and to the security of its neighbours as any territorial gain; but the eighteenth century shrank from drawing the logical conclusion from this fact. Only Justi, in the most penetrating attack ever made on the balance of power idea, pointed out that its strict application would place the states of Europe in a kind of 'reciproque Sklaverei', since each would be subject to interference from others who feared that internal change and development would strengthen it and therefore make it more of a threat to them.[31] Less logical writers were forced to take refuge in the argument that the strengthening of a state by natural internal growth threatened the balance of power less than

[28] *Nouveaux intérêts des princes de l'Europe* (Cologne, 1685) pp. 2–3, provides an early statement of this point of view.

[29] L. M. Kahle, *La Balance de l'Europe considerée comme la règle de la paix et de la guerre* (Berlin-Göttingen, 1744) p. 147.

[30] *Histoire de la grande crise de l'Europe* (London, 1743) pp. 1–3. For similar arguments see e.g. Fénelon, *Oeuvres* XXII, 309; and *Two Essays on the Balance of Europe, loc. cit.*, 773.

[31] *Op. cit.*, p. 60.

its growth by territorial gains; or at least in protestations that only very sudden and violent internal development of a state could legitimately provoke interference by its neighbours.[32]

Eighteenth-century ideas of the balance of power inevitably altered in response to changes in the political, economic and intellectual life of Europe. The period saw a striking increase of international trade, and in particular of Europe's trade with the rest of the world. Not only the older colonial powers—Spain, Portugal and the Dutch—but also France and above all Britain now based their economic strength and European position to varying extents on their possession of colonial empires and oceanic trade. This meant that commerce, colonies and maritime strength bulked larger than in the past in discussions of the nature of the European balance. English pamphleteers were already very conscious by the end of the seventeenth century of the degree to which the influence of their country in Europe depended on her trade, and therefore of the ease with which it could be shaken or destroyed by a successful attack on that trade. 'Can a nation be Safe without Strength?', Davenant asked in 1696. 'And is Power to be compass'd and Secur'd but by Riches? And can a country become Rich any way, but by the Help of a well Managed and Extended Traffick?'[33] Almost simultaneously Marshal Vauban, in two remarkable memoranda of 1699 and 1700, urged that France should not seek further expansion in Europe, which would now mean transcending her natural territorial limits. She should concentrate rather on obtaining a good understanding with her immediate neighbours to free her hands for a maritime war with her real enemies, the English and the Dutch, and for the creation of large colonies of settlement in Canada and the Mississippi basin. Only by colonial expansion, he asserted, could France become a real world power.[34] Though his discussion was not couched in terms of the balance it was perhaps the most explicit admission hitherto by any European statesman of the extent to which the power of the Atlantic states now

[32] Kahle, 106–7; Campbell, [?], *Memoirs of the Duke de Ripperda*, Appendix, p. 358; Brougham, *loc. cit.*, pp. 36–7; Gentz, p. 112.

[33] *An Essay on the East-India Trade* (London, 1696) pp. 7, 61.

[34] The memoranda are printed in E. E. A. de Rochas d'Aiglun, ed., *Vauban, sa famille et ses écrits. ses oisivetés et sa correspondance* (Paris, 1910) 1, 413ff. They are discussed in W. Gembruch, 'Zwei Denkschriften Vaubans zur Kolonial-und Aussenpolitik Frankreichs aus den Jahren 1699 und 1700', *Historische Zeitschrift* CXCV (1962) 297–330.

rested on colonial and maritime foundations. As he wrote, English resistance to possible domination of Spain and her empire by France was being inspired mainly by the economic strengthening of France and weakening of England which it was alleged would inevitably result, and by the repercussions which this might have on the relative standing of the two states in Europe. Even in Germany, which had little oceanic trade of its own, an interesting pamphlet of 1701 accused Louis XIV of aiming at world domination not merely through political power but also through 'Alleinkauf oder Monopolio', since he wished to control all the best harbours of the world and to monopolize trade in the Baltic and North Sea as well as the Spanish, Levant and colonial trades.[35]

By the middle decades of the century the idea that power was indissolubly linked with large-scale trade and with strength at sea was very widely accepted in western Europe. Even in backward Spain publicists and ministers were eager to stress the connection,[36] of which Britain seemed the outstanding example. 'Après tout', wrote a Dutch pamphleteer in 1743,

> il est si visible que les trois avantages, l'un d'être Puissance Maritime, l'autre d'avoir un Commerce fleurissant, et le dernier de tenir l'Équilibre du Pouvoir, sont tellement liés entre eux, par rapport à la Grande Bretagne, que ce seroit perdre son tems que de s'amuser à le démontrer.[37]

A British writer even argued that 'we may safely say, that the Ballance of Power . . . was created by Trade, and must continue to be the Object more especially of Trading Countries, as long as they preserve their Commerce and their Freedom'. This was because states combined against a dangerously strong neighbour largely 'from the just Apprehensions that this may, and indeed must, prove extremely prejudicial to Commerce in general, and to that of several Nations in particular who, to prevent this, will not scruple to take up arms'.[38]

From these very high estimates of the importance of trade and seapower emerged naturally, above all in France, the idea that a territorial and military

[35] *Die an der Licht gebrachte Wahrheit des österreichischen Rechts und frantzösischen Unrechts zur spanischen Succession* (Cologne, 1701) summarized in Kaeber, p. 74.

[36] e.g. B. de Ulloa, *Restablecimiento de las fabricas y comercio espanol* (Madrid, 1740) I, 2 ff.; G. de Uztariz, *Theoria y practica del comercio* (Madrid, 1742) pp. 2, 17–18, 324.

[37] *Le Système politique de la Grande-Bretagne dans la conjoncture présente* (The Hague, 1743) pp. 123–4.

[38] J. Campbell, *The Present State of Europe*, pp. 24–5.

balance in Europe was worth little unless it could be backed by a colonial and maritime one overseas, above all in America. 'Le balance du commerce des Nations en Amérique', wrote J. N. Moreau during the Seven Years War, 'est comme la balance du pouvoir en Europe! On pourroit même ajouter que ces deux balances n'en font qu'une.'[39] The Duc de Choiseul, the outstanding French statesman of the mid-century, was deeply impressed by the need, in the interest of the balance of power, to check the colonial and commercial growth of Britain and to foster that of France. In 1759 he wrote despondently that 'Le véritable équilibre consiste actuellement dans la commerce et en Amerique. La guerre d'Allemagne, même mieux faite qu'elle ne l'est, ne préviendra pas les maux qui sont à craindre par la grande superiorité des Anglais sur mer.' A year later, depressed by news of the fall of Quebec, he believed that since France had for the time being ceased to be a commercial power she had also ceased to be a firstclass power in any sense.[40] This idea was echoed by the most influential English pamphlet of the period, which argued that if Britain could dominate the Caribbean, the French, 'the great source of their wealth being cut off with their islands', would be unable to act effectively in Germany.[41]

This growing emphasis on the importance of colonies and intercontinental trade as elements in the European balance was in some ways perceptive. It showed a growing consciousness of the fact that the position in Europe would, in the long run, become merely an element in a world balance of power. Yet it was clearly pushed much too far. It was absurd for Choiseul to pretend in 1760 that France had ceased to be a first-class power; by doing so he ludicrously undervalued the importance of her economic and military strength in Europe.[42] The fact that the traditional

[39] *Mémoires pour servir à l'histoire de notre tems* (Frankfurt-Leipzig, 1757–60) I, 56, 58; quoted in A. Rein, 'Über die Bedeutung der überseeischen Ausdehnung für das europäische Staatensystem', *Historische Zeitschrift* CXXXVI (1927) 64.

[40] G. de R. de Flassan, *Histoire générale et raisonnée de la diplomatie française* (Paris, 1811) VI, 160, 279. In July 1760 Choiseul was in hopes that her alliance with Prussia might draw Britain into large-scale military operations on the continent. This would prevent her becoming commercially dominant, and then 'l'Europe sera heureuse, car le commerce sera partagé': To Voltaire, 13 July 1760, in T. Besterman, ed., *Voltaire's Correspondence* XLII (Geneva, 1959) no. 8310.

[41] I. Mauduit, *Considerations on the Present German War* (London, 1760) pp. 64, 137.

[42] A fact which was seen by at least some observers. One English pamphleteer pointed out that all her colonies combined were worth hardly half as much to France as dominance of the Austrian Netherlands would be: J. Perceval, *Things as They Are. Part the Second* (London, 1761) p. 45.

criteria of power—territory, population and armies—had not been invalidated by the new emphasis on colonies and colonial trade was shown most clearly by the emergence of another new element in the eighteenth-century balance. This was the rise of Russia as a great power.

No writer in the first years of the century envisaged Russia as having a rôle of much significance in Europe. Few indeed thought of her as a part of Europe at all in any fundamental sense. In 1711, for example, Defoe spoke of 'Sweden or Muscovy, Hungary or the Turks, which tho' it is True they are in Europe, yet as this [i.e. the west] is the governing part of Europe, it has been a Word Legitimated to this Part by the Custom of the Times'.[43] The victories won against Charles XII of Sweden, and the great personal prestige which Peter I enjoyed by the end of his reign, made it easier to think of Russia as a European power.[44] Yet for long writers, especially in France, were reluctant to recognize her as one in the fullest sense.[45] Nevertheless a long series of successes—her share in the destruction of the Swedish empire and the partition of Poland; her victories against Frederick II in the Seven Years War; her triumphs against the Turks in 1768–74—made it increasingly impossible to ignore the fact that a great new power had arisen in Europe. By the last years of Catherine II Russia's great-power status was beyond all reasonable doubt. Indeed by then her victories had aroused serious and widespread fears of her eventual domination of Europe. In 1787 the economist and statistician Sir John Sinclair, who had just returned from a visit to Russia, urged that 'all Europe must unite to check the ambition of a sovereign who makes one conquest only a step to the acquisition of another',[46] while two years later a pamphlet probably written by Freiherr von Borcke, the Prussian minister in Stockholm, called on the states of Europe to unite to halt the dangerous growth of Russian power.[47] In the 'Ochakov Crisis' of March–April 1791 the argument that Russia now threatened the balance of power,

[43] *The Ballance of Europe* (London, 1711) pp. 25–6.

[44] M. S. Anderson, *Britain's Discovery of Russia, 1553–1815* (London, 1958) chap. 4 *passim*; H. Doerries, *Russlands Eindringen in Europa in der Epoche Peters des Grossen* (Berlin, 1939) chap. 5 *passim*.

[45] e.g. J. N. Moreau, *Manloveriana, pour servir de supplément à l'Europe ridicule* (N.P., 1762) pp. 22–4, which denied, as late as the 1760s, that she was an integral part of the European state system as, for example, Denmark was.

[46] *Observations regarding the Present State of the Russian Empire* (London, 1787) p. 17.

[47] *Du Péril de la balance politique: ou exposé des causes qui l'ont alterée dans le Nord, depuis l'avènement de Cathérine II au trône de Russie* (London, 1789).

and should not be further strengthened by being left in possession of this allegedly important Black Sea fortress, was one of the foundations of the case put forward by Pitt and his supporters.[48] It was also accepted by the most famous British diplomat of the period, the Earl of Malmesbury.[49]

The rise of Russia is the best illustration of the way in which the balance of power during the eighteenth century was becoming more complex than ever before, with the geographical extension of the European state system and the emergence of new political forces. Until the end of the seventeenth century it had still been envisaged as a simple equilibrium between the two great dynasties of Bourbon and Habsburg in which all the other states of Europe played secondary rôles. 'Ce qui a fait jusques ici la sûreté des Princes de l'Europe,' wrote a pamphleteer in 1685, 'a été l'Égalité qui a subsisté entre les Maisons de Bourbon et d'Autriche.'[50] Down to the War of the Austrian Succession this simplified picture could still find acceptance.[51] The events of the 1740s and 1750s, however, destroyed it almost completely. By the second half of the century the rise of Russia, of Britain, and to a lesser extent of Prussia to great-power status, the new importance of events in America and in eastern and south-eastern Europe, had made it far more sophisticated and complex. New rivalries, from 1689 that between Britain and France, half a century later that between Prussia and the Habsburgs, had emerged and acquired the force of tradition.[52] The simple Bourbon–Habsburg balance had been replaced by a multiple one involving half a dozen great or semi-great powers; and this more sophisticated political reality probably did a good deal to encourage the development of more sophisticated theories of the balance.

[48] Anderson, p. 169.

[49] *Diaries and Correspondence of James Harris, first Earl of Malmesbury* (London, 1844) II, 436–7, 441.

[50] *Nouveaux intérêts des princes de l'Europe*, p. 1. Similarly an English pamphleteer spoke of 'Spain, which one while hath divided with France Europe into two, with which all other Princes have taken part according as their Interests required': *The Spirit of France and the Politick Maxims of Louis XIV laid open to the World* (London, 1689) p. 30.

[51] e.g. *The Original Series of Wisdom and Policy* (London, 1739) p. 72.

[52] *Das entlarvte Frankreich, oder das entdeckte Projekt von der europäischen Universalmonarchie* (The Hague, 1745), appears to be the earliest pamphlet to recognize rivalry between Austria and Prussia as a basic factor in the politics of Germany and a very important one in those of Europe: Kaeber, p. 91.

The whole idea of a balance of power was often dismissed by disgruntled politicians, especially by British politicians in opposition, as unreal. It was easy to attack it as camouflage for the self-interest or party prejudice of those who affected belief in it.[53] It could sometimes be contended that its vagueness made it meaningless,[54] while a moralist could see in it, in spite of its alleged unreality, a fertile source of wars and international tensions.[55] Yet balance of power theories, whatever their defects, also reflected the most constructive aspect of the Enlightenment—its faith in science and in the ability of man ultimately to control his own environment and future. Professor Gollwitzer is quite justified in seeing some connection between the rise and fall of the balance of power idea and that of liberal and optimistic ideas generally in Europe.[56] Both by some of its critics and by many of its supporters the workings of the balance were seen as introducing greater certainty, and above all a manmade certainty, into international affairs. Reliance upon it, wrote a critic early in the century, 'is indeed no other than to take the Government of the World out of the hands of Providence, and Entrust it to our own Skill and Management. Instead of *Dieu et Mon Droit*, it is *Je Maintiendrai*.'[57] Three generations later Brougham, approaching it from a diametrically opposed point of view, defended the balance because 'by the modern system of foreign policy, the fate of nations has been rendered more certain; and the influence of chance, of the fortune of war, of the caprices of individuals upon the general affairs of men, has been exceedingly diminished'.[58] The traditionalist (at least in some sense) of 1712 had little in common with the radical of 1803. But both agreed that an international balance of power,

[53] Thus Lord Chesterfield while in opposition, to quote only one of very many examples, spoke of the balance idea as 'introduced among us by corrupt and designing ministers, to subject and fleece their deluded countrymen': *Natural Reflexions on the Present Conduct of His Prussian Majesty* (London, 1744) p. 33. Even the elder Pitt, when not in office, denied the reality of the balance of power in Europe: J. Almon, *Anecdotes of the Earl of Chatham* (London, 1793) I, 278–9.

[54] e.g. *A modest Enquiry into the Present State of Foreign Affairs* (London, 1745) p. 4; *The True and Real Interest of Great Britain Impartially considered with Regard to the Impending Rupture among the Northern Powers* (London, 1749) pp. 26, 30, 31.

[55] The best example of this is Justi, pp. 9 ff., 26.

[56] H. Gollwitzer, *Europabild und Europagedanke: Beiträge zur deutschen Geistesgeschichte des 18 und 19 Jahrhunderts*, 2nd edn (Munich, 1964) p. 75.

[57] *Natural Reflections upon the Present Debates about Peace and War* (London, 1712) pp. 62–4.

[58] 'The Balance of Power', *Works* VII, p. 49.

properly organized and effectively maintained, would give man greater control over his political fate. They agreed that it would tend to make human needs and desires the measure of political action and to protect man against the unpredictable, whether dignified as providence or dismissed as mere chance.

Much eighteenth-century theorizing about the balance of power was therefore typical of many other aspects of the thought and feeling of the period. This is true of its underlying optimism and belief in the ability of man to control his own fate, though equally true of its sometimes naïve materialism and frequent superficiality.

II

W. MEDIGER

Great Britain, Hanover and the Rise of Prussia

Frederick the Great explains in his memoirs, *Histoire de mon temps*, that at the beginning of his reign Prussia was 'a sort of hermaphrodite', being a kingdom in name and an electorate in fact; and that he deemed it his duty to decide her status, i.e. to raise her to the rank of a great power.[1] When he became king in 1740, Prussia, indeed, as regards her influence in European affairs, ranked with her neighbours Saxony and Hanover, both of which competed with her for leadership in North Germany. Saxony enjoyed the glamour of a royal court at Dresden and wasted her economic strength owing to her connection with Poland by personal union. And the elector of Brunswick-Luneburg—which was the official title of the Hanoverian state—was His Britannic Majesty, George II. The king in Prussia also derived his royalty from that part of his territories which lay outside the Empire, a German enclave in a Slav state. From the Memel his dominions stretched to the Rhine, scattered all over North Germany, exposed to attacks, to political and economic pressure from all sides, involving Prussia in all kinds of troubles that arose in the east or in the west of Europe.

The dangers resulting from this disadvantageous territorial structure stimulated an urge to expand and a dynamism which the more consolidated and less imperilled rivals of Prussia lacked. Whoever ruled this state strove of necessity to unite the fragments of which it was composed and to form them into a coherent body by means of new acquisitions. Frederick William I, anxious to raise the inherent strength of his country out of proportion to its scanty economic resources in order to maintain its political independence, strained every nerve to build up a numerous and

[1] Frédéric II, *Histoire de mon temps* (*Redaktion von 1746*) (Leipzig, 1879) IV, 213–14.

highly effective army. This became Prussia's trump card in the hand of his son and successor. Frederick II's genius and ambition met the needs of the state he governed. He resolutely seized the unique opportunity that offered at the death of the last male Habsburg ruler, the Emperor Charles VI, and claimed, overran, and finally by 1745 won Silesia. By gaining this rich province, Frederick materially increased Prussia's resources and improved her strategic situation. The decisive step was taken towards consolidating a great power between the Elbe and Vistula.

With Silesia an immense amount of real strength and prestige shifted from Austria to Prussia. This change in central Europe was due not only to Frederick's efforts, but also to the intervention of France. Cardinal Fleury, to whom she owed her diplomatic predominance in Europe at this time, had skilfully prepared for the decisive struggle with Great Britain, her rival all the world over. But his plans were thwarted by the emperor's death and Frederick's action. A younger generation of ambitious generals and politicians pushed the sagacious old statesman aside. Instead of concentrating her forces on the maritime and colonial war, planned by him, France sided with the pretenders to the Austrian succession and sent an army to Germany in order to destroy the Habsburg monarchy and thus establish her own domination over central Europe.[2] Since Frederick realized that he could not get Silesia by negotiation, but had to fight for it, he no longer hesitated to join hands with France. The two powers were united by common enmity. Their co-operation, for years to come one of the pivots of European international relations, was mainly directed against Austria, who suffered most by it. At the same time the Franco-Prussian alliance, concluded in June 1741, spelt distress for Hanover.

George II and Frederick William I, though cousins and brothers-in-law, had for long hated each other; and their enmity had embittered the relations between Hanover and Prussia. Nevertheless, the elector-king had looked forward to the reign of his nephew Frederick, relying on his gratitude, since he had lent considerable sums to the young prince and

[2] For French policy see: M. Sautai, *Les préliminaires de la guerre de la Succession d'Autriche* (Paris, 1907); P. Vaucher, *Robert Walpole et la politique de Fleury, 1731–42* (Paris, 1924); A. M. Wilson, *French Foreign Policy during the Administration of Cardinal Fleury, 1726–43* (Cambridge, Mass., 1936).

thus enabled him to pay his debts.[3] When Frederick at last came to the throne, Britain was in dire need of allies. She was waging an unsuccessful war with Spain, and she was alarmed at the prospect of war with France, since she had been manoeuvred by Fleury into almost complete isolation. Threatened by the imminent clash of arms in his capacity as king, George as elector took the initiative in trying to win over the young king of Prussia with his fine army and to prevent his entering the league Fleury was just then busy building up in central and eastern Europe. To accomplish this important task, George sent his ablest German minister to Berlin.[4]

Gerlach Adolph von Münchhausen is famous in Germany as the founder of the University of Göttingen; and his picture hangs in a conspicuous place in the university library. He was an excellent and careful administrator, whose activity has to this day left traces in Hanoverian public life, for instance the well-known stud-farm of Celle and the sluice at Hameln. Long before he was given the title, he was in reality prime minister, the head and moreover the soul of the regency which governed the electorate in the absence of the sovereign. Münchhausen himself attached most importance to the conduct of foreign affairs. His predilection for diplomacy was ridiculed in the remark of a contemporary: 'Il ne se mouche pas sans politique.'[5]

Yet Münchhausen was indeed a farseeing, though not always successful statesman of rare disinterestedness. Personally free from ambition and greed, he served the interests of the Hanoverian state; but at the same time he had always in mind that Hanover was but part of a greater unity, the Holy Roman Empire. Münchhausen's policy centred round the welfare of the Empire, which he placed above the particular interests of his state. For he and his colleagues were deeply convinced that the Empire was indispensable for preserving order and peace between its members and

[3] Niedersächsisches Staatsarchiv, Hannover (hereafter cited as H[anover] A[rchives]), Hannover 92 LVIII 5 a: 'Einen von S.K.M. dem Kronprinzen Friederich von Preussen gemachten Geldvorschuss betr. 1739 ff.' In 1739 Frederick received £10,000 from George. He repaid the sum in 1740. Cf. K. Grünhagen, *Geschichte des Ersten Schlesischen Krieges* (Gotha, 1881) I, 20.

[4] For Münchhausen's mission to Berlin see: H.A., Hannover 11 IV Berlin I, Bestallungen Nr. 7 a, 1–157 fol.; Nr. 7 b, 1–38 fol.; F. Frensdorff, 'G. A. v. Münchhausens Berichte über seine Mission nach Berlin im Juni 1740', *Göttinger Akademie-Abhandlungen, phil.-hist. Klasse, Neue Folge* VIII, Berlin, 1904; Grünhagen, I, 19–24.

[5] F. Frensdorff, 'G. A. von Münchhausen', *Allgemeine Deutsche Biographie* XXII (Leipzig, 1885) 733.

for protecting the minor German states from encroachments of their stronger neighbours. They thought, moreover, that the Empire, being the centre of Europe, was in spite of its intrinsic weakness still capable of maintaining the balance and tranquillity between the powers, as long as its members remained united.[6] For this reason the Hanoverian statesman cherished the idea of close co-operation with Britain. In his eyes the kingdom and the electorate were united not only by their common sovereign, but even more by common dangers. Britain's maritime commerce suffered from the ever growing competition of the French, and she now had to face war with France. Simultaneously the Empire was threatened by the tendency of France to expand eastwards and by her more and more successful endeavours to control German affairs.

Münchhausen, therefore, wished to bring about an alliance between Prussia and Hanover under the auspices of Britain in order to defend the integrity and independence of the Empire against France. For that purpose he advised George II to pay the price of an agreement with Frederick and to help him to secure the West German duchy of Berg, including the city of Düsseldorf, to which he asserted a dynastic claim. Münchhausen did not grudge an increase of power to Prussia, as he wanted her to become the bulwark of the Empire against France.[7]

But Frederick gave up his claim and ambitions in the west and placed Silesia instead of Berg, the Oder instead of the Rhine, in the centre of Prussian policy. The reaction of George II to the news of his nephew's attack on Silesia was an outburst of fury, hatred, and jealousy.[8] Yet before he made up his mind how to tackle the new situation, he consulted his German ministers. They were equally alarmed and disconcerted, being afraid that the Empire would disintegrate and fall a victim to France if Frederick had his will and succeeded in disrupting the Habsburg monarchy. They recommended, therefore, in striking accordance with Robert Walpole's view and intentions, building up a coalition under British

[6] The Hanoverian ministers to George II, 11 November 1740, H.A., Cal.11E I 430 g; 17 January 1741, H.A., Hannover 92 LXXI 17 b vol. 1; W. Mediger, *Moskaus Weg nach Europa. Der Aufstieg Russlands zum europäischen Machtstaat im Zeitalter Friedrichs des Grossen* (Braunschweig, 1952) pp. 363–73, cf. Frensdorff, 'G. A. von Münchhausen', p. 731.

[7] The Hanoverian ministers to George II, 22 August 1740, H.A., Hannover 92 LVIII 8.

[8] Grünhagen, I, 275–6.

leadership and bringing pressure to bear on Frederick to force him to give up Silesia and renounce his claim.[9]

George II eagerly adopted this suggestion and at once designed, instead of mere demonstrations, a real concentric attack on Prussia by the forces of Austria, Saxony and Hanover together with Danish and Hessian regiments in British pay, Dutch troops and a Russian army, hoping to obtain from the defeated enemy some spoils for his electorate.[10] This policy miscarried. When the danger of French interference in the struggle for the Austrian succession became apparent, the British prime minister and the regency in Hanover, independently of each other, changed their course. But neither British nor Hanoverian diplomacy succeeded in reconciling the two contending powers at the expense of Austria, since Maria Theresa steadfastly refused to sacrifice an inch of Silesia. Desperate efforts to win Frederick over and to prevent his joining France came to nothing.

The first victim of the Franco-Prussian alliance was Hanover. In the autumn of 1741 the electorate was threatened with a pincer attack. A Prussian army was being assembled on its eastern frontier, a French army crossing the Rhine and approaching the Weser. George II, then in Hanover, yielded to pressure, and saved his country from ruin by signing a convention with France by which his German dominions were neutralized. In return he gave his vote to the French candidate for the imperial throne, the elector of Bavaria.[11]

Thus Hanover had felt the grip of Franco-Prussian military cooperation. This grim experience made a deep and ineffaceable impression both at Hanover and in London. The defeat of Münchhausen's German policy, however, was soon repaired. When Frederick concluded a separate peace with Austria in 1742, France loosened her hold on the electorate and the Hanoverian government recovered freedom of action. Notwithstanding the obligations of the convention, Hanoverian troops in British pay fought shoulder to shoulder with British forces against the French at

[9] Marginal note of George II; George II to the Hanoverian ministers, 16/27 December 1740; the Hanoverian ministers to George II, 17 January 1741, H.A., Hannover 92 LXXI 17 b vol. I.

[10] George II to the Hanoverian ministers, 20/31 January 1741, rescript and P.S., H.A., Hannover 92 LXXI 17 b vol. I.

[11] M. Sautai, *Les débuts de la guerre de la Succession d'Autriche* (Paris, 1909) pp. 285–304; H.A., Hannover 92 LXXI 17 d vol. IV.

Dettingen and in the Low Countries. And after the Wittelsbach Emperor Charles VII, the puppet of France and Prussia, had died in 1745, Münchhausen enjoyed the greatest triumph of his diplomatic career in skilfully bringing about the election as emperor of Maria Theresa's husband Francis. At the same time he as well as George hoped that Frederick, who was then waging his second war for Silesia against Austria and Saxony, which were backed by the Maritime Powers, would succumb to this coalition.[12] But Frederick held his own, defeated Austria and in a few weeks' campaigning crushed Saxony. The treaty of peace, which confirmed him in the possession of Silesia, was signed at Dresden in December 1745.

Prussia's resounding victory revealed her amazing strength and overwhelming superiority over her former competitors in North Germany. Henceforth the central and almost sole problem of Hanoverian policy was the quest for security. Some weeks after the peace of Dresden had been concluded, Münchhausen and his colleagues planned a European defensive organization to guarantee the safety of Hanover and to protect her integrity and independence against possible encroachments by Prussia. The Hanoverian ministers now dreaded Frederick's animosity against their country.[13] To be sure they were wrong in ascribing to him evil designs upon Hanover. Frederick's plan for Prussia's future aggrandizement comprised Saxony, Polish Prussia, Swedish Pomerania, and Mecklenburg;[14] but he never intended to conquer Hanover. His intimidated neighbours, however, could not be sure of that. Moreover the very fact of his unbroken connection with France, which was to grow more and more intimate, was a constant threat to His Britannic Majesty's German dominions.

The Hanoverian regency, therefore, ardently welcomed a proposal by Maria Theresa to George in his capacity as elector to join a defensive alliance against Prussia, which should be formed between Austria, Saxony, and Russia. In approving this scheme the Hanoverian ministers emphasized, however, that the intended league could not work without the support

[12] Mediger, *op. cit.*, pp. 401–12.

[13] Opinion of the Geh. Kammerrat Karl Diede zum Fürstenstein, 5 February 1746, H.A., Cal. Br. 24 Österreich I 216.

[14] Frederick the Great, 'Testament Politique, 1752: Rêveries politiques', *Die politischen Testamente Friedrichs des Grossen*, ed. G. B. Volz (Berlin, 1920) pp. 59–65.

of Britain, as the contracting powers were in dire need of money. Britain alone could put the machine in motion by means of financial aid.[15] Moreover, they argued, as a ministerial opinion of 5 February 1746 runs: 'Judging from the king of Prussia's conduct, there are two considerations that can check his lust of conquest, namely his apprehension of Russia and his anxiety not to lose the favour of the English nation.'[16]

In the eyes of Münchhausen and his colleagues Russia was the mainstay of Hanover's security, since they wanted to use her as a counterpoise to neutralize the superiority of Prussia. Yet they were well aware that Russia could not mobilize her forces without subsidies. For a decade to come the Hanoverian ministers, therefore, strove to combine British wealth and Russian manpower so as to keep Frederick in check by bringing to bear upon him the pressure of a Russian army in British pay, ready to invade his eastern provinces.

So long as the British government had to carry on the War of the Austrian Succession against France, it pursued just this policy of hiring a Russian army and keeping it assembled on the Prussian frontier in order to restrain Frederick from taking up arms once more. But when the peace of Aix-la-Chapelle had ended the Anglo-French struggle, without settling any of the questions that had caused it, the Pelham Cabinet dismissed the idea of paying further subsidies to Russia. In view of the heavy debt incurred during the war Henry Pelham himself shrank from contracting any engagement whatever on the Continent. His brother, the Duke of Newcastle, was on friendly terms with Münchhausen and the other Hanoverian ministers. In accordance with their view, he was intent on opposing some sort of defensive league on the Continent to the Franco-Prussian alliance in order to divide the forces of France and prevent her from concentrating on naval warfare. But he disagreed with his Hanoverian friends as to the importance of Russia and the necessity of securing her assistance by paying subsidies in time of peace. As an alternative Newcastle embarked on a policy of rallying the minor German states to the support of Austrian predominance in the Empire. When he began to court them, the electors and princes scented their chance to get money; and he had to wring from his brother a reluctant consent to

[15] The Hanoverian ministers to George II, 8 February 1746, H.A., Cal. Br. 24 Österreich I 216.

[16] Opinion of Diede, 5 February 1746.

one subsidy after another to buy Bavaria, Saxony and the other states.[17]

Münchhausen was not optimistic about the outcome of these endeavours, but his cautious warnings were disregarded. Meanwhile the Russian Grand Chancellor, Alexis Petrovich Bestuzhev-Ryumin, himself solicited a new subsidy treaty with Britain.

Frederick the Great called Russia a machine, which was put in motion by Britain.[18] His Hanoverian antagonists, too, considered Russia a mere tool which could and should be employed at will by the British paymaster. But Russia had a will and a policy of her own, though it was represented by a single man, Bestuzhev.

> Fléau de la Russie, exécrable ministre,
> Monstre, que la Discorde a vomi des enfers,

thus Frederick characterized his most dangerous and implacable enemy.[19] And indeed, the very appearance of the man was sinister—his always sullen, pale face with the piercing little eyes and the toothless mouth, which was occasionally distorted by a diabolical grin.[20] His ruling passion was to domineer. Yet he did not content himself with the power he exercised for some years within Russia, a power so great that he could be compared by foreign diplomats to a Grand Vizier.[21] He found a grim satisfaction in the thought that half of Europe was in dire fear of what he might do.[2]

Bestuzhev's policy derived its aggressive and overbearing character from his lust of power, and from his passions, especially his animosity

[17] D. B. Horn, 'The cabinet controversy on subsidy treaties in time of peace 1749–50', *English Historical Review* XLV (1930); D. B. Horn, *Sir Charles Hanbury Williams and European Diplomacy 1747–58* (London, 1930), pp. 48–52, 68–110, 149; Mediger, pp. 331–41, 437–43. Newcastle outlined his policy in a letter to Hardwicke of 6/17 November 1748: *Archives ou correspondance inédite de la maison d'Orange-Nassau*, 4th series, ed. Th. Bussemaker, I (Leyden, 1908) 190–5. For Hanoverian influence on the forming of Newcastle's policy see H.A., Cal. Br. 24 England 148: 'Korrespondenz zwischen dem Herzog von Newcastle und dem Grossvogt Geh. Rat Gerlach Adolph von Münchhausen betr. die allgemeine Politik. 1748–49'.

[18] *Histoire de mon temps*, p. 209.

[19] Ode: 'Les troubles du nord', *Oeuvres de Frédéric le Grand* X (Berlin, 1849) 34.

[20] S. Goriaïnow, ed., *Mémoires du roi Stanislas-Auguste Poniatowski* (St Petersburg, 1914), p. 159.

[21] Graf Finckenstein, *Rélation générale de la cour de Russie*, St Petersburg 1 October 1748: Deutsches Zentralarchiv, Abteilung Merseburg, Rep. 11. Russland 56 B.

[22] Funcke to Brühl, Moscow 28 September 1749, Sächsisches Landeshauptsarchiv, Dresden (hereafter cited as D[resden] A[rchives]), Loc. 3031 vol. II.

against Frederick. But on the whole it was the outcome of the development of Russia's international relations since the reign of Peter the Great.

In conquering Sweden's Baltic provinces, Peter had gained access to one of the main routes of European maritime commerce and had broken the power of Sweden. Henceforth Russia's preponderance in eastern Europe and her rank among the great powers was based on these conquests. They were safe so long as not only Sweden, but also Russia's other once formidable neighbour, Poland, remained in the state of weakness and decay to which Peter's arms and diplomacy had reduced them. So Russian foreign policy under his successors consistently pursued the course of keeping Poland and Sweden weak by interfering in their domestic affairs, by fostering and utilizing the party strife that was rending and paralysing both countries, and, if need be, by threats and by armed intervention.

To this end Russia contracted alliances with Austria, Prussia, and Saxony. She needed support to ward off the endeavours of France to wrest from her control of the area beyond her western frontiers, by trying to help Sweden and Poland to recover and to combine their regenerated forces with the still redoubtable power of Turkey against her. French diplomacy was busy erecting a barrier in the east—the famous *barrière de l'est*—to keep Russia away from central Europe that she might not overturn the balance of power in the Empire to the detriment of France.

Bestuzhev inherited antagonism to France from his predecessor Ostermann; but the situation was now aggravated by the sudden rise of Prussia. Although Frederick evaded the tempting offers of Polish and Swedish politicians, Prussia with her amazing striking power appeared as the potential backbone of an anti-Russian coalition under French auspices. Her very existence roused hopes and emotions from Stockholm to Constantinople that frustrated Russian influence. Also Bestuzhev perceived that the Franco-Prussian alliance was based on common interests: it therefore seemed to him indissoluble. Moreover he erroneously imagined that Prussia under the rule of Frederick's father and grandfather had been not merely allied with but dependent on Russia. He therefore regarded her co-operation with France as a defection. And he supposed that Prussia, in order to maintain her independence, would of necessity do her utmost with the aid of Sweden, Poland, Turkey and Persia to shut Russia up within her borders and prevent her intervention in European affairs.

Bestuzhev, however, claimed Russian ascendancy over Europe. He revealed the ultimate aim of his policy in the aspiration that Russia should command Europe, should give the law to her.[23] He was determined not only to hold his ground, but to extend Russia's sphere of influence from Poland to North Germany. Saxony was already under Russia's sway owing to her fear of Prussia and to the dependence of the elector-king on Russian assistance in Poland. Now Bestuzhev was bent on disrupting and subduing Prussia so as to reduce her also to the rank of a Russian satellite. For this reason he strove to bring about a war with Frederick, in order 'to weaken the king of Prussia'—a favourite expression of his which implied a partition of Frederick's dominions. As Russia's share of the spoils he proposed East Prussia, which province should be handed over to Poland in exchange for her territories to the east of the Dvina and upper Dnieper, and for Courland.[24]

But the chancellor could not realize his design without being authorized and backed by the tsaritsa. The Empress Elizabeth was confirmed in her aversion to the risks and troubles of power politics by the opposition of the Russian nobility and clergy to Bestuzhev's warlike policy, which meant that as many troops as possible must be kept assembled in the Baltic provinces, ready to attack Prussia as soon as an opportunity offered. Bestuzhev's opponents in the empress's council protested that the

[23] Memoir of Bestuzhev, 19 January 1756 o.s., *Arkhiv Knyazya Vorontsova* IV (Moscow, 1872) 83; Bestuzhev to Vorontsov, 11 Aug. 1744 o.s., *Sbornik imperatorskogo russkogo istoricheskogo obshchestva* (hereafter cited as *Sbornik*) CII (St. Petersburg, 1898) 472.

[24] For Bestuzhev's policy see Bestuzhev to Vorontsov, 11 Aug. 1744 o.s., *Sbornik* CII, 469–74; memoir of Bestuzhev, 13 Sept. 1745 o.s., *ibid.*, 453–69; draft of Bestuzhev's memoir, composed in French by the secretary of the Saxon legation, Funcke, D.A., Loc. 3028 vol. X; cf. Pezold to Brühl, 27 July, 17 Aug., 20 Oct. 1745, *ibid.*, Loc. 3028 vol. X, Loc. 3029 vol. XI; memoirs of Bestuzhev, 7 May 1753 o.s., S. M. Soloviev, *Istoriya Rossii s drevneishikh vremen* (Moscow, 1964) XII, 192–6; 1754, *ibid.*, 227–8; 19 Jan. 1756 o.s., *Arkhiv Knyazya Vorontsova* IV, 69–85; 3 March 1756 o.s., *ibid.*, III, 357–61; Mediger, pp. 597–616. For Bestuzhev's territorial designs see Tyrawley to Carteret, 8 Oct. 1744 o.s., 12 Nov. 1744 o.s., *Sbornik* CII, 129–30, 153; war aims, sanctioned by the Conference 15 March 1756 o.s., *Sbornik* CXXXVI, 31–34; Esterhazy to Kaunitz, 30 Nov. 1756, *Publikationen aus den K. Preussischen Staatsarchiven* LXXIV, 643; for opinion of Bestuzhev and Vorontsov see 3 May 1757 o.s., N. M. Korobkov, *Semiletnyaya voina. Materialy o deistviyakh russkoi armii i flota v 1756–1762 gg.* (Moscow, 1948) p. 142; Prasse to Brühl, 28 June 1757, D.A., Loc. 3034 vol. IIa; report of St Poniatowski, 6 Aug. 1757, W. Konopczyński, *Polska w dobie wojny siedmioletniej* (Cracow and Warsaw, 1909) I, 427.

concentration of such forces in this area was too expensive, since the cost of supplies was much higher there than in the interior of Russia. They demanded that the troops should be scattered all over the Russian Empire, which could not but diminish their efficiency through lack of training, let alone their mobility. To cut the ground from under their feet, the chancellor wanted Britain to defray the cost by hiring a Russian army, which was to be kept permanently on the western frontier for the protection of Hanover.[25]

For this reason Bestuzhev wished the British government to enter into negotiations about a new subsidy treaty. But Newcastle, entangled in his German policy, turned a deaf ear to his pleading, until the awkward question of Hanover's security became really urgent and forced his hand.

During the War of the Austrian Succession British privateers had captured a number of Prussian merchantmen. Frederick in vain claimed compensation for the losses his subjects had suffered and at long last in 1752 retaliated by stopping the repayment of money he owed to British financiers as successor of the Habsburgs in Silesia: he deposited the remainder of the sum due with the *Kammergericht* in Berlin until his subjects should be indemnified. British public opinion reacted violently. Anglo-Prussian relations became strained to breaking point and war seemed imminent. Wild rumours had it that Frederick was preparing an attack on Hanover.[26] George II was frightened into giving the desperate order that the troops and young men fit for service should retire to the fortress of Stade in case of a Prussian invasion.[27] At the same time Newcastle, behind the back of his colleagues, inquired of the regency how Britain could provide for the safety of the electorate and above all how the navy could be employed for its defence.[28]

The Hanoverian ministers composed their answer on 23 February 1753 under the influence of alarming news from the Prussian frontier,

[25] Mediger, *op. cit.*, pp. 295–329.

[26] Reports of Hanoverian civil servants from the Prussian frontier, H.A., Hannover 9 Preussen 191.

[27] George II to the Hanoverian ministers, 16 Jan. 1753 P.S., H.A., Hannover 92 LXXV 16 a; the Hanoverian ministers to George II, 1 Feb. 1753, H.A., Hannover 9 Preussen 191; George II to the Hanoverian ministers, 20 Feb. 1753, P.S., H.A., Hannover 9 Preussen 194; 7 March 1753, H.A., Hannover 92 LXXV 16 a.

[28] George II to the Hanoverian ministers, 13 Feb. 1753, P.S.; enclosed 'Minute', secret inquiry of Newcastle, H.A., Hannover 9 Preussen 193.

which later proved to be misleading. They emphasized that naval operations would not bring immediate relief. Nothing could save Hanover from a sudden attack but prompt succour from Austria and Russia. This, however, could not be secured unless Russia was enabled by subsidies to mobilize her army. The present opportunity should be seized to engage Russia by a subsidy treaty to the protection of the king's German dominions.[29]

This advice from Hanover turned the scales. Scarcely had Newcastle received the memoir of the regency, than a courier was sent to Moscow with instructions for the British envoy to ask for Russian military aid in case of a Prussian attack on Hanover and to offer a subsidy in return.[30]

This proposal enabled Bestuzhev to overcome his opponents and to enforce his policy. For under the new circumstances the empress gave her sanction to it, as she detested Frederick because of his insulting comments on her and was now eager to go to war with him.[31] Bestuzhev took control of the administration of the army and succeeded in concentrating the troops as he wished. Thus the bulk of the Russian forces had been assembled in the north-western borderlands when at long last, after toilsome negotiations spun out over two years, an Anglo-Russian agreement was reached in the autumn of 1755.[32] Meanwhile

[29] The Hanoverian ministers to George II, 13 Feb. 1753, H.A., Hannover 9 Preussen 193.

[30] Ph. Münchhausen to the Hanoverian ministers, London, 13 March 1753, P.S., H.A., Hannover 9 Preussen 193; Newcastle to Guy Dickens, 9 March 1753, *Sbornik* CXLVIII, 409–13.

[31] Memoir of Bestuzhev, 7 May 1753 O.S., as in fn. 24; Funcke to Brühl, 17 May, 16 July 1753, D.A., Loc. 3032 vol. VIII; Guy Dickens to Newcastle, 7/18 July 1753, *Sbornik* CXLVIII, 437; A. Beer, *Aufzeichnungen des Grafen William Bentinck über Maria Theresia* (Wien, 1871) p. cxlv; 'Result', formulated as the outcome of the sessions of the Council of State on 14 and 15 May 1753 O.S., French translation in *Sbornik* CXLVIII, 458–62.

[32] Mediger, pp. 474–6; D. F. Maslovsky, *Russkaya armiya v Semiletnyuyu Voinu* (Moscow, 1886) I, tables 9 and 10; memoir of the War College, 22 July 1755 O.S., *Arkhiv Knyazya Vorontsova* III, 658–9; *ibid.*, VII, 272–3, 336–7, 339; Funcke to Brühl, 20 June 1753, 11 Oct. 1754, D.A., Loc. 3032 vol. VII, Loc. 3033 vol. X; Guy Dickens to Newcastle, 31 May/11 June 1753, *Sbornik* CXLVIII, 428; Hyndford to Newcastle, 24 May 1748 O.S., *Sbornik* CX, 11; memoir of Bestuzhev, 19 Jan. 1756 O.S., p. 72. For the conclusion of the Anglo-Russian subsidy treaty see Horn, *Sir Charles Hanbury Williams*, pp. 182–3, 186–92; H. H. Kaplan, *Russia and the Outbreak of the Seven Years' War* (Berkeley and Los Angeles, 1968) pp. 15–16, 22–4; cf. Funcke to Brühl, 7 July, 22 July, 4 Aug., 11 Aug. 1755, D.A., Loc. 3033 vol. XII.

the international situation had changed. In signing the subsidy treaty, the British consented to Bestuzhev's demands, which Newcastle called 'very monstrous',[33] because war with France now stared them in the face.

Hostilities in North America had broken out, and the Newcastle Cabinet decided to try and bring France to terms by exploiting British naval superiority. This involved the risk of provoking a French counter-attack on the Continent, where Britain was vulnerable.

'Hanover robs us of the Benefit of being an Island, and is actually a Pledge for our good Behaviour on the Continent', wrote Chesterfield in 1742.[34] It was he who in 1747, as Secretary of State, concluded the first Anglo-Russian subsidy treaty to guarantee Hanover against a Prussian attack. His grumble voiced the general feeling of the British public against the king's German dominions. They were considered a burden, hampering British policy, and the wish to get rid of them was widespread. This resentment was exploited and exacerbated by the agitation of the Parliamentary Opposition. Playing to the gallery, Pitt thundered against the 'despicable Electorate'.[35] But even he, confronted by responsibility, had to admit in confidential conversations with Newcastle and Hardwicke that Britain was bound in honour not to suffer the king to be deprived of his German dominions in consequence of a British war.[36]

Yet the necessity of defending Hanover was not merely a question of prestige. It also involved material British interests. For Hanover controlled the mouths of the Elbe and Weser and the shore between them, i.e. the electorate held a position that might be of vital strategic and economic importance if it fell a prey to the French. In this respect it resembled the Austrian Netherlands. At the end of the War of the Austrian Succession the British had been forced to restore all their oversea conquests in exchange for the evacuation of the Low Countries by the French. In the same way a French occupation of Hanover was

[33] Newcastle to Guy Dickens, 24 Aug. 1753, *Sbornik* CXLVIII, 483–6.

[34] *The Case of the Hanover Forces in the Pay of Great Britain, impartially and freely examined* (London, 1742), p. 13, quoted in Wilson, p. 87.

[35] P. C. Yorke, *The Life and Correspondence of Philip Yorke, Earl of Hardwicke, Lord High Chancellor of Great Britain 1737–1756* (Cambridge, 1913) I, 292.

[36] Hardwicke to Newcastle, 9 Aug. 1755, Yorke, II, 231–2.

likely to counterbalance any successes the British might gain in America.[37]

This is the key to Newcastle's continental policy, to his desperate efforts in 1755 to assemble forces to ward off any attack on Hanover as well as on the Austrian Netherlands. Yet Austria, Britain's traditional ally, refused to take her share in the defence of the British strategic position on the Continent. For Maria Theresa's chancellor, Kaunitz, who was conducting Austrian policy, contemplated an overwhelming concentric attack on Prussia and not a risky and unprofitable defensive war against France. When this became obvious, Newcastle conceived the idea of winning Frederick over by using the threat of the new Anglo-Russian subsidy treaty to force upon him an agreement safeguarding Hanover's neutrality.[38]

The Hanoverian policy of employing Russia as a bugbear to overawe Frederick now bore fruit. For years he had been anxious at the prospect of a combined attack by Austria and Russia. He knew by experience that France would do nothing to relieve his eastern frontier of the ever growing pressure of the Russian armies. He therefore consented to an agreement with Britain, which in return for his pledging himself to protect Hanover freed him from his fear of Russian attack. For in signing the convention of 16 January 1756 he supposed that Russia would follow the lead of Britain, and that Austria, thus isolated, would not be able to stir.[39]

But contrary to his expectations the French government regarded his step as an unpardonable defection and were by the skill of Kaunitz lured into an alliance with Austria. Russia, however, proved to be more than a tool of British policy. Frederick little by little perceived that she was drifting from her British paymaster and yet was mobilizing her army and navy, that in doing so she was preparing for the offensive on Prussia

[37] Sir J. Corbett, *England in the Seven Years' War* (London, 2 vols, 1918) I, 22–3, 39; R. Waddington, *Louis XV et le renversement des alliances. Préliminaires de la guerre de Sept Ans* (Paris, 1896) pp. 114–16.

[38] Newcastle to Münchhausen, 25 July, 8 Aug. 1755, H.A., Hannover 91 v. Münchhausen I 22; cf. Münchhausen and Steinberg to Newcastle, 26 July 1755; Münchhausen to Newcastle, 11 July, 2 Aug. 1755, *ibid.*; Waddington, pp. 199–203; Horn, *Sir Charles Hanbury Williams*, pp. 199–204; Kaplan, pp. 16–19; Mediger, pp. 500–9.

[39] *Politische Correspondenz Friedrichs des Grossen* (Berlin, 1879–1939) XI and XII *passim*; Horn, *Sir Charles Hanbury Williams*, pp. 206–11; Mediger, chap. 7; Kaplan, pp. 19–22, 29–35.

which Bestuzhev for years had been planning. The king felt the ring of a powerful coalition closing round Prussia and saw no other way out of his awkward position than 'to cut the Gordian knot with the sword'.[40] So he took up arms, that his generalship might outweigh the statecraft of Kaunitz.

British and Hanoverian statesmen had done their utmost to guarantee Hanover against invasion. Their efforts resulted in the outbreak of a war that imposed upon Hanover too the heavy task of supporting both Britain's struggle for empire and Prussia's struggle for existence. The French strove to seize the electorate as a pawn which might counterbalance their oversea losses, and as a basis of operations against Prussia. So the little country had to sustain the onslaught of the bulk of France's land forces. Thanks to the generalship of Ferdinand of Brunswick, the commander-in-chief of the combined Anglo-Hanoverian army, the efforts of the French armies, in spite of their vast numerical superiority, ended in failure. Ferdinand for five years kept them in check. In doing so he enabled Pitt to take the offensive overseas and to conquer Canada and India. At the same time he preserved Frederick from being overwhelmed by the junction of his eastern and western enemies. Eleven days before Frederick's crushing defeat at the hands of the Russians in the battle of Kunersdorf, Ferdinand had beaten the French at Minden and thus prevented them from overrunning Hanover and joining hands with the Austrians and Russians.

Before the Seven Years War Hanoverian diplomacy had done a great deal to pave the way for Russia's advance towards Germany. During the war, however, the Hanoverian army, shoulder to shoulder with British and other German forces and backed by British financial aid, contributed essentially to save Prussia from destruction and thus to block that same advance.

[40] Frederick to Mitchell, 17 Aug. 1756, *Politische Correspondenz Friedrichs des Grossen* XIII, 230.

12

ALICE CARTER

How to Revise Treaties without Negotiating: Commonsense, mutual fears and the Anglo-Dutch Trade Disputes of 1759

Obsolescence clauses were not built automatically into treaties as early as the seventeenth century; nor were treaties always, or even usually, limited as to their operation by terminal dates.[1] Anglo-Netherlands relations in mid-eighteenth century were still governed by agreements made in the 1670s; eighty years later the terms of these were considerably out-of-date. The political treaty, made in 1678, had been renewed and revised on several occasions,[2] but even so was not really applicable to the Republic's or to England's needs by the time of the Seven Years War, as I have argued elsewhere.[3] But the commercial treaty of Westminster, dating from December 1674, though it had been once reinforced and once renewed,[4] had never been revised at all. It regulated with some precision the terms on which one contracting power could trade with the enemies of the other. But there had been such enormous changes in the direction of trade, and in the strategic and other importance of some of the articles mentioned in the treaty, that the arrangements come to in 1674 bore little relation to circumstances prevailing by mid-eighteenth century.

The agreement was badly in need both of revision and of explanation, especially as to how far it applied to trade with colonial possessions of the belligerent party's adversaries. This had been a matter of compara-

[1] Sir Ernest Satow, *A Guide to Diplomatic Practice* II (London, 1917) 174.

[2] Georg F. van Martens, *Recueil de Traités d'Alliance*, supplément I (Göttingen, 1835) p. 116.

[3] *Britain and the Netherlands in Europe and Asia*, ed. John S. Bromley and Ernst H. Kossmann (London, 1968) pp. 121–2.

[4] Jean Dumont, *Corps Universel Diplomatique du Droit des Gens* (The Hague, 1731) VII, part I, p. 282.

tively minor importance in 1674, but was to become of the greatest moment eighty years on.[5]

England and the Netherlands were both, as will be shown, anxious to reach an understanding on the vexed question of what trade rights the neutral power could claim. Neither party, however, wanted to face up to possible complications consequent on negotiating a settlement in form. Therefore both were reasonably satisfied with the solution eventually arrived at, a rule-of-thumb set of principles established by decisions in the English Prize Courts of Appeal, on ship cases sent up from Doctors' Commons and other maritime courts of first instance. These, taken together, guided Dutch merchantmen into safe channels of trade. Simultaneously English regulation of her privateers removed genuine grievances arising from speculative captures; and undercapitalization of privateers, which could rob those owners and masters whose vessels had been wrongly detained of costs, was rectified by enlarging the cautionary down payments exacted before commissions were issued.[6] After these principles became clear, the treaty was in effect, though not actually, renegotiated. Merchants now knew how they could safely conduct their trade, insurance risks once more became calculable, privateering captains could make a guess at what would be declared lawful prize. Above all the large capital represented by ships lying idle, with rotting cargoes and demoralized crews, could be put once more to profitable use.

Let us begin by considering the defects of the Treaty of 1674, seen in relation to conditions prevailing eighty years after it had been made. Like nearly all Netherlands commercial treaties,[7] it favoured the neutral trader, even though at the time it was negotiated the neutral power was England, not the Republic. Contraband of war was narrowly defined; and the following article listed commodities, lead, precious metals and even including naval stores, which were specifically not to be regarded as contraband in any circumstances. An explanatory article of the following

[5] In 1674 attempts were made by the Dutch to secure the treaty's application beyond Europe, with a view to their East Indies trade. See an historical study of the negotiation of the treaty, with copies of supporting documents, compiled for the Grand Pensionary Steyn: A[lgemeene] R[ijks] A[rchief], H[andschriften van de derde] A[fdeeling], 33.

[6] 32 Geo. II c. 25; cf. B.M. Add. MSS. 32890, fos. 401, 486.

[7] Philip Jessup and Francis Deak, *Neutrality, its History, Economics, and Law* I (New York, 1935) 35 ff.

year favoured the neutral still further, for in it trade between enemy ports, as well as trade between neutral and enemy ports, was declared free; the only limitation was the already usual one of prohibiting trade with *places blocquées ou investies.*[8] So resounding a declaration of the Dutch-favoured principle of *Free Ships, Free Goods* had become, of course, a major embarrassment to England in eighteenth-century wars, especially since Dutch merchants, though without encouragement from their government, applied the principle to trade between French home ports and Caribbean settlements.

By mid-eighteenth century, France was a major maritime power. But in spite of much detailed planning she was still unable to provide herself with every class of naval stores, the principal lack being the long pine mast timbers, most readily acquired from the Baltic, and needed to carry the enlarged spread of canvas required by bigger first-raters. The Dutch timber trade to the Baltic had by mid-eighteenth century become almost an affair of hereditary skill; the fly-boats in this service had been modified with vertical hatches astern and there was much expertise in the choice especially of mast-timber. There was also the possibility, under the terms of the explanatory article of December 1675, that Dutch timber ships could be used to supply French dockyards with assorted locally grown timbers, assembled from interior forests at French river-mouth depôts but not easily transferred from there to areas where they were needed in French ships which were at great risk from English privateers.[9]

In carrying home French colonial produce, and supplying French dockyards, the mid-eighteenth-century neutrals were prolonging, not shortening wars. But by mid-eighteenth century specialists in international relations such as Vattel and Hubner were already declaimin gthat to prolong a war was unneutral. Neither in practice nor in theory could the Dutch hope to enjoy both the strict terms of the Treaty of 1674 and their preferred policy of remaining neutral in eighteenth-century wars.[10]

By 1759 the difficulty about naval stores, acute in the early years of the war, had been more or less solved because timber from the Baltic was,

[8] Dumont, VII, part 1, p. 319. The limitation as to *places blocquées* is in article IV of the original treaty.

[9] Paul W. Bamford, *Forests and French Sea-Power, 1660–1789* (Toronto, 1956) pp. 132–4, 173 ff.

[10] Alice C. Carter, 'The Dutch as neutrals in the Seven Years' War', *International and Comparative Law Quarterly* XII (July 1963).

after all, an article of trade in demand in England; and English dockyard contractors were in wartime quite happy and entitled[11] to purchase this from owners of cargoes in captured Dutch timber ships. These owners were generally equally happy to sell it wherever a market could be found. There were in fact several captures of Dutch Baltic timber fleets early in the Seven Years War; but as the cargoes were quickly disposed of, and the ships allowed to go free if there were no aggravating circumstances, this matter did not greatly inflame Anglo-Dutch relations.[12] It is noticeable that insurance premiums on Dutch voyages to the Baltic did not vary, at least until the end of 1757, beyond the customary seasonal quarter to half per cent.[13] The main difficulty came over the Caribbean trade, for if not the treaty itself at least the explanatory article of 1675 could be extended to justify Dutch ships engaging in the direct trade between French home ports and their settlements in the West Indies—a trade which in peace time was strictly reserved for the subjects of the King of France. Amsterdam merchants were specially invited to engage in this carrying trade in March 1756 even before war had officially broken out.[14] It was Dutch participation in this trade which made vitally necessary a revision in some way of the Treaty of 1674–75.

Why then did the special commission, sent in 1759 from the States to London for this very purpose, return with no formal success? In fact circumstances were such that both Dutch and English were afraid to grasp

[11] 29 Geo. II c. 34: An Act for the Encouragement of Seamen, and the more speedy and effectual Manning His Majesty's Navy [copy in A.R.A., H.A. 33]; see especially section xxxviii.

[12] See correspondence between the Earl of Holdernesse, Secretary of State for the Northern Department, and Colonel Joseph Yorke, son of the Lord Chancellor Hardwicke, who was the English representative at The Hague, in July 1756: P.R.O., S.P. 84/474. If timber cargoes were sold to English dockyard contractors, the Dutch ships would be let go and the skippers indemnified as to freight. Correspondence between Hendrik Hop, Dutch representative in London, and his correspondents in the Netherlands, also for July 1756, reflects some satisfaction over this arrangement: B.M. Add. MSS. 17677 DDDD [Intercepted and copied letters, or Netherlands Transcripts].

[13] G[emeente] A[rchief] A[msterdam], Bib[liotheek] No. N.35.003. 24.

[14] Yorke to Holdernesse, 30 March 1756, and enclosures: S.P. 84/473; cf. G.A.A., Arch[ives of the] Burg[omasters], Vr[oedschap] Res[olutien] (Resolutions of the Town Council) 63 fos., 41–53, and Vr[oedschap] Mun[imentenboeken], 40 ff., 603v–605v. The latter is a series of documents supporting or explaining resolutions of the Town Council.

this nettle firmly. The Dutch reasons for fearing a full-scale engagement in diplomacy are fairly obvious. The Republic had twice in effect refused to send the auxiliary force of six thousand men, due under the terms of the Treaty of 1678 if England were threatened by invasion by a hostile power, as she felt herself to be in 1756 by France.[15] England had at least twice threatened to set the Treaty of 1678 in the scale against that of 1674,[16] to penalize the Republic for not complying with engagements under the one, by failing to fulfil her own duties under the other, as it were *refondre* all Anglo-Netherlands treaties.[17] Furthermore, should the Dutch press too hard for *Free Ships, Free Goods* in the Caribbean they might easily see this right being cut down in European waters where the Treaty of 1674–75 still operated to some extent to Dutch advantage, though much coastwise French trade in Dutch vessels was being interrupted on one pretext or another.[18] But what really weighed most in the Netherlands was the delicate balance of the domestic political situation. The allegedly anglophile Princess Gouvernante, Anna of Orange, daughter of George II, who had ruled in the name of her under-age son, died after a short illness in January 1759, in the middle of all the tensions created by the weakness of the commercial treaty. It would have been virtually impossible, in conditions prevailing just after her death, for any Dutch minister to put his name to a formal document retreating from long held rights sanctioned by ancient agreement.[19]

[15] The treaty had been invoked in February and August 1756 but had never been officially denounced by the States. From the Dutch standpoint these exchanges are explained in full detail by Nicolaas A. Bootsma, *De Hertog van Brunswijk* (Assen, 1962) pp. 318–70.

[16] Richard Pares, *Colonial Blockade and Neutral Rights* (Oxford, 1938) pp. 244, 249. The late author's Dutch references are to be viewed with a certain amount of caution.

[17] Quoted as from a Dutch source by Yorke on 4 August 1758: S.P. 84/481.

[18] G.A.A., Rech[terlijke] Arch[ieven] (legal records) contain a series of volumes, normally one *per annum* in peacetime, two *per annum* in time of war, which admit an insurance claim in respect of any disaster to a ship. These documents, signed by the insurers, give particulars of the voyage, though not generally of the cargo. In the first half of 1757, out of 156 claims, 115 concerned French coastal voyages. In the second half of 1758, out of 107 examined, 24 had visited French coastal ports, but usually on the way to or from the West Indies.

[19] Nicolas A. Bootsma, 'Prinses Anna van Hannover', *Voor Rogier*, ed. van den Eerenbeemt, Manning en Winkelman (Hilversum, 1964) pp. 127 ff., gives an account of this unfortunate woman, the English Princess Royal, not as 'silly', certainly not as partial to England, as Pares would have us believe (*op. cit.*, pp. 262, 253).

Yet something had to be done. For in the summer of the preceding year England had staged an all-out attack on the West Indies trade of the French,[20] deliberately aiming not only at trade by neutrals 'on behalf of' French islands but also at all trade of these islands. Now the situation in the Caribbean trade did not accord in the slightest with eighteenth-century opinion on what trade was, and what trade was not, permissible. The French islands were on the whole productive, but not over-favoured with harbours, and France was anyway always short of seamen and shipping in time of war. The Dutch settlements were not productive but had magnificent anchorages and warehousing, especially at St Eustatius. All islands, of whatever nationality, inevitably traded, both in peace and in war, with each other and in each other's produce; such trade though illegal in theory was in practice impossible to prevent. When England decided to wage economic warfare against the French islands, a fivefold problem emerged in respect of neutral traders. There was neutral participation in the direct trade between French home ports and French settlements. There was trade between French settlements and neutral home ports. There was trade on French account in produce of French islands, between neutral home ports and neutral settlements, and there was a similar trade on neutral account. Lastly there was direct trade, on neutral account, between neutral home ports and their own islands, in their own islands' produce. Natural law and justice placed this last category above interference by belligerents' privateers. But in the context of Netherlands trade with their own colonies as well as with those of the enemy of their English ally, lurked the difficulty of establishing whether the coffee, sugar or whatever it might be, was in fact Dutch property or whether or not it was the produce of the far from fertile Dutch settlements. Moreover it was still unclear whether the terms of the Marine Treaty of 1674–75 applied in extra-European waters. In the face

[20] G.A.A., Recht. Arch. 2996–8 inclusive. These three volumes cover 1758 alone, 2997 being only for the months of July and August. Cf. A.R.A., Archief Steyn, 23–5. These contain letters written to Steyn from representatives abroad in the years 1758, 1759 and 1760. Included is a lively series from J. Palairet, an assistant in the Dutch embassy in London whose functions seem to have somewhat resembled those of a present day commercial counsellor. On 10 October 1758 Palairet wrote that intensified English attacks on all trade with the West Indies were preparatory to the reduction of French islands to be attempted in the following year.

of all these prickly uncertainties, from the Netherlands' standpoint a full-scale negotiation presented many hazards.

Equally from the English viewpoint, 1759 was not a year in which to undertake a difficult negotiation. There was a genuine fear that the Republic was about to throw in her lot with the French, either as a member of an armed neutrality, or as an actual ally. Here again, the uncertainties of the Dutch political situation must be taken into account. No one in England quite knew what would happen once it became clear that the Princess Gouvernante was seriously ill, nor after the news came of her death. That it was her own ill-exercise of the powers inherited from her husband which created so much of the domestic tension was not well understood in England. In fact her death enabled the States Party, opponents of the House of Orange, to recapture the patronage which was what was mainly at stake. Indeed her death helped considerably to relax political unrest and ultimately enabled trade disputes with England to resume their correct proportions of an irritant, demoting them from being a possible cause of Anglo-Dutch war. But early in 1759 this was not clear in London; and gloom about Anglo-Netherlands friendship prevailed. We find, for instance, in December 1758, Charles Jenkinson confidently expecting that in order to keep the Netherlands out of the arms of France England would have to surrender at least a portion of what she regarded as her 'rights'.[21] This was partly because, coupled with the decision to send special commissioners to England, Amsterdam and the two Admiralty Colleges of the States of Holland had successfully pressed in that assembly a motion to equip further ships of war to add to those already available to convoy Dutch merchant ships. This might make it feasible to provide regular and effective convoys across the Atlantic as well as in the Narrow Seas, with added danger of a flare-up between Britain and the Republic.

Further, the chances of an armed neutrality between Denmark and the Dutch Republic began to seem fairly high. For in January 1759 letters were intercepted between the Hague and Copenhagen which revealed that the Danes had become interested in such a league, influenced by French

[21] Ed. Groen van Prinsterer, *A[rchives . . . de la] M[aison d'] O[range-] N[assau]*, ed. Theodoor Bussemaker, 4th ser. III (Leiden, 1912) 619, n. 2. Charles Jenkinson, future first Earl of Liverpool, became undersecretary of state in 1761: John Steven Watson, *The Reign of George III* (Oxford, 1960) p. 65, n. 3.

diplomacy. English understanding of Baltic politics was not sufficient for this Danish move to be seen in its true light, which was anti-Swedish not pro-French (and of course least of all pro-Dutch). That the Dutch were aware of this, and would anyway prefer to preserve neutrality and save on defence costs, was likewise not understood in England.[22]

There were also divisions between different sections in the English ministry, and a ministerial as well as dynastic succession question as George II came nearer to his long-expected death. English political tensions were not as acute as those in the Netherlands, but they were sufficient to enter into career calculations. The opinion of Lord High Admiral Anson, that to allow *Free Ships, Free Goods* to the Dutch without limits, would help the French as much as giving French troops Dutch colours to fight under,[23] we can more or less discount; for Anson though Hardwicke's son-in-law was not at the centre of English politics. But Pitt, whose alliance with Newcastle and Hardwicke was born of necessity not affinity, was determined to regulate British privateers and thus to cut down Dutch complaints. His co-secretary Holdernesse was, however, always reluctant to yield anything to Dutch Republicans, since he was married to the Greffier Fagel's favourite niece and so very much 'in' with the Orangists. The heir to the English throne was steeped in opposition influences; and it would be difficult whilst negotiating a new commercial treaty with the Dutch not to put weapons into the armoury of Leicester House. In 1759 the English were as unwilling as the Dutch to engage in diplomatic warfare over the terms of a treaty of such moment, signed so long ago.

Moreover, earlier attempts at negotiation had all failed. Sir Joseph Yorke, England's representative at The Hague, had from time to time come up with solutions to the difficulties posed by the obsolete treaty. He has been derided, perhaps rather unfairly, by Pares, who regarded him as too volatile, above all too optimistic to negotiate realistically.[24] Some of Yorke's ideas and suggestions were, however, quite sensible, especially about what could be done to remove reasonable Dutch objections to the

[22] *A.M.O.N.* III, 632–4; B.M. Add. MSS. 32837, Memorandum of 24 Jan. 1759.

[23] The Duke of Newcastle to Yorke, 17 November 1758; B.M. Add. MSS. 32885, fo. 365; cf. *A.M.O.N.* III, 568–72.

[24] Pares, p. 246.

conduct of the English privateers.[25] But Yorke did not get much encouragement from home; and the Dutch were slow to take the initiative for their own domestic political reasons. There were protests through diplomatic channels about individual cases of captured ships; but no initiative had been taken towards wholesale negotiation until the summer of 1758, when the situation became critical because of England's intensified measures against the trade of the French Caribbean settlements.

The States of Holland had begun to consider seriously the equipment of a few convoy vessels at the end of June 1758.[26] The news of this decision, which if agreed on by the majority of this provincial assembly would be likely to pass the States General, was not officially conveyed to Yorke until August; but he had heard, of course, about it; nothing could be done secretly in the Republic and Yorke's ear was fairly well to the ground. There was no definite move in the negotiation until August: but meanwhile Yorke had heard from Holdernesse that England would in no circumstances allow Dutch ships to trade direct to French islands, whether from French or from Dutch home ports. He was also told to remind the Dutch that the Treaty of 1674 had incorporated the declaration, usual in such agreements, that adjudication on disputed captures was reserved for the maritime courts and not a matter for negotiation between the powers concerned. With these rather uncompromising statements went an unrealistic reference to closer Anglo-Dutch union once the trade disputes had been settled.[27] Yorke gave the Pensionary a note stressing England's refusal to permit direct trade with the French islands and making clear that she would not extend *Free Ships, Free Goods* to the colonies of the belligerent party's adversary. Simultaneously the Dutch West Indies Company weighed in with a petition about its own losses suffered in trading with the Caribbean, but making no distinction between 'legitimate' dealings with the Dutch settlements and those with the French islands, which were arguably not covered by treaty. Yorke seized on this

[25] Yorke to Holdernesse, 30 September (separate) and 14 October (with enclosure), 1757: S.P. 84/479.

[26] A.R.A., [Derde Afdeeling] Res[olutien] St[aten van] Holl[and] 204, pp. 492–500, 14 June 1758, and pp. 552–66, 24 June 1758. The whole issue was then thrashed out in the Town Councils of the constituents of the provincial states. Cf., for example, G.A.A., Arch. Burg. Vr. Res. 64, fos., 32, 34–39v; Vr. Mun. 41, pp. 630–1; 42, 31–46v.

[27] Holdernesse to Yorke, 21 July: S.P. 84/481.

opportunity to tax the Dutch with having themselves confused their innocent Caribbean trade with that of the French, hence of being the authors of their own misfortunes.[28]

There were three official documents emanating from the Dutch side in the formal negotiations on the Treaty of 1674. None of them was promising of a solution, though that of September 1758 foreshadowed the final arrangement, by agreeing to adjudicate in Admiralty Courts over vessels taken in accordance with the terms of the Treaty of 1674. The question what 'in accordance with' implied had to be decided; and prior to negotiation the Dutch demanded extrajudicial release of ships taken up whilst trading *de bonne foi* with French islands. In return they agreed to withdraw convoy or diplomatic assistance from any of their merchantmen trading directly with the French Caribbean settlements.[29]

Yorke's orders on an answer to the Dutch proposals were long delayed, only reaching him in December.[30] The extravagant demand for extra-judicial release of the captured ships was countered by an equally unrealistic reference to Dutch non-fulfilment of the Treaty of 1678. The most substantial point made was that the Dutch had not yet availed themselves of their legal remedy—appeal in maritime first-instance courts against those decisions over which they felt themselves aggrieved. The bringing up of Dutch ships on suspicion was justified because some owners and/or skippers undoubtedly had provided themselves with false or double papers.[31] The reaction of the Dutch ministers was to despair of an accommodation; of the merchants, to storm at the ailing princess about

[28] Yorke to Holdernesse during August: *ibid.*

[29] Yorke to Holdernesse, 26 September (and enclosure): S.P. 84/482. The French were not at all pleased. A.A.E., C.P., Hollande, vol. 499 contains letters between the Comte d'Affry, French representative at The Hague, and his court in September 1758. Cf. A.R.A., Archief Steyn, 23, letters from Berkenrode, Dutch representative in Paris, for the same period.

[30] They were dated only 28 November: S.P. 84/482. Cf. B.M. Add. MSS. 32886, fos. 54–67. Pares thought the delay was due to Hardwicke's desire to prolong his stay at Bath (*op. cit.*, p. 259). But was not the 'obstinately negative' attitude of the English, condemned by Pares (p. 246), due to a desire not to negotiate?

[31] It should be noted that even in Rotterdam, held to be most anti-English of all Dutch towns, the authorities were extremely concerned that their merchants should trade according to treaty. The records of the maritime courts there are full of prosecutions for fraud. See especially G[emeente] A[rchief] R[otterdam], Zee[gerecht] 15, 16.

convoy vessels and a neutral maritime league.[32] Yorke tried to patch things up; but as neither he nor the Dutch ministers knew what the English wanted he was not very successful. All the same he met some of the Amsterdammers informally at the house of the Pensionary, and a little light began to dawn. The deputies agreed 'after much mumbling of the thistle', as Yorke put it, that the hope of rapid release of their ships might induce their merchants to give up, not only the direct trade to the French settlements but also the so-called 'overshipping' of French produce, from barques in Dutch colonial harbours into Dutch vessels. The deputies also appealed for better regulation by England of her privateers.[33] With these faint hopes to spur him on, Yorke produced a written paper, copied to the Amsterdam deputies. In it he stressed that to proceed against already-captured ships except by due legal process would be impossible. But he was able to announce that listing of ships awaiting adjudication was in hand.[34] He deliberately glossed over the outstanding difficulty of proving property in cargoes taken on board from French barques in Dutch colonial ports, whilst stressing English anxiety to see justice done (where appropriate) against her own privateers. This paper was under consideration in the States of Holland when the princess died.

Yorke received an answer only on 25 January, and as it still demanded an extrajudicial release of Dutch ships prior to negotiation he was very disappointed. However, the Dutch remained willing to surrender the direct trade to the French West Indian islands. In return, they expected complete freedom for trade to and from their own islands, whatever the property in the cargo. Elementary attempts were now made at defining ships' papers and there were further requests for regulating privateers. But though this Netherlands document did provide a basis for negotiation, Yorke was told that the Dutch ministers at The Hague deplored its terms and that it was to be taken as the expression of extreme merchant

[32] *A.M.O.N.* III, 587, 589, 590. G.A.A., Vr. Res. 64, fo. 98; Vr. Mun. 42, fos. 175–81; Bib. M. 951. 003.

[33] Yorke to Holdernesse, 15 December: S.P. 84/482. Cf. a Dutch account of this meeting in G.A.A., Nieuw Muniment Vroedschap, 1749–1795, R.6, 14 December 1758. The Amsterdammers were two Ruling and one Former Burgomasters, and the senior Pensionary, influential citizens indeed. Yorke speaks of them with contempt. It is clear that the meeting had been arranged on the initiative of the Grand Pensionary and Bentinck van Rhoon, and that the Princess Gouvernante knew and approved of it. I am indebted to Dr Simon Hart for this reference.

[34] Holdernesse to Yorke, 13 Dec.: S.P. 84/482.

opinion, yet further indication that official Dutch sources were realistic about what agreement would be possible. In his reply, Yorke referred again to the unfulfilled Treaty of 1678, and reiterated that to release the already captured ships extrajudicially was out of the question. Stalemate best describes the position.

How far was stalemate acceptable to, even welcomed by, either party? So legalistic a nation as the Republic must surely have been aware that in matters of prize law there could be no other authority in disputed cases than the maritime courts. Yet so far, in spite of much complaint and a considerable number of captures, it agreed that only two Dutch ship cases had been brought from maritime courts of first instance to the High Court of Admiralty Appeal. This was rationalized from the Dutch side; it was said that necessary papers were unavailable because retained by the inferior courts.[35] And it is arguable that owners might hope either to agree with captors outside the courts, so saving legal costs, or for a rapid negotiated settlement between the two countries which would make their position clear. But to go on raising the impossible demand for extrajudicial release seems unrealistic to the point of fatuity. Did the Dutch seriously want to negotiate?

Similar doubts arise over the reiterated English reference to the Treaty of 1678, its terms twice unfulfilled by the Republic. Six thousand Dutch troops had been sent to England in 1745 under the terms of this treaty. They were of poor quality; yet their departure from their own country, along with those of England stationed between the Republic and the French, had left the Dutch frontiers dangerously open to attack. The military position of the Republic was almost as bad in 1759 as it had been in 1745. It is true that the landward provinces had a 4–3 majority in the States General against the areas bordering on the sea, and that they were naturally in favour of augmenting the Dutch army. But all hope of their being able to get this policy implemented had disappeared when Holland adopted that of equipping convoy ships instead.[36] It was therefore hardly

[35] *A.M.O.N.* IV, 1, 11. Yorke to Holdernesse, 19 Jan. 1759: S.P. 84/483.

[36] Dutch political tensions affect Anglo-Netherlands relations at this time because it had become a point of honour with the maritime provinces, contributing 80 per cent of the revenue of the Union, but outnumbered in the States General 4–3 by the landward provinces, that (as the Amsterdam Pensionary Graafland told Bentinck) 'quand il s'agissait de soutenir la République, cela ne dépendoit pas de leur 20 per cent'; *A.M.O.N.* III, 616. The 80 per cent is emphasized also in documents urging the

likely that any troops would be spared from Netherlands frontier defence to protect England from possible French attack; and if Dutch troops were available they would surely be more valuable in Germany than in England as Frederick had earlier hoped.[37] The English threat to reiterate their demand for the terms of the Treaty of 1678, like the Dutch demand for extrajudicial release of captured ships, seems merely to underline the paper-tiger nature of the whole exchange.

The next step in the Anglo-Dutch *impasse* (for negotiation is no longer an appropriate term) was the formal Dutch decision to send commissioners to England. This move originated in the Admiralty Colleges of the Maas and of Amsterdam.[38] The leader of the delegation was Jacobus Boreel,[39] fiscal of the Admiralty of Amsterdam, far more moderate, one could even say more patriotically Dutch in his outlook, than Denick, his fellow functionary of the Admiralty of the Maas.[40] With him was Jan van der Poll,[41] whose signature occurs regularly, until the spring of 1758, as an insurer on documents accepting that an insurance claim had been made out in respect of ships suffering loss, damage or detention whilst at sea. A third commissioner, Meerman, Pensionary of Rotterdam, was added

---

landward provinces to help pay for additional convoy vessels: Res[olutions of the] St[ates of] Holl[and], 20 September 1758, vol. 205, pp. 862, 885. But the landward provinces had the last word. Though they agreed to contribute to this equipment of extra vessels, they failed to find even their small share of the costs: *ibid.*, 24 Aug. 1759, vol. 207, pp. 965–75.

[37] *Politische Correspondenz Friedrichs des Grossen* XIII (Berlin, 1881) 130 ff., 147, 202, 216–18, 228.

[38] The States of Holland agreed these on 22 March, and the States General on the following day: A.R.A., *Res. St. Holl.* vol. 206, p. 481; *ibid.*, *Res[olutien] St[aten] Gen[eraal]*, vol. 3814, p. 213.

[39] *N[ieuw] N[ederlandsch] B[iografisch] W[oordenboek]*, ed. Molhuysen en Blok (Leiden, 1911–37) IX, cols. 80–81; Johan Elias, *De Vroedschap van Amsterdam* (Haarlem, 1905) I, 538 ff.

[40] *N.N.B.W.* I, col. 707. Rotterdam and the Admiralty College of the Maas were violently anti-Orangist at this time, partly because the Princess Gouvernante had lately discharged her major domo, Jan de Back, whose brother was secretary there: *Nederlandse Leeuw* (1907) pp. 89–90; *N.N.B.W.* I, col. 208; H. W. Unger, *De Regeering van Rotterdam* (Rotterdam, 1892) p. 546. Note once again the influence of Dutch domestic politics on Anglo-Netherlands relations.

[41] Elias, *op. cit.*, II, 752–5. Van der Poll was liked and trusted. Yorke and d'Affry applauded his choice as commissioner, and the Amsterdammers were overjoyed: Yorke to Newcastle, 9 March, B.M. Add. MSS. 32888; d'Affry to his court, 22 March, A.A.E., C.P. Hollande, vol. 500. G.A.A., Coll[ectie] Pers[onalia] legkast I.l.376, F.Pol.

at the last moment, Yorke thought because Rotterdam was more interested in the Caribbean trade than were the Amsterdammers.[42] Meerman's appointment was rushed through at the last moment, at a Town Council meeting from which half the members were absent, a very unusual state of affairs, and seemingly at the instance of the Grand Pensionary. Meerman was a director of the insurance company of his home town, but a man it would seem of letters rather than of business when he could follow his own bent.[43] Like his colleagues he had had a legal training and administrative experience. None of the three had diplomatic experience and the choice of these persons, perhaps above all the by-passing of Hendrik Hop, experienced Dutch representative in London,[44] and his even more experienced Huguenot commercial assistant, Palairet, seems to be a yet further indication that the 'negotiation' was not to be regarded very seriously. (Of course neither Hop nor his assistant was at all pleased at being replaced in such a manner and by such inexperienced negotiators.)[45]

Before the commissioners arrived in England the Prize Judges, perhaps rather unexpectedly, reversed the lower court's decision condemning the *Maria Teresia*.[46] The *Maria Teresia* had voyaged from Amsterdam to Cork and from thence to St Eustatius with a cargo of provisions, the bulk though not all of which had been landed there. She had taken on as return cargo West India produce mainly from warehouses at St Eustatius; but she had additionally loaded from a couple of barques in the harbour, one of which was flying Dutch colours, the other being unidentified. The choice of this ship's case, as one which could be decided in favour of the Dutch,

[42] Yorke to Hardwicke, 13 Feb., B.M. Add. MSS. 35357; G.A.R., Res[olutien van de] Vr[oedschap] 85, fos. 63v–66v. A.R.A., H.A., 115 (correspondence between Steyn and Meerman).

[43] *N.N.B.W.* I, col. 1320. Among Meerman's literary and historical interests was concern for the orderly arrangement of the Rotterdam municipal archives.

[44] Hop had been in England since 1723. He was a member of a well-known Amsterdam regent family. *N.N.B.W.* II, col. 602.

[45] Palairet to Steyn, 2 May 1760: A.R.A., Archief Steyn, 25. In this letter Palairet more or less apologizes for 'difficulties' between himself and Boreel, evidently expecting that Boreel, who had just left for the Netherlands, would not bring Steyn a good account of the way Palairet had co-operated with the commissioners. Hop's correspondence with Steyn, previously fairly voluminous, dwindles markedly when the commissioners were appointed.

[46] P.R.O., H[igh] C[ourt of] A[dmiralty] 32/216. Pares deals thoroughly with this case: *op. cit.*, especially pp. 258, 268, 272–4.

may well have been deliberate,[47] and did much to soften opinion in the Netherlands. For the skipper was not asked to prove that all his cargo had been shipped on Dutch account, 'the weight of the evidence being that the said cargo belonged to subjects of the States General'.

The decision on the *Maria Teresia* was naturally unpopular among the English 'hawks', who wanted to take a hard line. But the 'doves' had been alerted by Yorke of the temper of the Rotterdam merchants, who on 5 March had passed no fewer than six inflammatory resolutions, against England's conduct, in favour of a defensive alliance with Denmark, and ordering the recall of all Dutch seamen in foreign service on pain of death.[48] A milder mood in England was clearly prevailing, and one that favoured also the rapid creation of well-defined legal precedent. For the next notable case considered by the Lords of Prize Appeal was that of the *America*,[49] a particularly flagrant example of direct trade to Port au Prince, requirements as to port dues and papers conforming to French practice and of the voiding overboard French passes and correspondence when chased by an English vessel. Any concealment even, much more destruction of papers, if proved in the Admiralty Courts, was held good cause for condemnation of the vessel as well as of the cargo. The choice of this ship is doubly significant. It had become necessary not only to prove to the Dutch that the direct trade to the West Indies would lead to condemnation, but also to the opposition in English government circles that too much was not going to be ceded. The sentence on the *America* caused only a minor revulsion in the Republic. And it served to stifle criticism at home.

We can see such political considerations working also over the bill to restrain the English privateers. This bill was at the committee stage when the three Dutch commissioners arrived in England. It was important that the Appeal Lords should have clear grounds for their decisions since this

[47] A scribbled memorandum in the Newcastle Papers, dated 29 March 1759, 'This ship for the Dutch, the next probably against them', indicates the possible prior choice of the *Maria Teresia* and perhaps also of the *America*, in which appeal against sentence was dismissed: B.M. Add. MSS. 32889, fo. 291.

[48] Yorke to Holdernesse, 6 March (separate), S.P. 84/483. A.R.A., Res. St. Holl. 206, pp. 479, 501–6; cf. Charles R. Boxer, 'Sedentary workers and sea-faring folk in the Dutch Republic', in *Britain and the Netherlands* II, ed. John S. Bromley and Ernst H. Kossmann (Groningen, 1964) pp. 148–68.

[49] P.R.O., H.C.A., 42/53.

was not the moment, or so Hardwicke thought, to consider in court any case which might bring on parliamentary discussion on the activities of the privateers.[50] As in this case the captors were declared to be in the right, no such issue was raised in court, or reflected in debates on the bill in the House.

The Dutch commissioners were furnished with instructions alleged to have been drawn up by the excessively anti-Orangist, francophile fiscal Denick of the Admiralty of the Maas.[51] But it was so clear to Yorke that these were only ostensible, that he did not even trouble to procure himself a copy of them.[52] They had been agreed in an *ad hoc* committee set up for the purpose by the States of Holland and had gone through the appropriate bodies of the States General, before the sentence releasing both ship and cargo of the *Maria Teresia* had become known. The commissioners were officially instructed to insist on the extrajudicial release of all captured Dutch ships before proceeding to negotiate. But there was always room to manoeuvre in Dutch diplomatic instructions; and in spite of Pares's rejection of any such idea,[53] it would be entirely in accordance with Netherlands practice that the commissioners should correspond only in general terms with the Pensionary and a small group of moderates who were advising him from Amsterdam. This was done to keep matters out of the hands of extremists, who were anyhow becoming less and less sure of an overall majority considering the change in political *tempo* after the death of the Princess Anna.

The French ambassador viewed almost with despair what he described as the *faiblesse* of his erstwhile cronies.[54] His lamentations and those of Yorke on the confusions, as they saw it, of Dutch government, coupled with Pares's unfamiliarity with the way the Netherlanders conducted their

[50] B.M. Add MSS. 32889, fo. 272, cf. *ibid.*, 32885, Hardwicke to Newcastle, 22 Oct. and 2 Nov. Their informant was Charles Viry, in touch with opposition personalities; cf. Sir Lewis Namier, *The Structure of Politics at the Accession of George III*, 2nd edition (London, 1961) p. 26.

[51] A.R.A., *Sec. Res. Stat. Holl.* XII, 511–22.

[52] Letters between Yorke and Holdernesse, and Yorke and Hardwicke, in April 1759. S.P. 84/484; B.M. Add. MSS. 35357.

[53] Pares, *Colonial Blockade . . .*, pp. 272–3.

[54] Even in January 1759 the French were beginning to despair of using Dutch services to their own ends. See d'Affry's letters to Choiseul in the first months of 1759: A.A.E., C.P., Hollande, vol. 500.

foreign affairs, have obscured what was really a modest initial triumph for the Dutch; the retention of their right to carry French produce from their own colonies to Europe, provided it could be colourably held to be their own property, as hinted at in the decision over the *Maria Teresia.* This was not, of course, *Free Ships, Free Goods* in all its glory. But if the commissioners had stood fast for this principle in extra-European waters, which the treaty did not vouchsafe them, they could have risked losing it in areas where it did pertain. And as the decision over the *Maria Teresia* gave room to hope, the balance of probability as to ownership might well be weighted on their side. Anyhow as time went on the question became more and more academic, as Moore's Caribbean squadrons began to win over the French; and the French had therefore diminishing need for Dutch shipping services.[55]

The commissioners were received by the king on 17 April, and had their first conference with Holdernesse the following day. They began, on the lines of their official orders, with the formal but derisory claim for extrajudicial release. Then came a demand, equally derisory and not even in accordance with the treaty, for the freedom from search of all Dutch vessels homeward-bound from Dutch settlements (they were not so insistent, it seems, on freedom from search for outward-bound ships). They were prepared for a mutual renunciation of wartime trade by the subjects of the non-belligerent with the colonies of the belligerent's enemy, but tried at first to obtain a most-favoured-nation clause.[56] This tough attitude was discounted by the British ministry as being the fruit of the official orders, from which a retreat would be sounded ere long.[57] Having asked, in a phrase, too much in matters of commerce, it was expected the Dutch commissioners would soon be authorized to render up more than a little.

Things did not, however, move all that fast. Holdernesse's answer to the commissioners was curt; no extrajudicial release, no needed delay over agreement to eschew trade with French settlements, since the trade of the

[55] Guadeloupe and Mariegalante fell in May 1759. Moore was able to convoy British merchantmen home and even for a time to blockade St Eustatius, preventing French produce being conveyed from there to Europe: Sir Julian Corbett, *England in the Seven Years War* (London, 1907) I, 390–2.

[56] Vide Article XI of the Commissioners' instructions: A.R.A., Secr. Res. Stat. Holl., XII, p. 519.

[57] B.M. Add. MSS. 32890, fos. 60, 350.

Dutch with their own colonies had been safeguarded by the decision over the *Maria Teresia.* This the commissioners, inexperienced in diplomacy, regarded as an ultimatum, and reported it as such in despair to the Pensionary by express. Steyn showed their letter to Yorke, before Yorke had received Holdernesse's own account. Therefore Yorke was unable to make effectively to the Pensionary Holdernesse's reasonable point that the right of search still presented very considerable difficulties.[58] Captains of English ships would still have to signal Dutch ships to heave to, and would still have to board to inspect papers if only to establish that the voyage had been to and was from a Dutch settlement. Within a week the commissioners had put in writing their agreement to retaining, in as unobjectionable a form as possible, the right to inspect in wartime the papers of merchantmen on the high seas. For this they were roundly denounced at home by the ardent Republicans.[59] But the Pensionary wanted a settlement, as quickly but also as quietly as possible; and support for the ardent Republicans was gradually falling away. D'Affry really despaired of the Dutch, a sure sign that a pro-Dutch, not a pro-French, line of policy was beginning to prevail in the Republic, in the early summer of 1759.[60]

There were also divisions on the English side, not only, as Pares makes out,[61] between insurers and captors of Dutch ships but also, more acutely than ever, between different groups within the English ministry. Like the Pensionary, Pitt wanted a rapid and uncontroversial settlement. He rightly thought that better control of privateers, with declining opportunities for illicit Dutch trade to French colonies and rapid adjudication of ship cases in the appeal courts, would do the trick, as it undoubtedly did. The lord chancellor and his sons (if we exclude the colonel at The Hague), were all for a strictly legal solution through the courts. The colonel naturally hoped for a negotiated settlement, he to negotiate. Bentinck, the arch-Orangist, still in the summer of 1759 hoped for personal

[58] This difficulty was not overlooked at The Hague: A.R.A., Sec. Res. Stat. Holl., XII, p. 530.

[59] A.R.A., Archief Steyn, Invent. 2, Grand Pensionary to the Commissioners, especially July–September 1759; *ibid.*, Invent. 24, Commissioners and Palairet to the Grand Pensionary, July–September.

[60] d'Affry to Choiseul. May–June 1759, A.A.E., C.P., Hollande, vol. 501; *A.M.O.N.* IV, pp. 73–5.

[61] Pares, *op. cit.*, p. 274.

intervention on the part of all people, of the king and of the Duke of Newcastle.[62]

The commissioners had a further shot at a formal negotiated settlement on 6 June. They produced yet another memorial and counterproject in reply to Holdernesse's dismissal of their opening move of April. In these papers they returned, with a flurry, to the position of January, reiterating once more the demand for extrajudicial release of ships where cases had not yet been heard or settled out of court, and urging yet further safeguards for their own colonial trade.[63] They argued that England had released ships extrajudicially, which was untrue;[64] and they maintained even that the 1674 Treaty applied to extra-European waters, on the grounds that its terms were to be made known to colonial governors. Further, they retreated from their earlier concession that property in the cargo could not be proved without inspection of papers. They seemed ready to surrender the indirect trade on French account, as well as the direct trade to the French islands. But how could property in the cargo be established without inspection of papers, or inspection of papers at sea be denied without agreeing that the ship would have to be taken into harbour? Such contradictory attitudes argue either negotiating naïveté or a desire not to reach a conclusion, especially as by June further decisions in the Appeal Court had gone some way to elucidating these matters, not by any means always against the interests of the Dutch, as Pares has shown.[65]

In thus returning to the form of their official instructions, the commissioners succeeded in wrecking any lingering hopes of a negotiated settlement. The situation bordered on comedy, for Yorke was told by the Pensionary that the commissioners' actions would be disavowed, and informed Holdernesse of this before the commissioners were so informed

[62] *A.M.O.N.* IV, 81–3.

[63] B.M. Add. MSS. 17677, DDDD, Commissioners to Fagel, *sub dato.*

[64] Some Dutch ships homeward-bound from Surinam had been released by the British government but only on payment of costs and with the consequent agreement of the captors. A Rotterdammer taken within Dutch territorial waters had also been released when the captain of the man-of-war whose prize she had become was pressured into relinquishing her. But neither of these was strictly extrajudicial.

[65] As in the case of the *Novum Aratrum*: Pares, *op. cit.*, pp. 215–17. This took a long time to settle, with a consequent grievance to the respective owners of ship and cargo.

by the Pensionary—with consequent confusion all round.[66] After such an unpleasant experience, the commissioners retired from 'active' negotiation, attending instead such occasions as a formal meeting of the heads of Oxford colleges to install a Chancellor, described by Palairet as the most pompous and absurd ceremony in the world.[67] Boreel spent some of his time in advising owners or their agents when an appeal case was pending. But he was less well informed on whom to brief than was Palairet, who had been long resident in London and was a faithful attendant at the courts, which the commissioners, if we can believe Palairet, were not.

What really caused this stop in the commissioners' proceedings? Besides political uncertainties in both countries, and an understandable fear in the Netherlands that a negotiated settlement would leave their merchants worse off than before, the events of the year 1759 undoubtedly made such a settlement more difficult than ever. The changing balance of power in the West Indies, rendering the French islands' trade less attractive to the Dutch, has already been surveyed. But on the Dutch side there also developed a further threat to their neutrality, posed by the French who wished to send actual munitions of war, purchased from Sweden, via Amsterdam and Southern Netherlands waterways to be stockpiled in French dockyards.[68] By the autumn of 1759 only eight or so Dutch ships still awaited adjudication in the English Admiralty Courts.[69] One of these was particularly damaging to the Netherlands cause because her papers clearly revealed fraud on the part of the Governor of St Eustatius.[70] So that although by then the two remaining commissioners[71] were living like lords according to Palairet and had been joined by their wives and families,[72] they were glad to complete their business. Boreel was the last

[66] Holdernesse to Yorke, 19 June, Yorke to Holdernesse, 26 June: S.P. 84/484; Newcastle to Yorke, 29 June: *A.M.O.N.* IV, 96–101; Commissioners to Fagel, 19 June: B.M. Add. MSS. 17677, DDDD.

[67] Palairet to Steyn, 3 July, A.R.A., Archief Steyn, Invent. 24.

[68] Carter, *loc. cit.*, p. 216, fn. 10 above.

[69] Bentinck's notes of a conversation with Yorke, 27 Dec. 1759, *A.M.O.N.* IV, 215.

[70] This was *de Snip,* or *Snep*: P.R.O., H.C.A., 42/96. See also Boreel to Fagel, 28 March 1760 (copy), which states the law of the war of '56 in connection with this case. A.R.A., Archief Steyn, 25.

[71] Meerman returned to his post as Pensionary in Rotterdam in October: Boreel to Steyn, 9 October: A.R.A., Archief Steyn, Invent. 24. Meerman's commission as Pensionary to the Rotterdam Vroedschap had been renewed for five years in November 1758: G.A.R., Vr. Res. No. 84, fo. 91v.

[72] Palairet to Steyn, 3 July, 9 October 1759: A.R.A., Archief Steyn, Invent. 24.

to go, sailing in style from Greenwich in a royal yacht on 2 May 1760.[73] The famous so-called law of the war of '56 had at length been clearly stated, in judgments on the ships *Vriendschap*, *Resolutie*, and *Amstel*. The situation with regard to the French colonial trade was at length both stated and underlined.[74]

On the English side until the French defeat at Quiberon Bay some anxiety about a Jacobite invasion, with consequent falls in English debt stock prices, caused fears about the raising of supplies for 1760.[75] The Dutch in their turn feared a new demand, consequent on rumours of invasion, to fulfil the terms of the Treaty of 1678. Should the six thousand troops due to England under this long-ago treaty be again requisitioned, and again refused, the Treaty of 1674, with its *Free Ships, Free Goods* principle still viable in European waters, would be in greater danger than before.[76] If the troops should be sent, in order to obviate danger to the Treaty of 1674, the Republic would be open once more, to the new ally, Austria, of the old enemy, France. With this French ally, the Republic now had a common frontier, equivalent almost to the common frontier with France that the whole former Barrier policy had been designed to obviate. And there no longer existed an adult member of the House of Orange to 'save' the Republic, as William IV had been called on to 'save' her in 1747. Substitutes, the German Prince Louis of Brunswick-Wolfenbuttel,[77] the inactive officebound bureacrat Fagel, the pacifist Steyn, least of all the obsessed anglophile Bentinck van Rhoon, would none of them command support enough in the Republic to be able to govern, even in a manifest emergency. A combination of English and Dutch alarms, with clarifications in respect of permitted trade though the English Admiralty courts, put an end to the charade of these so-called negotiations on the

[73] Palairet to Steyn, 2 May 1760: *ibid.*, Invent. 25.

[74] Palairet to Steyn, 25 March 1760: *ibid.* Boreel stated this 'law', that a trade reserved to nationals in time of peace could not be carried on by neutrals without interference from belligerents, whatever treaty rights were enjoyed, in a letter to Fagel on 28 March 1760; copy *ibid.*

[75] Alice Carter, *The English Public Debt in the Eighteenth Century* (Historical Association, London, 1968) pp. 23–4.

[76] Cf. Steyn to the Commissioners, 16 October 1758: A.R.A., Archief Steyn. Invent. 2.

[77] Prince Louis had been brought into Dutch from Austrian service in 1751 to reform the Netherlands army: Bootsma, *Hertog van Brunswijk*, pp. 12 ff. Cf. Pieter Geyl, *Willem IV en Engeland tot 1748* (The Hague, 1926) p. 36.

terms of the Treaty of 1674. Trade disputes ceased for a time to bedevil Anglo-Dutch friendship, and Anglo-Dutch treaties the trade of Dutch merchants. Henceforth the Republic could enjoy and profit[78] by its neutrality, untrammelled by the actions of the warring powers.

[78] Johannes de Vries, *De economische achteruitgang der Republiek in der achttiende eeuw* (Amsterdam, 1959). The author prints fifteen graphs of yields from taxes, and of numbers of outward-bound and of home-coming ships based on port dues and other particulars (section 2 pp. 1–12). These show upward trends towards the end of the Seven Years' War. It is difficult to reject Professor van Dillen's conclusion, though it has been contested, that the Seven Years' War presented opportunities for profit to the neutral Netherlands: 'De Beurscrisis te Amsterdam in 1763', *Tijdschrift voor Geschiedenis* XXXVII (1922). Price material from Nicolaas W. Posthumus, *Nederlandse Prysgeschiedenis I* (Brill, 1943) shows increases which reflect scarcities, suggesting increased exports or other pressures on domestic resources.

13

MICHAEL ROBERTS

Great Britain, Denmark and Russia, 1763–1770

I

It is perhaps understandable that the history of Anglo-Danish relations in the eighteenth century should remain a bypath not much frequented by English historians. Nevertheless it presents, in the closing years of the ministry of J. H. E. Bernstorff, some features of general interest, and sheds some light on the wider problems of British foreign policy in a comparatively unexplored period. It reveals the real difficulties and dilemmas with which successive secretaries of state were confronted in the postwar Europe of the sixties. And it illustrates with painful clarity the obsessive thinking, the uncritical acceptance of inherited assumptions, the parochialism and mental inelasticity which vitiated British statesmanship in the years after the peace of Paris.

After 1763 ministers were in search of a 'system'. The 'Old System', based on alliance with Austria and the Dutch, was dead, and no amount of nostalgia could revive it; the new system, based on the Prussian alliance, had been shattered by Bute's peace. Failing either of these, the only road to security against Choiseul's plans for revenge seemed to lie in collaboration with Russia. A Northern League, resting on the foundation of an Anglo-Russian alliance, had both real and speculative advantages: it translated into political terms those strong economic ties which not even the Seven Years War had been able to sever, and which led many Englishmen to think of Russia as a 'natural' ally; it might serve to attract the Scandinavian powers, and so wean them from dependence on France; and it was expected to pave the way for the much-desired reconciliation with Prussia. It was with prospects such as these in view that British diplomacy in the mid-sixties became unwontedly active in Stockholm and in Copenhagen.

In the 1720s and early 1730s Anglo-Danish relations had been cordial. But the breakdown of the Anglo-French *entente* after 1731 eventually forced Denmark, as it also forced Sweden, to choose between a French and a British system. In 1742 Denmark finally turned to France, and on 15 March 1742 concluded with that country a treaty of alliance: it was renewed in 1749, and again in 1754. Popular feeling in Denmark remained stubbornly anglophile;[1] and Denmark had at least one common interest with Britain, in that both were concerned to keep foreign armies out of Hanover; but still it was true that in 1763 Denmark had for twenty years been reckoned by British ministers as a French puppet, bound to the court of Versailles by indispensable subsidies, a state whose system was 'trifling', and whose subordination to France partook of servility.

This attitude, though intelligible, was based on a misconception of the motives behind Danish policy and of the nature of Denmark's relations with France. Despite the French minister's ascendancy in Copenhagen, despite Choiseul's rather condescending attitude to his Danish client, the French did not find their ally servile. The paid dear in guarantees and subsidies for Denmark's fidelity, and in return they gained advantages which at best were negative. The alliance ensured that the small but respectable Danish navy should not be at Britain's disposal; and France could feel that Denmark protected the rear of Sweden, who was the real linch-pin of the French system in the North. Denmark's essential rôle, as seen from Paris, was to be passive, to be benevolently neutral, and to be prepared to defend her neutrality: in short, she was to be paid for doing what it was in any case her interest to do. In the jargon of the day, Sweden was to be the 'active' power, Denmark the 'inactive'. For Denmark, on the other hand, the connection brought some solid benefits, without (as a rule) any very onerous burdens. Thus Bernstorff, who had been directing Danish policy since 1751, declined to be involved in the Seven Years War, despite the fact that Danish shipping suffered much from the outrages of British privateers, the operation of the 'Rule of 1756', and the costly delays of the Admiralty Courts: though Denmark concurred with Russia and Sweden in forming an armed neutrality to protect her marine, Bernstorff

[1] S.P. 75/118 fos. 287–9, Titley to Sandwich, 21 Dec. 1765.

took great pains to avoid provocative anti-British measures.[2] It was true that he was a close personal friend of Choiseul. It was also true that he was of Hanoverian origin, and had at one time considered entering the service of the Prince of Wales. But neither circumstance was allowed to affect his policy; though Britain and France each suspected that at heart he was the friend of the other.

The truth was that his policy was neither pro-French nor pro-British: it was pro-Danish.[3] Bernstorff was among the most remarkable of that large contingent of eighteenth-century statesmen who, entering the service of a foreign country, devoted themselves absolutely to the interests of their employer. He looked on Britain and British policy with detachment, complaining at times that ministers in London were prone to equate the interests of their own country with those of Europe. Yet he regarded a strong Britain as necessary for the preservation of the European balance; and he had no intention of allowing France to become the arbiter of Denmark's destiny.[4] But as long as French ministers behaved with moderation and restraint, as long as the French system could be made to serve Denmark's purpose, Bernstorff was content to stick to it.[5] His foreign policy was directed to three main objectives: to preserve peace in the North; to maintain the constitution of 1720 in Sweden and block any attempt to enlarge the powers of the Swedish monarchy; and to conclude, with other members of the house of Oldenburg, an agreement for the exchange of ducal Holstein for Oldenburg and Delmenhorst.

Since the middle of the sixteenth century the house of Oldenburg had

[2] *Riksrådet Anders Johan von Höpkens Skrifter* (Stockholm, 1890) II, 368; *Correspondance entre le comte Johan Hartvig Ernst Bernstorff et le duc de Choiseul, 1758–1766* (Copenhagen, 1871) pp. 62–3; E. de Barthélémy, *Histoire des Relations de la France et du Danemarck sous le Ministère du Comte Bernstorff* (Copenhagen, 1887) p. 127. For the neutrality convention, *Danske Tractater 1751–1800* (Copenhagen, 1882) pp. 172–180. For the exorbitancies of the Admiralty Courts, and Danish complaints, see B.M. Add. MSS. 35425, fo. 140, Sir John Goodricke to Lord Royston, 25 March 1759.

[3] For Bernstorff's foreign policy in general see P. Vedel, *Det ældre Grev Bernstorff Ministerium* (Copenhagen, 1882); E. Holm, *Danmark-Norges Historie fra den store nordiske Krigs Slutning til Rigernes Adskillelse*, (*1891–1912*) III; Jørgen Schoubye, 'J. H. E. Bernstorffs udenrigspolitikk i dansk historisk forskning', *Historisk Tidsskrift*, XII Series, I (1966).

[4] For his attitude to Britain, see Friis, II, 190, Vedel, pp. 25–6; for his independence of France, *Correspondance ministérielle du Comte J. H. E. Bernstorff, 1751–1770*, ed. P. Vedel II (Copenhagen, 1882) 105.

[5] *Bernstorff-Choiseul Corr.*, p. 141.

been divided: a senior line sat upon the throne of Denmark; a number of cadet branches were established in various north German territories, of which the most important was the duchy of Holstein-Gottorp. In the latter half of the seventeenth century the political and dynastic connections of the dukes of Holstein-Gottorp with the crown of Sweden had exposed Denmark to the danger of simultaneous attacks in front and rear. That danger had indeed been removed by the collapse of the Swedish empire, and the failure of Charles Frederick of Holstein to secure the succession to Sweden on the death of Charles XII. But it had very soon been succeeded by another, more formidable still, as a result of Charles Frederick's marriage to a daughter of Peter the Great. Successive Russian sovereigns now embraced the cause of Holstein; a Holstein prince, Adolf Frederick, was placed on the Swedish throne as the result of Russian insistence; and Charles Frederick's son was designated by the Tsaritsa Elizabeth as her heir. A permanent settlement of the dynastic feud within the house of Oldenburg had thus become vital to Denmark's security; and the least costly and most promising method of achieving that end seemed to be the surrender of the outlying lands of Oldenburg and Delmenhorst in return for Holstein-Gottorp—a project which it will be convenient to refer to henceforward by its Danish name of *Mageskiftet*.

Denmark's anxiety to maintain the Swedish constitution of 1720, as amended in 1756, was derived from memories of the exploits of Charles X and Charles XII: it was based on a fear that if the Swedish monarchy ever freed itself from constitutional checks it might turn again to an aggressive foreign policy of which Denmark would be the first victim. No doubt it was a fear which rested on an exaggerated estimate of the actual and potential military strength of Sweden at this time; but however that may be, it led Danish statesmen to interfere in Swedish domestic politics. In the perennial Swedish party dog-fight Denmark supported the ruling party of the Hats: naturally so, for the Hats had in 1756 imposed upon the monarchy both personal humiliation and an abridgment of the prerogative. They were the watch-dogs of the constitution. They were also the friends and pensioners of France, who for nearly twenty years had kept Sweden a member of the French system. The preservation of Swedish liberty, moreover, was also a Danish interest in that it had a bearing on the plan for *Mageskiftet*; for in 1750 Adolf Frederick had renounced his claims upon Holstein, and Bernstorff feared that if he were to make himself absolute he would use his freedom from parliamentary control to revive them.

Such, then, were the main objectives of Bernstorff's foreign policy. In pursuit of them he could on occasion manifest a certain flexibility; but the objectives themselves remained essentially unchanged. It was a policy prudent, but also courageous; a policy which attempted to confront real dangers by measures appropriate to the resources at his disposal. If it pleased him at times to dress it up in the trappings of high idealism and general principles, it was always a policy based on Danish interests. The slightly smug piety of his private life tended, no doubt, to colour his official communications; but that did not alter the fact that where his adopted country was concerned he had a sharp eye to the main chance.

At the beginning of the sixties, however, it seemed that he had disastrously miscalculated. In 1762 the death of the tsaritsa placed the Holstein claimant on the Russian throne, in the person of Peter III. He had always been inaccessible to negotiation on the Holstein question; and within a few months of his accession Denmark found herself threatened by a Russian onslaught, cynically backed by Frederick the Great, with no prospect of aid from any quarter. Bernstorff's attempts to induce the powers to treat *Mageskiftet* as a matter of general European concern had no success.[6] Choiseul did not lift a finger to help; he even refused to pay six millions of arrears of subsidy which Denmark desperately needed for defence.[7] At the last moment Denmark was saved, not by her French ally, but by Peter's deposition. And Bernstorff emerged from the crisis profoundly disillusioned with Choiseul.

Hard on the heels of France's desertion of Denmark came disquieting indications that the French court might be considering a change of course in Sweden. If Bernstorff was disenchanted with Choiseul, Choiseul was equally disenchanted with Bernstorff's friends the Hats. Sweden's military performances during the Seven Years War had been deplorable; and her clamour for subsidies had not been matched by a punctual discharge of her obligations. To Choiseul there seemed little point in continuing to pour

[6] *Bernstorff-Choiseul Corr.*, pp. 26–7, 101, 116, 137–47, 182; [P. Vedel] 'Grev v.d. Ostens Gesandtskaber', *Historisk Tidsskrift*, IV Series, I (1869–70); *Souvenirs de Charles Henri Baron de Gleichen* (Paris, 1868), p. xxviii; Barthélémy, pp. 172–9.

[7] *Bernstorff-Choiseul Corr.*, p. 227 n. 1; *Corr. ministérielle* II, 62, 74, 83; Barthélémy, pp. 241–4.

out money into the pocket of an ally who could not or would not do what was expected of her. Thus in the closing stages of the war, and in the first years of the peace, French ministers began to wonder whether after all the best policy in Sweden might not be to support a curtailment of 'liberty' and an increase in royal power, as being the most hopeful means of ensuring that France's supposedly 'active' ally in the North should be efficient as well as expensive.[8] As yet this evolution of French policy was only beginning to be debated; but it would soon manifest itself in a reluctance to pay arrears of subsidy, and in 1766 it would be complete. It was matched by internal developments in Sweden, where the Hats were in disarray, discredited by the ignominy of the war, and in danger of defeat: a state of affairs which made their leaders welcome the good offices of the Queen in arranging a party truce, and led them to promise moderate concessions to the crown. Thus from Bernstorff's point of view neither the Hats nor the French were any longer sound on one of the fundamental points of his programme. Moreover, in the autumn of 1763 came an important change in the policy of Russia. Catherine upon her accession had at once called off the Holstein war; she was not inaccessible to the idea of *Mageskiftet*; and she was not prepared to commit herself unequivocally to the support of the prerogative in Sweden.[9] On the other hand, she felt that the example of 1757 had shown that aggressive and irresponsible action in the field of foreign policy was as much to be feared from the Swedish senate as from the Swedish monarchy. Her object therefore gradually defined itself as the restoration of the constitution of 1720 in its original form, shorn of later king-yoking amendments. This would provide a system of checks and balances adequate to insure Russia against a sudden attack either by an all-powerful ministry or by an absolute king. It was with this idea in mind that she invited Denmark, in December 1763, to concert with her a common line in Stockholm, including a guarantee of the constitution of 1720. After some hesitation, Bernstorff accepted this proposal.[10] The reorientation of Danish policy was completed by the signature, on 11 March 1765, of a Russo-Danish treaty of

[8] For all this, see Olof Jägerskiöld, *Hovet och författningsfrågan 1760–1766* (Uppsala, 1943) *passim*.

[9] *Udvalgte Breve, Betænkninger og Optegnelser af J. O. Schack-Rathlous Arkiv* (Copenhagen, 1936) p. 271.

[10] *Sbornik* [*imperatorskogo russkago istoricheskogo obshchestva*] LI, 49, 494; 'Ostens Gesandtskaber', pp. 564–6; *Corr. ministérielle* II, 158 fn. 3.

mutual aid and guarantee, to last for eight years. The treaty included three secret articles, two of them of great importance: one promised an early opening of negotiations on *Mageskiftet*; the other pledged each party to common action in Sweden to preserve the constitution of 1720, and bound them never to permit the Swedish branch of the house of Oldenburg to succeed to ducal Holstein.[11]

But if Denmark had thus become Russia's ally, Bernstorff hoped to avoid becoming Russia's satellite.[12] He desired the tranquillity and independence of all the nations of the North; and he had no idea of making himself the accomplice of Russian aggression, least of all in Sweden.[13] Moreover, in accepting the friendship of Russia he did not at first conceive himself to be necessarily forfeiting that of France, or to be deserting his old Hat friends in Stockholm. He took care to inform them of the progress of his negotiations with the tsaritsa;[14] and in the summer of 1764 he made it clear that he was ready to renew the French alliance (it had expired in March) provided France were willing to renew her subsidies: he would be glad, he wrote, to forget France's desertion, and the tardiness of French remittances, if only he could be sure of her attitude in Sweden; and in any case he was not prepared to engage in recriminations.[15] The French could not feel so magnanimous. They saw in Denmark a renegade, and a renegade who had allied herself to the chief opponent of French policies both in Stockholm and in Warsaw. To such a power they could certainly not be expected to pay subsidies; nor even, perhaps, outstanding arrears.

II

The swing of Danish foreign policy from France to Russia presented British ministers with an opportunity to re-establish British influence in

[11] *Danske Tractater*, pp. 183–202.

[12] *Corr. ministérielle* II, 195; Friis, *op. cit.*, II, 178.

[13] Denmark, he wrote, 'ne regarderoit . . . jamais avec indifférence qu'aucune puissance, quelle qu'elle puisse être, sans en excepter aucune sur la terre, voulût envahir hostilement la Suède et la mettre sous sa dépendance': *Corr. ministérielle* II, 223.

[14] 'Ostens Gesandtskaber', p. 618. Panin was complaining of this as early as 24 Feb. (o.s.) 1764: *Sbornik* LI, 220–1.

[15] *Corr. ministérielle* II, 175–6, 177–8. As he wrote to Choiseul, 14 Jan. 1759, 'il n'y a que la France seule qui puisse le [Frederick V] détacher de la France': *Bernstorff-Choiseul Corr.*, p. 14.

Copenhagen; since what was bad for France must, by an axiom of politics which it never occurred to them to question, be good for Britain. The chances of exploiting this potentially favourable situation depended, however, on whether any inducement could be offered to Denmark which it was worth her while to accept; for a connection with Britain was much more directly provocative of France than a treaty with Russia. Something, too, would turn on personalities. On Danish personalities, since Denmark was an absolutism run by a council of state for a more or less *fainéant* monarch, and would soon be in the hands of a schizophrenic prince and his unscrupulous or irresponsible favourites. On British personalities, because much would depend upon the skill and judgment of our minister in Copenhagen. But, as it happened, the Copenhagen legation during this period provided no very favourable picture of the diplomatic service. In 1763 the minister was Walter Titley, who had been appointed Resident as long ago as 1728. He was now old, cynical, and gouty; anxious to disburden himself of the drudgery of the office, and not given to avoidable initiatives. From 1764 to 1765, it is true, he had the assistance of a Resident, in the person of Dudley Cosby; but though Cosby had some intelligence and a desire to be active, he was effectively disabled by a mental breakdown in December 1764. His successor as Resident, and subsequently (on Titley's death in 1768) as minister, was another novice, Robert Gunning: a man who was certainly able, as his subsequent career in Russia was to make clear, but diffident, touchy, obstinate in his opinions, and given to gloom: Osten once referred to his 'spleeny constitution'.[16] Titley still wrote some of the dispatches, and secretaries of state addressed themselves sometimes to Titley, sometimes to Gunning, occasionally to both. But in general the situation, as Gunning complained, was that in summer Titley went off to the country, and in winter he was incapacitated by gout.[17] And this was the more unfortunate, since Gunning soon developed erroneous notions about Danish politics and politicians which became a real obstacle to any Anglo-Danish *rapprochement*.

If British diplomats in Copenhagen did little to improve relations, their chiefs in London can scarcely be said to have compensated for their

[16] P.R.O., N. Ireland, Macartney Papers (DOD 572) II, no. 40: O[sten] to Macartney, 25 Sept. 1771.

[17] H.M.C., *Weston-Underwood*, p. 400, Gunning to Weston, 12 April 1766; P.R.O., N. Ireland, Macartney Photocopies, T. 2513, Gunning to Macartney, 2 August 1766.

deficiencies. Between September 1763 and September 1770 five Northern Secretaries—Sandwich, Grafton, Conway, Weymouth, Rochford—were responsible for Britain's dealings with Denmark. Their attitudes show some personal and temperamental differences, but basically they were remarkably similar in that not one of them (unless perhaps Lord Rochford) ever really grasped the realities of Danish domestic politics, or the motives which inspired Danish statesmanship. Lord Sandwich, certainly, saw the situation in simple terms of black and white. For him Denmark was a power which need scarcely be taken into account, the tool of French designs, the gull of French artfulness, the needy pensioner. But if he made no effort to understand Bernstorff's policy, it was not for want of information: from Sir John Goodricke in Stockholm, and later from Cosby, he received analyses which he might well have taken *ad notam*.[18] It seems that Sandwich had made up his mind that Denmark must subordinate all other considerations, and postpone all other interests, to the paramount necessity of inducing France to continue the payment of subsidies: it was an error which he shared with Frederick the Great.[19] He was indeed prepared for a dynastic connection in the old style, and there was no difficulty about giving assent to the engagement of Princess Caroline Matilda to the Crown Prince Christian. But his only real interest in Denmark was in the state of her fleet; and though Cosby made a favourable report on it, Sandwich declined to be impressed.[20] As to Bernstorff's views on the Swedish constitution, he considered them to be of only marginal interest, and he had little patience with a minister in Copenhagen who allowed himself to be concerned with such things.

It was an attitude which illustrated one of the weaknesses of British diplomacy in this period. Though ministers abroad were indeed always instructed to correspond with one another, the instructions with which they were sent out were usually confined strictly to the business likely to arise at their place of residence, and they were given little or no guidance upon the broad principles of British foreign policy, or the state of our relations with other European powers; and this was true even in regard to states whose politics were most closely linked with those of the country

[18] S.P. 75/117 fos. 197–201, Cosby to Sandwich, 16 Oct. 1764; S.P. 95/104 fos. 42–3, Goodricke to Sandwich, 10 April 1764.

[19] *Pol*[*itisches*] *Corr*[*espondenz Friedrichs des Grossen*] XXIV, 9, 180 n. 1.

[20] S.P. 75/117 fos. 227–9, 230–1; 118, fos. 68–79.

where they were to reside. Macartney was sent to Russia without any information about British policy in Sweden, and when he asked for it was informed by Sandwich that no addition to his instructions was deemed necessary.[21] The contrast with the elaborate instructions provided by France, and even by Russia, was striking;[22] and it was not to our advantage. It is of course true that Sandwich was not blind to the interaction of Swedish and Danish politics; but he did not take kindly to suggestions based on a recognition of the fact that it existed. When Panin produced a plan for Anglo-Russian collaboration in Stockholm and Copenhagen, with the idea of making Sweden the 'inactive', and Denmark the 'active', power in the North, Sandwich curtly turned it down: partly because it had been thrust upon him without prior consultation; partly because he feared that it might be a trick to leave England with the main burden of expense for Swedish corruption (in which, as it happened, he was entirely mistaken); but partly also because he did not trust Denmark to continue 'active' on the right side.[23] There were, to be sure, some grounds for Sandwich's prejudice against Denmark. In one aspect it was the inevitable result of Bernstorff's delicate balancing between France and Russia, which had led him to keep France and the Hats informed of his negotiations with Panin. To Sandwich this appeared to be mere duplicity. Yet he might have reflected that Bernstorff could hardly afford an open breach with France until he was certain of his treaty with Russia; and he ought to have been reassured by the panic created in Hat circles by the news of the Russian negotiation.[24] Once the Russian alliance was actually concluded, however, it might have been expected that British suspicions of Denmark would be allayed; but before that had a chance to happen they were revived

[21] S.P. 91/75, fos. 59, 75–7. As late as 1/16 Nov. 1765 he complained to Grafton of being 'entirely in the dark as to what system His Majesty intends to observe with regard to other Courts': *ibid.*, 76, fo. 331. Cf. a similar complaint by Henry Grenville at Constantinople, 16 March 1765: Frank Spencer, *The Fourth Earl of Sandwich. Diplomatic Correspondence 1763–1765* (Manchester, 1961) p. 64 n. 3.

[22] See, e.g., the instruction for Filosofov on his appointment to Copenhagen in July 1766, in *Sbornik*, LXVII, 20.

[23] S.P. 95/106, fos. 13–15, 100–3; S.P. 91/75, fos. 75–7. Panin, for his part, regarded it as 'too obvious in its value to need comment': *Sbornik* LXVII, 162.

[24] S.P. 95/105, fos. 208–11, Breteuil to Praslin, 16 Nov. 1764 (intercept) in Sandwich to Goodricke, Separate and Most Secret, 14 Dec. 1764; cf. R.A. Stockholm, Tengberg Avskr. Danska ministrarnas i Stockholm depescher, Schack to Bernstorff, 30 Oct. 1764.

in full force by the unfortunate affair of the Hat senators. The Caps, triumphant in the Diet of 1765, were determined to attack the still-subsisting Hat senate, and threatened proceedings against some of its leaders. Three of them—C. F. Scheffer, Hamilton, Ekeblad—were old and tried friends of Denmark, and Bernstorff, with characteristic chivalry, determined to support French efforts to secure them an honourable retirement.[25] He therefore agreed to contribute 400,000 copper *daler* to the French corruption chest in Stockholm, to be used solely for buying votes on this issue. The British government got wind of this, and lost no time in passing on the information to Panin. Panin, naturally enough, was furious;[26] and Bernstorff succeeded in appeasing him only by paying Russia 50,000 roubles (which were promptly forwarded to Stockholm to reinforce the Caps' party funds) and by promising that he would not do it again.[27] In St Petersburg the affair was thus smoothed over; but the impression it produced was not so easily effaced in London.

By the autumn of 1765, however, some improvement in Anglo-Danish relations began to appear likely in the relatively near future. It was now scarcely possible to doubt that Denmark was committed to Russia; though Choiseul (who shared the British habit of viewing politics in terms of Anglo-French rivalry) considered that, by the mere fact of being lost to France, Denmark had become attached to Britain.[28] Frederick V of Denmark was now obviously near the end of his life (he was to die on 14 January 1766), and his death might well lead to changes. The Crown Prince Christian, soon to become Christian VII, was engaged to a British princess; he was anxious to improve the army, and would probably hope to do so with British money; and his attitude to Bernstorff was uncertain. Of this Bernstorff himself was well aware; and the possibility of an early dismissal was perhaps one of the considerations which pricked him to fresh efforts to complete *Mageskiftet* as soon as possible. In England, too, the situation had altered. With the coming of the Rockinghams to power in July 1765 Grafton had replaced Sandwich as Northern Secretary; and despite his youth and inexperience foreign observers were disposed to

[25] *Corr. ministérielle*, II, 215–18, 223, 230–4, 242–3.

[26] *Sbornik*, LXVII, 373, 409; S.P. 95/107, fos. 47–8, 54–5, 155–6, 190–1; S.P. 75/118, fos. 236–7.

[27] *Sbornik*, LXVII, 432; S.P. 91/66, fo. 7.

[28] *Mémoires du Duc de Choiseul*, ed. F. Calmettes (Paris, 1904) pp. 390–1.

hope that the change would mean a less insular attitude to the concerns of Europe.[29] In regard to Denmark, at all events, it appeared that these hopes might be justified; for on 12 November 1765—stirred to action, perhaps, by the news of Frederick V's breaking health—Grafton sent to Titley the first major policy dispatch to be received by that minister for some years.[30] It is true that it went no further than to order him to use every effort to strengthen the new connection between Denmark and Russia; but at least it was a recognition of the fact that Britain could no longer be wholly indifferent to what Denmark was doing.

It was followed by other signs of a thaw in Anglo-Danish relations. In Copenhagen, the accession of Christian VII moved old Titley to an unwonted spurt of initiative: on 21 January 1766 he urged Grafton to offer a subsidy-treaty in return for a Danish contingent in the event of war.[31] But this was to misunderstand the motives which lay behind Grafton's tentative approaches. Grafton had no idea of concluding an old-fashioned, Newcastle-style, troop-hiring treaty: he was interested in Denmark primarily as a factor in Britain's relations with Russia. In St Petersburg, Macartney had recently put his signature to a new commercial treaty, and the British government might hope that when it was ratified the way would be clear for the resumption of the large question of an Anglo-Russian alliance which would lay the foundations for the much-desired 'System of the North', and to which it was reasonable to suppose that Denmark would ultimately accede. But in the meantime Denmark might be more immediately useful as a lubricant. For Macartney's signature of the commercial treaty, far from making all smooth, had produced serious friction between the two courts. The Rockingham administration, rightly or wrongly, felt that the treaty could not possibly be ratified as it stood. They had invincible objections to a sentence in art. 4, which reserved to Russia, 'in reciprocity for the Navigation Act', the right to make such regulations for her shipping as the empress might think appropriate. It was in an effort to break the deadlock on this article that Grafton on 24 December 1765 ordered Macartney to inform Panin that Britain was 'in no ways averse to enter into a Negotiation of Alliance with the Court

[29] See, e.g. R.A. Stockholm, Diplomatica, Anglica: Nolcken to K.P., 26 July 1765; *Sbornik*, LXVII, 432, Panin to Osterman, 6 Jan. [O.S.] 1766.

[30] S.P. 75/118, fos. 261–3.

[31] S.P. 75/119, fos. 33–5; cf. *ibid.* 118, fos. 287–9.

of Denmark'—*provided* that Russia in return would agree to removing the obnoxious reservation in art. 4.[32]

It was an interesting proposal, if only because it embodied in concise form many of the delusions and errors of British foreign policy in the sixties. It would have given Denmark few advantages, for it did not offer a subsidy, while in a military point of view Denmark must obviously look to Russia rather than to Britain for protection; it might well have involved Bernstorff in commitments to defend Hanover; it assumed that alliance with Britain required no bait in order to make it, by some ineluctable logic, a desirable object to any continental power. In regard to Russia the suggestion was redolent of all those calm assumptions and arrogant attitudes which Panin found most distasteful in British statesmanship: it reflected British parsimony in the matter of subsidies; it advanced a claim to Russian gratitude for doing what (in Russian eyes) it was in any case Britain's interest to do; it ignored the fact that in so far as the influence of France at Copenhagen had been destroyed (the professed objective of British policy in Denmark)[33] that result had been attained wholly by Russian, and not at all by British, action; it gave Russia no advantages in return for a Russian concession; and the concession it demanded was of the most offensive kind, since the abandonment of art. 4 involved possible prejudice to Russia's economic interests together with a real denial of Russia's claim to equality of international status, which was a matter of prestige more important to Catherine than any commercial consideration. And finally, whatever the merits or demerits of the idea, it was a proposal of more than dubious sincerity. Macartney was permitted to give 'the fairest general professions'; but he was plainly told that he must avoid any firm commitment. An Anglo-Danish alliance was to be dangled as a bribe to Panin; but once the commercial treaty was safely concluded according to British ideas, Grafton would pay, or decline to pay, as best might suit his book.

Nevertheless, despite this ominous beginning, the idea of a closer connection with Denmark continued to engage the attention of ministers at

[32] S.P. 91/76, fo. 353, Grafton to Macartney, 24 Dec. 1765.

[33] 'The first and main Object of His Majesty's Aim in all the Northern Courts must be the entire Overthrow of the French System; and from whatever Motive Russia may act, she so far effectually promotes the Interest of Great Britain': S.P. 75/119, fo. 418, Conway to Gunning, 19 Dec. 1766.

home and diplomats abroad. In St Petersburg the Danish minister von der Asseburg from time to time made encouraging signals to the ever-zealous Macartney;[34] in Copenhagen Christian VII, in a private audience kept secret from his ministers, sounded Titley on the possibility of an alliance, offensive as well as defensive, to be gilded by British subsidies.[35] Conway, who had no taste for offensive alliances, politely evaded this proposal;[36] but Christian did not relinquish the idea. He wanted British money, certainly; but he wanted even more, perhaps, to show that he was master in his own house by striking out his own line in foreign policy, even though by doing so he should compromise Bernstorff's plans for bringing off *Mageskiftet*. Bernstorff, for his part, was not prepared to enter into a commitment with Britain until he had *Mageskiftet* in his pocket. And as yet the negotiations for the exchange had not begun. They were waiting for the arrival of Catherine's negotiator, the Holsteiner Caspar von Saldern: in fact they did not start until 30 December 1766. But this did not prevent the British ministers from entangling *Mageskiftet* in the conversations about a possible alliance. In September Conway threw out a suggestion that Britain might offer her good offices in the Holstein question, instead of paying Denmark a subsidy.[37] It was not a proposal which was likely to appeal to Bernstorff, who rightly believed that his negotiations with Saldern had a better chance of success if they were kept confidential, and was justifiably confident of his ability to conduct them without British assistance. Nor was it calculated to commend itself to Saldern and Panin, who would have looked upon it as an attempt to cover up British meanness by meddling in a matter which did not concern us.[38] But if Conway's offer of good offices was ill-considered, it was no worse than the zareba of misunderstandings produced by Titley's and Gunning's suggestion that we might evade a subsidy by offering a *guarantee* of the exchange.[39] Conway could not possibly underwrite in advance a settlement as yet unmade, and outside his control; and even when Gunning explained that the guarantee would not have been called for until the negotiations had been completed, he did not much mend matters; the

[34] S.P. 91/77, fos. 82–4, 87, 191.
[35] S.P. 75/119, fos. 130–2, Titley to Grafton, 13 May 1766.
[36] S.P. 75/119, fos. 144–8, Conway to Titley, 13 June 1766.
[37] S.P. 75/119, fos. 240–1.
[38] S.P. 91/77, fo. 296, Macartney to Conway, 12/23 Oct. 1766.
[39] S.P. 75/119, fos. 120–7, 282–4, 301–4, 322–5, 370–2.

difference between giving a guarantee now, and undertaking to give one later, not being very material.

Thus the question of *Mageskiftet* had contrived to get itself involved with the perennial controversy about subsidies. To Titley and Gunning it seemed obvious that Denmark could not do without foreign gold. If the alliance were to be secured at all, Britain must be prepared to offer a subsidy, if only to remove the otherwise irresistible temptation to turn once more to the old paymaster in Paris.[40] But here they found the way barred by one of the sacred cows of British foreign policy: the great principle of No Subsidies in Peacetime. All secretaries of state in the sixties were obsessed by the political impossibility of inducing the House of Commons to violate this principle; and in any case they were firmly convinced that any state with a proper sense of its dignity and interest ought to jump at the chance of a British alliance, without any financial inducement. Foreign powers, alas, were curiously obtuse about this. Both Grafton and Conway protested earnestly that if ever it were conceivable that Britain should abandon her objection to subsidies, it would be in Denmark's favour (the Danish fleet, after all, was a consideration);[41] but if a concession were made to Denmark, how would it be possible to deny a subsidy to Sweden—or even perhaps to Russia? Gunning, with one eye on our very unfavourable balance of trade with the Scandinavian countries, made the tempting suggestion that Denmark might offset a subsidy by lowering her protective tariffs;[42] Titley argued, with some force, that simple defensive alliances were useless, since their effectiveness depended upon agreement upon who was the aggressor, while subsidy treaties were free of such ambiguities.[43] It was all in vain: Conway was not to be shifted. In July 1766 Pitt had at last condescended to take office. He came in determined to expose the incompetence of his predecessors by the speedy conclusion of a Northern League of Great Britain, Russia and Prussia; and almost his first act was to nominate Hans Stanley as ambassador to St Petersburg, and to direct him to settle all difficulties with

[40] S.P. 75/119, fos. 127, 170–5, 282–4; B.M., Egerton MSS. 2696 fo. 124.

[41] S.P. 75/119, fos. 69–71, Grafton to Titley, 14 Mar. 1766; 119, fos. 144–8, Conway to Titley, 13 June 1766; *ibid.*, fos. 292–6, same to same, 30 Sept. 1766; cf. S.P. 95/107, fos. 221–2, Grafton to Goodricke, 6 Dec. 1765, where he argues that from a naval point of view Denmark is a better candidate for a subsidy than Sweden.

[42] S.P. 75/119, fos. 170–5.

[43] S.P. 75/119, fos. 372–3, Titley to Conway, 18 Nov. 1766.

Frederick the Great on his way there. In London it seemed obvious that once the alliance with Russia was made, Denmark would have no option but to become a party to it: instead of wasting time and energy on the outworks in Copenhagen, Stanley was to storm the citadel in St Petersburg. To Conway, somewhat winded by Chatham's impetuosity but not indisposed to believe in his ability to perform miracles, the urgent appeals of Gunning to grasp the fleeting opportunity in Denmark appeared misconceived and indeed irrelevant.[44]

By the end of 1766, however, the situation had altered considerably. Hans Stanley, not surprisingly, had got cold feet; Sir Andrew Mitchell in Berlin had left his government in no doubt that even the name of Pitt did not avail to soften the animus of Frederick;[45] from St Petersburg the supplanted and humiliated Macartney was relaying, with evident *Schadenfreude*, Panin's devastating comments on the ineptitude of British policy. Chatham's grand diplomatic offensive had collapsed ignominiously before it had well begun. Perhaps after all a Danish alliance might, in a modest way, do something to repair the damage. So Conway seems to have thought; for on 19 December 1766 he wrote to Titley and Gunning ordering them to begin negotiations. He admitted all Titley's arguments as to the uselessness of simple defensive alliances without subsidies; but he concluded, with dispirited inconsequence, that this was the only kind of offer that was open to him, and they must make the best of it.[46] They did what they could. On 16 January 1767 they made their proposal to Bernstorff: they even offered to let him draft the treaty himself.[47] But Bernstorff, though courteous, was unresponsive. He was approaching the crisis of his negotiations with Saldern, and he could not afford to risk offending that jealous and overbearing personage by separate negotiations with the British ministers.[48] Conway found this quite inexplicable: he could see no connection, he wrote, between *Mageskiftet* and the question of an Anglo-Danish alliance.[49] Obliquity in a secretary of state could hardly go further; but at least he accepted the facts of the

[44] *Ibid.*, fos. 292–6, Conway to Titley, 30 Sept. 1766.

[45] S.P. 90/85, fos. 223–8, Mitchell to Conway, 4 Dec. 1766.

[46] S.P. 91/77, fos. 296, 304; 78, fos. 30–5, 39–41. S.P. 75/119, fos. 412–15.

[47] S.P. 75/120, fos. 13–14; *Corr. ministérielle* II, 306.

[48] S.P. 75/120, fos. 13–14, Gunning to Conway, 7 Feb. 1767.

[49] *Ibid.*, fos. 32–4.

situation, even though he could not understand them: by May 1767 he confessed that he had abandoned all hope of an alliance with Denmark—and characteristically blamed Russia for his disappointment.[50]

Meanwhile Bernstorff had reaped the reward of concentrating on essentials. On 22 April 1767, after patient diplomacy, agreement was reached on the provisional *Mageskiftet* treaty.[51] No report of the progress of the negotiation had leaked out to Titley and Gunning; nor had any word of it reached London from other quarters. A month later Conway could write to Titley agreeing that *Mageskiftet* 'makes no part of M. Saldern's business at Copenhagen' (it was, in fact, his only business there): 'the only exchange in view', he thought, was of 'some trifling territory whose name has at present escaped me'.[52] It was August before Gunning became aware of strong rumours that the treaty had been signed; and his comments on them were singularly obtuse.[53] In Copenhagen, it seemed, British intelligence was on a par with British statesmanship.

III

The responsibility for this state of affairs, and for the bad relations between the British ministers and their Russian colleagues to which it bore witness, lies squarely on the shoulders of Gunning, and to a less extent on those of Conway. Gunning arrived in Copenhagen very soon after the opening of the new reign, at a moment when the domestic politics of Denmark were in an unwontedly labile condition. Around the young king the ambitions of rival politicians clashed, coincided, and diverged again, so that the most experienced of diplomats might well have lost his way in the labyrinth. Christian's jealousy of his father's counsellors; the natural hope of those who had been excluded from power under the old king to regain it under the new; desire for, or resistance to, reforms; squabbles and rivalries among Bernstorff's friends or allies, such as that which set Moltke against

[50] *Ibid.*, fos. 140–2.

[51] *Danske Tractater*, pp. 229–63; O. Brandt, *Caspar von Saldern* (Erlangen-Kiel, 1932) pp. 153–7.

[52] S.P. 75/120, fos. 140–2, Conway to Gunning, 22 May 1767.

[53] *Ibid.*, fos. 166–8. Goodricke and Shirley (in St Petersburg) both got wind of the treaty in June: B.M. Add. MSS. 37054, fo. 3; Uppsala Univ. Library MS. F.386, Shirley to Goodricke, 22 June 1767. Choiseul, it is only fair to add, was equally sceptical and uncomprehending: *Sbornik* CXLI, III (to Bausset, 10 July 1766); 380, 402 (to Rossignol, 31 Dec. 1767, 2 March 1768).

Reventlow; genuine differences of opinion on the great question of *Mageskiftet*—all these various antagonisms contributed to make the picture unusually complex and difficult to interpret.

Gunning might have been forgiven if he had taken some time to get his bearings in this tumbled landscape. But in fact he sought no such indulgence. Within a fortnight of his arrival he was confidently pronouncing that Bernstorff was insincere in his professions of goodwill, and recommending threats rather than blandishments as the method most likely to be effective with him.[54] Within a month he was writing of d'Ogier, who for thirteen years had ably upheld the French cause in Denmark, that he was 'more formed for a *contrebandier* than a minister'.[55] This easy dogmatism, so much at variance with that strain of diffidence which his friends deplored, reflects the prejudices and preconceptions which he had acquired in London before setting out: he came with a stereotyped system of ideas which was much in need of re-examination; he measured men with a meteyard which he had picked up in the secretary's office. Were they 'French', or were they 'English'? No doubt it was true that under Christian VII, as under Frederick V, some Danish statesmen *were* 'French', and others 'English'; but such alignments were not the only, nor even the main, determinants of politics: indeed, if men were to be pigeonholed according to their *penchant* for a foreign power, the true categories were now rather 'Russian' and 'anti-Russian'. Certainly the old French–English antithesis was no longer a useful way of estimating men and policies, and might easily be a very misleading one, as may be seen from the extraordinary absurdities and contradictions which bestrew the reports of British diplomats on Danish personalities. For example, with regard to Ditlev Reventlow. On 5 February 1763 two letters from Copenhagen reached Lord Halifax. One, from Titley, reported that Reventlow was strongly 'French'; the other, from Goodricke, described him as the warm friend of England.[56] But by February 1766 Titley had changed his mind; for Reventlow, after all, was the enemy of Moltke, and Moltke was incontrovertibly 'French'.[57] And yet, on the other hand,

[54] S.P. 75/119, fo. 110, Gunning to Grafton, 19 April 1766.

[55] B.M., Egerton MSS. 2704, fo. 75, Gunning to Sir J. Yorke, 10 May 1766.

[56] S.P. 75/116, fo. 20; *ibid.*, 115, fo. 13: cf. a similar contradiction in 1764, *ibid.*, 117, fos. 232–4, 246.

[57] S.P. 75/119, fos. 259–60; 118, fos. 124, 162; 119, fos. 196–8; 'Grev Adam Gottlob Moltkes efterladte Mindeskrifer', *Hist. Tidsskr.* IV Series II, (1871–2) 268.

Reventlow was also the intimate friend and supporter of Bernstorff, who was (of course) France's lackey. . . . It was all most confusing. It was still more confusing in regard to St Germain. St Germain was a French officer whom Bernstorff had imported to reorganize the Danish army. Choiseul, however, disliked and distrusted him;[58] in June 1766 Bernstorff dismissed him from the War Directory; and thereafter he allied himself with Bernstorff's enemies, and intrigued to bring about his fall. Thus a man whom British ministers naturally considered as 'French' was curiously transformed into an ally of the friends of Britain; and by a final confusion was eventually to be dismissed from the Danish service altogether at the instance of Saldern, as being an enemy of Russia. It is of course true that a man such as Charles of Hesse did correspond to British stereotypes better than Reventlow or St Germain; but our interests were not well served by a habit of thought which led secretaries of state and envoys to forget that foreign statesmen—even in a small country—might be moved by other strings than attachment to a French or British system, that support of British policies was not a universal moral obligation, and that domestic disagreements, personal rivalries, concern for national interests, might be more powerfully operative factors than regard for the wishes of a foreign power, or greed for the cash it could provide.

The most important of all such misconceptions, of course, was that which concerned Bernstorff himself. If Gunning by any chance still had an open mind about Bernstorff when he arrived in Denmark, a few weeks in Copenhagen sufficed to close it. He very soon decided that Bernstorff was still 'French'; and if Danish words and deeds did not seem to square with that idea, that must be because Bernstorff was also 'hypocritical'.[59] Within a very short time of his arrival in Copenhagen, Gunning became the intimate associate of the Prussian minister, Baron von Borcke;[60] and Borcke's influence reinforced existing prejudices. Borcke's father was in disgrace in Berlin, and Borcke himself was beginning to think that there was much to be said for transferring his talents to another employer. His present object was to find a niche for himself in Denmark, and he had his eye on the post of minister of finance.[61] As long as Bernstorff was in

[58] *Bernstorffske Papirer* II, 660.

[59] S.P. 75/119, fos. 336–8.

[60] B.M., Egerton MSS. 2704, fo. 74.

[61] *Schack-Rathlous Archiv*, p. 409; 'Breve fra Slutningen af det 18de Aarhundrede', *Danske Magazin*, v Ser. III (1893) 13: Gregers Juel to Schack-Rathlou, 6 Dec. 1766.

power, however, his chances in this direction were extremely slim; and Borcke therefore set himself to engineer Bernstorff's removal. He found a suitable ally in Count Danneskjold-Samsøe. Danneskjold at one time had been minister of marine; he had been out of office throughout the reign of Frederick V; he hated Bernstorff and his friends; and he was now importuning Christian VII to reinstate him. In this he was successful, entering the council on 1 August 1766. Danneskjold was an old friend of Titley;[62] he was a man of ability, with a real concern for administrative reform; and he sincerely differed from Bernstorff on the expediency of negotiating *Mageskiftet* at this time. But his jealousy, vindictiveness, and atrabilious humour made him an impossible colleague, and an inconceivable alternative to Bernstorff.[63] Nevertheless both Gunning and Conway speedily decided that Danneskjold was the man for them, and proceeded to back him against Bernstorff. By the end of 1766 Conway was describing Bernstorff as 'the most artful and the most able, and therefore to Us and Russia, the most dangerous Supporter of the French Cause in Denmark'.[64] In pursuance of these curious notions Gunning gave at least tacit support to a determined attempt by Borcke, Danneskjold and St Germain to overthrow Bernstorff in August 1766. The attempt failed: Bernstorff survived. But Borcke and his clique of malcontents did not give up the game; neither did Conway and Gunning change their opinions.

In November 1766 Caspar von Saldern had arrived in Copenhagen to begin the long-promised negotiations for *Mageskiftet*. He was well esteemed in London as a proved friend of Britain and the advocate of an Anglo-Russian alliance; and he came heralded by warm recommendations from Macartney in St Petersburg and Ralph Woodford in Hamburg.[65] On his way to Denmark he had called in at Berlin, where he had striven hard to mollify Frederick's anti-British mania.[66] He had told Woodford

[62] S.P. 75/119, fos. 271–6.

[63] Dorothea Biehl thought him 'the most opinionated, choleric and vindictive man ever to draw breath': 'Charlotte Dorothea Biehls historiske Breve', *Hist. Tidsskr*, III Series IV (1865–6) 357; Saldern called him 'an Incendiary, blinded by his personal animosity': S.P. 75/119, fo. 427; and even Gunning admitted that he was not 'versatile': *ibid.*, fos. 430–1.

[64] S.P. 95/110, fo. 217, Conway to Goodricke, 19 Dec. 1766.

[65] S.P. 75/119, fos. 158–60, 241; 91/75, fo. 231; B.M., Egerton MSS. 2696, fo. 166.

[66] Brandt, *Saldern*, pp. 134–40; B.M., Egerton MSS. 2696, fos. 36–9. Frederick's tart comments are in his *Oeuvres posthumes* (Berlin, 1788) V, 23–4.

that he intended to secure the dismissal of any friends of France before he would consent to begin negotiating with the Danes.[67] In short, he embodied in his own person all that a British statesman could hope for from a representative of Catherine II. And he knew Danish politics well. From the point of view of Gunning and Conway, however, he suffered from one fatal defect: he did not share their distrust of Bernstorff and their *penchant* for Danneskjold. Conway was grieved to find that 'the Court of Russia has been so far imposed upon, as to direct Monsr Saldern to support Bernstorff'. He accordingly wrote to Gunning ordering him to set Saldern right on this point, and to open his eyes to the true state of Danish politics.[68] No doubt it was the case that Bernstorff was the man who had sponsored the *rapprochement* with Russia, that he was the champion of that *Mageskiftet* which was also Saldern's personal policy, and that on Christian VII's accession Panin had signified his hope that Bernstorff would be retained in office.[69] It was true, also, that Danneskjold was among the most vigorous opponents of the *Mageskiftet* negotiations, and was reckoned by Panin as an enemy. But it was clear to Conway that the Russians did not know their own business, and that it had now become his duty to instruct them in it. And with a zeal born of presumptuous ignorance he hastened to discharge that friendly office.

On 19 December 1766 Macartney was ordered to inform Panin that 'we think ourselves very well informed of what passes in Denmark and of the real sentiments entertained by the Leading Men of that Country'; and that Danneskjold was 'undoubtedly by Inclination, Principles and Interest the most avowed and determined Foe of the French System (that he was also the foe of Russia was, it seemed, irrelevant), while 'Mr Bernstorff . . . whatever fables he may now from necessity be obliged to, is from his own opinion and habit devoted to the cause of France'.[70] By the time these instructions reached him Macartney was too preoccupied with his own personal grievances to have space in his dispatches for much besides the insolent irony in which he clothed his resentment of Conway's ill-treatment. He did indeed obey his orders, but he did not trouble to

[67] B.M., Egerton MSS. 2696, fo. 39, Woodford to Gunning, 13 June 1766.

[68] S.P. 75/119, fos. 396–9, Conway to Gunning, 5 Dec. 1766.

[69] *Denkwürdigkeiten des Freiherrn Achatz Ferdinand von der Asseburg* (Berlin, 1842) p. 123.

[70] S.P. 91/77, fo. 320, Conway to Macartney, 19 Dec. 1766.

report on how his insinuation had been received.[71] As for Gunning, who had been similarly instructed, he lost no time in acting upon orders so conformable to his own opinions. On at least two occasions he wrestled with Saldern in an effort to open the eyes of that deluded minister to Danneskjold's merits and Bernstorff's iniquity.[72] To his surprise and chagrin he found that he made not the least impression. Even when he enlisted the aid of Borcke the effect remained curiously disappointing.[73] Borcke was by this time preparing a second and more dangerous attempt to bring about Bernstorff's fall. The intrigue came to a head in March 1767, at a moment when the negotiations for *Mageskiftet* were on the eve of success. In the circumstances, Saldern did not hesitate to intervene in Bernstorff's favour; but it required three minatory interviews with Christian VII, and a formal Russian Note, before the plot was finally defeated.[74] Gunning found it expedient to send home an explicit denial that he was implicated in this tenebrous affair;[75] but Bernstorff certainly thought he was, and from Saldern's point of view he might just as well have been.[76] For he had chosen to associate himself with Russia's most inveterate enemies in Copenhagen; he had striven to destroy Russia's chief friend there; and all this at a moment when Chatham's crazy administration was feebly debating why Russia should be so blind to her own interests as to decline to enter into a British alliance on Britain's terms.

It was no wonder if Saldern's relations with Gunning thereafter left much to be desired. Saldern was certainly not a very conciliating character:

[71] We know that he spoke to Panin about it: Asseburg, *Denkwürdigkeiten*, p. 398, Asseburg to Bernstorff, 14 Feb. 1767.

[72] S.P. 75/119, fos. 424–7; 120, fos. 15–18, 25–7, 29.

[73] Saldern is said to have lured them on to reveal their intrigues against Bernstorff, and to have replied with a laugh, 'Ja meine lieben Herren, sind Sie denn eigentlich dazu hier, um das dänische Ministerium zu stürzen? Ich für meiner Person bin es nicht': Brandt, p. 158.

[74] For this affair see 'Depeche af 12 (13) April 1767 fra Gehejmraad C. v. Saldern og Generalmajor Filosoffof til den russiske Regering' *Dansk Magazin*, v Series III (1893); 'Breve fra Slutningen af det 18de Aarhundrede', *ibid.*, pp. 13, 16; *Corr. ministérielle* II, 315–16; *Bernstorffske Papirer* II, 86–8, 201–2, 315–16, 447; E. Holm, 'Caspar von Saldern og den dansk-norske Regering', *Hist. Tidsskr.*, IV Series III (1872–3) 101–9.

[75] S.P. 75/120, fo. 113, Gunning to Conway, Private and Confidential, 4 May 1767.

[76] Russian reactions can be gauged from Panin's dispatch of 4 Feb. o.s. 1767: *Sbornik*, LXVII, 338–47.

gross and greedy, obstinate, opinionated, jealous and suspicious, prone to hector and to bully, taking a brutal pleasure in the exercise of power;[77] but he was a good friend to those who treated him as one. Gunning might complain that 'His behaviour to me, Mr Titley, and the few friends we have here, is such as would be hardly excusable, even if war was declared between his Court and Ours';[78] but he was hardly entitled to be surprised, for in Denmark, as far as Saldern could see, Britain was indeed almost a hostile power.[79] One consequence of this situation was that for some months Gunning lost all credit in Copenhagen; while Saldern, if he did not quite treat Denmark as Repnin was treating Poland, at least went to great lengths to secure Bernstorff against any rival. Within a short time the anti-Bernstorff gang appeared to have been routed. And at the beginning of 1768 even Conway at last brought himself to face the truth and acknowledge that he had been mistaken. The alienation of Saldern, he frankly confessed, must be attributed to British support for Danneskjold. But now that Danneskjold was out of office, and Bernstorff professed himself an adherent of the Russian system, and the banishment of St Germain [Gunning's former ally!] had demonstrated the destruction of French influence; 'It seems to me no business of ours to meddle with the endless intrigues of that Court, but to make the most of the natural influence His Majesty . . . ought to have there.' In pursuance of this prudent, if somewhat belated, resolution, Gunning was ordered to reconcile himself somehow with Saldern; and on 2 February 1768 he was able to report that this delicate task had been accomplished. Saldern, it seemed, had entertained the absurd suspicion that Gunning did not think well of Bernstorff, and was a supporter of Danneskjold and Borcke. . . . This strange misconception was now happily removed. Which did not prevent Gunning from commenting, when Saldern returned to Russia in the following month, that it was incredible that he should have put his trust in a set of men whom he came to Denmark to overthrow.[80]

[77] For Saldern's difficult personality see, e.g., *Bernstorffske Papirer*, II, 475 n. 1. Mme Plessen plaintively wondered 'par quelle fatalité l'Impératrice s'est elle toujours servie de bêtes féroces': *ibid.*, 416.

[78] S.P. 75/120, fos. 122, 156.

[79] Brandt, *Saldern*, pp. 159–78.

[80] S.P. 75/121, fos. 5–6, Conway to Gunning, 9 Jan. 1768; *ibid.*, fol. 115 for Gunning's despatch of 2 Feb. 1768.

IV

In reality (whatever Gunning might think) there had been a sharp change for the worse in Franco-Danish relations during the preceding eighteen months. Choiseul, on his resumption of the direction of foreign affairs in April 1766, had subjected French policy in Denmark to a sceptical scrutiny, and reached the conclusion that it had been extravagant, futile and absurd.[81] He did indeed reopen his correspondence with Bernstorff, but only to send him a letter in which he announced that France had reconciled herself to the fact that she could entertain no hope of Danish assistance against Britain, and that Denmark was now to be considered as attached to the Anglo-Russian system.[82] From this moment the old friendship between them was at an end. And when Blosset, the new French minister to Denmark, received his instructions on 14 October 1766, they were couched in terms which would have astonished Gunning if he had been aware of them; for they included a strict injunction to give no encouragement to the idea that France would ever pay another subsidy, and referred to 'the known attachment of the majority of Danish ministers to the Court of London'.[83] By this time Bernstorff had got wind of Choiseul's final decision to change his policy in Sweden and work for the re-establishment of monarchical sovereignty; and before the end of November he was horrified to receive details of the plan to precipitate a constitutional revolution by Adolf Frederick's temporary abdication.[84] The final disillusionment came when France reacted to the news of the *Mageskifte* treaty of 11 April 1767 by refusing to pay any further instalments of subsidy arrears, on the ground that Denmark 'had undertaken engagements directly contrary to France'.[85] And when, on the last day of his administration, Bernstorff looked back on Choiseul's record, it seemed to him that for a decade 'il ne se souvint du Nord que pour le négliger, le haïr, et le troubler'.[86]

Nevertheless, though France might repudiate and contemn, Bernstorff showed no desire to revive the negotiations for a British alliance. It was

[81] *Receuil des Instructions* XIII, *Danemark* (Paris, 1895) p. 177.

[82] *Bernstorff-Choiseul Corr.*, pp. 234–7, Choiseul to Bernstorff, 15 April 1766.

[83] *Recueil des Instructions . . . Danemark*, pp. 179–84.

[84] *Corr. ministérielle* II, 299–300, Bernstorff to Schack, 22 Nov. 1766.

[85] *Ibid.*, II, 337–40, 351–3; cf. S.P. 75/121, fo. 95.

[86] *Ibid.*, II, 482, Instructions for de Blome, 14 Sept. 1770.

not that he bore a grudge because Gunning had been the intimate of his most inveterate domestic enemies. But he had no desire to place Denmark in a position where she might be dragged into Britain's worldwide quarrels.[87] He saw, as many of his contemporaries did, the enervating effect upon British foreign policy of ministerial instability;[88] and he felt the contrast between the ignorant and parsimonious indifference which dominated Britain's continental policy, and the arrogant and tyrannical spirit which she displayed in mercantile affairs. Yet even in July 1767 he could be sufficiently objective to give to British statesmanship such credit as was due to it: 'Mais au défaut de l'entendue des vues et de l'ardeur du travail, vous observerez beaucoup de modération et beaucoup de droiture'; and he added that apart from those countries who were disappointed of subsidies, 'il n'y en a point qui ait sujet de se plaindre de la Grande Bretagne'.[89] But an alliance seemed unnecessary from the point of view of security, now that Denmark could count on Russia; Catherine put no pressure upon him to conclude it; and he was content to wait until the long-expected Anglo-Russian treaty should provide the natural opportunity for Denmark's adhesion.

Thus throughout 1768 Anglo-Danish relations remained in a state of suspended animation. For most of the year the Northern Secretaryship was in the idle and incompetent hands of Lord Weymouth. During his tenure of the seals ministers at the northern courts were lucky if in six months they received a single dispatch worth reading: British diplomats, he believed, should '*hear* as much and *say* as little as possible';[90] and he took care to supplement precept with example. Gunning was accordingly left to occupy himself with refurbishing Titley's country house;[91] with organizing a gift of staghounds to Christian VII;[92] and with preparations for Christian's visit to England, which took place in the autumn. Though it was regarded by George III as a great nuisance, the visit proved an

[87] *Ibid.*, II, 256–8.

[88] 'Ses ministres, chancelants et reduits ou à craindre ou à désirer une démission prochaine, ne peuvent se former ni de plan ni de système': *ibid.*, II, 329; cf. S.P. 75/120, fo. 234.

[89] *Corr. ministérielle* II, 332.

[90] S.P. 91/79, fo. 22, Weymouth to Cathcart, 30 Sept. 1768.

[91] B. M. Egerton MSS. 2697, fo. 242.

[92] Which the secretary's office managed to bungle: S.P. 75/120, fos. 189, 198; 121, fo. 143.

unexpected success: Christian was popular with the crowds, Horace Walpole thought well of him, Oxford gave him an honorary degree; and though he subsequently went on to Paris, ministers were not unduly perturbed. Bernstorff accompanied him; and made a decidedly good impression. The official British view of him underwent a rapid, and as it proved a permanent, alteration: in January 1769 Rochford (who had succeeded Weymouth in the previous October) could write to Gunning that 'the good dispositions of Monsr de Bernstorff towards His Majesty and the alliance with Great Britain are not to be doubted'.[93] And from that good opinion even Gunning no longer audibly dissented.

Before Bernstorff returned to Denmark from western Europe, two events had occurred which precipitated a crisis in the affairs of the North. In November 1768 the Turks declared war on Russia; in December came the long-expected royalist *coup* in Stockholm, when Adolf Frederick declined to exercise his constitutional functions until the Cap ministers should agree to summon an extraordinary Diet. Both events were showy successes for Choiseul; and to many observers there seemed to be a sinister connection between them: the restoration of monarchical power in Sweden, it was feared, would be the preliminary to a diversionary attack on St Petersburg. Great Britain, Denmark and Russia had now a common and urgent interest in defeating French designs in the North; and there was much discussion about the expediency of presenting a joint declaration in Stockholm, designed to keep Sweden out of the war, or to bolster up the tottering Cap senate.[94] It proved difficult, however, to reach agreement either on the content or the timing of such a declaration; and though the ministers of the three powers collaborated to fight the election which followed in the spring of 1769,[95] their efforts were

[93] S.P. 75/121, fos. 26–7, 123, 133, 140–1, 184; *Bernstorffske Papirer* I, 404; III, 50–1; *The Letters of Horace Walpole*, ed. Toynbee, VII, 213, 215; R.A. Stockholm, Diplomatica, Anglica: Nolcken to K.P. 26 Aug., 20 Sept. 1768; Gallica: Brev till amb. Cretuz. Sprengtporten to Creutz, 20 Sept. 1768; S.P. 75/122, fos. 1–4, Rochford to Gunning, 17 Jan. 1769.

[94] *Corr. ministérielle* II, 362 n. 1, 374–8, 395 n. 1; S.P. 95/113, fos. 141–3; 114, fos. 3–8, 13–14, 21–3, 33–4, 139–46, 155, 185–6; 115, fos. 7–8, 16–17, 55–7; S.P. 75/122, fos. 10–11, 23–4, 117–18; R.A., Tengberg Avskr. Danska ministrarnas i Stockholm Depescher, Juel to Bernstorff, 6, 16 Dec. 1768.

[95] *Ibid.*, Juel to Bernstorff, 3 Feb. 1769; and see Goodricke's plan for joint operations in S.P. 75/122, fos. 96–7, Gunning to Rochford, 1 April 1769.

unavailing in the face of the universal unpopularity of the Caps' economic policies. The result was a triumph for France and the Hats; and when the *riksdag* met at Norrköping in April, the only question seemed to be whether its sessions would lead to the kind of constitutional reform which France now desired, or whether the Hats, despite French pressure, would remain faithful to their old belief in 'liberty'.[96]

The *débâcle* in Sweden, though it thus drew Britain and Denmark closer together, revealed also how widely divergent their policies and objectives were. Bernstorff's essential concern, as always, was to preserve the constitution of 1720, of which the Caps, rather than the Hats, were now the most reliable guardians. When it became apparent that the Caps would be powerless to defend it, he was driven back on a choice between two policies: either forcible intervention in conjunction with Russia, or an understanding with the 'true Whigs' among the Hats which would encourage them to resist the Court's designs. For some months he pursued both. But his alarm at developments in Sweden led him to order a partial mobilization of the fleet; and France retorted with a threat of war. Bernstorff declined to be bullied; and in a reply which even Gunning considered 'spirited' defied Choiseul to do his worst.[97] Rochford reacted to the situation by giving an immediate promise of assistance if the French fleet should attempt to intervene. For this Bernstorff was not ungrateful; though privately he expressed doubts whether the pledge would in fact be honoured.[98] The best hope of aid in a crisis, he felt, still lay in Russia; and he determined to draw even closer the ties which linked Denmark with the tsaritsa. Already in February 1769 he took the initiative in offering a new and more binding alliance;[99] and ten months later that initiative bore fruit. The treaty of 13 December 1769 provided for mutual assistance, maintenance of the constitution of 1720 in every detail, if need be by force, and in the last resort territorial gains for each party at Sweden's

[96] As C. F. Scheffer tried to argue that they would: *Schack-Rathlous Archiv* p. 382, C. F. Scheffer to Schack, 24 Feb. 1769.

[97] He had foreseen the possibility of a Hat victory as early as 1767, and had been careful to warn his minister in Stockholm to do nothing to alienate them irrevocably; *Corr. ministérielle* II, 309–11, 382. For the mobilization and its repercussions see *ibid.*, II, 280 n. 2, 381, 396; S.P. 75/122, fos. 10–11, 63–5, 69–70, 77, 112.

[98] S.P. 75/122, fo. 78; *Corr. ministérielle* II, 399 n. 1.

[99] *Corr. ministérielle* II, 383–90, 409, 417.

expense.[100] Potentially, it was a partition treaty; actually, it seemed to bind Denmark irrevocably to Russia.

Lord Rochford, on the other hand, made it clear that he was interested only in destroying French influence in Sweden, and not in a rigid defence of the constitution in defiance of Swedish wishes:[101] a realistic and intelligible policy, but almost the opposite of Bernstorff's.[102] He hoped, as Goodricke did, that the Swedish crisis would produce the Northern League which had so far eluded his predecessors: a Quadruple Alliance of Russia, Denmark, Great Britain and Prussia, designed to prevent Sweden from disturbing the 'Tranquillity of the North', would be able to compel Sweden's adhesion—without a subsidy.[103] But this, alas, was a naïve delusion. It was a solution which disposed of difficulties by ignoring them. Frederick the Great's views on Sweden by no means coincided with those of the other three powers,[104] and in any case it was his object to obstruct the formation of any Northern League (above all, any league that included Britain) and to monopolize Russian friendship for himself. Secondly, even if Prussian opposition were ignored, the plan denied the constant Russian claim that any alliance with Britain must stipulate for some tangible concession by George III, to match the concessions which Catherine felt that she was making. For months Cathcart had been toiling in St Petersburg to devise an 'Expedient' satisfactory to both parties: the plan for a Quadruple Alliance assumed that he had been imagining difficulties where none existed. Moreover, there was an inconsequence about British policy which cannot have inspired Bernstorff with much confidence. Soon after the Swedish Diet met, the Danish and Russian ministers in Stockholm had reached an agreement with the

[100] *Danske Tractater*, pp. 301–10.

[101] S.P. 95/114, fos. 3–8, Rochford to Goodricke, 13 Jan. 1769.

[102] Bernstorff himself acknowledged the difficulty, and doubted the justification, of maintaining the Swedish constitution 'si toute la nation était unanimement resolue de la changer': *Corr. ministérielle* II, 390–1; and added 'il parait très-douteux au roi qu'une puissance puisse s'attribuer vis-à-vis de l'autre le droit de défendre et de maintenir une constitution et des lois qui lui sont étrangères'—a sentence which imposes some modification of the argument about his view of international law set forth in Schoubye, *loc. cit.*

[103] S.P. 95/114, fos. 69–70, 90–1; S.P. 91/80, fos. 70–84, 230; 81, fos. 18–22.

[104] As Rochford, indeed, knew: S.P. 75/122, fo. 13; S.P. 95/114, fos. 33–4; for Frederick's attitude, see G. Olsson, 'Frederick den Store och Sveriges författning', *Scandia* XXVIII (1961) pp. 353–5.

frondeur Pechlin,[105] as a result of which he undertook to bribe sufficient members to defeat the attempt to carry constitutional reform. He offered three plans: the most radical (for which he demanded £120,000) promised a total change in the Senate and the destruction of French influence; the least expensive (a mere £30,000) undertook simply to preserve the constitution intact. Goodricke transmitted these options to his government;[106] and the cabinet without hesitation plumped for the cheapest.[107] No matter that it contradicted Rochford's definition of British interests in Sweden: it was the cheapest, and that was sufficient. It did indeed secure Denmark's main objective; but it may be doubted whether this was a consideration which weighed very heavily in London.

To this confusion in British policy Gunning added his own modest contribution. His judgment on personalities had latterly undergone revision: with the Russian minister Filosofov he was now on terms of confidence, and of Bernstorff he was beginning to write with respect.[108] But he still thought of men as 'French', if they were not plainly 'English': he wrote, for instance, that all the ministers were French except Bernstorff, Reventlow and Schack[109]—which was scarcely less absurd than his delusions of two years earlier. And having formerly attacked Bernstorff as the tool of France, he now fell into the opposite error of crediting him with anti-French policies which he would certainly have repudiated: it was a particularly unfortunate mistake to inform his government that Bernstorff's concern in Sweden was not so much to defend the constitution as to eradicate French influence there.[110]

Nevertheless, though the Swedish crisis of 1769 did not produce an Anglo-Russian alliance, nor bring the prospect of an alliance with Denmark any nearer, the close collaboration of the three powers in Stockholm did give them a certain community of feeling. Rochford in the end was able to persuade his colleagues to sanction expenditure of unprecedented magnitude; and though Britain's contribution was

[105] R.A. Stockholm, Riksdagsjournaler, G. Reuterholms Dagbok öfwer början af 1769 års riksdag, pp. 46–54; Tengberg Avskr. Juel to Bernstorff, 26 April 1769.

[106] S.P. 95/115, fos. 91–3, Goodricke to Rochford, 28 July 1769.

[107] *Ibid.*, 115, fos. 80–2, Rochford to Goodricke, 25 Aug. 1769.

[108] S.P. 75/122, fos. 67, 112, 119–20, 205–7.

[109] *Ibid.*, 122, fos. 239–45, Gunning to Rochford, 25 Nov. 1769.

[110] *Ibid.*, 122, fos. 119–20, Gunning to Rochford, 13 May 1769.

probably not much bigger than Denmark's,[111] and far less than the sums poured out by Catherine, it did at least blunt the edge of their gibes at British parsimony. And the effort was successful: by the end of 1769 Pechlin had earned his money; the constitution was saved (and a revolution in the next reign thereby made highly probable); Goodricke, for the first time in six years, could take some well-earned leave; and the three powers could devote themselves in concert to planning their revenge at the next Diet. The basis had been laid, it might be hoped, for more cordial relations between London and Copenhagen. In May 1770 even the sceptical Gunning could write: 'I flatter myself . . . that the System of this Court is become too solid to be easily shaken.'[112]

But Gunning had a genius for being wrong. By 1770 Bernstorff's political existence was hanging by a hair. Christian VII was sinking into insanity; the irresponsible and essentially apolitical intriguers around him were reinforced by enemies of Bernstorff (and of Russia) such as Rantzau-Ascheberg; and already Struensee was advancing from behind the throne to seize the power in the state.[113] By a final irony the English Queen and her lover became the instruments for overthrowing the minister who had at last come to be recognized as the best remaining friend that England had in Denmark—or at least as the minister whom it was now England's interest to keep in power. When on 15 September 1770 Bernstorff received his dismissal and retired from Denmark, his fall was regarded in London, no less than in St Petersburg, as a heavy blow;[114] and Robert Gunning was soon made to regret the statesman whose principles he had never understood, whose character and ability he had consistently underrated, and whose ministry he had twice attempted to destroy.

V

It needs no great penetration to divine why British ministers failed to secure the alliance of Denmark in the years after 1763. For it takes two to make an alliance, and from Bernstorff's point of view there were only two inducements with which Britain could hope to tempt him: a guarantee of

[111] Britain spent about £32,000: S.P. 91/82, fos. 283–4.

[112] S.P. 75/123, fo. 59.

[113] France, of course, suspected that Struensee was a tool of England: Barthélémy, p. 322.

[114] S.P. 75/123, fo. 154, Rochford to Gunning, 12 October 1770.

Mageskiftet was one, the offer of a subsidy was the other; and both appeared to be out of the question. The disadvantages to Denmark of a British alliance were obvious, while the benefits might probably be had without any explicit commitment, since no British ministry could permit France to overpower the Danish navy. But of course it was not possible for British ministers, any more than it was possible for Bernstorff, to consider Anglo-Danish relations in isolation. The securing of Denmark was desired in London not so much for its own sake, but as one element in a broader diplomatic strategy. It was certainly desirable to eliminate French influence in Copenhagen, just as it was desirable to eliminate it in every other European capital. But the main object of British policy in the late sixties was an alliance with Russia; and the importance of Denmark lay in the possibility that one road to St Petersburg (but by no means the only one) might well lie through Copenhagen. Since no British ministry felt able to accept the terms which Catherine demanded, it occurred to diplomatists in both camps that this obstacle might be circumvented if Britain were to give active support to Russian designs in areas in which Catherine was especially concerned. The two most promising of these seemed to be Sweden and Denmark. In Sweden Sir John Goodricke established close relations with Count Ostermann, his Russian colleague; and he did succeed in persuading his superiors in London to pursue a policy of active collaboration with Russia which at times entailed heavy drains on the Civil List for purposes of corrupting Swedish politicians: for a moment there seemed at least a chance that an Anglo-Swedish alliance might provide the foundation for Panin's League of the North. But whereas in Sweden the Anglo-Russian *entente* was solidly established, this was not the case in Denmark. In Denmark everything went wrong. British ministers displayed an extraordinary obtuseness as to the importance of *Mageskiftet*; they made no effort to comprehend Bernstorff's attitude to Sweden and to France. Danish politics gave no chance to demonstrate goodwill to Russia by sharing the expense of a concerted plan of corruption. Conway and Gunning seemed oblivious of the fact that the destruction of French influence in Copenhagen was really the work of Saldern and Bernstorff, and they persisted in misconceptions and intrigues which menaced the one and exasperated the other. So far from propitiating Catherine, they seemed in Denmark to go out of their way to provoke her.

One measure, and one measure only, could have retrieved these blunders: a subsidy to Denmark. The essential objection to paying subsidies in peacetime, if successive secretaries of state were to be believed, was not that they were expensive (though in the financial climate of the sixties that was always a serious consideration), but that experience had proved their uselessness. As regards any armed assistance which Denmark might give, this might well be near the truth; but was it still true if the equivalent was not merely the Danish fleet, but the Russian alliance?—if by a moderate subsidy to Denmark Britain could avoid a much bigger subsidy to Russia, and above all avoid surrender on the Turkish clause? The only answer to this question that ministers could supply was that it was beneath the dignity of a great nation to appear thus to *purchase* the Russian alliance, and that in any case the House of Commons would hardly agree to it. To which it could be retorted that if we wanted the Russian alliance at all, we could hardly expect to get it for nothing, and were very unlikely ever to get it on less onerous terms. But this in turn provoked the reflection that perhaps after all a mere *entente* with Russia would give us all we really needed, without the sacrifices which an alliance entailed; that Russia was our 'natural' friend in any foreseeable international crisis; that it would be foolish to pay for what, in any event, must probably be ours for the asking; and that, after all, there was something to be said for keeping our hands free.

Thus the case of Denmark provides a good example of the doubts and hesitations, the mixture of common sense and self-deception, the half-volitions and obstinate preconceptions, which helped to shape—or perhaps to wreck—British foreign policy in the exceptionally difficult years of the postwar era.

14

STEWART OAKLEY

Gustavus III's Plans for War with Denmark in 1783–1784

It was the lifelong ambition of Gustavus III of Sweden to enable his country to play a decisive and independent role in European affairs. Such a policy implied firm government, a healthy economy, sound finances which would eliminate dependence on foreign subsidies, a powerful army and fleet, and the prestige which was most readily gained in the eighteenth century by the acquisition of territory at a neighbour's expense. As far as the last was concerned, two possibilities seemed open to Gustavus. Either he could attempt to regain the lands which had been ceded to Russia at the Peace of Nystad, or at least the part of Finland which had been lost in 1743, or he could revive those pretensions to Norway which had been entertained by a number of his predecessors since the break-up of the Kalmar Union.[1] Of these alternatives the latter appeared to him the more attractive, at least during the first half of his reign. Denmark was a less formidable antagonist than the Russia of Catherine the Great, and there was hope that Norwegian discontent might be fanned into open revolt against Danish rule.[2] Gustavus also regarded Denmark with particular aversion for the wrongs she had done the House of Holstein-Gottorp, of his own ties with which he was deeply conscious.[3] Blood ties also played an important part in his attitude to his cousin in St Petersburg.[4] But he could not hope to strike at Denmark with any

[1] J. A. C. Hellstenius, *Försök till Framställning af Konung Gustaf den Tredjes Dansk Politik* (Uppsala, 1862) pp. 3–4: O. Jägerskiöld, *Den Svenska Utrikespolitikens Historia* Pt. 2, II (Stockholm, 1957) p. 271.

[2] *Konung Gustaf III:s efterlemnade och femtio år efter hand död öppnade papper*, ed. E. G. Geijer I (Uppsala, 1843) 231–2; Hellstenius, p. 4; Jägerskiöld, p. 271.

[3] Y. Nielsen 'Gustav III:s Norske Politik. Et Tillæg til Gustavianska Papperen,' *Historisk Tidskrift*, Kristiania, II R I Bd. (1877) p. 38; Hellstenius, p. 3.

[4] Jägerskiöld, p. 271.

likelihood of success until certain conditions were fulfilled. Either he must persuade the tsaritsa to abandon the Russo-Danish alliance which had been forged in the Era of Liberty with the object of keeping Sweden weak and replace it with a Russo-Swedish entente or he must at least ensure that she was so preoccupied by events in other parts of Europe that she would be unable to come to Denmark's aid before that power had been decisively defeated, so that Sweden would not have to cope with a war on two fronts.[5] It was also desirable that other powers interested in the Baltic, especially Britain with her fleet and Prussia with her army, were not in a position to intervene.

At the very beginning of his reign the same international situation which encouraged him to carry out his *coup d'état* in August 1772 also encouraged him to consider making a bid for Norway; above all Catherine was preoccupied with Turkey and Poland. Before the *coup* was launched the acquisition of Norway seemed a very desirable preliminary to it, while after it had been successfully executed the temptation to launch a preventive war against Denmark before Russia was again free to join her in an attempt to restore the constitution of 1720 was strong.[6] While, however, Denmark became alarmed by reports of the Swedish king's reception of a delegation of Norwegian peasants and by his inspection of the Norwegian frontier during his *eriksgata* and took steps to put her defences in a state of readiness, she was careful to avoid any incident which would provide the Swedes with an excuse to open hostilities. There was a certain amount of unrest in Norway, but it was not such as to suggest that a revolt there was imminent.[7] Gustavus did not feel strong enough to risk a war in which he was openly the aggressor, for which, in any case, under the terms of the new constitution, he would have to obtain the consent of the Estates, and the crisis passed. He continued to watch developments in Europe closely, but there was for several years no sign of the emergence of conditions which might give him a free hand in the west. Indeed Denmark and Russia seemed to draw closer together, and Russo-Swedish relations,

[5] *Ibid.*, pp. 271–2.

[6] C. T. Odhner, *Sveriges Politiska Historia under Konung Gustaf III:s Regering*, I (Stockholm, 1885) 192; Geijer I, 231–2; Nielsen, pp. 28–9; Jägerskiöld, p. 263.

[7] L. Wahlström 'Gustav III och Norrmännen', *Gustavianska Studier* (Stockholm, 1914) pp. 128–30; Odhner, I, 179, 190–1, 193–5; Hellstenius, pp. 9–15; Nielsen, pp. 9–27, 29–34; Jägerskiöld, p. 264.

for all Gustavus's attempts to bring about a rapprochement, remained strained.[8]

But in 1777 came the crisis over the Bavarian succession which seemed to promise a European conflict, and at the same time Catherine's relations with the Turks reached a point at which a new Russo-Turkish war appeared likely in the near future.[9] In the same year Gustavus at last persuaded France, his only sure ally, on whose subsidies he was heavily reliant, to allow him to fulfil his long-cherished ambition to visit Catherine in St Petersburg.[10] He was in fact unable to persuade her even to give specific approval to the new Swedish constitution.[11] But he was far from discouraged by the encounter and hoped that frequent correspondence between the two monarchs, even if confined largely to family matters, might lead to cooperation in wider fields.[12] That he was again seriously contemplating war with Denmark at this time is suggested by the visit made to that country in 1778 by his ambitious intimate J. C. Toll, a strong advocate of a bold foreign policy, who after it presented the king with two encouraging reports on the political situation in Denmark and the state of her defences.[13]

The War of the Bavarian Succession came to an end without the upheaval for which Gustavus had hoped, and a Russo-Turkish war failed to materialize. But the growing British interference with neutral trade during the War of American Independence provided Gustavus with an opportunity to strengthen his links with Russia which he was not slow to exploit. Denmark's more cautious attitude to the question of a League of Armed Neutrality, due to Bernstorff's distrust of Sweden and his wish to secure an agreement with Britain, played into Gustavus's hands.[14] It is significant that in 1780 Henrik Trolle, who had shortly before spoken

[8] C. T. Odhner, 'Gustaf III och Katarina II åren 1783–4', *Nordisk Tidskrift* (Stockholm, 1879) pp. 139–40; Geijer, II, 108; Odhner, I, 396–7, 479; Jägerskiöld, pp. 264–7.

[9] Jägerskiöld, p. 277.

[10] *Ibid.*, p. 272; Odhner, I, 286–9, 481–3.

[11] Odhner, I, 484–8; II, 242–3.

[12] Odhner, I, 489–90.

[13] K. Mellander, *Johan Christopher Toll som Militär och Politiker under Gustav III* (Stockholm, 1933) pp. 92–3; Odhner, I, 528–9; Hellstenius, pp. 16–17; Jägerskiöld, p. 278.

[14] I. de Madariaga, *Britain, Russia and the Armed Neutrality of 1780* (London, 1962) pp. 185–91, 233; Odhner, II, 96–7, 229; Jägerskiöld, pp. 281–6.

of taking Norway in Copenhagen, was appointed admiral-general to take charge of a great build-up of Sweden's naval strength which would give her a fleet as large as those of Denmark and Russia combined in seven years, and that shortly afterwards Toll presented plans for the army which obviously envisaged a Norwegian campaign.[15] We also know that while Gustavus was in Germany that same year he discussed with Gustav Creutz, his ambassador to France, plans for a war with Denmark with the object of adding Norway to his dominions.[16] These discussions followed a letter which Creutz wrote to his master in November 1779 in which he advocated such a policy after speaking with the king's friend, Evert Taube, who had arrived in Paris shortly before. Creutz envisaged the crisis which might follow the deaths of Frederick of Prussia or Maria Theresa, or the overthrow of the governments in Copenhagen or St Petersburg, as a suitable occasion.[17]

Bernstorff's fall at the end of 1780, which led to an improvement in Russo-Danish relations, was a blow to Gustavus's hopes.[18] But for some time before this he had been under pressure from his more cautious councillors, led by his chancellor Ulrik Scheffer, whose judgment he respected, to curb the ambition which he had done little to conceal and to tread warily while the situation in Europe was so uncertain; even Trolle thought that any moves should be delayed until more of the shipbuilding programme had been completed.[19] Gustavus seems as a consequence to have again decided to bide his time.

Catherine's proclamation of the annexation of the Khanate of the Crimea in the middle of April 1783 caused him immediately to revive his plans; a Russo-Turkish war, which would draw Russia's military and naval forces from the Baltic, seemed inevitable. And other factors appeared to be in favour of a 'forward' policy by Sweden. While her financial situation was still far from satisfactory, both her army and her navy were

[15] A. Munthe, *Svenska Sjöhjältar* VI (Stockholm, 1911) 241; Odhner, II, 99–101, 232; Mellander, pp. 105–10, 123; Jägerskiöld, p. 280.

[16] Uppsala University Library (U.U.B.), F 418: Gustavus III to Trolle, 3 June 1783; Hellstenius, p. 19; Odhner, II, 229; Jägerskiöld, p. 280; Odhner, 'Gustaf III', p. 142.

[17] G. Castrén, *Gustav Philip Creutz* (Helsingfors, 1917) pp. 283–5; Odhner, II, 229; Mellander, p. 123.

[18] Odhner, 'Gustaf III', p. 142.

[19] Munthe, p. 242.

stronger than they had been for many years; Frederick of Prussia was ageing; Britain, humiliated by the loss of her American colonies, was suffering from political instability; and the Guldberg regime in Denmark seemed unlikely to react to any situation with much vigour.[20] Toll had returned to Sweden in March after a lengthy tour of Germany, France and Poland, and Gustavus now began discussing with him the details of a war with Denmark.[21] It was decided that this should begin in the summer with a planned incident between a Swedish frigate and the Danish guardship at Kronborg accompanied by the delivery in Copenhagen of a strongly worded note on the subject of the Sound Dues. The Danish fleet was then to be blockaded in the harbour of Copenhagen by a Swedish squadron from Karlskrona, a landing effected in Zealand by a large army covered by the rest of the high-seas fleet and Norway invaded and occupied.[22]

Catherine kept a wary eye on Sweden while she prepared for her Crimean enterprise in the full knowledge that Gustavus might seek to take advantage of her preoccupation with, she suspected, the blessing and encouragement of Prussia and France.[23] But she was concerned principally by Swedish troop movements in Finland, where Gustavus had announced his intention to attend manoeuvres.[24] She decided to seize the opportunity presented by this latter news to write on 2 May reminding the king of an agreement made during his stay in St Petersburg in 1777 to meet her on the frontier between their dominions whenever he should again find himself on the eastern side of the Gulf of Bothnia.[25] Such a meeting would not only give her a chance to gauge his intentions more accurately but could also be used to put pressure on the Turks by suggesting that

[20] Hellstenius, p. 19.

[21] I. Andersson, 'Johan Christopher Toll: Biografiska Problem', *Scandia* (Stockholm-Cophenhagen-Oslo) VIII (1934) 55; Odhner, II, 235; Mellander, p. 123.

[22] Jägerskiöld, p. 290; Mellander, p. 125. No record of these discussions has survived, but it appears from the subsequent correspondence that the plans had already reached this stage by the time Toll left for Karlskrona.

[23] K. Kumlien, 'Storbrittanien och Sverige under den Orientaliska Krisen 1783–1784' [I], *Historisk Tidskrift* LXI (Stockholm, 1941) 277; Odhner, II, 244; Jägerskiöld, p. 289.

[24] Odhner, II, 243; Kumlien [I] (*H.T.*, 1941), pp. 275–6.

[25] U.U.B., F 488: Catherine II to Gustavus III, 21 April (o.s.); Odhner, II, 245; Odhner, 'Gustaf III', p. 144.

their ally was willing to enter into a bargain with her at their expense.[26] The invitation raised in Gustavus the hope that the tsaritsa might be willing, in exchange for the renunciation of his obligations to the Turks, to allow him a free hand against Denmark.[27] A quarrel between Rosencrane, the Danish foreign minister, and the Russian envoy in Copenhagen provided further grounds for optimism.[28] Before replying to Catherine's letter, however, he sent Toll to Karlskrona to discuss the Danish plan with Trolle.[29]

Toll reached the naval base on 19 May, having given out as the reason for the trip the need to make arrangements for a visit the king intended to pay to Germany.[30] After he had talked with the admiral both men on the 20th informed Gustavus of their opinions in separate letters. They agreed that the operation was feasible on condition that there was no danger of interference by Russia or another maritime power, that sufficient funds were available and that adequate supplies of grain could be ensured, though Trolle had hoped that he would have been allowed more time to build up his fleet and complained that his shipbuilding programme would be interrupted. Toll believed that the attack should be launched preferably at the beginning of August. He admitted that the weather made this a risky time of year for naval operations, but most of the harvest should by then have been gathered and the risk of foreign intervention would be less. Trolle believed that the sooner the campaign began the better, before the secret had leaked out and Denmark had had time to arm. He proposed that the squadron to blockade the Danish fleet should consist of eight men-of-war and two frigates which could be prepared as if intended to escort the king to Germany, but warned that the rest of the fleet could not be made ready for a further six weeks.[31]

Two days later, after Toll had left to join his regiment in Skåne,[32] the

[26] Odhner, 'Gustaf III', p. 144.

[27] Munthe, p. 245. I have found no evidence to suggest that Gustavus, as Kumlien contends, wished to avoid meeting Catherine.

[28] E. Holm, *Danmark-Norges Historie under Kristian VII* II (Copenhagen, 1906), 372. Kumlien [I] (*H.T.*, 1941), p. 273.

[29] U.U.B., F 418: Gustavus III to Trolle, 15 May; Geijer, III 17–18; Jägerskiöld, p. 289.

[30] Mellander, pp. 125–6.

[31] U.U.B., F 428; Trolle to Gustavus III, 20 May; Toll to Gustavus III, 20 May; Geijer III, 18–21; Odhner, II, 236–7; Jägerskiöld, p. 290; Andersson, p.56.

[32] Mellander, p. 126; Munthe, p. 247.

Admiral wrote again. He had now become more impressed by the difficulties involved in operating so late in the year, when winds might prevent the fleet from leaving harbour, and pleaded for postponement until the early summer of 1784, when three more men-of-war and three more frigates would be available. It was true that the risk of intervention by another power would be greater then, but a war begun in the current year might last until the next anyway, and Swedish forces would then be no longer fresh.[33] Toll also began to discover additional obstacles. On 25 May he warned the king of the danger that even if Prussia did not enter the war as a belligerent, Frederick might still send troops to aid Denmark. These could reach Zealand in a few weeks, that is before the second Swedish squadron was ready. To guard against such an eventuality he proposed that the army fleet be sent from Finland to cut communications across the Great Belt.[34] He must, however, have known from his correspondence with Trolle that the army fleet could not be made ready until the following year[35] so that he was in effect also arguing for postponement. He may have avoided making the suggestion at this stage in order to allow Trolle to do so first and give the impression that he was more enthusiastic about the project than the admiral in order to increase his standing with the king.[36] But ten days later he did choose to be more specific. He reported that news of rumours of an imminent war with Denmark had reached Trolle from both Östergötland and Stockholm and that the Danish admiral Bille had expressed his intention to visit Karlskrona, which suggested that his suspicions had been aroused. If Gustavus felt that, in view of all this, postponement was advisable, the enterprise, he thought, could still be launched in 1784 and with even greater hope of success since there would have been more time to prepare.[37]

As soon as Gustavus had received the first reports from Toll and Trolle he wrote to Catherine accepting her invitation and asking her to name a

[33] U.U.B., F 428: Trolle to Gustavus III, 22 May; Jägerskiöld, p. 290; Munthe, p. 251.

[34] U.U.B., F 428: Toll to Gustavus III, 24 May; Mellander, p. 126; Andersson, p. 57. The army fleet (also known as the galley or archipelago fleet) was made up of small ships able to operate inshore and within the archipelagos off the coasts of Sweden and Finland.

[35] U.U.B., F 428: Trolle to Gustavus III, 20 May, 6 June.

[36] Andersson, p. 58.

[37] U.U.B., F 428: Toll to Gustavus III, 5 June; Geijer, III, 32–3; Andersson, pp. 57–8.

place of meeting.[38] He counted a good deal on the effects that his conversations with the tsaritsa might have on other rulers and gave to Trolle as one of the reasons against postponement of operations that by the following year such effects could no longer be exploited. In other ways also, he argued, the situation might then be less favourable for Sweden: the Russo-Turkish war might have ended in a Russian victory which would enable Catherine to turn all her attention to the Baltic; the crisis in Russo-Danish relations might have been solved; the death of either Christian VII or the Danish queen-mother might lead to the establishment of a stronger régime in Copenhagen; and Britain might have overcome her political difficulties.[39] Nor was he very concerned by the rumours reported by Toll. Stockholm, he wrote to Trolle, was always a hot-bed of rumour and some of the wiseacres' guesses were almost bound to be right by pure chance. Similar warnings, he pointed out, had been conveyed to him in 1772, and what, he asked, would have happened then if he had because of them decided to postpone the coup? As for Bille, he was probably only coming to Karlskrona out of idle curiosity and if the worst came to the worst his frigate could be seized and the Danish navy weakened thereby. 'My first principle', he concluded, 'is never to change the course of something which has already been resolved on.'[40]

He wrote the letter on the eve of his departure for Finland on 9 June, when his forthcoming encounter with Catherine was looming very large in his thoughts. Indeed he told Trolle that 'everything depends on my interview with Catherine. This is the step which will decide everything. If I find on my return from Viborg [one of the possible meeting places] that nothing can be done then the squadron can on my arrival in Karlskrona have a day's exercise and be laid up.'[41] His earlier and later statements suggest that the outbreak of a Russo-Turkish war was still to be a signal for action and that what was in his mind was that *if* the occupation of the Crimea had not led to an open breach between St Petersburg and the Porte by the time agreed for the beginning of operations *and* he had failed

[38] U.U.B., F 418: Gustavus III to Trolle, 27 May; Odhner, II, 246; Jägerskiöld, p. 290.

[39] U.U.B., F 418: Gustavus III to Trolle, 3 June; Geijer, III, 27–32; Odhner, II, 237–8; Jägerskiöld, p. 290; Munthe, pp. 251–2; Holm, p. 372; Kumlien, [I] (*H.T.*, 1941), p. 273.

[40] U.U.B., F 418: Gustavus III to Trolle, 9 June; Geijer, III, 33–4.

[41] U.U.B., F 418: Gustavus III to Trolle, 9 June; Geijer, III, 33–4.

to reach an agreement with the tsaritsa which would free him from the fear of Russian intervention, the attack on Denmark would at least have to be postponed. His policy during the following twelve months was to depend to a large extent on the fulfilment or non-fulfilment of either of these conditions. A pact with Russia *and* a Balkan conflagration was, of course, even more desirable.

By the time Gustavus sailed, a fourth party had been made privy to the great secret. The king had decided that the time had come to accept the resignation of Ulrik Scheffer, who, conscious that he no longer enjoyed his sovereign's confidence, had for some time been offering to step down. Creutz, who was known to be more favourable to a bold foreign policy and whose large debts made him very dependent on Gustavus's favour, was chosen to succeed him and recalled from France. When he landed in Skåne on the last day of May, he was met by Toll and informed what was afoot.[42] No evidence of his immediate reactions has survived, but the advice which he later tendered suggests that he always had serious doubts about the possibility or indeed the desirability of a Russian alliance in view of its possible repercussions on Sweden's relations with France, which he felt must not be jeopardized for uncertain gains, and about the advisability of attempting anything until the European situation had become clearer.[43] But how far he communicated these fears to Gustavus at this stage we do not know. He arrived in Stockholm on 7 June and accompanied the king across the Gulf of Bothnia two days later.[44]

Gustavus's visit to Finland lasted a month. He had to postpone his meeting with Catherine because of a fall from his horse soon after landing which broke his upper left arm. But he finally arrived at Fredrikshamn on 29 June and stayed for three days closeted with the tsaritsa. No record was kept of the two rulers' discussions, which were conducted in the strictest privacy, and not even Creutz seems to have been informed of their contents. Gustavus, however, appears to have offered to conclude an alliance with Russia by which both parties should bind themselves not to interfere in each other's wars and Catherine to have countered with a proposal for a triple alliance between Russia, Sweden and Denmark directed mainly against the Bourbon Powers. She did not apparently

[42] Odhner, II, 240–2; Jägerskiöld, p. 290; Castrén, p. 381.

[43] Castrén, p. 384.

[44] Odhner, II, 242; Castrén, pp. 381–2.

reject Gustavus's project outright, but her own must have made it plain to him that she was not prepared, for the time being at least, to abandon Denmark, while he had given her a fairly clear idea of the object of his ambitions.[45]

Gustavus put on a brave face and professed himself satisfied by the meeting, but it must have been a sad disappointment to him. He continued, however, to believe that war between Russia and Turkey would break out and that Swedish preparations should be hurried on so as to be completed by the middle of July. He wrote to Trolle immediately after his return to Sweden on 9 July that if Turkey gave way it would be as if Denmark were to give up the Sound Dues.[46] Toll had drawn up a plan of campaign, which he reckoned would last three months and was to involve an invasion of Zealand by 14,200 troops, and one of Norway by three columns: one of 3000 men from Jämtland which was to aim for Trondheim, one of 5000 from Värmland which was to seize Kristiania and one of 5500 to capture the fortress of Fredrikshald.[47] His brother, whom he had sent to reconnoitre its defences, reported back that the Danes were not taking any special precautions and that the general public seemed concerned solely by internal affairs such as the shortage of money and the fate of the Danish East India Company.[48] Trolle dispatched a frigate to Gothenburg to be ready to cut communications across the Kattegat.[49]

But the middle of July came and went without any sign of the hoped-for Near Eastern conflagration; Albedyhll in St Petersburg reported that there seemed little likelihood that the Russian fleet would be sailing for the Mediterranean in the near future.[50] Trolle continued to warn of the

[45] Geijer, III, 37–9; Odhner, II, 247–51; Jägerskiöld, pp. 290–2; Odhner, 'Gustaf III', pp. 144, 146–7; Kumlien [I] (*H.T.*, 1941), pp. 263, 287–9. Kumlien doubts whether Catherine suggested a triple alliance at the Fredrikshamn meeting and is followed in this by Jägerskiöld. The Russian approaches to the Swedish representatives in St Petersburg a short time later about such an agreement were couched, however, so as to suggest that the Swedes were expected to be already familiar with the idea (see below, p. 280).

[46] U.U.B., F 418: Gustavus III to Trolle, 10 July; Geijer, III, 39–41; Kumlien [I] (*H.T.*, 1941), p. 294.

[47] U.U.B., F 428; Toll to Gustavus III, 7 June; Geijer, III, 35.

[48] U.U.B., F 428: Toll to Gustavus III, 17 July; Geijer, III, 49; Odhner, II, 253; Mellander, p. 126.

[49] U.U.B., F 428: Trolle to Gustavus III, 24 June.

[50] Kumlien [I] (*H.T.*, 1941), p. 296.

dangers of navigation in the autumn months, and at the beginning of August Creutz wrote to Gustavus of his fears to 'agir dans les tenebres' and of the need for 'combinaisons qui vous assurent qu'un revers n'entraine point la perte de Votre Gloire, le bouleversement de l'État, l'amertume et des regrets qui empoisonneront la reste de vos jours'.[51] In addition, the Marquis de Pons, the new French ambassador who arrived in Stockholm on 24 July bearing instructions which reflected his government's fears of a Russo-Swedish alliance following the Fredrikshamn meeting and its desire for peace in the Baltic, urged restraint.[52] At the end of July Gustavu, appears still to have been hoping that it might be possible to launch the attack as planned in a few weeks and called Trolle from Karlskrona for consultations. Toll followed the admiral to Stockholm shortly afterwards.[53] But then came news of the peaceful occupation of the Crimeas and at a conference at Drottningholm on 19 August it was formally decided to postpone operations until July 1784 in the hope that the necessary prerequisites—an agreement with Russia and/or a Russo-Turkish war—would by that time be fulfilled.[54] Gustavus was to help conceal the preparations and dispel rumours by making his long dreamed-of ourney to Italy, using as an excuse his accident in Finland; the waters of Pisa were adjudged by his doctors likely to help heal his broken arm which was still giving him some trouble.[55]

While he was away a committee consisting of Toll, Trolle, Creutz and von Carlsson, the able head of the Chancery's war department, who had been informed of the Danish plans as soon as Gustavus returned from Finland, was to make the necessary preparations for the war and send a monthly progress report to the king. It was to be chaired by Creutz and meet at his house, but it was dominated by Toll, who was now higher in the king's favour than ever. He was to have his troops, increased now to a total of 34,000, ready by May, while Trolle promised an army fleet of two frigates and forty-two smaller ships for June and a high-seas fleet of sixteen men-of-war and nine frigates for July. All that either the Council

[51] U.U.B., F 511: Creutz to Gustavus III, 3 August; Geijer, III, 45–7; Kumlien [1] (*H.T.*, 1941), p. 293; Munthe, pp. 257–9.

[52] Odhner, II, 246–7; Jägerskiöld, p. 293; Kumlien [1] (*H.T.*, 1941), p. 295.

[53] Geijer, III, 47–50; Odhner, II, 254–5; Munthe, p. 259.

[54] Geijer, III, 50; Odhner, II, 255; Kumlien [1] (*H.T.*, 1941), p. 296.

[55] H. Stålhane, *Gustav III:s Resa till Italien och Frankrike* (Stockholm, 1953) pp. 9, 13, 16; Odhner, II, 258–60; Odhner, 'Gustaf III', p. 148.

or the College of War was told was that a Defence Committee (*Beredning för försvarsverket*) had been set up to supervise the apportionment of defence expenditure for the coming year and had been given full powers to act in the king's name.[56] Liljencrantz, the secretary of state for trade and finance, was asked to provide a total of 1,617,000 Rdr for a special effort in this sphere (it had been decided that 942,000 Rdr would be needed for the campaign) and, after some protest, managed to do so with the help of two Dutch loans.[57]

The meeting in Fredrikshamn had caused a considerable flurry in the courts of northern Europe, and in Sweden itself the volume of rumour grew after the king's return from Finland. Evert Taube, who had been let into the secret by Gustavus, wrote to him on 23 July that talk of war with Denmark was general and that he had heard from Scheffer, who appeared to be *au fait* with all the details of the plot, that the British envoy Wroughton in particular was alarmed.[58] Wroughton's dispatches, however, show him to have been no more than puzzled by the preparations in Karlskrona, and Scheffer may have chosen to exaggerate the danger in order to persuade the king to adopt a more cautious policy.[59] Johan Könemann, the Danish chargé d'affaires in Stockholm, was also interested in Swedish naval preparations, but was as little concerned by them; their most likely purpose, he thought, was 'de donner à la marine Suèdoise si négligée jusqu'icy au moins un air plus respectable et de la mettre avec le tems réellement sur le pied où elle devoit etre'.[60] His government seems to have been quite unaware of any impending danger.[61]

On the evening of 27 September Gustavus slipped quietly away from Drottningholm and made his way to Ystad, where a yacht was waiting to take him to Warnemünde.[62] He had been preceded by Taube, who acted as his consultant on the Danish enterprise during his journey, and by Sparre, the member of the Council officially responsible for defence, who

[56] Geijer, III, 63–4; Odhner, II, 255–6, 299; Mellander, pp. 127–30; Stålhane, pp. 13, 302–5; Munthe, pp. 260, 262.

[57] U.U.B., F 441: Rådsprotokoller, 27 August, 3 September; K. Åmark, *Sveriges Statsfinanser 1719–1809* (Stockholm, 1961) pp. 630–1; Geijer, III, 50–60; Odhner, II, 256–8.

[58] Geijer, III, 41–5.

[59] Kumlien [1] (*H.T.*, 1941), pp. 272, 290–3.

[60] D.R.A., Dept. f.u.A., Sverrig II, Depecher, Könemann, 29 July, 19 September.

[61] Kumlien [1] (*H.T.*, 1941), p. 285.

[62] Odhner, II, 263–4; Stålhane, pp. 30–4.

had associated himself with Liljencrantz and Scheffer in warning against foreign adventures and who had consequently been kept in ignorance of the war plans. Sparre's absence from the country was deemed desirable both to help the concealment of these plans and to give the Committee a freer hand.[63]

The Committee held its first meeting on 1 October but had nothing of importance to report until after its second on 12 November, when Toll, who was always worried by the supply problem, pressed for the invasion of Norway to be made by the southernmost of the three armies alone while the other two were held in reserve.[64] Gustavus discussed this proposal with Taube, who advised that the original plan should be adhered to but that the Värmland corps should be made the largest and aim for Bergen, thus cutting the country in two, while the Jämtland army should be reduced in size. The king accepted this argument and the Committee fell in with his wishes, although Toll continued to protest that it would be easier to operate with one army than three.[65]

Unknown to Gustavus, Creutz's letters to him during his journey, letters in which the Danish plans were discussed, were from the beginning intercepted in Hanover and their contents communicated to Lord Carmarthen in London.[66] He in turn instructed the British representatives in Copenhagen and St Petersburg at the end of December to pass on the information to the Danish and Russian governments. Neither took the reports very seriously for some time. Too many factors appeared to militate against Sweden's attempting such an enterprise; she was, it was thought, not strong enough militarily to act alone, and the poor harvest of 1783 and the harsh winter which set in at the beginning of 1784 caused

[63] Odhner, II, 261–2; Stålhane, p. 29.

[64] Odhner, II, 300; Mellander, p. 131; Stålhane, pp. 91, 95–6, 312–13; Wahlström, p. 132.

[65] Stålhane, pp. 97, 313–14; Mellander, p. 132; Wahlström, p. 132. For the king's acceptance see Mellander, p. 132; Stålhane, pp. 91, 143–4, 314.

[66] For the interception of correspondence to and from Scandinavia in Hanover at earlier periods, see the author's 'The interception of posts in Celle, 1694–1700' *William III and Louis XIV: Essays 1680–1720 by and for Mark A. Thomson*, ed. R. Hatton and J. S. Bromley (Liverpool, 1968); B. Peterson, ' "The correspondent in Paris": en engelsk informationskälla under 1700-talet', *Scandia* (Stockholm, Copenhagen and Oslo) XXVII (1961); and H. Stiegung, *Den engelska underrätelseverksamheten rörande Sverige under 1700-talet: en studie i Londonkabinettets politiska spionage med särskild hänsyn tagen till åren 1770–1772* (Stockholm, 1961).

considerable distress to a large number of her inhabitants.[67] Könemann and Wroughton continued to treat the rumours with scepticism; Könemann did not even discover the existence of the Defence Committee until May.[68] At the end of November 1783, however, Creutz reported military activity in Norway which led Gustavus to order spies to be sent to the country both to investigate the situation and, if possible, to play on Norwegian discontent.[69] Two men were in fact sent under the direction of Henrik af Låstbom, a Värmlander devoted to the king, who himself visited Kristiania. Their reports, sent to Gustavus at the beginning of March 1784, spoke of widespread fear of a Swedish attack, but they could find no evidence that any special preparations were being made to meet it. Toll undertook a journey to the frontier but could not get very far because of deep snow.[70]

Soon after landing in Germany, Gustavus had received a letter from Staël, Creutz's replacement at Versailles, warning him to expect an invitation to visit the French court.[71] Creutz encouraged him to accept this when it came, arguing that one should humour old friends, that the growing influence of Breteuil, recently appointed secretary of state for the *Maison du Roi* at the expense of the more cautious Vergennes, promised more vigorous French support for his plans and that the trip might make the tsaritsa, on whom he thought the king should not rely too much, more amenable.[72] Gustavus, however, hesitated. He feared that Catherine might be offended by any negotiations with France, against whom the triple alliance, which she was again proposing to Gustavus through his representatives in St Petersburg, was principally directed, and that he might spoil his chances of the rapprochement with Russia of which

[67] L. Trulsson, 'Engelskt Underrätelseväsendet under Sjuttonhundratalet med hänsyn till Svensk Politik', in *Gottfried Carlsson 18.12.1952* (Lund, 1952) p. 308; Kumlien [2] *Historisk Tidskrift* LXII (1942) 26–9; Jägerskiöld, p. 294; Holm, p. 379.

[68] D.R.A., Sverrig II: Könemann, 20 January, 2, 10, 17 February, 2, 8, 30 March, 13 April, 21 May; Odhner II, 321; Holm, p. 378; Kumlien [2] (*H.T.*, 1942) p. 31.

[69] Odhner, II, 302; Stålhane, pp. 92, 100–1.

[70] U.U.B., F 499: Carlsson to Gustavus III, 17 February 1784; Odhner, II, 302–3; Mellander, p. 131; Hellstenius, p. 25; N. Staf, 'Gustav III och Norge: Major F. A. U. Funks Resa till Norge 1785', in *Historiska Studier Tillägnade Sven Tunberg* (Stockholm, 1942) p. 374; Wahlström, p. 133.

[71] Jägerskiöld, p. 293; Stålhane, p. 39.

[72] Geijer, III, 132; Castrén, pp. 389–90; Stålhane, p. 91; Kumlien [2] (*H.T.*, 1942), p. 17.

he was still dreaming.[73] He had toyed with the idea of returning through Vienna; but his meetings with Joseph II in Florence and Rome, though he did his best to create the impression that he and the emperor had reached full agreement, dashed his hopes of any kind of Austrian alliance, and finally, at the end of December, he decided to reply affirmatively to the French proposal, which had reached him in Pisa.[74] It seems, however, that he did so in order to put pressure on Catherine and that he was prepared to change his plans if she should react favourably. At the same time he sought other ways of insuring himself against Russian interference with his plans. Heidenstam, his minister in Constantinople, was instructed to urge the Turks to declare war and Count Johan Hård was sent to Berlin to sound out the possibility of an alliance with Prussia, which had been on bad terms with Russia since a dispute over Danzig in the summer of 1783.[75]

On 12 February in Naples, Gustavus was told by the Russian minister Razumovskii of the Russo-Turkish agreement on the Crimea which had been signed on 8 January.[76] It was a sad blow; only two weeks before, he had written to Trolle that 'all seems to foretoken a great upheaval in Europe'.[77] But he persuaded himself that the conflict was only briefly postponed thereby and ordered the Defence Committee to continue its preparations.[78] On 7 March he wrote to Creutz with a suggestion for engineering an incident between Rosencrane and Sprengtporten, his envoy in Copenhagen, as a prelude to war.[79] Creutz, however, was much less optimistic. He had long entertained doubts about the Danish enterprise; his constant harping on the distress at home caused by the harsh winter may have been calculated to dampen Gustavus's enthusiasm and his strong advocacy of the visit to France was possibly motivated by a hope that the French government would impress upon the king the need for caution.[80]

[73] Geijer, III, 131; Odhner, II, 273–4; Jägerskiöld, p. 273.

[74] U.U.B., F 418: Gustavus III to Trolle, 27 January; Geijer, III, 87, 114; Odhner, II, 271, 281; Jägerskiöld, p. 273; Castrén, p. 391; Stålhane, pp. 80–1, 88, 105.

[75] U.U.B., F 418: Gustavus III to Hård, n.d.; Odhner, II, 272–3, 281–2; Jägerskiöld, pp. 293–4; Kumlien [2] (*H.T.*, 1942) pp. 18–19.

[76] Odhner, II, 284–5; Jägerskiöld, p. 294.

[77] U.U.B., F 418: Gustavus III to Trolle, 16 March; Geijer, III, 113.

[78] Odhner, II, 285; Stålhane, p. 115.

[79] Odhner, II, 302; Stålhane, pp. 98–9, 322–4.

[80] Geijer, III, 129; Kumlien [2] (*H.T.*, 1942), p. 47.

Now he became bolder. At the end of February he wrote advising the putting off of any attack on Denmark, unless some sort of agreement had been reached with Catherine, until the death of Frederick II. Then Joseph would probably seek from Prussia the compensation for Russian gains which he had not sought in Turkey and would set off a large-scale conflict, of which Sweden would be able to take advantage. He had already warned against any dealings with Frederick, whom he distrusted deeply.[81]

Gustavus received this letter on 16 March, when he was back in Rome.[82] Combined with the continuing peace in the East, the absence of any promising response from Catherine and the unfavourable reaction of Prussia to his approaches, its arguments finally persuaded him to give way so far as to order in his reply on the 22nd, that preparations for an imminent offensive should be halted. Even now, he could not bring himself to give up all hope that circumstances might allow him to attempt something before the end of the year; the Committee was told to continue assembling supplies and to do whatever else seemed feasible to improve the state of readiness.[83] A breach might yet occur between Russia and Turkey. Catherine, to whom he had written to ask what Joseph had told her of their meetings, might still agree to abandon Denmark. He might obtain French support; he told Creutz that twenty French warships would be sufficient to hold off both the English and the Russian fleets. Denmark, who was reported to be arming, might even anticipate a Swedish attack by launching one herself. Gustavus ordered that if the latter should happen, his brother the duke of Södermanland should take charge of the main army on the Norwegian frontier, but that care should be taken to provide him with bold advisers as he was easily influenced and was inclined to be stubborn once his mind had been made up; the king himself would lead the army in Skåne as soon as he could get home.[84]

A series of events during the following three months finally drove Gustavus to change the whole direction of his foreign policy. Catherine had by March begun to take more seriously the reports of his aggressive intentions in the Baltic, to which additional colour had been given by his

[81] Odhner, II, 283–6; Castrén, p. 391; Stålhane, p. 131.

[82] Stålhane, p. 130.

[83] Odhner, II, 285–6, 305; Jägerskiöld, p. 294; Stålhane, pp. 132–3; Kumlien [2] (*H.T.*, 1942) p. 17.

[84] Geijer, III, 120; Stålhane, pp. 134–6.

remarks to the emperor and Razumovskii. She began to mobilize her forces; on 17 March wrote a sarcastic reply to his letter, in which she professed to discount all the rumours which had reached her; and ordered Arkadij Markov, who had been appointed envoy to Sweden in March 1783 but was at this time in Paris, to meet Gustavus in Rome, where he was both to make a last attempt to win the king over to her plan for a triple alliance and to discover how far the projected visit to Paris was motivated by promises of French help for designs against Denmark or herself.[85]

Gustavus and Markov talked for two hours in St Peter's on Good Friday, 5 April. In the course of the conversation Gustavus firmly rejected the idea of any alliance with Denmark, whom he attacked bitterly, especially for her Holstein policy, and renewed his offer of a pact by which Russia should abandon Denmark in exchange for the renunciation of his own alliance with Turkey, backing it up with an ill-considered threat. 'Vous savez', Markov reported him to have said, 'que de ma frontière à Petersbourg il n'y a pas grande distance.' When he went on to claim that if Sweden and Russia were united, 'le Danemark bientot n'aura rien à livrer ni à disposer de rien', the Russian asked him if he was proposing a conquest of Denmark and if France could be expected to support this. Gustavus replied that it would not and this was an additional reason why Catherine should allow him a free hand; she could use her influence to gain compensation for Denmark in Germany. After Markov had attacked France for fomenting trouble between neighbours in the Baltic, Gustavus concluded the discussion by asserting that he would nevertheless be compelled to renew his ties with that power unless Catherine accepted his proposals before he reached Paris.[86] The result of the meeting was much the same as that at Fredrikshamn the previous year; the king offered the tsaritsa further insight into his ambitions while he remained as far from his objectives as ever.

A few days after the interview, Gustavus received news of Trolle's death on 12 March.[87] The king had come to rely heavily on the admiral,

[85] U.U.B., F 488: Catherine II to Gustavus III, 17 March; Geijer, III, 120–2; Odhner, II, 288–90; Jägerskiöld, p. 294; Odhner, 'Gustaf III', p. 149; Stålhane, p. 179; Kumlien [2] (*H.T.*, 1942) pp. 33–4, 49.

[86] *Historiallinen Arkisto* III (Helsinki, 1871) 61–75; Jägerskiöld, pp. 294–5; Odhner, 'Gustaf III', pp. 149–51; Stålhane, pp. 149–50, 335–42.

[87] Geijer, III, 124–6; Odhner, II, 286.

whose loss must be regarded as a further blow to his plans; he was undoubtedly deeply distressed. Trolle was, in accordance with instructions left by Gustavus before he left Sweden, replaced on the Defence Committee by Colonel Ehrensvärd, who continued to build up the fleet in accordance with the plan adopted in 1780, but who was never informed of the original purpose of his predecessor's activities in Karlskrona.[88]

A month later two even more disturbing pieces of news reached the king, now in Venice. He was informed of the coup d'état in Copenhagen on 14 April which, he remarked laconically, 'changed much'.[89] His forebodings of the effects of the overthrow of the Guldberg régime proved to be justified, for the new Danish administration immediately took vigorous measures to meet the threat from Sweden.[90] Then a few days later, on 10 May, Catherine's letter of 17 March was delivered to Gustavus by her special courier; he could no longer be under any illusion about Russia's attitude to an attack on Denmark, and at the beginning of June the tsaritsa issued a specific declaration of her determination to stand by her ally.[91]

Gustavus's last hope—of using the Russian and Danish threats to persuade France to grant him powerful military and financial aid which might be used for aggressive purposes—was dashed soon after he reached Paris at the end of the first week of June. Vergennes wanted peace in the Baltic and urged the Swedish king to seek a rapprochement with Denmark and Russia; only with difficulty could Gustavus obtain even a subsidy agreement for a sum considerably smaller than that for which he had asked.[92]

At the same time Creutz's assurances in reply to Catherine's manifesto that Sweden's military build-up was purely defensive calmed both her neighbours, who halted their mobilization.[93] By the end of July the crisis

[88] Geijer, III, 64 n. 1, 124; Odhner, II, 303–4; Stålhane, pp. 17, 152; Munthe, pp. 263, 269.

[89] U.U.B., F 479: Gustavus III to Creutz, 7 May; Geijer, III, 141–4.

[90] H. G. Garde, *Efterretninger om den Danske og Norske Søemagt* IV (Copenhagen, 1835) 288; Odhner, II, 322; Hellstenius, pp. 24–5; Stålhane, p. 228; Kumlien [2] (*H.T.*, 1942) p. 32. In D.R.A., Dept f.u.A.: Sverrig Ie, there is a large collection of reports on Swedish military preparations, mainly from May 1784.

[91] Odhner, II, 293, 322; Jägerskiöld, p. 295; Odhner, 'Gustaf III', p. 153; Hellstenius, p. 22; Stålhane, pp. 178, 242.

[92] Odhner, II, 331–6; Jägerskiöld, pp. 295–7; Odhner, 'Gustaf III', pp. 153–5; Kumlien [1] (*H.T.*, 1942) p. 266.

[93] Geijer, III, 161–2; Odhner, II, 322–3; Odhner, 'Gustaf III', p. 153; Stålhane, p. 142.

was at an end. So also was an important stage in Gustavus's foreign policy. From this time onwards he directed his ambitions eastwards and when the Russo-Turkish war, on the likelihood of which he had built so much in 1783–84, finally broke out in 1787 he hurried forward preparations to strike, not at Denmark, with whom in fact he tried to conclude an alliance,[94] but at Russia. Not that he seems ever to have completely abandoned his hopes of acquiring Norway. A Major Funk was sent to explore the area around the Kristiania Fjord in the summer of 1785 and discover the extent of discontent: the Lofthus Rising in west Norway of 1786–87 resulted in the appointment of a Swedish consul-general in Kristiania to keep an eye on developments; and in 1790 Armfelt conducted negotiations with Norwegian dissidents.[95] It became obvious, however, that the prospect of replacing Danish with Swedish rule aroused little enthusiasm in Norway and that what most Norwegian patriots wanted was either an improvement in the status of their country within the Twin Monarchy or full independence. Toll urged his master to encourage hopes of the latter, but Gustavus feared that an independent Norway might become a breeding ground for dangerous doctrines and refused to countenance the proposal.[96]

[94] S. J. Boëthius, *Om Orsakerna till Gustaf III:s Krig med Ryssland* (Uppsala, 1884) p. 13; Hellstenius, p. 33; Wahlström, p. 142.

[95] Odhner, II, 360; Hellstenius, pp. 30–2, 39–41; Nielsen, pp. 41, 44–52, 54–72; Staf, *loc. cit.*, pp. 374–92; Wahlström, pp. 134, 138, 151–4.

[96] Hellstenius, pp. 29–30, 42–3; Nielsen, p. 41; Staf, *loc. cit.*, pp. 393–4; Wahlström, p. 152.

15

C. A. MACARTNEY

The Compromise of 1867

To writers on the Compromise of 1867 it is a perpetual temptation, to which nearly all of them succumb, to devote their remarks not to the Compromise itself, but to the Dualist System. Compromise and Dualist System, although closely interconnected, are, however, different things. The Compromise which, *pace* the usual British nomenclature, should properly be so called, without the prefix 'Austro-Hungarian', is the bilateral agreement concluded in 1867 between Franz Joseph, *qua* King of Hungary, and the representatives of the Hungarian nation, and set out in the Hungarian Law XII of that year. The Dualist System is the wider political structure constructed partly on, partly round, that law, the whole forming the framework within which the constitutional life of the Habsburg Monarchy was conducted from 1867 to 1918. Under it the Monarchy, now officially entitled the Austro-Hungarian Monarchy, consisted of two political entities, the one composed of the Lands of the Hungarian Crown, the other, of the remaining dominions of the Habsburgs. The former was a unitary state, or near-state, except that Croatia-Slavonia enjoyed a fairly wide measure of autonomy inside it (this was recodified in 1868), while the other half of the Monarchy, technically known as 'the Kingdoms and Lands represented in the Imperial Council', was, as its name implies, a federation of provinces, each of which sent representatives to a central parliament competent for the questions of common interest to them all. Each half was entirely independent of the other as regards its internal affairs, in respect whereof each formed a constitutionally limited monarchy. The two entities, however, besides recognizing the same member of the House of Habsburg as monarch, also formed a unity in respect of the subjects, described in the Austrian law as 'common' and in the Hungarian as 'of common interest', of foreign policy and defence, and there were three 'common' ministers: one for foreign affairs, one for defence and the third for the finances required by the other two. These ministers were responsible, up to a point (there were certain limits, especially in respect of defence, beyond which parliamentary control ceased) to the two parliaments, and those bodies, or their representatives, also decided what quota of the necessary expenditure should be borne by each half; this being reconsidered every ten years.

Besides these 'pragmatic subjects', so termed because Hungary recognized them as of common interest in virtue of the Pragmatic Sanction issued by Charles VI, there were other so-called 'questions of common interest', on which the two halves of the Monarchy adopted a common policy by agreement. These included commercial policy towards other states and towards each other, the latter being regulated by a tariff and commercial treaty, subject to reconsideration every ten years—in practice, the first agreement of 1867 established a customs union and this was still in force in 1918—and also some aspects of indirect taxation, weights and measures and monetary standards, and certain questions relating to the railway system.

The two parliaments enjoyed equal rights in all these respects, and the basis of the whole system was that of strict parity between them. The quotas of taxation were not equal—they began at 70:30, rising by 1907 to 63.6:36.4; but they were calculated on the basis of taxable capacity, so that here, too, there was parity of burden, as the contingents to the common army, while not equal, were proportionate to the populations.

Nearly all of this derives directly from, where it does not simply repeat, the Hungarian Law, which further sets out in detail the political philosophy of the system, as seen from the Hungarian angle. It is very bulky, for it contains an enormous amount of preamble and argumentation—it is really a committee report, hurriedly and roughly thrown into the form of a law—but can be summarized as follows:

It begins by pointing out that under her existing laws, confirmed by various members of the Habsburg dynasty, most recently Leopold II in 1791 and Ferdinand I in April 1848, Hungary has no internal constitutional link with any of the Habsburgs' other dominions. But when accepting the Pragmatic Sanction, in 1722–23, she recognized that defence constituted 'a common and mutual obligation' between herself and them: and 'the suitable guidance of foreign affairs'—a subject not mentioned in

1722—is ingeniously brought in as a function of defence. Now that constitutional institutions have been restored in Hungary after the absolutism, and are being introduced in Austria, these questions must be subject to constitutional control in both halves of the Monarchy; and the rest of the Law is chiefly devoted to laying down the machinery whereby this control can be exercised and harmonized without infringing the mutual independence of the two parties: the establishment of the common ministries, the definition of their parliamentary responsibility, the devices for exercising a control which shall at once be joint and not joint (this is achieved by a polygonizing of the circle so ingenious as to render the remaining logical contradictions almost imperceptible), the treatment of the non-pragmatic subjects of common interest, and certain other points of detail.

The Law does not touch on Hungary's internal structure—this had been settled shortly before, or provision made for its settlement, in the course of the negotiations which will be described presently. Still less, of course, does it dictate the internal structure of the other half of the Monarchy—Austria, as it may be called for convenience—although it does insist that a condition for Hungary's acceptance of it was that the Austrian Lands should have due influence over the constitutional treatment of the common affairs, and it speaks of a Cis-Leithanian parliament (in the singular) as a counterpart to the Hungarian. This, however, is less a stipulation than an assumption, based on what was then the *de facto* constitutional position in Austria, as it had evolved in the preceding years.

Writers on the subject, whether they profess to be writing on the Compromise or on the Dualist System, nearly always in fact make the latter their theme, and their essays are usually expressions of the author's views on the merits or demerits of Dualism; which they praise or blame—most often the latter, since it is easier to find fault with other people's work than to praise it, and makes the critic sound cleverer—according to its effects as seen by them in the hind-sight of history. The humanly interesting question is, of course, whether the Dualist System provided the best answer, or any satisfactory answer at all, to the 'problem of the Monarchy', and it is one on which the present writer holds his own views; nor is he averse from making himself sound clever. He will come to them in due course. He does, however, hold most strongly that any criticism of a historic achievement is valueless, and indeed meaningless, which does not take into account its historical setting and the circumstances in which it came into being. This is most particularly true of the Compromise, which was the result of a long and complex process of trial and error, and the writer makes no apology for turning next to a sketch of its antecedents, beginning with those which were more immediate: with the development, that is, of the opposition to the pan-Monarchic absolutism legally imposed by Franz Joseph under the so-called Sylvester Patent of 31 December 1851, which annulled the so-called Stadion Constitution of March 1849, which in its turn had annulled the 'April Laws' passed in Hungary in April 1848 and rendered nugatory the near-complete Kremsier draft Constitution worked out for the Western Lands by the *Reichstag* of 1848–49.

Speaking dogmatically, as the limitations of space require, it may be said that there proved to be in the Monarchy three factors which in the end made the neo-absolutism untenable. The first was the Italian opposition, reinforced from Piedmont, and ultimately from France. The second was the opposition which is usually described as emanating from the 'Liberal' German-Austrian bourgeoisie; but this description is not to be accepted without reservation. The German-Austrian bourgeoisie was Janus-faced. A considerable number of its members consisted of Josephinian-minded bureaucrats, with their families and associates, who were opposed only to certain aspects of the absolutist régime, notably its 'feudal' characteristics, while strong supporters of other aspects of it, in particular, of its centralism. They, however, shaded into the business interests, and these again into the Jewish financial interests, which were only half inside the Monarchy, the other half being international. These interests were often the most important of all, because the Austrian Government after 1848 was, as it had been before that date, chronically in the red, and obliged to borrow from them to pay its way. The financiers, inside and outside Austria, were strongly anticlerical and antimilitarist, and also against the bureaucratic absolutism on account of its expense, and this Janus-face of the German Austrians and Jews was anticentralist also in respect of Hungary and Italy.

The third real opposition force was the Hungarian, which again was not homogeneous: one can distinguish in it three main groups—*Richtungen*—which, of course, overlapped. At one extreme stood the true rebels, who looked to the exiled Kossuth: numerically considerable, but for the time being cowed into silence. At the other extreme stood the so-called Hungarian Old Conservatives, the feudal magnates who were against Bach's centralizing bureaucracy, but also against the liberal tenor of the April Laws, and wanted, broadly, a return to the *status quo ante* 1848. Then there was a central party, as leader of which Ferenc Deák emerged after about 1855. Deák was antiseparatist, and accepted the Pragmatic Sanction. He, too, thought that the April Laws had gone too far in respect of the common services—defence, etc.—and did not exclude the possibility of their being revised by the constitutional method of agreement between the Crown and the Hungarian Diet; but he insisted that the laws were legally valid and that the Crown must recognize the fact before the negotiations opened.

There was in the 1850s no other noteworthy opposition. The Poles had been *de facto* bought off—the buying off of the Galician Poles is of much earlier date than is generally recognized. The Czech and Slovene nationalists were passive in this decade, and the Bohemian Feudalists, for various reasons, equally so. The Clericals were on the side of the régime.

In 1859 Austria was defeated in Italy and lost Lombardy. Many causes contributed to this—irredentism in the Italian provinces themselves, the role of Piedmont, the ambitions of Napoleon III, Buol's and Franz Joseph's own inept diplomacy, Gyulai's incompetence as a military leader; but Hungarian discontent played a considerable part—troops had to be kept in Hungary, Hungarian units deserted, Hungarian émigrés influenced foreign opinion. Bigger still was the contribution of the financiers. Owing to their hostility to the régime, Austria had simply been unable to raise the money, inside or outside the Monarchy, to maintain an efficient, adequately equipped army. The three factors listed above had between them made the continuance of absolutism impossible.

After this there began the story of Franz Joseph's retreat towards constitutionalism, his object being to find the ally which would help him to hold the Monarchy together at the least cost to his own authority. It was a zigzag course, during which one such ally after another was tried and proved ineffective. It is often written, even by Austrian historians, that his concessions to Hungary began on the morrow of the armistice of Villa Franca. This is not the case. In those first days, Franz Joseph was still entirely against any concessions to any group of Hungarians. The first ground yielded, by the dismissals of Bach and Kempen, and in the

Laxenburg manifesto and the government programme of 23 August 1859, was exclusively to the German constitutionalists and the financiers: what was promised was effective control of expenditure, both civil and military, concessions to the legally recognized non-Catholic Churches and to the Jews; extended local self-government, and subsequently, a series of practical alleviations for the Jews. And the second step, taken when these half-measures had been received with near-derision, the convocation of the old *Reichsrat*, the investment of it with a quasi-representative character by the inclusion in it of elected members from the *Landtage*, was again really in the same direction: the *Reichsrat*'s functions (which were only advisory) were, as first defined, purely financial, and the purpose of the move was to restore the confidence of Austria's foreign and domestic creditors.

The move did, however, entail a political concession towards Hungary, although a reluctant and paradoxical one. Under Bach, Hungary had been divided into five *Regierungsbezirke*, and one possible course would have been to appoint a *Landtag* for each of them. Several of Franz Joseph's advisers recommended this: they said it would be less dangerous than giving Hungary back her single central Diet. Others, however, warned him that there would be tremendous storms if the division of Hungary were institutionalized, and he adopted this view, without pleasure, but bowing before what seemed to him necessity. The *Regierungsbezirke* were abolished and the administration centralized. The Hungarian Diet was to supply six of the thirty-six elected members who, with twenty-one life members, were to make up the 'Reinforced *Reichsrat*'.

In view of this important concession, one can describe the institution of the Reinforced *Reichsrat* as a step towards the final Dualism of 1867. But it did not lead there directly: it proved another zig of the zigzag, which ended in another road block. All the thirty-six non-life members were nominated, for the occasion, by Franz Joseph himself, and for Hungary he nominated six Old Conservative magnates. But the Old Conservative political philosophy favoured provincial historical rights all round: not only for Hungary, but also for Bohemia, Galicia, etc. Consequently, when the six Hungarians arrived in Vienna, they allied themselves with their fellow-magnates from elsewhere, notably with a newly formed group of Bohemian magnates under Count Jaroslav Clam-Martinitz—the first emergence of this force since 1849—to form a 'Party of the Federal

Nobility'. They turned the *Reichsrat* into a sort of Constituent, which was not within its terms of reference at all, and produced a strongly decentralized, federalist, draft constitution for the Monarchy. The other members of the *Reichsrat* had no recourse left but to counter with an alternative draft, more centralized; and Franz Joseph, unable to defy both, found himself left with no choice but to take one or the other. He chose the Federal Nobility's draft, because his Hungarian confidants told him that Hungary would accept it, and issued the so-called October Diploma, which was based on its ideas. There was to be a central Parliament, of 100 members, to which Hungary was to send representatives; but the special position of Hungary was recognized in so far that the other Provinces were to meet without the Hungarians when questions came under discussion 'which had long been "handled and decided" by them as a unit' (actually there were no such questions, because they had never sat as a unit except at Kremsier, which had not decided anything; but to insist on this would perhaps be pedantry).

The Crown promised—this was a move forward which was never retracted—to exercise its legislative powers only with the cooperation of the *Reichsrat* or the *Landtage*. The *Reichsrat*'s consent was necessary for taxation.

For Hungary, the historic Diet was to be reconstituted; new statutes were to be drafted for the other *Landtage*, which were to have wide powers.

This experiment again was a complete failure. Although further concessions had been made to Hungary, including the reestablishment of its Court Chancellery and the reintroduction of Magyar as the language of internal administration, the country solidly rejected the idea of any central *Reichsrat* at all. The reception in the west was little better: quotations of Austrian bonds sank to a new level, and the government had to pay nearly 9 per cent for new accommodation.

In view of this it was clear that the idea of aristocratic federalism for the Monarchy was out: but what should replace it? Franz Joseph was not at this stage going any further to meet Hungary, which seemed to him insatiable short of concessions which in his view were incompatible with the continued existence of the Monarchy. He did, however, think that it might be possible to placate liberal opinion and to put the finances in order; while another factor which weighed strongly with him at the time was the hope of attracting opinion in the German states by a display of constitutionalism and Germandom. Accordingly, he appointed a new ministry, with the Archduke Rainer minister president and Anton von Schmerling minister of state, and on 1 February 1861 issued the so-called February Patent. Nominally an elucidation of the October Diploma, and in fact not altering the powers retained by the Crown under the Diploma and also retaining the quasi-Dualist provision that the *Reichsrat* could sit as a full body, or as a 'narrower' (*engerer*) one without the Hungarians, it changed the balance by replacing the Diploma's *Reichsrat* by a much larger body. The franchise for this gave much larger representation to the German bourgeoisie, although it is important, for the understanding of the next years, to stress that the common description of the franchise as 'establishing the predominance of the German bourgeoisie' is exaggerated. That class was still underrepresented by comparison with the great landowners; and it was possible to tip the balance one way or another by exerting pressure at the key points. As it happened, the balance was so delicate that pressure on the great landlords' electoral colleges in the 'mixed' crownlands of Bohemia and Moravia could change the majority in the whole *Reichsrat*. In 1861, however, the pressure was the other way; and the parties calling themselves Liberals, or German Liberals, although not quite united, emerged as the largest single grouping in the *Reichsrat*.

They had been brought into power to provide a government which should support the régime, and *qua* Josephinians they did so; but that very centralism alienated many of the other political factors in the Monarchy, and the German nationalism with which they contrived to combine it estranged others. The Hungarians, now rallied behind Deák—Kossuth and the émigrés were losing credit, and when the elections were held not a single Old Conservative was returned to the Diet—refused to attend the *Reichsrat*, and denied its competence to legislate for Hungary. The Croats, although anti-Hungarian, yet also boycotted the *Reichsrat* for their own reasons, so that the only representatives of the Hungarian Lands to attend it were the Saxons and Roumanians from Transylvania. In the west, the Poles withdrew from it in 1863 when martial law was proclaimed in Galicia; and the Czechs walked out in the same year, after the Germans had grossly insulted them. Meanwhile, the Liberals had also turned the German federalists and clericals against them by premature attacks on the Corcordat of 1855. The Germans had thus driven everyone else into opposition to the government, leaving themselves its only nominal prop; and at the same time they proved themselves, *qua* Liberals, rather the opponents of the system than its supporters, by their refusal to vote essential taxation: their only remedy for the Government's continued financial difficulties was to cut expenditure, especially expenditure on the army. Thanks to their remorseless cheese-paring, Austria's army was so visibly weakened that when it seemed clear, in 1864, that war with Prussia was inevitable, Franz Joseph, although not despondent about the outcome of the war, still felt that he could not face it with a disaffected Hungary in his rear. He got into secret touch with the Hungarians, this time approaching Deák, who now did not dismiss the possibility of interparliamentary discussion of the 'common' subjects; and Franz Joseph demonstrated his hope of coming to terms with Hungary by visiting the country—that was in June 1865—and promising convocation of the Diet.

This was a clear repudiation of Schmerling, who had hoped to starve the Hungarians into subjection. 'We can wait,' he had said when the Hungarians refused to attend the *Reichsrat*. He and the archduke resigned, and the field was clear again for a new combination, if such could be found. Franz Joseph seems to have been thinking, at the time, in the terms of a reversion, in the west, to the federation of the original October Diploma, for his new minister president was Count Richard Belcredi, a man connected by birth and career with the Bohemian federalist aristocracy. Belcredi said indeed that he would show that Austria could be governed without the Germans, but no immediate structural change was made. The *Landtage* were left in being, only the operation of the *Reichsrat* 'suspended' (*sistiert*), pending the outcome of the negotiations with the Hungarian and Croat Diets, which were convoked for the following December. These negotiations narrowed the gap in important respects: Franz Joseph recognized the validity of the April Laws, although still insisting that those relating to common affairs would have to be amended. The Hungarians agreed to some form of discussion of those affairs between the two parliaments. But it must be two parliaments, and Franz Joseph still stipulated for one. Thus the gap was still unclosed when there came the Austro-Prussian War of 1866.

Among the many effects of Austria's defeat in this was the great weakening, not perhaps to be explained in terms of logic, but very real, of the political position of her Germans. Whatever shape the Monarchy took in the future, it could be neither that of Bach absolutism, nor of the February Patent. The Germans were curiously slow to realize this; but the other peoples felt it, and prepared to take advantage of it. And now it was very important that the Slavs played their hand very badly, and the Hungarians theirs very well. Polish, Czech and Croat leaders met in Vienna for a 'Federalist Conference', but entirely failed to reach an agreed programme, even between themselves. Moreover, not only had the Pole ignored the Ruthenes, and the Croats the Serbs of Slavonia, but the Czechs had deliberately arranged that the Slovenes, whose views on how ths Monarchy should be constructed differed from theirs, should not be invited. Czechs and Slovenes further indulged in outbreaks of hostilite against the Germans which made the latter determined not to accept ay inch more of federalism than they could help. Deák, on the other handn held his following together (with some difficulty, but in the end firmly, enough) and asked by Franz Joseph what his terms were after Königgrätz, replied that they were the same as before it.

It was also important that the man now emerging as Deák's right-hand man was Count Gyula Andrássy. Andrássy was a man of charm and of lineage, *hoffähig*; and he struck up a personal friendship with the Empress Elizabeth which caused her to press the Hungarian case on her husband, who seems to have been influenced by her—so far as is known, the only instance in all his reign of his letting his policy be affected by feelings of his heart. Moreover, Andrássy was not an Old Conservative in politics, but a Liberal. He also came from the Slavonic north of Hungary, and was strongly impressed by the Slav danger and thus inclined to seek the alliance of the Germans of the Monarchy (later, when he was foreign minister, of the Reich) against the Slavs. 'You take care of your Slavs,' he is reported to have said once, 'and we will take care of ours' (the version 'barbarians' is not authenticated, although it would have been characteristic enough)—a lapidary formulation of what is usually said to have been the philosophic basis of Dualism.

Hardly less important was the emergence on the other side of a German Austrian politician, the Styrian Kaiserfeld (incidentally, a Germanized Slovene) who appreciated the realities of the situation and worked for partnership between the German Austrians and the Hungarian Liberals, so that his wing of the German Austrians were not, like Schmerling's, the opponents of Deák and Andrássy, but their allies—a transference of weight from one scale to the other which tipped the balance decisively.

Given these developments the end was now inevitable, although there was still much opposition to what proved to be the ultimate solution. There was some in Hungary, where a considerable party still thought that Deák was going too far in conciliation; and even more in Austria, from the federalists, headed by Belcredi, on the one hand, and the German centralists on the other. Franz Joseph could not even find a minister president from among his own subjects to carry through the negotiations—a Hungarian would have been impossible, and Kaiserfeld simply did not come into consideration because at that stage Franz Joseph never made anyone under a count minister president, and he had run out of archdukes. He had therefore to call on the Saxon, Beust (it is always said that Beust was appointed to organize *revanche* against Prussia, but it seems likely that the appointment was made, at least in part, with an eye on the Hungarian negotiations). In a showdown between Beust and Belcredi, in February 1867, Franz Joseph opted, although with personal reluctance, for the former, and the remaining negotiations were concluded quickly enough. Ten days after Belcredi's resignation, Franz Joseph issued a rescript appointing Andrássy president of a responsible Hungarian ministry. Law XII was adopted by the Diet on 29 May, and sanctioned by Franz Joseph, *qua* King of Hungary, on 28 July.

In the event, not only were the representatives of Cis-Leithania not consulted during these negotiations; they were not even allowed an *ex post facto* voice on their result. This had not been the original intention, for when the *Reichsrat* was *sistiert* the Cis-Leithanian *Landtage* had been promised that results of the negotiations with Hungary and Croatia should be laid before them 'for the hearing and appreciation of their views, which should be given equal weight' (*um ihren gleichwertigen Ausspruch zu vernehmen und würdigen*). Some of them had even been dissolved and new elections held under the appropriate pressure, so that a *Reichsrat* majority had been got together prepared to vote the Compromise. But meanwhile Beust had become converted to Deák's standpoint that the law was no concern of Austria's, so that the sanctioned Compromise was simply laid before the *Reichsrat*, in the autumn of 1867, as a *fait accompli*, with a request to it to vote the necessary implementing legislation, providing the Austrian machinery for the common consultations.

The supplementary and consequential measures referred to above were the five Austrian laws known as the December Constitution, in which the *Reichsrat* worked out its own internal composition, relations with the Crown, etc.; the subsidiary Hungaro-Croat Compromise, which should have come simultaneously with Law XII but had got stuck on reefs, and was concluded only in 1868; the Hungarian so-called Nationalities Law, again of 1868; and finally, the Army Act for the whole Monarchy, accepted by the two parliaments, once more, in 1868.

The Compromise, when it was concluded, was very ill received in a number of quarters, especially by the Czechs, but also by the diehard German centralists and others; and the condemnations of the Dualist system have not died away to this day. It is common enough to find even relatively serious historians writing that because the Compromise set up the artificial hegemony of the Germans in one half of the Monarchy and the Magyars in the other, it dealt the deathblow to the Monarchy, in stifling the legitimate aspirations of its other peoples and driving them into irredentism. On a somewhat lower plane, we get the Germans' complaints that the principle of parity was unfair to Cis-Leithania, the population of which was considerably larger than that of Hungary, and that the Hungarians, while shouldering less than half of the burden, contrived to exercise more than half the influence.

There is something in this last point, although not, perhaps, a very great deal. The Hungarians, on their side, were always complaining that they got less than full parity, and this was certainly the case with the army, and with the National Bank. For the rest, it is obvious that the Compromise was no ideal solution for the national and social problem of central Europe. It not only did not satisfy the aspirations of many peoples and political factors, but did not do equal justice to them all. The nationalities of Hungary came off particularly badly: the weaker nationalities in the West less so, but some of them did not receive full justice, although to say that the 'oppressed nationalities' were driven into irredentism, and the Monarchy destroyed, is absurd: the strongest irredentism in the whole Monarchy was among the Italians, who, Heaven knows, had little to complain of. Yet when their antecedents are considered, the futility surely becomes apparent of complaining that something else 'ought to' have been devised, other than the Compromise and the Dualist System. For in fact a whole long series of experiments had been tried, each of them without success. Absolutism had proved unable to maintain itself; so had aristocratic federalism; so had neo-Germanic centralism; so had Austro-Slavism (the decisive crash of this came later, in 1871); so, for that matter, had Hungarian separatism *à la* Kossuth. All of them had failed because the forces opposed to them were stronger than those in favour of them. Only Dualism, the core of which was the Compromise, had stronger backers than opponents; and thanks to this it succeeded in coming to birth alive, and what is more, in living for fifty-one years—a very long life for any structural arrangement of central Europe, about three times as long as that with which the Allies tried to replace it after 1918. The proof of the pudding, to change the metaphor, is in the eating; and by that test the Compromise, if not generally palatable, at any rate contained enough vitamins to support fifty million people for fifty years.

And finally: this historical sketch has confined itself to immediate antecedents, but it would be possible to go back much further than 1851 and to show that there was nothing essentially new in the Dualist System. It simply adapted to parliamentary conditions relationships which went back far in the history of the Habsburg Monarchy. It was not in 1867 that Hungary first achieved legal recognition of her independence of the Habsburgs' other territories, except in respect of defence and foreign affairs. This had been assured her by many solemn promises, including those made by Charles VI or III in connection with the Pragmatic Sanction and Leopold II's laws of 1790–91. It was also a fact that when the Hungarian constitution had been annulled, as by Leopold I, or ignored, as by Joseph II, Hungary had fought back and had recovered it. Her 'April Laws' of 1848, which formed the Hungarians' *point de départ* in the later negotiations, had been questionable in their treatment of the 'common subjects', but not in asserting her complete internal independence; nor, indeed, were they so questioned in Vienna itself, when first enacted.

Nor was the Cis-Leithania which emerged under the December Constitution anything new. In its structural provisions, the *Reichsrat* of 1867 simply took over, with very slight modifications, the provisions of the February Patent; and they again took over, hardly altered except for the extended franchise, the structural provisions of the Stadion Constitution of March 1849, which again followed closely the Kremsier draft of the 1848 *Reichstag*. Even that went back to the original convocation, announced in March 1848, of representatives of the Cis-Leithanian Lands, to work out a constitution for themselves; and the treatment of those Lands as a unit—not, of course, a parliamentary one, but an administrative one—goes back to 1749, when Maria Theresa abolished the Bohemian and Austrian court chancelleries in favour of the *Directorium* and the *Oberste Justizstelle*. In this respect again, the Dualist System was simply an adaptation to the new conditions of constitutional institutions of a very old structure.

16

V. G. KIERNAN

Diplomats in Exile

From the later eighteenth century Europe was entering into regular political relations with Asia, and to the old kingdoms of Asia were soon added the new republics of Latin America. In the history of European diplomacy this blazing of trails in the backwoods, far from its traditional setting of Paris or Vienna, stands as a chapter by itself, instructive in various ways, not seldom ludicrous.

Like so many European things, the system of international relations and the diplomatic profession that grew with it from early modern times were specific to their continent of origin. In old Asia only sporadic analogies can be recognized. Nadir Shah's pretext for invading India in 1738, alleged want of courtesy by the Mogul government to his newly founded dynasty, bore a striking resemblance to Louis XIV's pretext, as reported by Voltaire, for invading the United Provinces. But Delhi was too remote from the other capitals it had dealings with—Isfahan, Bokhara, Stamboul—for such refinements to grow into a system. China recognized no equals, whereas an art of diplomacy presupposes equality of rights or status, if not of strength, in a 'family' or 'comity' of nations, or at least of sovereigns. Japan since the early seventeenth century had refused intercourse with anyone else. Latin America was as inexperienced, and outgrew its *gaucherie* more slowly.

Neighbouring Turkey had been Europe's introduction to Asia, and many an envoy had experienced the imposing ceremony of reception in the grand court of the Seraglio, amid flashing scimitars and waving plumes.[1] This was a plane on which West and East, each steeped in monarchic habits of pomp and display, could meet. When Morier's

[1] N. M. Penzer, *The Harem* (London, 1936) chap. V.

fictitious Persian embassy arrived in England, in the reign of Jeremy Bentham, it was informed that Europeans had ceased to care about niceties and trifles of ceremonial;[2] but the ingrained diplomatic fondness for them was about to take on a new lease of life in the Orient, where sparrings and skirmishings turned very much on the etiquette of royal audiences. This happened above all in China, and a plain man, whether Celestial or Cockney, might have laughed at the absurdities on both sides when a Son of Heaven was induced to manifest himself, in 1894, to envoys arrayed like Solomon in all the glory of 'cocked hats with feathers, helmets with spikes and eagles, képis with plumes, busbies and astrakhan caps'.[3] A last echo from innermost Asia of this kind of ritual was the reception, smaller but stage-managed with equal care, of an American military mission in the Second World War by the Dalai Lama, with the guests presenting ceremonial scarves and throwing grains of rice over their shoulders.[4]

Ruder forms of contact had been worked out as well, by English and French emissaries enlisting Red Indian allies with fire-water and blankets, or Portuguese factors palavering with African chiefs. Europe's empires were swelling, small peoples being swallowed up in them. This background of imperial expansion was bound to colour the diplomatic outlook. Anywhere in Afro-Asia, occasionally in Latin America, a man would have at the back of his mind the thought that the country he was posted to might before long be someone's colony; as Burma suddenly became in 1886 just when it was endeavouring to 'come out' in the world. Two philosophies clashed with each other. One, the more pacific and truly diplomatic, was expressed by Lord Macartney, after the failure of his mission to Peking in 1792, in a masterly survey of how to improve relations with China: not, he emphasized, by impatience or force.[5] But trade was not prepared to wait, even if diplomacy was; and it was by force that relations with the Far Eastern countries were inaugurated. Some of those concerned had misgivings. 'I never felt so ashamed in my life',

[2] R. Morier, *The Adventures of Hajji Baba of Ispahan in England* (London, 1828) chap. 21.

[3] W. J. Oudendyk, *Ways and By-ways in Diplomacy* (London, 1939) p. 52.

[4] Lt.-Col. I. Tolstoy, 'Across Tibet from India to China', in *National Geographical Magazine* xc, no. 2 (Aug. 1946) 208–12.

[5] Lord Macartney, *An Embassy to China*, ed. J. L. Cranmer-Byng (London, 1962) pp. 211–15.

Lord Elgin wrote in December 1857 while British troops prepared to attack Canton.[6] Six years later a note was delivered to the Japanese on which an Englishman who had a hand in it reflected, rereading it in later life: 'The language is perhaps rather stronger than more modern taste would approve, but with a powerful, almost overwhelming squadron of men-of-war at one's back, the temptation to express one's feelings with frankness is not easy to resist.'[7]

The most notable exponent in the Far East of the diplomacy of 'frankness', before American aircraft-carriers appeared on the scene, was Sir Harry Parkes, who fairly earned his statue at Shanghai as the man who did more than any other to promote trade 'and to make China know her place'.[8] In 1865 he was transferred to Japan, where he vigorously applied the same methods. Envoy and empire-builder were rôles between which such a man never learned to draw fine distinctions. When he was minister at Peking in 1885, near the end of his life, and Britain arbitrarily took possession of Port Hamilton in Korea as a naval base against Russia, there was speculation about what subtle plans he might have in mind: but a younger Briton then at Tokyo thought Parkes was simply an Englishman of the old school who believed in taking anything that was worth taking, and troubled his head about it no further.[9] He had a German counterpart in Max von Brandt, scion of a Prussian army family and minister at Peking for eighteen years after winning his spurs in Japan, who practised a hectoring policy which too many of his successors in the Far East emulated.[10]

By the later nineteenth century an equilibrium was being reached: to those Asian states that survived, the usages and civilities customary in Europe were being extended, and they were learning to reciprocate them. 'Damns have had their day.' Decorum was still far from perfect. Sir R. F. Thomson at Teheran had to remind a subordinate at Meshed, accused of interfering with the local administration, that the right way to deal with

[6] A. Michie, *The Englishman in China* (London, 1904) p. 324.

[7] Sir E. Satow, *A Diplomat in Japan* (London, 1921) p. 82.

[8] T. R. Jernigan (former U.S. consul-general at Shanghai), *China's Business Methods and Policy* (Shanghai, 1904) pp. 251–2; and see generally S. Lane-Poole and F. V. Dickins, *The Life of Sir Harry Parkes* (London, 1894).

[9] Sienkiewicz to Freycinet, no. 113, 2 Oct. 1885, Paris, Archives du Ministère des Affaires Etrangères (henceforth referred to as A.A.E.), Japon, vol. 31.

[10] H. Stoecker, *Deutschland und China im 19 Jahrhundert* (Berlin, 1958) p. 95.

Persian officialdom was 'unremitting patience and courtesy'.[11] His counsel of perfection was soon being neglected again, like Macartney's, because Persia unlike Japan failed to make good its title to respect. High-handed treatment of Persians easily led Westerners into similar behaviour to one another. Britain and Russia each obtained the grant of a district in the foothills above Teheran for their summer quarters, and refused to allow any other envoys who rented villas there to hoist their flags—'an absurd situation', protested a Dutch representative, 'the like of which existed nowhere else in the world'.[12]

Diplomatic life in the outposts had many discomforts to roughen tempers. Each region had its special annoyances in the way of troublesome insects, native servants, or climate. Housing was a frequent grievance: the Foreign Office in London was besieged with petitions for repair or improvement of buildings, which it often could not find money for. At Peking the British and French had the advantage of being able to help themselves to princely palaces, after the second Anglo-Chinese war; the British unlike the French paid a rent for theirs, kept a good garden, and made themselves relatively snug. 'Very few races in the world have any idea of comfort', the famous Orientalist Sir Denison Ross once confided to his diary as he sweated his way through an eastern tour.[13] Doubtless what could be achieved at Peking fell far short of the standards of 'British comfort', and service there, an Englishman familiar with it declared, ought to be reserved as 'a special punishment for diplomatic criminals—men who have systematically neglected to endorse or number their dispatches, or who have insisted upon having an opinion of their own . . .'.[14] On this reckoning Bangkok might have been a purgatory for souls of erring diplomats departed. Here the British legation was housed in a big, tumbledown pile of brick, dangerously ruinous it was complained in 1880. Life was 'monotonous, damp, and depressing'.[15] Bangkok indeed united every drawback of climate, fever, mud, and solitude; it was one of several

[11] Sir R. F. Thomson to Lord Granville, no. 25, 27 Feb. 1885, enclosing correspondence with Meshed, in P.R.O., F.O. Persia, 60/469.

[12] Oudendyk, p. 165.

[13] Sir E. D. Ross, *Both Ends of the Candle* (London, 1943) p. 236.

[14] Sir E. Hornby, *An Autobiography* (London, 1929) p. 227. Hornby was in the Far East for many years as a British circuit judge.

[15] W. G. Palgrave to Alston, private, 5 April 1880, F.O. Siam, 69/73.

places that men in the profession might well feel ought to be annexed by somebody, out of consideration for them.

A favourite grumble in the British service was that no extra allowance was given for transport of furniture to more distant posts, to which a diplomat had to go more or less like a snail, carrying his house on his back. This lends added pathos to the misfortune of Mr Kennedy in Chile in 1891, whose official residence and private furniture perished in the biggest fire anyone could remember at Santiago. It started in the small hours at 'a German eating house opposite', and martial law, which happened to be in force, delayed the arrival of the fire brigade.[16] Nearly all the archive was lost; it was in any case incomplete, 'and contained much rubbish', as must have been the case with nearly all small missions, in tropical latitudes where damp and insects were always eating documents away, in days before the typewriter—then just making its blessed appearance in the service. In a private missive Kennedy feelingly lamented the straits he and his wife were reduced to in a chilly hotel. 'Our latest experience in this uncomfortable country makes us feel very "sick". . . . We are at the height of our winter season with much cold rain wh. adds to one's misery —I hope that before long Lord Salisbury may be able to offer me promotion somewhere outside of South America.'[17] It was standard practice for each individual to keep privately in touch with some acquaintance in the Office, according to his rank, and a steady croaking, as of frogs, could be heard from all these marshes and backwoods.

Risks to health were among the trials and tribulations borne by the martyrs of a noble profession, as all these exiles felt themselves to be. Thomson impressed on the Office that he and his staff could not dispense even temporarily with a doctor.[18] A man might fall ill and have to stick at his post until a relief could be sent, as befell a French representative, Duprat, at Santiago.[19] At the port of Callao in Peru in 1883 Acting-consul Fisher was commended for laudable conduct during a yellow fever epidemic, visiting sick Britons and the Foreign Seamen's Hospital and reading the burial service.[20] Worse yet were the hazards to life and limb

[16] J. G. Kennedy to Lord Salisbury, no. 55, 5 June 1891, F.O. Chile, 16/265.
[17] Kennedy to Sanderson, priv., 9 June 1891, F.O. 16/265.
[18] Thomson to Granville, no. 32, 20 Mar. 1885, F.O. 60/469.
[19] F. de Bâcourt to Freycinet, no. 1, 18 Jan. 1885, A.A.E., Chili, vol. 26.
[20] Papers in F.O. Peru, 61/349.

that either domestic broils or anti-foreign passions might give rise to. Few diplomats aspired to an actual crown of martyrdom, any more than the prelate in Scott's *Fair Maid* who talked so feelingly of the barbarous Highlanders—'We hear some of them are yet utter heathens, and worship Mahound and Termagant'—when the frivolous Duke of Rothesay suggested that he would no doubt be eager to find a speedy way to heavenly bliss by undertaking an embassage to them.[21] Anywhere near salt water a Briton could count on the navy being not too far away; and his European colleagues and their nationals were glad to bespeak its protection when danger threatened, loudly as they might declaim in quiet times against Britannia's bent for ruling the waves. North-west Persia was beyond range of naval gunnery, and the consul-general at Tabriz asked for an extra guard. He had four men already, but one of them, who had been on sentry-go for forty-eight years, could plausibly be described as 'old and infirm'.[22] Peking too lay inland, and it was in the siege of the legations during the Boxer outbreak in 1900 that diplomatic nerves were tested most severely, and showed up, for the most part, badly.[23]

A diplomat was trained to find reasons, and he could generally find a good many for not being banished into the wilds. Men of the first chop, with suitable influence, might dodge it altogether; though a country like Italy never seemed at a loss for counts and barons to adorn even the most out of the way places. There was often the same disgust at being outside Europe that a French civil servant felt at being outside Paris. Apart from social amenities and creature comforts, everything of professional importance was thought of as confined to Europe. From this point of view Constantinople might uneasily be included. It was a hybrid, one of the plums of the service, but blighted by many of the inconveniences of further Asia. 'Certainly this is no country of delight and joy', Henry Grenville had written from there to George III; 'fire and plague possess it merely.'[24] Wherever there were Russians, there was some experience to be gained in baffling their knavish tricks; most of the western hemisphere had not even any Russians, and on Ecuadorians or Venezuelans finesse was

[21] Sir Walter Scott, *The Fair Maid of Perth* (1828) chap. 13.

[22] Thomson to Granville, no. 10, 27 Jan. 1885, F.O. 60/469.

[23] See 'B. L. Putnam Weale' (B. L. Simpson), *Indiscreet Letters from Peking* (5th edn, London, 1906).

[24] D. B. Horn, *The British Diplomatic Service 1689–1789* (Oxford, 1961) p. 86.

thrown away, while the highest rank that could normally be hoped for was minister-resident.

At mid-century foreign secretaries were at the stage of trying to persuade the diplomatic service that the whole world must now be its regular sphere of action. In 1853 Lord Clarendon made an offer of Montevideo (Uruguay) to an excitable secretary of legation at Madrid, L. C. Otway, who was clamouring for promotion. 'Montevideo would *not* suit me *at all*', Otway replied promptly: he had already declined Lima, and what he wanted was a good berth in Europe. He added that, 'en attendant better and more substantial things', he would welcome a knighthood.[25] This latter request was soon repeated, as one 'to which I attach extreme importance!!!'[26] Even Clarendon ,whose enormous correspondence with his agents rendered him proof against most of what could be expected from them, was staggered. 'I must frankly tell you', he wrote back, 'that I have not often been more surprised than at your request to be made a knight.' If granted it would only make Otway ridiculous. As for South America, 'I consider all these posts diplomatic, and strictly in the order of diplomatic promotion.'[27] A couple of years later he made a far more flattering offer, Rio de Janeiro. Otway was much obliged. 'I know however that with my constitution and temperament to go there would be for me certain death'; he hoped he need not go for six months, and that his lordship would sanction the arrangement if in the meantime 'I can prevail on any gentleman in Switzerland or Germany to exchange'.[28] Clarendon laid it down that he could not allow individuals to pick and choose, 'to say which places they will accept and which they will refuse', any more than a commander could with his officers.[29] Rio was rejected; but ultimately Otway found himself marooned in Central America, like a remittance-man, it may be guessed, packed off to the colonies to be out of the way, and there, thrown on his own resources, he went to pieces.

Clarendon's principle was not strictly enforced in the following decades: excuses went on being accepted. In career records the phrase:

[25] L. C. Otway to Lord Clarendon, 9 Dec. 1853: Clarendon Papers (private papers of the 4th Earl, in the Bodleian Library, Oxford), vol. c.9. This and the following letters are quoted by kind permission of the present Earl of Clarendon.

[26] Otway to Clarendon, 2 Jan. 1854, vol. c.20.

[27] Clarendon to Otway, 14 Jan. 1854, vol. c.127.

[28] Otway to Clarendon, 9 Oct. 1855, vol. c.28.

[29] Clarendon to Otway, 16 Oct. 1855, vol. c.134.

'appointed to ——, but did not proceed' was a recurrent one. Liberal use was made of juvenile attachés, paid or unpaid, for whom a short spell in the tropics might be a not too unwelcome adventure. But there had to be some senior men in charge of them, and the bluest blood was not always a safeguard against being sent. Those on whom the lot fell were apt to wend their way to their destination as sluggishly as Shakespeare's schoolboy creeping to the classroom, and as soon as they got there to beg for the earliest possible transfer, and meanwhile to solicit long leaves of absence at short intervals. A Frenchman in South America lamented that an opportunity to push foreign interests was being lost because the European representatives were not ready to seize it. 'Malheureusement Carcano part;—le Ministre d'Angleterre, après un an de séjour, n'est pour ainsi dire pas encore arrivé—le Ministre d'Allemagne est à Berlin.'[30] In 1886 a new British envoy was appointed to Colombia. 'It is rumoured however', it reached the ear of the Office, 'that Mr Dickson hopes not to have to go to Bogotá at all.'[31] In November 1887 a Hugh Fraser who had only come out to Santiago in February 1885 was requesting six, or at least four, months' leave.[32]

There was criticism of the cream of the profession for its refusal to learn new ways and tackle what could now be regarded as the 'really important missions' far away.[33] Its horizon was widening, but only by slow degrees. In 1864 Britain had five men of ambassadorial rank. One of the five had never served outside Europe; three had been earlier at Constantinople; two had been at Washington, and one, briefly in youth, at Rio. In 1891 there were seven ambassadors, all still at European capitals (including Constantinople). Two had never served outside Europe; three others only in Turkey, Egypt, or the U.S.A., though two of these had also been viceroys of India. Two had ranged as far afield as South America, and of these one had also been at Peking.[34] At this date Fraser, who started in

[30] A private letter of May 1886 from a member of the French legation at Santiago, A.A.E. Chili, vol. 27.

[31] Minute on H. Fraser (Santiago) to Lord Salisbury, no. 6, 22 Jan. 1886, F.O. 16/242.

[32] Fraser to Salisbury, no. 83, 9 Nov. 1887, F.O. 16/248.

[33] 'Foreign Office Sketches', from *Vanity Fair* (London, 1883), section on Sir Thomas Wade.

[34] The five ambassadors in 1864 were: Lord Cowley (Paris), Sir H. Bulwer (Constantinople), Lord Bloomfield (Vienna), Lord Napier (St Petersburg), Sir A. Buchanan (Berlin). In 1891 the seven were: Sir A. B. Paget (Vienna), Lord Dufferin

1855 and was now minister at Tokyo, had seen fifteen posts in his thirty-five years, six of them outside Europe. As in the Indian army, names of the Scottish and Anglo-Irish gentry tend to recur in the borderlands of diplomacy. A younger son of an Earl of Fingall, like Sir F. R. Plunkett who was in harness in these years, might be less supercilious about what was offered him than the *jeunesse dorée* of England. It is observable too that among the Irish it was often the Catholics—the Plunketts and Pakenhams—who were drawn to diplomacy, while the Church of Ireland, as the Anglican Church called itself there, supplied the fighting generals.

In 1885 it was still impossible to provide Teheran with a second secretary. 'It is very difficult to get members of the Diplomatic Service to go there at all', an Office minute explained apologetically.[35] The simple expedient of opening the service to less fastidious entrants was, needless to say, overlooked. As late as 1896, by which date travel and residence in the East were at any rate less painful than they had been, there was astonishment when a secretaryship at Teheran was accepted by a young sprig of the aristocracy with a father-in-law rich enough to come out to visit him at Constantinople by special train.[36] At Teheran he found Sir Mortimer Durand, seconded from India, making the best of a bad job by spending his mornings in a cool bath, reading French novels, and his afternoons at polo.[37]

Another mode of adaptation to such a post, by an unambitious loafer content to rest on his oars in a backwater, was practised by an Irishman named Knox at Bangkok. Here some of the old nabob habits of the European in the East, which had a marked resemblance to those of the gentry in Ireland, could still be indulged in. When he retired to his native land in 1879 to seek still deeper repose as a Master of Hounds, the Office was left with an embarrassment on its hands in the shape of an illegitimate half-caste daughter, married 'under circumstances qui laissent à désirer', so it heard,[38] to a dignitary named Pra Pre Cha who was in political hot

---

(Rome), Sir E. B. Malet (Berlin), Sir R. B. D. Morier (St Petersburg), Sir W. A. White (Constantinople), Lord Lytton (Paris), Sir F. C. Ford (Madrid).

[35] P. Currie, minute on Thomson to Granville, no. 24, 25 Feb. 1885, F.O. 60/469.

[36] Lord Hardinge of Penshurst, *Old Diplomacy* (London, 1947) pp. 60, 23.

[37] *Ibid.*, p. 63.

[38] Memo by J. Pauncefote in F.O. 69/80. T. G. Knox began in the army, served in India and China, then with the Siamese army, before rising from Interpreter (1857) to Agent and Consul-general (1875); on his retirement he was knighted.

water; she called herself 'Madame la Baronne'. By the time his successor William Gifford Palgrave, wafted from Bulgaria, had got into his stride, it was felt in London that Knox had been the easier of the two to bear. A man of brilliant gifts and romantic feats in Arabian exploration and many other fields, a late recruit to the service long condemned to languish in obscure corners, Palgrave was jumping heavily now at a chance to mould policies of his own and sway the destinies of Asia. From the moment of his arrival, he reported, he adopted a courteous tone with the king and ministers, but made it perfectly plain that he expected them to mend their ways, and in short order. 'Fairly frightened, they begged me to dictate.'[39] He proceeded to do so, but managing these Siamese proved harder work than he had bargained for. 'I feel like a man who has a couple of dozen monkeys to keep in order', he wrote before long, 'with a baboon or two among the lot!'[40] By now the Office too was fairly frightened, and decided that his private letters should be left unanswered.[41] It was also indignant because he had absented himself on the plea of health to Japan, and the legation there had to be cabled to send him back. 'That dreadful man Palgrave', as someone feelingly called him,[42] was presently got rid of to Montevideo, where he could do less harm and soon died.

There were men as ambitious as Palgrave and less unbalanced who were content to make their whole careers in the outlands. It was not after all easy to get into the service, still harder to rise in it, and men without family connections to help them might be as glad to embrace any opening as the Vicar of Wakefield's son was to catch at a prospect of being made secretary to 'an embassy talked of from the synod of Pennsylvania to the Chickasaw Indians'.[43] They could appreciate moreover the opportunities held out by these new regions where all was still in flux; and there was no telephone or radio yet to stifle the enterprise of the man on the spot. Some of the early Americans in the Far East were of this stamp: men like

[39] Palgrave to Tenterden, priv., 2 May 1880, F.O. 69/78.

[40] Palgrave to Hervey, priv., 7 Nov. 1881, F.O. 69/78.

[41] Note on foregoing, by Hervey.

[42] J. G. Kennedy, acting chargé d'affaires at Tokyo, to Parkes, priv., 20 April 1881, F.O. 69/78. Kennedy accused Palgrave of intriguing with the Japanese. 'He wants your place! and has also an idea of entering Japanese service! . . . but I tell them that he is a person of no account and a mere schemer.'

[43] *The Vicar of Wakefield*, chap. 20.

Townsend Harris,[44] or Peter Parker, 'a missionary diplomat, scheming to capture Formosa', though their real effectiveness was limited by their government's lack of interest.[45] Parkes was the triumphant example: he looked on Japan, as the 'Great Elchi' did on Turkey, as his fief. 'Jusqu'à ces derniers jours', it was said of him near the end of his career by a Frenchman who knew him, 'Sir Harry Parkes . . . qui avait vu grandir peu à peu les personnages qui sont devenus les Ministres du Mikado, a pu exercer dans ce pays une quasi-dictature.'[46]

One other type attracted by remote Asiatic posts was the man of scholarly tastes, such as Sir Thomas Wade who went to China in 1842 as a young soldier, turned to Chinese studies, and in 1871 became minister at Peking. He was one of a small handful of heads of mission in that generation who had never served anywhere else. This specialization was criticized as narrowing men's vision, and making them useless for any other capitals.[47] More truly it might be called a waste of talent when a Japanese scholar like Satow was shifted, much against his grain, to Uruguay and Morocco. But by this time the old pioneering generation was being replaced by a quick sequence of envoys serving a brief sentence and hurrying away. Compared with these the man of literary tastes and long residence was likely to acquire a more sympathetic interest in his second homeland. Thomson is an example. Of Wade it was said that it gratified him to be saluted in the street by the meanest Chinese coolie.[48] His official duty of helping to poison China with British opium must have grated on him. 'I do not for a moment slacken in my zeal', we find him writing in one of his notebooks, 'for such a termination of the Opium discussion as will be satisfactory alike to the Government of China and to my own.'[49]

It might be an old civilization rather than a living people that bookish men felt an affinity with. Oudendyk fell in love with Chinese gardens and

[44] See C. Crow, *Harris of Japan* (London, 1939).

[45] Akira Iriye, *Across the Pacific* (New York, 1967) p. 15.

[46] Sienkiewicz to Ferry, unnumbered, 25 April 1884, A.A.E.. Japon, vol. 30. There was now a reaction against Parkes's tutelage, he added, which the Germans were seeking to exploit.

[47] *Foreign Office Sketches*, section on Sir R. Thomson.

[48] Hornby, p. 233.

[49] No. 6 of a bundle of notebooks or scribbling-pads, pp. 46–47, in the Wade Papers, Cambridge University Library: Add. MS. 6318.

classical poetry; he felt very much at home too in Persia, another land of refinement and misery, and in Russia, where he thought the peasants looked very picturesque and the tsaritsa 'inexpressibly sweet'.[50] Diplomats of all shades were as a rule firmly conservative in their politics, and had no objection to oriental despots or Latin-American dictators so long as these were amenable to the diplomatic approach. It was part of what they had to endure in their banishment to be haunted by thoughts of the democratic rot setting in at home. Sir Horace Rumbold could not sleep easy when Gladstone was in office.[51]

After the Boxer rising, when order had been restored by the allied sack of Peking, the diplomats set to work to seal off their legation quarter into another Forbidden City, with walls and barriers and cannon to keep out Chinese intruders. Oudendyk deplored this creation of 'a veritable fortress within the capital', as a 'permanent insult' to China.[52] But it was only the logical climax of a self-seclusion that Western *corps diplomatiques* in Asia habitually practised; a reflex of the separate existence led by Europeans in their colonies, British India first and foremost. At Constantinople Vambéry found the foreign area, Pera, completely aloof from the old city across the Golden Horn. 'I was surprised to see how little the Pera world knew of what was going on in Stambul.'[53] Within these enclaves there was often nearly as strict a segregation between diplomatic and commercial society, and the *chers collègues* were thrown very much on their own company.

One drawback for the younger fry must have been the limited scope for those flirtations or gallantries, those games of *chercher les femmes*, with which the profession in Europe was popularly associated, a smooth manner and persuasive tongue being equally an asset in both pursuits. In the West there was no doing anything, Hajji Baba discovered, 'without women and eating'.[54] It may be conjectured that diplomatic wives, like

[50] Oudendyk, p. 146.

[51] Sir H. Rumbold, *Further Recollections of a Diplomatist* (London, 1903) pp. 194–6.

[52] *Op. cit.*, p. 113.

[53] A. Vambéry, *The Story of my Struggles* (London, 1904), Nelson edn, p. 145. To the same self-isolating habits, persisting much later, 'Western Governments probably owe a very great deal of the misinformation from the East which has misled them': C. Sykes, *Troubled Loyalty. A Biography of Adam von Trott zu Solz* (London, 1968) p. 217.

[54] Morier, chap. 41.

those of colonial officials, often did little to improve relations with the exotic countries they—still more reluctantly than their husbands—had to live in. When the old empress Tzu Hsi had to curry favour after the Boxer trouble by inviting the ladies at Peking to an entertainment, they were all agog. Mrs Conger, the American minister's wife, led them in rehearsing their curtsies; but at the palace they exchanged rude comments among themselves, heedless of whether any of the Chinese understood what they were saying, and even went off with valuable cups or ornaments as souvenirs.[55]

Thrown so much together, diplomatic castaways were likely to get on with one another either better or worse than at home. At Tokyo Sienkiewicz and Plunkett were on the best of terms, and the Anglo-Irishman was willing to agree when the Franco-Pole blamed British policy in Egypt for his country's resentful attitude.[56] Abuse of Britain was the best passport to Franco-German amenities, and Sienkiewicz wrote with satisfaction of his German colleague: 'Il s'élève vivement contre les intolérables prétensions de l'Angleterre à une sorte de domination sur tous les pays d'Afrique ou d'Asie où d'autres nations ont également des intérêts.'[57] It was the Russians who were supposed, correctly enough perhaps since Russian society was still so feudal, to be most adept at the personal approach. A British alarmist drew an imaginary picture of a Russian diplomat somewhere in Asia being supplied, in advance of a new Englishman's arrival, with an elaborate dossier on his private tastes and characteristics.[58] Applied to dealings with Asians, this way of doing things might take the form of threats, less well wrapped up in civil verbiage than they usually were, or of bribes, sometimes swallowed with a good grace Britain, though more straitlaced, was not altogether ignorant of the utility of palm-greasing.[59]

Europeans far from home acknowledged an obligation to stand together, and the *corps diplomatique*, an institution resembling a guild of foreign merchants in olden days, made a tangible embodiment of their

[55] I. T. Headland, *Court Life in China* (New York, 1909) p. 101; Oudendyk, p. 119.

[56] Sienkiewicz to Ferry, no. 87, 30 Mar. 1885, A.A.E., Japon, vol. 31.

[57] Sienkiewicz to Ferry, no. 58, Conf., 9 Oct. 1884. A.A.E., Japon, vol. 30.

[58] A. Diósy, *The New Far East* (London, 1898) pp. 343–4.

[59] See e.g. E. B. D'Auvergne, *Envoys Extraordinary* (London, 1937) p. 190, on an episode in Stratford Canning's earlier life at Constantinople.

solidarity, the concert of Europe in miniature. By a delicacy of tradition the post of doyen went by seniority, not by national status, although this did not always make for effective conduct of a post that was often no sinecure in places like Tokyo, as Sienkiewicz remarked when it fell to him,[60] or Peking, as Oudendyk was to realize.[61] Often of course it was a country with an axe of its own to grind that invoked the principle of unity. In 1884 Sienkiewicz told Paris that his European colleagues, at first inclined to sympathize with China in the undeclared war over Vietnam, were coming round to the French viewpoint: 'On semble mieux comprendre que c'est en somme en faveur de la civilisation occidentale que nous combattons.'[62] In the decades of haggling over the 'unequal treaties' forced on Japan when it was first opened up, Britain was frequently accused of appealing for a united front against revision because British interests had most to lose.

American nonconformity was not seldom an annoyance. A Mr Bingham at Tokyo warmly espoused the cause of treaty revision, and was a thorn in the flesh of successive British representatives. 'I beg to mention in conclusion', one of these sufferers wrote home after an interview with him, 'that Mr Bingham's conversation is in the nature of a speech or lecture and that it is next to impossible for the listener to attempt argument or even remarks.'[63] Many tributes were paid him none the less when he left. 'Although Mr Bingham', said one of these, 'by the vehemence and length of his arguments in favour of Japan, frequently fatigued both Japanese and foreigners alike, it is due to him to say that he leaves behind him in this country many friends.'[64] But the subject of how European diplomats in that age smarted under the moralistic prolixity of Americans, in their eyes a parcel of untutored amateurs, harmless ignoramuses at the best, is a large one by itself.

Mere distance from home, when reports and instructions might be months on their way, exposed men to the risk of falling into imbroglios of one kind or another. Telegraph cables were proliferating; but the cost of telegrams between the Pacific coast of South America and London in

[60] Sienkiewicz to Freycinet, no. 116, 4 Nov. 1885, A.A.E., Japon, vol. 31.

[61] Oudendyk, p. 326 (this relates to 1923–31).

[62] Sienkiewicz to Ferry, no. 58, Conf., 9 Oct. 1884, A.A.E., Japon, vol. 30.

[63] Kennedy to Granville, no. 93, Conf., 16 Aug. 1881, F.O. Japan, 46/280.

[64] Hon. F. R. Plunkett to Salisbury, no. 191, 20 July 1885, F.O. 46/332; cf. Sienkiewicz to Freycinet, no. 101, 22 July 1885, A.A.E., Japon, vol. 31.

the 1880s was nine shillings a word.[65] A news-sender did well to bear in mind—a salutary discipline in its way, from which the modern journalist is free—that any prophecies he indulged in would be scrutinized weeks or months later. Kennedy closed a long dispatch in late April about the Chilean civil war of 1891 by predicting that it must be over by the end of next month, since neither side could stand the strain much longer. 'Interesting', a Foreign Office hand noted on this, '—but we are now past the middle of June and the prophecies of a termination of the struggle have not been fulfilled.'[66] A foreign minister at Paris assured the envoy at Tokyo, as Sherlock Holmes assured Watson on Dartmoor, that his reports were being studied with great interest, though mainly of a retrospective sort because they arrived so late and the Far Eastern situation fluctuated so rapidly.[67]

Languages were a further stumbling-block. 'On est exposé à ces accidents dans les pays à dragomans', another Frenchman at Tokyo wrote, explaining how he had misunderstood the Japanese view of some subject through a mistranslation.[68] Some of Russia's earliest treaty arrangements with China had been made incongruously in Latin, with the Jesuits at Peking as intermediaries.[69] In this department the man who stayed all or most of his life had a great advantage over the bird of passage. Wade was a scholar, and it speaks well for the linguistic resources of his legation that by 1880 he had the assistance of two Chinese Secretaries, E. C. Baber and W. C. Hillier, while even his secretary of legation, the Hon. Thomas Grosvenor, was making his second sojourn at Peking and could speak the language. At Teheran all correspondence with the government was carried on in Persian, and it was felt that Thomson, himself very proficient, must have an Oriental Secretary to aid him.[70] Frenchmen accustomed to regard their own tongue as the only one fit for a diplomat were vastly relieved at Tokyo to meet a vice-minister of foreign affairs, Shioda, who spoke it perfectly.[71]

[65] Office note by W.A.C. (Cockerell) to Currie, 4 Sep. 1886, F.O. 16/241.

[66] Kennedy to Salisbury, no. 41, 29 April 1891, and minute by T.H.S. (Sir Thomas Sanderson), F.O. 16/264.

[67] Freycinet to Sienkiewicz, no. 9, 14 April 1885, A.A.E., Japon, vol. 31.

[68] Geofrey to Bourée, private, 22 Jan. 1879, A.A.E., Japon, vol. 27.

[69] M. N. Pavlovsky, *Chinese-Russian Relations* (New York, 1949) pp. 102–3.

[70] Minutes on Thomson to Granville, no. 24, 25 Feb. 1885, F.O. 60/469.

[71] Count Raphael de Viel-Castel to Challemel-Lacour, no. 61, 23 Aug. 1883, A.A.E., Japon, vol. 29.

When Harmand was posted to Bangkok as French *consul et commissaire* he found it hard to get the hang of things: contact could be made only with a few suspicious 'mandarins', and the other European representatives kept their thoughts to themselves[72]—if they had any. Some years later when Satow was stationed here he found that there always seemed to be wheels within wheels. At one point he had to warn the Governor of the Straits Settlements against a Mrs Anderson: she was the daughter of 'old Bush, the harbourmaster, who is high in the King's confidence', and through her the latter might be getting word of official views at Singapore about Siam. In the same letter Satow mentioned that the Rajah of Singora in the Malay peninsula was dying.[73] 'I am afraid', his correspondent returned, 'that they have poisoned the old Rajah for his friendship to us.'[74] But while Bangkok was anything but plain sailing, Tokyo was more unfathomable still. A baffled German observed that Bismarck always looked for positive facts in reports, but nothing in Japan could ever be called positive.[75] In 1883 Sienkiewicz was groping for light on where authority really lay in the governing circles. 'Depuis mon arrivée ici, je cherche à en saisir le mécanisme. Mais il y a tels points obscurs qui échappent aux investigations des Européens.'[76] Two years later he had to confess that this still essentially Asiatic government remained shrouded in mystery.[77] 'Je dus procéder à une véritable interrogataire', he wrote after a long attempt to pump one senior functionary.[78] Whether there was any Pooh-Bah at Tokyo willing to mortify family pride by pocketing a *douceur*, or whether he was worth sweetening, must have been hard to decipher. Sienkiewicz recommended a cross of the Legion for a navy minister, Karamura, who stood out against the new craze for everything German.[79] And a little flattery, such as his predecessor bestowed on 'la

[72] Harmand to Freycinet, no. 2, 3 Mar. 1882, A.A.E., Siam, vol. 8. His predecessor Blancheton had died after only a year of Bangkok.

[73] Satow to Sir F. Weld, 16 Jan. 1887, P.R.O. 30/33(2): Satow Papers.

[74] Weld to Satow, Priv. and Conf., 24 Jan. 1887, *ibid.*

[75] Sienkiewicz to Ferry, no. 80, 17 Feb. 1885, A.A.E., Japon, vol. 31.

[76] Sienkiewicz to Challemel-Lacour, no. 15, 15 Dec. 1883, A.A.E., Japon, vol. 29.

[77] Sienkiewicz to Freycinet, no. 119, Conf., 15 Nov. 1885, A.A.E., Japon, vol. 31.

[78] Sienkiewicz to Ferry, no. 71, 2 Jan. 1885, *ibid.* He got some help from his military attaché, Capt. Bougouin, who had known the army leaders for years; no. 30, 17 April 1884, A.A.E., Japon, vol. 30.

[79] Sienkiewicz to Ferry, no. 31, 18 April 1884, A.A.E., Japon, vol. 30.

noble nation japonaise', advancing so speedily in civilization,[80] could do no harm, even though in this case, when an alliance against China was the object in view, it did no good. To a stiff-necked Briton it came less naturally to bestow compliments on Asiatics; but one enterprising man at Teheran, Sir H. Drummond Wolff, invented a totally unauthorized medal of his own, and his successor Durand went on distributing it to deserving Persians—to the unspeakable indignation of Edward VII when a war minister turned up in London proudly wearing it.[81]

Western clocks went at a very different tempo from those of other continents, and the immense wastage of time there was another perpetual irritation. 'Il y aura naturellement des lenteurs', a French diplomat wrote about some negotiations in hand, excusing himself in advance for their lengthiness, 'comme il arrive toujours; mais ces lenteurs sont dans le tempérament des hommes d'État du Chili et font partie de leur politique.'[82] All over Latin America it was the same thing; but this was nothing to the slownesses of Asia, where feeble régimes were trying to save themselves from extinction by playing for time, spinning everything out to some Oriental Kalends. At Constantinople British ambassadors lived, as the biographer of one of them wrote, in 'almost princely state', but a splendour 'dearly bought by the constant, thankless, and fruitless labour in which they are habitually engaged'.[83] Abdul Hamid's inability to make up his mind, or allow it to be made up for him, could be excruciating. Lord Dufferin is said to have waited at the Yildiz palace from ten in the morning until two hours after midnight for a decision about Egyptian affairs; after at long last going home to bed he was roused by a messenger from the Sultan with yet another draft—'but the English patience was exhausted and the fate of Egypt sealed'.[84] Constantinople and its wily or wooden heads were in fact so exhausting that they could be handed over on occasion to a William White, an east-European of Scottish origins and of vast ability, looked on in the service as a rank outsider, though a clever one. 'He was a very religious Roman Catholic', says Hardinge, who served under him, 'and I always knew when he was meditating some doubtful

[80] Viel-Castel to Challemel-Lacour, no. 62, 4 Sep. 1883, A.A.E., Japon, vol. 29.

[81] Hardinge, pp. 65–6.

[82] Duprat to Ferry, no. 46, 30 May 1884, A.A.E., Chili, vol. 26.

[83] Lord Newton, *Lord Lyons. A Record of British Diplomacy* (London, 1913), Nelson edn, p. 104.

[84] A. Vambéry, p. 353.

scheme as he would then spend hours walking up and down the corridors crossing himself all the time.'[85]

English patience ran out rather quickly, some critics thought. W. S. Blunt believed that the right man for Constantinople would have been his cousin Terence Bourke, whom he found living in Tunisia, an unpaid vice-consul, fluent in the local dialect and with a host of acquaintances: 'He has what Englishmen so seldom possess, an inexhaustible patience equal to the Oriental's own.'[86] Trollope displayed a good share of this virtue when he spent two months in Egypt in 1858 settling a postal treaty with Nubar Pasha, an amiably evasive Armenian who seemed to have no fixed place of business but would come hospitably to his hotel with servants bearing pipes and coffee, which the novelist smoked and quaffed 'with oriental quiescence but British firmness'.[87] At Peking he would have faced a labour of two years instead of months, for the Tsungli-Yamen or foreign ministry set up under Western pressure in 1861 was a breakwater against which waves of half-frantic diplomats dashed themselves in vain. 'China never voluntarily makes a concession without receiving a substantial quid pro quo', wrote Curzon at the end of the century,[88] with the naïve astonishment that the West often felt when it found the East behaving exactly as it did itself. Lord Salisbury once soothed a Chinese who was complaining of the Indian government's delays over some issue with the remark: 'The Minister must remember that we also have a Tsungli-Yamen at Calcutta.'[89]

From some evils of the East, including veils and unlearnable grammars, Latin America was free, but it had plenty of its own; it was a sort of bigger and more boring Balkan peninsula, unenlivened by occasional excursions to Vienna. Rio de Janeiro was the most bearable capital, because down to 1889 it had a monarchy and court and an aristocracy of slave-owners. At Asunción, in the depths of the interior, an Englishman of rank might be welcomed by a Guaraní Indian in jacket and canvas trousers, one bare room of whose house with four wooden chairs was all the foreign office Paraguay could boast.[90] Lady Salisbury once ran into Blunt in Paris and

[85] Hardinge, p. 41.
[86] W. S. Blunt, *My Diaries* (London, 1932 edn) p. 153 (the entry relates to 1894).
[87] A. Trollope, *An Autobiography* (1883) chap. 7.
[88] G. N. Curzon, *Problems of the Far East* (London, 1894) p. 284.
[89] Lady G. G. Cecil, *Life of Robert, Marquis of Salisbury* (London, 1921–32) III, 215.
[90] Lord Frederick Hamilton, *Vanished Pomps of Yesterday* (London, 1920) pp. 178–9.

told him she was busy paying calls on ambassadresses. ' "Of course," she added, "I don't include those of the South American Republics or any other of the people who live up trees." '[91] Catholic Irishmen may have been thought less unlikely than others to find Latin America uncongenial. Between 1852 and 1890 the Hon. F. J. Pakenham was subjected to six spells of duty there.

Most Latin-American states were undeniably faction-ridden, and rival politicians often played to the patriotic gallery by tweaking foreign noses, a fact that helps to explain the cavilling tone of so much diplomatic comment. 'My stay in these wretched Republics is drawing to a close', the chargé d'affaires in Costa Rica wrote in 1864 to Lord Malmesbury. He had been endeavouring to sustain 'the *prestige* that should attend an English Minister in these half-civilized countries', but he felt that for them to be taken over by any European Power would be 'a blessing to humanity, and a great boon to civilization and commerce.'[92] When Sir Spenser St John was in Haiti, from 1873, as chargé and then minister, he was much inclined to play the part of a European Power himself, and 'frequently took violent measures against native disturbers of the public peace':[93] he had been in Borneo with Rajah Brooke. To bully or be bullied might appear the only choice. When the very well-connected Rumbold went to Chile in 1873 he felt that firmness was required to restore the British name, drooping of late years. 'My predecessor, Mr Taylour Thomson, had on several occasions been subjected to much indignity.' He was promptly immersed in a typical storm in a South American teacup, and had to engage in altercations with a 'verbose and boastful' foreign minister named Ibáñez, really a mediocre lawyer, 'a small man of insignificant appearance, with thin sandy hair, and the address and bearing of a schoolmaster'.[94]

In 1886 London was wondering whether to resume relations with anarchical Bolivia. One impediment that might have been thought of was that in the course of a revolution some years earlier all the Bolivian

[91] Blunt, p. 58 (1891).

[92] Earl of Malmesbury, *Memoirs of an Ex-Minister* (Leipzig edn, 1885) III, 184.

[93] *Dictionary of National Biography*, s.v.

[94] Rumbold, chap. 4. Taylour Thomson's whole career, except for 1858–72 in Chile, was passed in Persia, where, as Sir W. T. Thomson, he was succeeded in 1879 by Sir R. F. Thomson.

archives—such as they were—had been flung out of the windows, though the ratification of the Anglo-Bolivian treaty of 1840 happened to be picked up by a passing Englishman.[95] Fraser at Santiago agreed with Colonel Mansfield at Buenos Aires that a renewal of relations would be futile; he went further, and recalled various unpleasant incidents at La Paz, among them a 'discomfiture' that befell the redoubtable Spenser St John. 'In truth, it has always seemed to me that Her Majesty's Government did far too much honour to the Spanish American Republics, and that the best that could be said for the greater number of the small Missions in this part of the world was that they were useless. It is well for those that are merely superfluous. This is not my first experience of Spanish America, and I think I could name a good half dozen Republics in treating with which it is hardly possible to maintain any dignity or self-respect.'[96] A year later Fraser had a grievance of his own to embitter him, when he suddenly found in the newspapers three confidential dispatches by the Brazilian member of an arbitration tribunal at Santiago, which the foreign minister at Rio had coolly read out to the Chamber: 'They mention my name freely, and . . . give a shape and colour to the history of those transactions . . . that I have some difficulty in recognizing.'[97]

Livingstone was exploring Africa, and Sir Richard Burton the globe, in the uniform of Her Majesty's consuls; Herman Melville pined for a consulate somewhere in his beloved South Seas.[98] In the average run of duty to be done, however, a consul's lot, like a constable's, was not a happy one. It was he who bore the brunt of the rougher duties, and belonged, particularly in the British service, to a separate cadre, socially as well as professionally inferior. But all these men, high or low, were playing a part, well or badly, in the weaving together of our modern world. They have left behind them a rich store of humours and ill-humours, buried in mountains of old papers. In their worst hours they can hardly have guessed at the experiences awaiting some of their descendants, such as the hundred and thirty sessions of the ambassadorial

[95] Sir E. Hertslet, *Recollections of the Old Foreign Office* (London, 1901) pp. 43–4.

[96] Fraser to Lord Rosebery, no. 44, 3 June 1886, F.O. 16/242. Rosebery noted on it: 'A good despatch.'

[97] Fraser to Salisbury, no. 66, Conf., 30 Aug. 1887, F.O. 16/248.

[98] L. Mumford, *Herman Melville* (rev. edn, London, 1963) p. 162.

talks between America and Communist China,[99] each side reciting its views over and over and over again, or the charity football match at Nairobi in March 1969 between diplomats and cabinet ministers.

[99] See K. T. Young, *Negotiating with the Chinese Communists* (New York, 1968).

17

I. H. NISH

Dr Morrison and China's Entry into the World War, 1915–1917[1]

George Ernest Morrison had three distinct careers: as doctor, journalist and government servant.[2] He was born in Geelong, Victoria, in 1862, the son of Dr George Morrison who had gone from Scotland to become headmaster of the Presbyterian school there. He began his training as a doctor at the University of Melbourne (1880–82) and, as a common custom then was, proceeded to the University of Edinburgh to continue his studies in 1884. In between he had fitted an adventurous journey to New Guinea during which he was attacked and had lodged in his chest a spear-head which was only removed at the Royal Infirmary of Edinburgh. He graduated in 1887[3] but, unable to settle in a medical career, he undertook

[1] The major sources for Morrison's career are the Morrison papers (uncatalogued manuscripts 312) at the Mitchell Library, Sydney, and it was by the kind permission of the Mitchell Librarian that I was able to consult them. These consist of Morrison's diaries and letters sent and received (cited subsequently as M.P.) They have been extensively used in the biography, Cyril Pearl, *Morrison of Peking* (Sydney, 1967), which deals only cursorily with the episode recounted here. For the important Japanese side of the story, the source used was the Japanese Foreign Ministry compilation, *Sekai taisen kankei, Nihon gaikō bunsho* [Japan's diplomatic documents during the (first) world war] vol. 1 (Tokyo, 1940) (cited as S.T., N.G.B.). Since this essay was written, the Japanese Foreign Ministry series, *Nihon gaikō bunsho* (Tokyo, 1936–) has been published down to 1917. The main sources for British policy have been the Foreign Office archives and the papers of Sir John Jordan, British minister in Peking, 1906–20 (F.O. 350), in the Public Record Office, London.

[2] I have dealt with other aspects of Morrison's career in my articles, 'Dr G. E. Morrison and Japan', *Journal of the Oriental Society of Australia* II, no. 1 (1963) 42–7; and 'Morrison and the Portsmouth Conference', *Journal of the Royal Australian Historical Society* XLVIII, part 6 (1963) 426–36.

[3] Morrison graduated M.B., C.M. in 1887 and, after completing a thesis in 1895, graduated M.D. While he was not a great enthusiast for the Edinburgh medical school, he was subject to recurrent tropical diseases and visited Edinburgh for an examination whenever he came home from the East right down to his death in 1920.

a journey in the unknown of central China, which he described in his book, *An Australian in China* (1895). This work brought him early success as a man of letters and he readily forsook his profession to join the staff of *The Times*, first temporarily and then from 1897 as its permanent correspondent in China. It was his good fortune that the Far East was front-page news in the decade that followed; and he became a member of the coterie of great scholar-journalists of Edwardian England. In 1912, when China became a republic, Ernest Morrison decided to leave *The Times* and accepted an appointment as one of the political advisers to the President of China through the good offices of Captain Ts'ai Ting-kan, one of the president's aides-de-camp.[4] Educated in the United States and fluent in English, Ts'ai occupied high office for the remainder of Morrison's service in China and was his most consistent ally among the Chinese.

Morrison's period as political adviser covered many important events in China. He gave the Chinese leaders regular advice on international developments but seldom with great effect; he was rarely taken into their confidence.[5] One of the instances where he did exercise influence was the case of China's entry into the First World War, which provides a useful case study of the functions and methods of one of the foreign advisers employed by the Chinese in the early days of the new republic.

China's initial reaction to the outbreak of the war in Europe was to announce her neutrality. Her entry did not become a burning issue until late in 1915, when Japanese forces were already in occupation of the former German leased territory of Kiaochow. Japan had also imposed on China the treaties of May 1915 which exacted special privileges and deeply humiliated her leaders. This gave the Chinese strong grounds for entering the war on the allied side in order to win allied support in their resistance to the concessions extorted by Japan. But there was no point in joining the Entente powers until it was more evident that they would emerge victorious from the war. Any such move was likely to be favoured as an essentially anti-Japanese device.

When China's entry into the war was urged by foreign governments, it was conceived rather as an anti-German device. Their underlying purpose was to encourage the Chinese to mobilize their arsenals in order to

[4] Ts'ai Ting-kan to Morrison, 2 Aug. 1912, M.P. 171.

[5] M.P. 178 for numerous letters of complaint from Morrison to Ts'ai in 1913: 'I am kept more in the dark than when I was a Correspondent.'

provide arms and other supplies for which Russia was especially desperate. There was also a desire to limit the clandestine activities of Germans and Austrians in China. As in other neutral countries, German consuls and merchants had been trying to damage the commercial and military prestige of the Entente powers. By proposing China's entry into the war, these powers intended not so much to induce the Chinese to send their troops to Europe as to secure the expulsion of enemy nationals from their territories. While Britain, France and Russia wished to see China involved, their allies, the Japanese, saw the proposal as one directed primarily against themselves and were thoroughly suspicious.

For Dr Morrison, the issue came to a head in the autumn of 1915.[6] On 28 October Britain, France and Russia had, at the instance of Japan, made representations to President Yüan Shih-k'ai against the scheme to install him as emperor. Morrison warned Yüan that such advice was bound to be tendered.[7] Yüan, without abandoning the monarchical movement, informed the powers that there would necessarily be some delay before his inauguration.[8] It was against this background that Morrison suggested that Yüan could best restore the confidence of the European powers by offering to join the Entente. After various consultations, he drew up a memorandum to this effect in association with his friend Ts'ai. At an interview with President Yüan on 1 November, he argued that China should declare war on Germany on the ground of the many unneutral acts of Germans on Chinese territory.[9] The arguments which Morrison advanced to the Chinese were telling enough. He claimed that China would profit from the manufacture of arms for the Allies; her arsenals would be re-organized and equipped with modern machinery; she would, after the war, have a voice at the peace conference; she could, without violating international law, confiscate the German and Austrian share of the Boxer indemnities, amounting to £14 million; she would recover possession of the German and Austrian concessions in Tientsin and Hankow and would be able to rid herself of her unequal treaties with

[6] Morrison to M. Allison (London), 17 November 1915, M.P. 104: 'I am determined that China shall come into this war on the side of the Allies. Japan is the doubtful factor.'

[7] Morrison to T. J. Henry, 11 April 1916, M.P. 105.

[8] Jordan to Grey, 11 Nov. 1915, F.O. 371/2340, [169333].

[9] Diary, 1 Nov. 1915, M.P. 104.

Germany and Austria.[10] This was a forcible—if optimistic—presentation of the advantages which China stood to gain.

Professing to be in favour of joining the powers, Yüan let it be known that China must first be invited by the Entente to join them and that he required a loan from them of £2 million for the expansion of his arsenals. Given these two conditions, he would force Germany to declare war by accepting a contract for the supply of munitions to the Entente. Yüan explained to Morrison that in August 1914 when Japan was preparing to attack Kiaochow he had offered to join these operations against Germany, 'pressing if need be 50,000 troops for this task'.[11] He had made such an offer to the British minister in Peking, Sir John Jordan, who had advised him to do nothing. Morrison had been out of China at the outbreak of the war and had not returned until 14 September. He had not hitherto known of the offer but now condemned Jordan's reaction as a diplomatic blunder of the worst kind. In retrospect, it is not unreasonable that this offer should not have been taken seriously by one who knew China's appalling financial state and felt that her military contribution would not justify the hazards involved. None the less, Yüan claimed that the rejection of his 1914 offer made him shy of taking a public initiative in 1915.[12]

Yüan avoided acting directly but left it to Liang Shih-yi, the head of the Revenue Council and his intimate adviser, to fly a kite. On 6 November Jordan reported a secret discussion in which Liang had said that 'it is better to throw off the mask and deal with the question of supplying arms and ammunition on a regular footing', though he insisted that the question should not be treated as China's initiative.[13] When this report found its way to London, the Foreign Office was already considering a different scheme for expelling Germans from China and obtaining the use of her arsenals which had been promoted by Sir Marcus Samuel, former Lord Mayor of London and a merchant-financier with interests in the Far East. On 11 November Sir Edward Grey, encouraged by the War Office, passed on an amalgam of the Chinese and Samuel proposals to Japan saying that, although the supply of Chinese arms to the Russian

[10] Morrison to Dr G. W. Prothero (London), 1 Dec. 1915, M.P. 104.

[11] Morrison to L. Fraser (London), 12 Oct. 1916, M.P. 142.

[12] *Ibid.*; T. F. Millard, *Democracy and the Eastern Question* (New York, 1919) pp. 95–6. I have been unable to trace Jordan's report of Yüan's offer of 1914 in the Foreign Office archives. But he made similar offers to Japan on 1 September.

[13] Jordan to Grey, 6 Nov. 1915, F.O. 371/2341, [183325].

government might give rise to German protests against China, ultimately involving her in war, he firmly believed that it would bring about important moral and material consequences for the general strategy of the European war.[14] The Japanese ministers professed to be astounded at the suddenness of this approach. But the British ambassador in Tokyo, Sir Conyngham Greene, took the opportunity to speak to the foreign minister on 15 November in support of the London proposals and felt that he had made some impression.[15]

Morrison wrongly suspected Jordan of not passing on Liang's overtures to London. He therefore lobbied the French, Belgian and Russian ministers in Peking, who were less aware of the pitfalls which the Japanese attitude involved; and these governments put pressure on London for a joint approach. Morrison also informed them that the initiative had come from China—a fact which Britain was anxious to conceal from the Japanese. Moreover, it was Morrison who first spelled out the financial conditions on which China would be prepared to cooperate since Liang had not made these known to Jordan.[16] Encouraged by the testimony of Jordan that the intrigues of Germans in China had reached considerable dimensions, Grey agreed to join the other powers in a more farreaching approach to Japan than the earlier British overture. On 22 November the ambassadors of Britain, France and Russia presented Japan with a note saying that the three powers proposed to ask China for the use of her arsenals and for energetic measures over German and Austrian agents and residents in China, which would probably be welcomed by the Chinese. It was, the note argued, nothing more drastic than inviting China to break off relations with Germany and Austria. The Japanese foreign minister agreed to lay the matter before his colleagues.[17]

Morrison was always inclined to leak his activities to the press.[18] On this occasion the matter received much publicity, which was distasteful to

[14] Grey to Greene, 12 Nov. 1915, F.O. 371/2340, [168694].

[15] Greene to Grey, 8 Jan. 1916, F.O. 800/68.

[16] Minutes on Jordan to Grey, 17 Nov. 1915, F.O. 371/2340, [173106]; a Foreign Office official minuted that Morrison took matters up with other legations as 'he finds he does not carry much weight with the British Legation'.

[17] Greene to Grey, 23 Nov. 1915, F.O. 371/2341, [176806].

[18] Morrison to Prothero, 1 Dec. 1915, M.P. 104: '*The Times* is being kept exceptionally well-informed by its correspondent, a fellow-Australian of mine, named Mr W. H. Donald.'

Britain,[19] and ill-informed speculation was rife. Particularly damaging in the eyes of Tokyo was a Peking message to the *Asahi Shimbun* on 25 November which suggested that, while the powers were trying to get China into the war, Britain was trying to negotiate an alliance with her and even quoted the alleged terms of the treaty. If true, this suggested extreme bad faith on Britain's part towards Japan. Jordan denied the rumour in Peking and Grey promptly scotched it:

> We have not contemplated anything of the kind and have no intention, except in consultation with Japan, of entering upon negotiations of a political nature with China. When the matter was merely one of purchase of guns and rifles, we dealt with it alone, but we approached Japan directly it assumed a political aspect and we have consistently refused, without the co-operation of Japan, to continue discussing the matter at Peking.[20]

This assurance was eventually issued to the press in the form of a public disclaimer by the British government. But even the *Japan Weekly Mail* commented that 'a section of British residents in Peking holds an opinion insisting on the establishment of special relations between Britain and China, Dr Morrison being reported to be a warm advocate of this plan'.[21] The rumour was highly plausible and even the denials did not discredit it completely. Some Japanese newspapers denounced Britain's attitude with a vituperation which was quite unprecedented and continued their campaign well into 1916.

In formulating their own policy, the Japanese took the natural course in making indirect inquiries in China and found that Liang Shih-yi and Morrison were implicated. Slippery as usual, Yüan told them that he did not want to give up neutrality and sacrifice German goodwill and that he would not welcome an approach from the allies.[22] While Japan's diplomats overseas tended to favour the allied proposal, army headquarters and the war ministry resisted any disturbance of China's neutrality. Accordingly, the Japanese cabinet on 3 December opposed the whole idea. The foreign ambassadors were told that the Japanese were prepared to

[19] Foreign Office memorandum, 11 April 1916, F.O. 371/2841, [68358].
[20] Grey to Greene, 26 Nov. 1915, F.O. 371/2341, [178314].
[21] *Japan Weekly Mail*, 27 Nov. 1915.
[22] Foreign Ministry memorandum, 30 Oct. 1916, S.T., N.G.B., no. 678.

consider what measures they could take in China to promote the supply of arms to Russia, 'without exposing China to the charge of an open breach of her neutrality', and to work with China for the extension and improvement of Chinese arsenals. They would cooperate in putting an end to Austro-German intrigues against the allies but did not think it advisable 'to take such measures as to involve China in the present war' or to encourage 'open rupture between China and Austria-Germany'.[23] Britain concluded that this reply was final: Japan would not allow China to become a belligerent. While the Entente powers had formally agreed to consider ways of dealing with German intrigues, Japan had virtually slammed the door on the allied use of China's arsenals. The overture had, moreover, dispelled the hope of improving relations between the Entente and Japan, where it had 'crystallized public opinion into an attitude of no surrender'; Japan would hear of no rôle for the powers in China other than one of 'hands off'.[24]

Morrison was widely blamed for the failure of this diplomatic initiative. He was disowned by Yüan, who issued an official statement that China had never considered the possibility of abandoning her neutrality.[25] Moreover, British diplomats did not welcome the activities of the political adviser, whose 'interference contributed to our embarrassment'.[26] As a result, whatever Morrison did thereafter he had to do on his own, unassisted by British diplomatic representatives; he had become *persona non grata* with them. Nor were the Japanese any kinder to Morrison. The elaborate apparatus of Japanese military intelligence in China at this time had clearly branded him as anti-Japanese and the central figure in intrigues to restrict Japan's activities in China.[27] It is doubtful how far Morrison knew of this distrust; and he continued to cling to his *idée fixe* with stubborn pertinacity.

Britain had been badly snubbed by the refusal of the Japanese government and the hostile campaign in the Japanese press which followed. Grey decided to continue with his policy of marking time in the Far East. As

[23] Greene to Grey, 8 Dec. 1915, F.O. 371/2341, [7242].
[24] Greene to Grey, 8 Jan. 1916, F.O. 800/68.
[25] Ishii to Inoue, 4 Dec. 1915, F.O. 800/68.
[26] Alston (Peking) to Grey, 16 Aug. 1916, F.O. 800/68.
[27] Foreign Ministry memorandum, 30 Oct. 1916, S.T., N.G.B., no. 678.

one of his assistants wrote, 'the Japanese had so misconstrued our attitude on the expulsion of Germans that we are inclined to move very warily in any fresh crisis'.[28] But the French and Russians were less inclined to let the matter drop. Russia was in a favourable position to ask for Japan's assistance since she was engaged in negotiating a treaty of alliance with Japan which was eventually signed in July. The Russians used the opportunity to press Japan to adopt a more helpful attitude over China. Grey, however, urged them not to confuse the alliance negotiations, of which he fully approved, 'by including the expulsion scheme [since the Japanese] are firm in their intention not to fall in with our proposals'.[29]

Meanwhile Morrison thought it wise to tread cautiously. China was in turmoil over the monarchical issue and was hardly interested in gaining admission to the ranks of the allies.[30] In the middle of January Morrison discussed this question with Yüan's elderly Japanese legal adviser, Dr Ariga Nagao, 'Methuselah Ariga' as Morrison described him. Morrison complained that the earlier representations had been bungled by the diplomats who had failed to convince the Japanese that the proposal was in their best interests; he hoped to go to Tokyo and discuss the matter thoroughly with Japanese statesmen of his acquaintance; but, since present circumstances would not permit this, he wanted to bring his views privately through Ariga to the knowledge of the Japanese authorities. Ariga reported to the Japanese minister in Peking who duly passed on a message to Tokyo.[31]

By the summer the situation in China seemed to change in Morrison's favour. Firstly, Yüan's bid to become emperor failed in April under strong Japanese pressure. Secondly, his death on 6 June removed from the scene the inveterate enemy of the Japanese. Thirdly, most of the members of the successor government of President Li Yüan-hung had been educated in Japan and had been associated with the Japanese before they came to power. It was not unreasonable to expect that Japan's attitude towards a more amenable government in China might be more favourable.

Morrison of course had to start from scratch and try to convert the new president, for whom he continued to act as political adviser. To this end

[28] Langley to Jordan, 15 Dec. 1915, F.O. 350/14.
[29] Grey to Buchanan, 3 March 1916, F.O. 410/65.
[30] Morrison to Henry, 11 April 1916, M.P. 105.
[31] Hioki to Ishii, 7 Feb. 1916, S.T., N.G.B., no. 663.

he presented him with a memorandum setting out the arguments in favour of China's entry into the war, as he had done before for Yüan. In July Morrison was granted two months' leave in order to take his wife and two sons for a holiday at Chuzenji, a mountain resort in Japan where foreign ambassadors went in retreat from the Tokyo summer. He used the opportunity to discuss his all-absorbing interest with the British military attaché in Tokyo.[32] On 7 August, the British ambassador, Sir Conyngham Greene, also saw him and reported that Morrison 'was quite discreet and did not ask me any questions but merely reeled off his own views as if he were dictating to a typist and not expecting any interruption or response'. Greene, however, told him that the whole question was absolutely stationary and there was no sign of its being ready for re-opening.[33]

Morrison had also conversations with many of his Japanese friends, including the newspaperman Mochizuki of the Liberal Press Agency. He reached the conclusion that, since Japan had become Russia's ally in July, 'the cause of the Entente was now in the ascendant, whereas this was far from being the case ten months ago'.[34] Morrison therefore thought that it would be worth while to put out feelers to the Japanese government. This he did, apparently without the authority of the Chinese government or its knowledge and unbeknown to the British embassy.

Morrison asked for an interview with Viscount Katō Takaaki, the leader of one of the opposition parties, who had formerly been foreign minister and had the reputation of being pro-British. There is no denying the boldness of this step: Morrison was not *persona grata* with the Japanese; he could hardly have served as political adviser to Yüan without incurring their suspicion and antagonism. To meet this point, Morrison told Katō that he wanted to discuss matters as an Englishman, not as one in the service of China. Nor were they more than distant acquaintances: yet Katō agreed to meet him.

On 15 August Katō came from his villa at Oiso to see Morrison in Tokyo. Always a skilful advocate, Morrison presented the China issue in the light most favourable to Japan, emphasizing the extent of American

[32] Report by Col. J. A. C. Somerville in Greene to Grey, 1 Aug. 1916, F.O. 800/68.

[33] Greene to Grey, 15 Aug. 1916, F.O. 800/68.

[34] Greene to Grey, 15 Aug. 1916, F.O. 800/68; diary, 15 Aug. 1916, M.P. 107; and diary, 25 May 1909, M.P. 81.

economic and financial activity in China and of the favour which it was shown. He spoke of the German activity, particularly in the consulate in Shanghai which gave small loans to China and thereby injured the interest of Japan directly and indirectly. Katō asked where the money came from and Morrison explained that every day China paid Germany £6000 on account of the Boxer indemnity and various other loans. Morrison went on to argue that the country which would benefit most from China's entry into the war was Japan. It was a pity that Japan had not so far recognized this: was there no way of bringing about better understanding on this issue? Katō replied that he did not know much about the question and thought that Britain's real motives had not been brought home sufficiently to the Japanese government. Morrison added that the method of putting forward the various proposals in the past had not been satisfactory and that present circumstances had greatly changed. In Morrison's version of the conversation, Katō admitted what does not feature in his own report, namely, that the matter had been presented to him in a new light and that he was ready to bring it to the notice of the ministry for reconsideration.[35]

Katō did indeed report to the Foreign Ministry; but Morrison would have been greatly disturbed if he had seen the Foreign Ministry's estimate of the conversation.[36] Katō reported that it was not clear whether Morrison's cordiality was because his position in China was now rather insecure or whether he really recognized the ascendancy of Japan in China and was speaking sincerely; if Japan's minister in China handled him aright, Morrison could be turned into an ally, a 'person in our own medicine basket'.

Morrison accidentally met Greene at Chuzenji on 28 August and later reported in writing about his interview with Katō. Greene sent only the briefest of acknowledgements; Morrison noted that 'it ought to have been written in invisible ink', so noncommittal were its contents.[37] When he returned to Peking in the middle of September, he spoke openly to foreign residents of what seemed to him 'a successful interview' and sent

[35] Kato's version of the conversation is found in Ishii to Hayashi Gonsuke (China), 24 August 1916, S.T., N.G.B., no. 671; Morrison's version is given in the enclosure to Jordan to Grey, 20 Sept. 1916, F.O. 405/220, no. 202.

[36] S.T., N.G.B., no. 671.

[37] M.P. 107. Jordan had warned Greene against talking to Morrison in case Japan associated Britain with his activities: Jordan to Greene, 8 Aug. 1916, F.O. 800/68.

details to a wide range of diplomats and journalists. The British legation was at pains to make clear that Morrison's approach to the Chinese president and later to Katō had been made without the knowledge of any British official, far less the British government. Morrison also sent a lengthy note to the Foreign Office, where his overtures to Katō caused quite a flutter. The London government, which was necessarily mindful of the needs of the Entente, could not afford to neglect any move which might improve its fortunes in the East. While dissociating himself from the project which Dr Morrison had brought forward again on his own initiative, Grey sent a cautious telegram to Japan:

> We had in fact decided not to raise this question again ourselves nor to encourage it being raised unless we were sure that the Japanese had changed their views on the subject. We should however be ready again to discuss the project at any time if the Japanese Government care to take the initiative but shall not ourselves propose discussion.[38]

When Morrison heard of this, he considered it to be too lukewarm; and he proceeded to bring the matter to public notice in Britain by addressing officials, friends and newspapermen. To one of his journalist friends, Lovat Fraser, who was leader writer on the Far East for *The Times*, he wrote:

> I can now see that Japan can be induced, provided the British government will act with reasonable firmness, to join in inviting China to become a member of the alliance. Surely you can help to induce the British government to adopt a new and more resolute attitude both in Tokyo and in Peking.[39]

It is doubtful whether this attempt to influence the British government and British opinion was fruitful. At any rate it was overtaken by a cabinet crisis in Japan: the Okuma ministry resigned on 6 October and, with the resulting change of foreign minister, China policy came up for lengthy review in which Morrison's views received some attention.[40]

The story of China's entry into the war now enters its final phase as the

[38] Grey to Greene, 23 Sept. 1916, F.O. 371/2648, [187336]; Chinda to Ishii, 28 September 1916, S.T., N.G.B., no. 672.

[39] Morrison to Fraser, 12 Oct. 1916, M.P. 142.

[40] Foreign Ministry memorandum, 30 Oct. 1916, S.T., N.G.B., no. 671.

result of pressure from an unexpected quarter.[41] On 4 February 1917 the American government sent China a note stating that it proposed to break off relations with Germany because of the programme of indiscriminate submarine warfare which she had announced and calling on other neutral powers to take similar action. It also asked its minister in Peking, Paul S. Reinsch, to try to induce the Chinese to adopt this course. When these instructions arrived, it was Sunday and Morrison was entertaining Reinsch at his cottage outside Peking. They both took immediate action. Reinsch went to the Chinese foreign ministry, the Waichiaopu, and later in the evening saw the premier, Tuan Chi-jui, the leader of the northern warlords, but came away discouraged by the interview.

Morrison visited President Li Yuan-hung early on Monday morning. He was accompanied by Admiral Ts'ai Ting-kan, who had become naval assistant to the new president. As one who had been Morrison's closest associate over the years, Ts'ai was known to be favourable to China's entry into the war.[42] It was left to these two to present those aspects of the case for China's entry which Morrison had been canvassing since 1915[43] but which Reinsch in his formal diplomatic capacity could not put. The president replied that as a student of war and a soldier who had been commander of the Revolutionary army in 1911, he was convinced that Germany would win the war; he therefore insisted that it was in China's interest to remain strictly neutral. Morrison left despondent and committed to his diary that the president was 'weak, vacillating and tremulous' and had a 'bovine intelligence'.[44] He was therefore certain that it would be an uphill task to convince the Chinese government.

Two days later Morrison, in the company of General W. S. Y. Tinge, called on Premier Tuan whom he found to be sodden with opium. It was confirmed at the interview that, as soon as Tuan had received the American request, he had put out feelers in Tokyo. But he had not yet been able

41 This story is relatively well covered in monographs such as: R. H. Fifield, *Woodrow Wilson and the Far East* (New York, 1952) pp. 62–78; T. E. La Fargue, *China and the World War* (Stanford, 1937) pp. 78–113; P. S. Reinsch, *An American Diplomat in China* (London, 1922) chs. 21 and 24; and T. F. Millard, *Democracy and the Eastern Question*, ch. 5.

42 M.P. 184–7. Ts'ai had known President Li personally from their early days in the Chinese navy together.

43 Above, pp. 324–5.

44 Diary, 30 Jan. and 5 Feb. 1917, M.P. 109.

to ascertain the Japanese view. The interview was indecisive and Morrison made a diary note that it had been a waste of time, except that everything counted.[45] Another leader who had to be taken into account was General Feng Kuo-chang, the vice-president, who was tuchun (governor) of Nanking and was therefore remote from policy-making in Peking. At the request of General Tinge Morrison at an early stage drew up for Feng a memorandum setting out the arguments in favour of China's entry. This was telegraphed to Feng in the hope that it might be useful in commending the proposal to the parties of the south.

The initial contacts made by his various foreign collaborators, who were mainly Americans,[46] left Morrison convinced that it was best to bring pressure to bear on the leaders through influential Chinese themselves. He noted in his diary that the net result of all the lobbying that was going on was that 'Young China' was in favour of the cause and 'the Old Gang' was opposed.[47] The chief object must therefore be to feed the Young China party with arguments in the hope that it would have some influence on the final decision. The majority of those through whom Morrison and his collaborators acted had been educated in the United States. They included one minister, Dr Ch'en Chin-tao, the minister of finance. More numerous were the officials on whom Morrison felt he could rely for some support: Dr Wu Chao-chu, son of the foreign minister; Quo Tai-chi, the secretary to the president; and Lu Tseng-tsiang, former prime minister and foreign minister and now member of the special foreign affairs council. Then there were other non-officials who played some part, like Eugene Chen (Ch'en Yu-jen), editor of the English language *Peking Daily*, and Dr Wang Chung-hui, a leading jurist. One of the intentions of these foreigners was to work up support among parliamentarians in the hope that this would put indirect pressure on the leaders. Apart from the Young China party, they sought the support of the Kuomintang—C. T. Wang had led them to expect this—and the Chinputang (progressive party). It was of course difficult to assess how effective these promises of support were likely to be; but there were grounds for confidence that

[45] Diary, 7 Feb. 1917, M.P. 109.

[46] These included Sam Blythe, Roy Anderson, Dr J. C. Ferguson, proprietor of the *Shanghai Times* and a supernumerary political adviser to China, and Stephenson Smith.

[47] Diary, 5 Feb. 1917, M.P. 109.

progressive opinion was moving towards the views of the foreign lobby.

The Chinese cabinet, which was left by the president to make the final decision, asked the Americans for all manner of guarantees: it wanted a loan of $10 million and the American share of the Boxer indemnity to be funded in long-term bonds. Because Reinsch was out of cable contact with Washington, he gave these assurances on his own initiative and without waiting for the approval of his government. Thus fortified, the cabinet thrashed the matter out on 8 February at a marathon meeting lasting six hours. Reinsch presented his case to some members of the cabinet just before the meeting opened, while Morrison tried to talk some of the younger generals into applying last minute pressure. Eventually at 6 o'clock on the following day it was announced that a remonstrance against the submarine menace had been made to Germany which was informed that 'in case its protest be ineffectual, the Government of the Chinese Republic will be constrained to sever diplomatic relations'.[48]

The diplomatic representatives of Britain, France and Russia were not particularly helpful in reaching this decision. They were not unreasonably fearful of a rebuff from Japan, as had happened in 1915, and took the view that this was an issue best left to the Americans to pursue. Morrison was indeed asked not to compromise the British legation by suggesting that his actions were in any way inspired by the British government.[49] The Foreign Office line was initially that Britain should encourage the American initiative unofficially but that China should decide only after seeking Japan's opinion. As it happened, there need have been no anxiety about Japan, where the cabinet met on 9 February and decided to support the American invitation since it was not dangerous for Japan and since China, because of her goodwill to the Americans, was likely to accept in any case.[50]

What had been achieved was a triumph for that group of foreigners who pushed the Chinese to a decision. Pride of place went to Reinsch with the influence of the American government behind him; but Morrison had a part to play. Influential too was a fellow-Australian, W. H. Donald, the editor of the *Far Eastern Review*, who had opportunities for contacts which

[48] Chinese Ministry of Foreign Affairs to Hintze (Peking), 9 Feb. 1917, Millard, p. 112.

[49] Diary, 5 Feb. 1917, M.P. 109.

[50] Resolution of Japanese cabinet, 9 Feb. 1917, S.T., N.G.B., no. 737.

were denied even to Morrison. Beyond this was a staunch group of Americans who, in the phrase of one of them, formed a 'flying wedge' which did not spare any pains to bring the American wishes home to influential Chinese.[51] But Morrison and Reinsch were not pursuing identical objectives. The Americans made it plain that they were asking China to join the United States and other neutrals in breaking off relations with Germany, not to join the allied side. Morrison on the other hand wanted them to enter the war and benefit from that act. While the German reply was awaited, the Chinese were busy. The cabinet set up a committee of foreign advisers, including Morrison, which met several times and drew up in French a memorandum on the likely consequences of breaking off relations with Germany.[52] On 15 February the Chinese informed the various allied governments of the price they demanded for breaking off relations: the postponement of payment of interest on their foreign loans during the war and an increase in the rate of duty on imports. Most of the powers were inclined to be evasive on these points and to view cast-iron undertakings without great enthusiasm.[53] But on 28 February the French minister to China, speaking on behalf of seven allied powers, replied accepting in principle her conditions for breaking off relations with Germany.

When the Germans replied in a spirit of no concession, the Tuan cabinet finally got its way and cut diplomatic ties on 14 March. Tuan and his supporters, the northern tuchuns, were in favour of participation in the war, because it would open up the possibility of greater financial assistance from overseas, help them to build up what they called their 'participation armies' and strengthen the position of the North against the South. Their stand was reinforced when the United States entered the war in April. But, in a note of 4 June, the Americans urged China to attend to her domestic situation and emphasized that 'the entry of China into war with Germany [was a matter] of secondary consideration'.[54] On the other hand, Morrison and the European powers recommended that

[51] On Donald, see above, p. 326, fn. 18. For the members of the 'flying wedge', see above, p. 334, fn. 46.

[52] The committee consisted of Morrison, Padoux (French), de Codt (Belgian) and Ariga (Japanese).

[53] Greene to Motono, 26 Feb. 1917, S.T., N.G.B., no. 781.

[54] Lansing to Reinsch, 4 June 1917, *Foreign Relations of the United States, 1917* (Washington, 1926) pp. 48–9.

China's entry was in her best interest, while the Japanese urged China to reject the American view. When all this advice descended on China, Premier Tuan was temporarily out of office, having been dislodged by President Li who continued to be unconvinced of the wisdom of breaking relations with Germany. But on 13 July he returned to power and his government eventually declared war on Germany on 14 August 1917.[55]

It cannot be said that China made a vital contribution to the allied victory; although she offered to send an expeditionary force to Europe, it was not accepted by the allies and only 'coolie' battalions saw service on the western front. Because of the outbreak of the Bolshevik revolution, the supply of Chinese arms to Russia was no longer required, though her decision for war led to the internment of Germans in China. Nor was she able to take full advantage of her standing as an ally because of the state of civil war between North and South which existed from the summer of 1917. For this reason, too, it was hard for her to gain the concessions which she sought at the Paris peace conference.

Morrison's wife was jubilant at China's entry into the war and congratulated him on his success: 'Your efforts of the last 2½ years have not been in vain. I always remember you saying to Sir John [Jordan] once "I am determined it shall go through" and I have often felt quite miserable that so far it hadn't gone through.'[56] It is true that Morrison had been one of the consistent advocates of China declaring war. In 1915 he had worked alongside the European powers; but they had withdrawn because of Japanese resistance. In 1917 he found himself in company with the United States; and later, when the Americans blew cold, it was the Japanese who advocated China's full participation. As governments changed their stance, Morrison remained constant: he still employed in 1917 the arguments he had used in 1915.

Morrison's problem was that he never had assured support. In China he was one foreign adviser among many. Since the Chinese were inexperienced in dealing with foreign advisers, he had no prescribed functions and no regular access to the president. When he wanted to win the attention of the leaders, he had to rally support wherever he found it. In

[55] This extremely complex domestic story in which Morrison had little part is told in Li Chien-nung, *Political History of China, 1840–1928* (Princeton, 1956) pp. 363–73.

[56] M.P. 192.

the crisis of 1917 he succeeded where he had earlier failed in mobilizing enough supporters with American help. Nor did he have the backing of the British Government. Though many Chinese found it hard to believe, he was not the appointee of his government nor did he receive instructions or advice from it. On the contrary, he was during his period as adviser never taken into the confidence of the British legation in Peking or of the Foreign Office. In these circumstances, his job might easily have turned into a sterile sinecure, had his own strong personality not made him campaign for causes in which he believed.

One such cause was China's entry into the war, in which Morrison felt that China's interest coincided with that of his own country and that he had a dual loyalty. It is possible to argue that the benefits which China could derive from entering the war were marginal and uncertain. Yet her leaders clearly thought it had advantages when they first took the initiative to raise the matter with Britain. Naturally they were worried about Japanese opposition. Morrison therefore felt that he was justified in trying to persuade Japan unofficially in 1916 as he had earlier tried to enlist the support of Russia and France for the proposal. This was personal diplomacy without the authority of the Chinese government of a kind which can only be understood in the context of the fluid diplomatic methods of China. It was certainly independent but probably not disloyal. For its part, the London government after 1915 chose not to press for China's entry for fear of a further rebuff from Japan. Yet Morrison persevered despite discouragement from British quarters. He considered that Britain would derive advantages from the proposal that were not recognized by those in Whitehall. We may concur in the view that it was only fair 'to credit him with the loyal desire to help [Britain] in time of need'.[57]

Thus Morrison, like an oriental marriage-broker who was on the point of completing arrangements for an important match, persisted against the opposition of reluctant neighbours and finally overcame the modest hesitancy of bride and groom.

[57] Greene to Grey, 15 Aug. 1916, F.O. 800/68.

18

ESMONDE ROBERTSON

Mussolini and Ethiopia: The Prehistory of the Rome Agreements of January 1935

Most authorities attempt to explain Mussolini's policy for war against Ethiopia by concentrating on events in 1934. Miss Elizabeth Wiskemann tells us that after the murder of Dollfuss in July of that year it was the Duce's aim first to overwhelm Ethiopia, and then to dispatch Italian forces to the Brenner. She thus, rightly, considers Mussolini's action in Ethiopia as an anti-German move.[1] According to G. W. Baer in a scholarly and exhaustive treatment of the subject: 'No single program of action was devised until Mussolini himself manifested an interest in Ethiopia and took complete and forceful command of the formulation and execution of Italian colonial policy in East Africa.'[2] He considers Mussolini's article 'Verso il riarmo' (Towards rearmament) in the *Popolo d'Italia* of 28 May 1934 to be the turning-point. But he goes on to say that the available 'evidence does not give us a conclusive explanation' as to why Mussolini acted when he did, and thus turns to the 'nature of Italian Fascism, the mind of Mussolini and the needs of his dictatorship', to account for Italian aggression.[3] Geoffrey Warner has provided us with by far the best account of French policy under Laval. 'Barthou' (foreign minister until 10 October 1934), he claims, 'had taken advantage of a growing coolness between Mussolini and Hitler' to try to draw Italy into an anti-German coalition. Laval continued the negotiations, but with a different end in view. 'I thought,'—he is taking Laval's own words, recorded in 1942, at their face value—'that the first thing to do was to bring France and Italy closer together. I thought that this was the first link

[1] E. Wiskemann, *The Rome-Berlin Axis* (London, 1966) pp. 57–8.

[2] G. W. Baer, *The Coming of the Italian-Ethiopian War* (Cambridge, Mass., 1967) p. 24.

[3] *Ibid.*, pp. 28–9.

in a chain which would one day lead to an agreement with Germany.'[4] Baer and Warner evidently had not at their disposal the French diplomatic documents covering the period July 1932–March 1933.[5] These, read in conjunction with earlier Italian publications,[6] render necessary a reinterpretation of the Rome Agreements and of the origins of the Italian-Ethiopian War.

The Italians had never forgotten the 'shameful scar', as d'Annunzio had called it, of their defeat at Adowa in 1896.[7] In 1906 they concluded a treaty with Britain and France for the division of Ethiopia into spheres of influence, should political order in that country disintegrate after the death of the Emperor Menelik I. Their fears seemed to be justified, for in the chaotic conditions in Ethiopia after the death of Menelik and the outbreak of World War I, Emperor Eyasu tried to win support from the Muslim population and turned to the Central Powers.[8]

In 1919 the Italians once again turned to East Africa. They claimed, in accordance with Article 13 of the Treaty of London, that in return for the occupation by Britain and France of former German colonies, Italy should be compensated in Africa: specific mention was later made of Djibuti in French Somaliland.[9] The Italians, though, were more successful in bargaining with the British than with the French. The British Foreign Office, under Curzon, was prepared to cede Jubaland on the border between British and Italian Somaliland only if Italy evacuated the Dodecanese in favour of Greece, as she had promised to do in 1920. In 1924 Austen Chamberlain, in need of Italian support to put pressure on Turkey to recognize Iraq as a British mandate, withdrew this condition and in 1925 Jubaland with its port of Kismayu was handed over to Italy.[10] While Britain and

[4] G. Warner, *Pierre Laval and the Eclipse of France* (London, 1968) pp. 63 ff.

[5] Ministère des Affaires Etrangères, *Documents diplomatiques français 1932–1939* (hereafter referred to as *D.D.F.*), ser. I, I, 9 July–14 Nov. 1932 (Paris, 1964) and II, 15 Nov. 1932–17 Mar. 1933 (Paris, 1966). The numbers of the documents are referred to below.

[6] R. Guariglia, *Ricordi, 1922–1946* (Naples, 1950) and R. Aloisi, *Journal, 25 Juillet 1932–14 Juin 1935*, edited by M. Toscano and translated by M. Vaussard (Paris, 1957). This important work has not been published in the Italian original.

[7] Baer, p. 4.

[8] R. Greenfield, *Ethiopia* (London, 1963) pp. 136–7.

[9] R. Louis, 'The United States and the African peace settlement of 1919: the pilgrimage of George Louis Beer', *Journal of African History* IV, no. 3 (1963).

[10] C. Seton-Watson, *Italy from Liberalism to Fascism* (London, 1967) pp. 683–4; and Baer, p. 14.

Italy had already, with great reluctance, agreed to Ethiopia's admission to the League of Nations in 1923, they had not abandoned the 1906 policy of dividing that country into spheres of interest. In 1925 they reaffirmed their respective spheres of influence. France was invited to accede to this agreement but refused to do so. Italy was to be allowed to construct a railroad linking Eritrea and Somaliland, as well as to have economic privileges in the area west of Addis Ababa; Britain, to control the waters of the Blue Nile near its source in Lake Tana. Since the terms of the treaty were ostensibly contrary to Article 20 of the Covenant, the regent Ras Tafari protested to the Council of the League, as a result of which the Treaty was repudiated by Britain and Italy.[11]

It is doubtful whether the regent would have succeeded in mobilizing the support of the League had it not been in the interest of one of the great powers that Ethiopia should remain a sovereign state. The French had completed their railway from Djibuti to Addis Ababa before 1919. They were thus able to tap much of the resources of the hinterland. Although traffic on this line was frequently disturbed, because of political unrest, it brought in sufficient revenue to enable the French to keep Djibuti operating as a port of call in their line of communications with Madagascar and the Far East. In face of strong Italian and also British opposition the French had supported Ethiopia's application for League membership in 1923; and they hoped to take the lead in developing that country's economic resources and promoting educational reform. They were prepared to adhere to this policy only on condition that Tafari made real progress towards the modernization of his country; failure would mean a reversion to the policy of 1906 for the delimitation of spheres of influence.[12]

Both Mussolini and Tafari were later to labour under certain delusions. Mussolini thought that it would be enough to square the French if Italy was to resume her expansion in Ethiopia, and gave insufficient thought to Britain;[13] the regent only too gullibly believed that admission to the League was tantamount to consecration to statehood, and that the League would rescue his country from falling a prey to the imperial ambitions of her neighbours. In the late twenties there was still no immediate danger. The Italians were busy 'restoring order' in Cyrenaica which had

[11] F. P. Walters, *A History of the League of Nations* (London, 1952) I, 397–8.

[12] *D.D.F.*, ser. I, II, 182; annexes.

[13] See the introduction to Aloisi, *op. cit.*

completely slipped from their control since the outbreak of World War I: not until 1931 was Graziani successful against the desert sect, the Senussi. In these circumstances Mussolini wished to remain on good terms with Tafari, and in 1928 a twenty-year Treaty of Friendship was concluded between Ethiopia and Italy.

After 1930 it was no longer believed that North Africa offered a favourable field for future Italian expansion. In March 1932 General de Bono, Italian Minister for Colonies, was sent to Eritrea with instructions from Mussolini to develop this colony as a base, at first for defensive operations against a supposed Ethiopian attack.[14] De Bono's contention that he and the Duce alone later knew of military plans of an offensive character is without foundation.[15] Guariglia, Political Director of Europe, the Near East and Africa in the Italian Foreign Ministry and a close friend of Grandi, the Foreign Minister, was a keen advocate of an expedition in a 'grand style' against Ethiopia. According to him, Ethiopia was the one area in the world where Italy could expand without colliding with the interests of other powers. This rich fertile country was not only capable of absorbing Italy's surplus population but could provide her with black troops for deployment in North Africa. Guariglia described the failure of existing Italian policy in Ethiopia under Mussolini and outlined the future lines of policy in a long memorandum of 27 August 1932 which was intended as his political testament.[16]

Ethiopia's irredentism was directed principally against Eritrea, the defence of which would become all but impossible after Ethiopia had been transformed from a feudal society into a centralized state. The 1906 agreement was in Guariglia's view the Magna Carta of Italy's rights and aspirations which had been given recognition by Britain and France. After France's refusal to cede Djibuti in 1919 two courses were open to Italy: first, to exert direct influence over the central government at Addis Ababa; second, 'to attract the more powerful chiefs in the neighbourhood of our territories under our influence'. The latter course, known as the *politica periferica*, had been practised by Baldissera before Adowa. Guariglia accused the government of Ethiopia after 1925 of trying to play off one of its European neighbours against the other. It had invited the Italian

[14] E. de Bono, *Conquest of an Empire* (London, 1937) p. 3.
[15] *Ibid.*, p. 13.
[16] *Ricordi*, pp. 164–7, 180; and Appendix A, pp. 763–73.

government to cede a corridor of territory connecting the interior with Assab on the Red Sea, in order to reduce Ethiopia's complete economic dependence on France. Although the transfer of this corridor could in no way endanger the position of Italy strategically, the Fascist government, for reasons of prestige alone, refused to alienate one single acre of territory. Instead, Ethiopia was offered the facilities of a free port at Assab in return for permission to construct a railway connecting Assab with Dessie in the south. Tafari showed little enthusiasm for this project, on the ground that Ethiopia would have to finance the part of the line within her own territory. As an alternative Baron Franchetti was sent to Addis Ababa to win Tafari's acceptance for a line constructed by a private company running from Setit in Eritrea to Gondar in the north of Ethiopia. From the Italian point of view this line was of great strategic as well as of economic value. Not surprisingly Tafari took no practical steps for its realization.

In 1932 Guariglia proposed that Italy should in future give the impression that the Setit-Gondar line was not a private but a public enterprise. Should the emperor refuse to fall into line with Italian wishes, the new minister to Addis Ababa should be instructed to denounce the Treaty of Friendship of 1928.[17] Recently Tafari (since 1930 Emperor Haile Selassie) had again advanced the idea of an outlet to the sea at Assab, but this time he offered Italy compensation—a 'miserable' tract of territory in Ogaden as well as permission to construct the Setit-Ogaden line. Guariglia strongly discountenanced negotiations on these proposals. Instead he insisted that the ground for the conquest of Ethiopia, like that of Libya, should be prepared diplomatically well in advance.

Ethiopia constituted one of many outstanding spheres of conflict between Italy and France in Europe, the Near East and Africa. In 1928 there were three main causes of dispute in North Africa alone: the frontier of Libya, the status of Italians living in Tunisia and the future of Spanish Morocco. In 1919 the French had ceded to Italy a few oases on the frontier between Libya and Tunisia. In 1928 Italian claims were still modest, but by 1932 they were multiplied tenfold. Not only did Mussolini demand the Tibesti Borku triangle north of Lake Chad, but also at least a large slice of the mandated French Cameroons, with a corridor linking it with Libya.

[17] *Ibid.*

These extravagant claims, if realized, would have severed French communications in central Africa, and were roundly rejected.[18]

Tunisia itself has been described as an Italian colony with a French government[19] in which the Italians outnumbered the French and were concentrated in areas of great strategic importance, Tunis, Bizerta and Cape Bon.[20] According to the Statute of 1896, which regulated Tunisia's relations with France, the Italians could claim Italian citizenship in Tunisia and French citizenship in Italy. During the war Italian irredentism caused such friction that even before the armistice the Statute was suspended, but remained provisionally in force pending agreement on a new one. In the general negotiations of 1928 on North Africa the French were prepared to compromise and allow the Italians a relatively privileged status within a liberal constitution. But Mussolini, moved by *amour propre*, demanded all or nothing. Either the 1896 Statute should come into full force for at least ten years, or France should be allowed outright annexation of Tunisia. Both alternatives were rejected by the French; the first because it would deny France a free hand in North Africa, the second because of the inevitable resentment annexation would cause among the entire Muslim population of the French empire, especially in Morocco.[21]

The only success Mussolini scored in North Africa was in Morocco. In 1928, after many fruitless negotiations, and with British backing, Italy was allowed to participate in the international administration of Tangier, thereby limiting French control of the Western outlet of the Mediterranean. This concession however only whetted Mussolini's appetite. There was also, as in Tunisia, a considerable Italian colony in Spanish Morocco. It was well organized locally and, like all Italian colonies overseas, subject to constant Fascist propaganda directed from Rome. Politically it proved a fertile ground for the extension of Italian interests in the western Mediterranean, an area which unexpectedly was to become a storm centre.

After the fall of the monarchy in 1931 Spain allowed herself to be used

[18] *D.D.F.*, ser. I, II, 182; annexes.

[19] S. H. Roberts, *The History of French Colonial Policy, 1870–1939* (London, 1963 edn) pp. 285–92.

[20] *D.D.F.*, ser. I, II, 41, 182. Mussolini also supported the movement for autonomy among the Italians in Corsica, an important French air base; see C. Seton-Watson, p. 692.

[21] *D.D.F.*, ser. I, II, 182; annexes.

as a base for antifascist propaganda organized principally by Italian freemasons. The following year Spanish counterrevolutionaries asked General Balbo, Italian minister for aviation, for arms. These were already on their way by sea when their revolt was crushed in July. There was evident fear in Rome that the Spanish Republic might allow the French to occupy the Balearic islands in return for support to maintain its authority on the mainland, for the aim of Italian naval manoeuvres in the summer of 1932 was to maintain communications between Italy and her North African colonies against this illusory French threat.[22] It was also mooted in left-wing newspapers in Madrid that Spain should withdraw altogether from her part of Morocco. If the Italians could not seize this colony themselves Mussolini was determined that the French should not cheat them, as they had done in Tunisia in 1882, and march in. The French for their part had not finally subjugated the Berbers in the interior and they feared that if Spanish authority broke down Spanish Morocco might be annexed by Italy.[23]

The French, though, were willing to pay their price for a free hand in North Africa; and certain pro-Italian newspapers in France thought they saw a way out. Why not let Italy realize her colonial aspirations in areas where they were not likely to come into serious conflict with French interests, for example in Turkey or Ethiopia? The Italians had been promised a large zone in Asia Minor by the agreement of St Jean de Maurienne of 1917. After the war they had to stand by and watch the British and French helping themselves to Palestine and Syria as mandates. In 1924 Mussolini still believed that the Turkish Republic would break up.[24] But he was soon disillusioned: under the strong rule of Kemal Ataturk any encroachments on Turkish territory would, with Russian support, be resisted. Hence in 1930 Italy concluded a Treaty of Friendship with Turkey. Mussolini gave full publicity to the unofficial hints, made in the French press, that Italy's claims could be met in Asia Minor, and the information was passed on to the government in Ankara. The upshot was a serious crisis in Franco-Turkish relations in 1932.[25]

[22] Guariglia, pp. 184, 198–9. See also his memorandum of 3 September 1932, pp. 773–89.

[23] *D.D.F.*, ser. 1, I, 105, 110 and 260.

[24] Seton-Watson, pp. 697–8.

[25] *D.D.F.*, ser. 1, II, 182; annexe 7.

By 1930 French policy towards Ethiopia had changed. In that year Haile Selassie had crushed a revolt, but failed to establish his authority fully over the chiefs. The French were now reluctant to throw in their lot with a semifeudal régime, and remained determined that the Djibuti–Addis Ababa line should fall within the French economic sphere of interest. News of this change of policy leaked to the Italians.[26] Nevertheless Haile Selassie, aware of the Italian peril, had been able to secure arms from France in 1930. Early in 1932 he went a stage further and in March proposed a treaty of alliance with France. The French, in no need of Ethiopian support in any case, turned down his offer on the spurious ground that France would only contract alliances within the framework of the League. Haile Selassie remained undaunted, and instead proposed a treaty of friendship and commerce with France, the outcome of which would have been the conversion of his country into a virtual French protectorate. The French gave no reply. Early in 1933 the emperor sent Taklé Hawariat, one of his ablest henchmen, first as a private citizen, later as minister, to Paris to explore the ground for agreement. Although Taklé took the view that French domination would be infinitely preferable to Italian he was cold-shouldered.[27]

Mussolini certainly knew that the French were reluctant to lend Ethiopia support; an agreement between France and Italy was thus logical. According to Guariglia negotiations for a general settlement, started on Grandi's initiative in 1928[28] were only taken seriously by the French after their evacuation of the Rhineland and Hitler's first electoral success in 1930. In spite of momentary fears of a Franco-German accord, on the occasion of Laval's visit to Berlin in 1931,[29] Marquis Theodoli, Chairman of the Mandates Commission of the League, was sent unofficially to Paris to sound out the French government. The choice of Theodoli was exceptionally good. While not a member of the Fascist party, he was *persona grata* with the Italian government. While working on the Mandates Commission he became friendly with Robert de Caix, the French representative, and he appreciated that the French needed Italian support in Syria, which was demanding independence and League

[26] *Ibid.*

[27] *D.D.F.*, ser. I, II, 174 and fn., 182, 197.

[28] Guariglia, pp. 127 ff., 173.

[29] Warner, pp. 42–4.

membership.[30] On Theodoli's return Mussolini, who knew about Theodoli's visit, insisted to Grandi that Fascism needed an impressive diplomatic victory, such as the cession of a real French colony.[31] There was much discussion on which colony Italy should claim. In June 1932 Grandi sounded the French on the possibility of the cession of a mandate, evidently the Cameroons.[32] In September Rosso, Grandi's *chef de cabinet*, rejected the idea that Italy should realize her ambitions in Ethiopia, because of the stout resistance he expected. Instead, the Italians should be allowed to establish a colony in Angola, under a chartered company so as not to violate Portuguese sovereignty.[33] There was thus much talk of a new partition of Africa. In Guariglia's view Italian expansion in the Cameroons, previously German, would encounter revived German claims, no less than French interests; in Angola, the interests of the Government of South Africa no less than those of Portugal. He was also worried on several occasions because the Fascist press had clamoured for the cession of Syria. Such 'absurd demands', he claimed, ought to be silenced by the Palazzo Chigi both on the ground that the French were unlikely to make a gift of Syria to Italy and because the acquisition of a country riddled with domestic strife would prove a liability.[34] Guariglia himself was anxious that Italy should win French as well as British acceptance for her aims in Ethiopia. According to his account the subject was raised for the first time at the end of 1931 or early in 1932 by Berthelot, General Secretary of the French Foreign Ministry, to Theodoli. News of the proposal leaked to Mussolini and surprisingly evoked a violent outburst of gallophobia. Mussolini wanted a gift of African territory from France, not a bribe to deflect him from his main aim which was a 'grand policy in Europe' and expansion at Yugoslavia's expense.[35]

Despite Mussolini's hostile reaction Guariglia succeeded in keeping open future negotiations with France. In a long letter to Grandi of 9 February 1932 he systematically formulated his objections to the *passione adriatica*

[30] Guariglia, p. 450; and *D.D.F.*, ser. I, II, 182; annexe.

[31] *Ibid.*, p. 139 ff.

[32] *D.D.F.*, ser. I, II, 182.

[33] *D.D.F.*, ser. I, I, 375 and II, 182.

[34] Guariglia, pp. 139–40. Berthelot preferred to conduct these negotiations with Theodoli, rather than with the Italian ambassador in Paris.

[35] *Ibid.*, p. 144.

which was likely to involve Italy in difficulties with France and Yugoslavia.[36] In these circumstances Berthelot, on being informed of Mussolini's attitude, had to tread with great caution in all his subsequent dealings with Italian diplomats, above all because one of the desiderata for discussion was the position of anti-Fascist refugees in France, a subject on which Mussolini was especially sensitive.[37] Berthelot, and his successors, also had to take into account the difficulties a deal over Ethiopia, which came up again for discussion between Theodoli and de Caix early in 1932, would encounter in his own country.[38] On the one hand annexation by Italy of a part of French Somaliland, and the right to establish a railway line from Assab on the coast to the existing line to Addis Ababa, would cause an outcry from the French colonial lobby. The price for this could be nothing less than a complete free hand for France in North Africa. On the other hand, were Italy allowed to construct the prospective line from Assab to Dessie, and thus threaten the integrity of Ethiopia, there would be an uproar in the League on which French security in Europe depended.

Nevertheless, despite the sacrifices entailed, a deal with Italy was attractive; for it would put an end to all the colonial disputes between France and Italy.[39] It is highly significant that the negotiations met with the approval of Laval, premier until February 1932. French officials, moreover, were not thinking solely in terms of the political situation in Africa. In a summary of the negotiations and related topics of 10 January 1933 they argued that 'the situation has developed in such a way since last spring that French opinion, anxious about the future, desires to neutralize Italian hostility'.[40]

French anxiety is easy to understand. On 11 December 1932 Germany had been granted equality of status in armaments in a 'system providing security for all nations'. French military staffs dreaded the day when German rearmament would become a reality. In 1932 they planned against two groups of potential enemies: Germany and Italy; Russia and Turkey.[41]

[36] *Ibid.*, pp. 144–64.

[37] *Ibid.*, pp. 175–6.

[38] *D.D.F.*, ser. I, I, 214 and II, 182.

[39] Guariglia for his part did not think that the difficulties encountered were sufficient to deter Italy from continuing with her plans, *op. cit.*, Appendix A.

[40] *D.D.F.*, ser. I, II, 182; annexes I and 2.

[41] *D.D.F.*, ser. I, I. For naval policy see 266, 271, 273; for the army's policy, 244, 250, 260, 272 and II, 203.

Of the two groups the former was incomparably more dangerous. Ever since the negotiations for the London Agreement of 1930 Mussolini had been clamouring for equal status in naval armaments, a prospect which caused dismay in the French admiralty.[42] With Britain showing almost no interest in the Mediterranean it would mean virtual Italian control of this sea, as the French had to keep a part of their fleet in the Atlantic and North Sea. The French had thus to maintain a margin of supremacy over the combined fleets of Italy and Germany. Moreover the French possessed few ships with speed and armament equal to the German pocket battleships of the *Deutschland* class or Italian cruisers. Nor could the French rely on the British to take on the defence of the Atlantic while they themselves concentrated in the Mediterranean, as they had done before 1914. There were also political difficulties. By the Treaty of Locarno Britain and Italy had guaranteed both France and Germany against an unprovoked attack. If France attacked Germany because the latter invaded the territory of one of France's allies in Eastern Europe Italy might, the French Admiraly feared, go to the aid of Germany and Britain remain neutral.[43]

In other respects the French were more dependent on sea power than they had been before 1914. During the colonial disturbances in 1925 troops had to be sent from metropolitan France to North Africa. Next year, after a provocative speech by Balbo to the Italian community in Tunis, the French held joint army and navy manoeuvres in Tunisia.[44] Since Franco-Italian relations did not improve the French had to maintain the greater part of their fleet in the Mediterranean, and (as late as 1935) approximately one-fifth of their army, seven divisions in North Africa, ten near the Alps, for possible war against Italy.[45] The fleet had to secure the passage of troops as well as material across the Mediterranean.

France had to be ready also to dispatch troops to help her allies in eastern Europe. According to General Weygand, in a memorandum for the Ministry of War dated 16 January 1933,[46] the best port of disembarkation

[42] *Ibid.*, 329.

[43] *D.D.F.*, ser. 1, 1, 266; annexe, note of 21 October 1932.

[44] Seton-Watson, pp. 692–3.

[45] *D.D.F.*, ser. 1, 1, 82 and 83.

[46] *D.D.F.*, ser. 1, 1, 203. It is of interest that General Weygand strongly criticized the view that French military planning should be based on the assumption that a future war would be defensive (*ibid.*).

was considered to be Salonica. The weakest point of all in the French security position was Belgium, with whom France had concluded an alliance in 1920. Political opinion in Belgium was divided, and it was believed by the French that Belgium would honour her obligations only if she were sure that France would be on the winning side and that her territory would not be used as a shock-absorber in the event of a German attack against France. The question was frequently asked in interdepartmental meetings: where could France secure troops to reinforce the north-east frontier? She could maintain a preponderance over Germany if Italy could be converted, as she had been in 1914, from a potential enemy to a neutral or better still an ally. No wonder that the service chiefs stressed the importance of conciliating Italy, which would also lead to better relations with Turkey.[47]

While Mussolini himself was not in any way alarmed by the prospect of German rearmament many of his advisers thought otherwise.[48] Grandi, while in office, had been anxious not only to reach a compromise settlement with France on the question of naval parity,[49] but also to cooperate with both France and Yugoslavia against Germany, within the framework of the League. He was thus in full agreement with the ideas expressed in Guariglia's letter of 9 February 1932, which apparently was never seen by Mussolini.[50] Moreover, Grandi's position was being undermined. In the summer of 1932 the League was under constant attack from Paulucci Baroni, the new Italian delegate. General Balbo too, one of Grandi's rivals, in an article in the *Popolo d'Italia* early in July threatened Italy's withdrawal.[51] Soon Mussolini was to become his own foreign minister: Grandi was sent as ambassador to London; Rosso to Washington; Guariglia to Madrid.

It is sometimes argued that the defenestration of the old guard inaugurated a major change in the direction of Mussolini's foreign policy.[52]

[47] *D.D.F.*, ser. 1, 1, 266.

[48] For Mussolini's view of German rearmament in 1932, see *D.D.F.*, ser. 1, 1, 116, 237; for the Pope's view which was identical to Mussolini's see *ibid.*, 246, 273.

[49] See *British Documents on Foreign Policy*, 2nd ser., 1 (London, 1946) chap. 5.

[50] Guariglia, p. 434.

[51] *Ibid.*, pp. 175–6.

[52] G. Craig, 'Totalitarian Approaches to Diplomatic Negotiation', in *Studies in Diplomatic History and Historiography in Honour of G. P. Gooch*, ed. A. O. Sarkissian (London, 1961) p. 110.

But this is not necessarily true. Suvich, the new deputy foreign minister, and Baron Aloisi, the *chef de cabinet* and later Italian delegate to Geneva, were not just cyphers, but tried with some success to continue the policies of their predecessors.

On 29 July, shortly after taking office, Aloisi discussed fully with Guariglia Italy's aims in Ethiopia. The same day he discussed with Suvich and Theodoli the possibility of resuming the negotiations with France.[53] On 13 September he learnt from Theodoli that the French might now be willing to cede the Cameroons. On 4 October he told the Duce emphatically that in view of the dangers of German rearmament agreement should be reached with France. Mussolini rejected Aloisi's pleas on the grounds that greater pressure could be brought to bear on France if Germany were allowed to rearm in stages. Hence he did not favour Aloisi's suggestion of starting negotiations with France over a mandate. He insisted that 'France must allow us complete liberty on the Danube where, united with Austria and Hungary, we will form a rampart which could prevent an *Anschluss* . . . on the Rhine we are against France, on the Danube with France'.[54]

In his famous Turin speech of 22 October 1932 Mussolini gave expression to some of these more moderate ideas; and he was far less bellicose than on previous occasions.[55] He proposed that Italy, France, Britain and Germany should cooperate within the framework of the League, an organization which, he felt, might prove effective for preserving the peace in Europe but not in the Far East or Latin America. One wonders whether Mussolini deliberately refrained from mentioning the Near East and Africa. The speech, which was described by Aloisi as the 'absolute apotheosis of Mussolini and the renaissance of Imperial Rome', found a relatively favourable response in France.[56] The upshot was that Theodoli was allowed to continue negotiations with de Caix, provided that they were restricted to general topics; no mention was made of Ethiopia, in which Mussolini was still uninterested.[57] New contacts were also made with Italophil French citizens. Bérenger, President of the Committee of

[53] Aloisi, 29 July.

[54] *Ibid.*

[55] *D.D.F.*, ser. 1, 1, 4, 172.

[56] Aloisi, 27 October and 6 November 1932; and *D.D.F.*, ser. 1, 1, 271.

[57] Aloisi, 3, 4, 25 December 1932.

Foreign Affairs of the French Senate, visited Rome at the end of the year.[58] He was told by Mussolini that Britain and France should be allowed to maintain their empires and Germany to expand in the Baltic. Italy's aims were confined to economic expansion in the Danube area and in the Near and Middle East. Officials of the Quai d'Orsay laid great stress on the fact that the name of Ethiopia was not so much as mentioned by Mussolini; and they drew the conclusion that if Italy sought aggrandizement at the expense of that country no agreement with France would be necessary. France was expected to be a benevolent spectator in face of Italian action. The French did however believe that Mussolini was probing Bérenger on the possibility of a deal by which France would no longer be molested in North Africa if, in return, she dropped Yugoslavia as an ally.[59]

Mention of Yugoslavia was indeed ominous. Mussolini had already, by sheltering Pavelić, leader of the Croat terrorist organization, the Ustaša,[60] committed himself to a policy of promoting terrorism in Yugoslavia, a state whose dissolution both he and the Fascist press believed to be imminent once it was deprived of French support.[61] Although the documents on the relations between Pavelić and the Italian authorities have not been published, Aloisi was reasonably well informed of what was afoot.[62] On learning that the Ustaša was to be armed by Italy and operate from Hungarian soil, he warned both Mussolini and Cortese, Pavelić's protector, of dangerous international repercussions.[63]

France and the Little Entente were already alarmed. On 28 October the Franco-Yugoslav Alliance of 1927 was renewed. Mussolini retaliated by proposing a customs union with Albania. Tension on the Italian-Yugoslav frontier and in Albania ran high. On 2 December certain public monuments in Italy were damaged by high-spirited Serbs, which resulted in a violent campaign in the Italian press, not only against Yugoslavia but also

[58] *Ibid.*, 6, 8, 10 and 12 November 1932; and *D.D.F.*, ser. 1, I, 329.

[59] *D.D.F.*, ser. 1, II, 182. The text of the conversation has not been reproduced in the French documents, but Mussolini described the interview to Aloisi. The Germans were also informed of what took place (Aloisi, 14 January).

[60] M. Broszat, *Der Kroatische Ustacha Staat, 1941–1945* (Stuttgart, 1964) chap. 1.

[61] *D.D.F.*, ser. 1, I, 110, 129. See also Aloisi, 28 November, on which date Mussolini claimed that the Serbs would rise before the Croats.

[62] On 15 December he noted: 'Affairs in Croatia are delicate and difficult. And they take up much of my time. I believe . . . they are the result of a plan decided before my arrival at the Ministry.'

[63] *Ibid.*, 28 and 30 November.

against France.[64] On Christmas Day 1932, always a grim one for the Duce, who was away from his office, he was furious to learn from a spurious source that General Weygand was on good terms with Paul-Boncour (the new French premier) and was contemplating a preventive war against Italy.[65]

While Mussolini was fully preoccupied with Yugoslavia[66] and France conditions could not have been less propitious for a warlike enterprise against Ethiopia. Yet on 15 December, the day Aloisi was alarmed by the extremely grave international situation, he told his colleagues in the Palazzo Chigi that it was necessary to resume immediately the famous *politica periferica.* Aloisi also expressed his disappointment that little progress in this direction had so far been made.[67] The ideas expressed in Guariglia's memorandum of the previous September were now, thanks to Aloisi and others, to be taken up rather unexpectedly by Mussolini himself. The instructions to be given to Vinci, the new minister to Addis Ababa, were a matter of some urgency and Mussolini had to adopt a clearer line in Ethiopia.[68] In the presence of Suvich and Aloisi on 3 January Mussolini told Vinci that Italy was to pursue a policy of friendship with Ethiopia, the aim of which was to disguise in every way Italy's plans. Without altogether sharing the optimism of his military staff, Mussolini believed that a 'warlike operation in Ethiopia would succeed, provided we were completely free in Europe'. The military committee, presided over by General de Bono, had already studied all plans. It was necessary that Vinci, during his mission, should remove all suspicion. 'If the Negus made proposals for an exchange of territory, negotiations must simply be postponed.' Aloisi stated that Italy should acquire a port giving her access to the sea comparable with that enjoyed by France in Djibuti. Mussolini also informed Vinci that the Italian government aimed at constructing a railroad from Assab to Dessie.[69]

Certain general conclusions can be drawn from the meeting of 3 January. It seems that the initiative for action in Ethiopia came from the

[64] *D.D.F.*, ser. I, I, 70 and II, 54, 110, 134, 142; Aloisi, 15 December.

[65] *Ibid.* See also entry for 5 March.

[66] *Ibid.*, 29, 30 December.

[67] *Ibid.*, 15 December.

[68] Perhaps Mussolini allowed himself to be talked into taking up the Ethiopian project. He was under constant pressure to do so, especially from de Bono.

[69] *Ibid.*, 3 January 1933.

conservative diplomats and soldiers such as Guariglia, de Bono, Theodoli, Aloisi and the Duke of Aosta, not to mention the Jesuits and the king.[70] The late Professor Toscano's contention that Aloisi had been opposed to the Ethiopia venture and Baer's that he had not been fully informed cannot be substantiated, at least for the period 1932–33.[71] It can be contended, but not proved, that Aloisi, alarmed by Mussolini's dangerous policy in Europe, tried to deflect his master's attention from Europe to a relatively 'safe' military operation in a more distant part of the world, in return for which Italy would win the collaboration of France against Germany.

Such a policy had no immediate prospect of success. Mussolini remained convinced that Yugoslavia intended war with Italy, and on 7 January ordered a publication of all public and clandestine measures directed against Italy by the government of Belgrade. This publication was evidently to be used to justify Italian action against Yugoslavia.[72]

As a result of a security leakage the crisis came to a head prematurely. On 8 January the Vienna socialist newspaper, the *Arbeiter Zeitung*, published details of the import of captured World War I weapons from Italy for repairs at the factory of their origin at Hirtenberg in Austria. A part of these arms were to be used by the Austrian Heimwehr; the rest, dispatched to Hungary for the Ustaša.[73] The next day Aloisi discussed at a meeting with the Italian High Command a plan submitted by Pavelić for a Croat revolt, the exact details of which are not known. All present had the impression that it would lead inevitably to war, and that Italy should extricate herself from a situation in which she might be arraigned before the League. Aloisi also dismissed Mussolini's contention that Yugoslavia was on the point of breaking up.[74]

In fact Yugoslavia won the full backing of the Little Entente, which pressed to have the Hirtenberg affair brought before the League. But Britain and France, not for the first or last time, were prepared to allow Italy immunity from international censure. They insisted, in a protest

[70] The King had visited Eritrea in September 1932 and took a keen interest in the defence of the colony; see de Bono, *op. cit.*, pp. 8–9.

[71] Toscano in his introduction to Aloisi concentrates on the later phase of Mussolini's policy: see also Baer, pp. 36–7.

[72] Aloisi, 7 and 9 January 1933.

[73] *Ibid.*, 8 January; and *D.D.F.*, ser. 1, II, 196.

[74] Aloisi, 9 January 1933.

addressed to the Austrian, but not the Italian, government, that the weapons should either be destroyed or returned to Italy.[75]

After Hitler came to power terror in Austria was fomented by both Germany and Italy. In these circumstances, which can only be referred to briefly here, Aloisi's original enthusiasm for the Ethiopian venture cooled. Positions were now reversed: Aloisi had to hold Mussolini back until Italy was secure in Europe.[76] Not only was there the threat of an *Anschluss*, combined with that of German rearmament, but Mussolini failed to keep his promises made to Aloisi on 27 April 1934 to clamp down on the Ustaša terrorists. On 10 October 1934 the inevitable happened. King Alexander of Yugoslavia and the French Premier, Barthou, were murdered in Marseilles. Italy was now fully involved in a major crisis in Europe between Yugoslavia and Hungary. On 14 December 1934, even after the Wal Wal incident, Mussolini maintained that an agreement with the Little Entente and France would prove unacceptable to the Fascist party. The stage was still not set for war in Africa. But by the end of the month Mussolini had turned a complete somersault. Aloisi was told on the 25th that the Ethiopian affair would 'come to a head' after Italy had concluded an agreement with France and that it was necessary to move with greater speed. On the 29th Mussolini had agreed to defend Austria within the framework of the League and the Little Entente and to drop Hungary.[77] The way was now open for a general agreement with France and for the Ethiopian campaign. Laval, for his part, had approved the earlier negotiations between Theodoli and de Caix. He knew what he was doing, and it can only be assumed that he was aware of the probable repercussions which an Italian 'free hand' in Ethiopia would have on the League of Nations.[78]

The horsedealing between France and Italy in 1932 throws light, not only on the Ethiopian war but on the Spanish Civil War and the future action of Pavelić in Yugoslavia. Mussolini wanted action for its own sake, but he restlessly switched from one objective to another. Symptomatic of his attitude was a remark to Aloisi on 14 January 1933. 'Ajaccio and Bastia

[75] *D.D.F.*, ser. 1, II, 209, 259, 342; and Aloisi, 12 February.

[76] Aloisi, 30 June, 12 July, 1 October.

[77] Aloisi, 29 December 1934.

[78] See also D. C. Watt, 'The secret Laval-Mussolini agreement of 5 January 1935', *Middle East Journal* (1961).

would be two beautiful Italian provinces. Possession of Corsica is better than that of Dalmatia. It would turn the Tyrrhenian Sea into an Italian lake. Whoever holds Corsica commands the eastern Mediterranean.'[79] But Italian policy under Mussolini was not merely hand to mouth improvization; there was some system. In 1932, when Mussolini still showed remarkably little interest in Ethiopia, his soldiers and diplomats were, on a local level, doing all the necessary spadework for the campaign. Italians were infiltrating into Ethiopia and establishing numerous consulates in areas where Italy had virtually no economic interests. Work, on a small scale, was also going ahead, with little or no supervision from Mussolini, to prepare Eritrea as a military base. Indeed, when Mussolini did take a personal interest in the plans late in 1934 he may have proved a hindrance.[80] His ministers were even more keen than he was on a deal with France, and the publication of the Italian and French documents for 1934–35 is eagerly awaited. These will enable us to tell the full story of the Rome Agreements.

[79] Aloisi, 14 January 1933.
[80] Baer does not take this view; *op. cit.*, pp. 23–4.

19

SIR HERBERT BUTTERFIELD

Diplomacy

I

When people began to be interested in diplomacy in early modern times, they tended to take the line that it was almost as old as the human race. One writer quoted Josephus's *Antiquities of the Jews* for the view that God had created angels so that they should act as his ambassadors.[1] In order to show that the art of negotiating went back to very early times, one or two of them pointed to Jacob in the Old Testament, and recalled the tricks that he played on his brother, his father and his father-in-law. In the seventeenth century there were writers of manuals for ambassadors who felt that, though lying was wrong, a diplomat might have to resort to it on occasion; and they liked to have biblical support for anything that they advanced. A good precedent here was Abraham who, in a foreign land, was afraid that the ruler would fall in love with his wife, Sara, and then would want to kill the husband. By adopting the device of pretending that Sara was his sister, the patriarch saved not only his own life but also the existence of a whole people, 'the seed of Abraham'.

The Tell el-Amarna letters—numbering a few hundred and belonging to a period near to 1400 B.C.—have acquired great fame as early documents of foreign policy. They no doubt deserve their fame; but one can brood over them at dead of night without finding a trace of the diplomatic craft, though there were occasions when diplomacy was sorely needed. In those days great importance was attached to the goods which one ruler would send to another as a present; and trouble repeatedly occurred because the recipient regarded the gift as inadequate. One king, who ought to have received from the Egyptian pharaoh a statue of solid gold, found that the

[1] Josephus, XV, 8, in A. Gentili, *De Legationibus* (London, 1585), Bk. I, chap. 20.

article, when it came, was under weight, and it turned out to have been made of wood, plated over with gold. But the reaction of the complainants was never particularly diplomatic; they would resort to straight bleating or begging, would withhold the return gift, or would detain the unfortunate messenger, perhaps for years.[2]

Earlier than this, the Hittites had been building up an empire from a centre in Asia Minor; and they provide foreign policy material that has stimulated considerable thought.[3] They seem to have regarded it as necessary to supply historical—even ethical—justifications of the wars on which they embarked. Even in war they seem to have abstained from the atrocious cruelties—and the attempt to strike terror in the world by advertising their severities—which characterized the Assyrians centuries later. Also they shrank from the policy of taking hostages. If a vassal-ruler rebelled and was defeated they seem to have favoured the policy of reinstating him, counting on his having had his lesson. In the peace treaty they would urge him to respond to this treatment in the right spirit, and it would be hard to discover elsewhere diplomatic instruments which so appealed to a man's sense of gratitude. There now exists quite a considerable scholarly literature which sets out to show how God's covenant with Israel follows the pattern of these treaties between Hittite emperors and their vassals. Indeed, amongst students of the Hittites there has been a good deal of controversy, because some would explain the story by saying that their empire must have been weaker than it pretended to be—must, indeed, have been camouflaging its weakness with a show of moderation. If this were the case, it would represent quite a remarkable example of diplomatic artistry; for, in any event, one rarely reads documents relating to foreign policy which so regularly bring a moral tone into international discussion—great emperors apparently moved by such an urgent, such an aching, desire to reason with their enemies. The Hittites seem in fact to have been a curiously mild people—milder in their internal legislation than the Children of Israel at a much later date—able, even in a political

[2] *The Tell El-Amarna Tablets*, ed. S. A. B. Mercer (Toronto, 1939) I, no. 27; Tušratta to Amenhophis IV, no. I, pp. 153–61. These tablets contain the correspondence of the Babylonian, Assyrian and Mitanni monarchs with Amenophis III and his son, the famous Ikhnaton, of Egypt.

[3] J. Friedrich, *Staatsverträge des Hatti-Reiches in hetitischer Sprache* in *Mitteilungen der Vorderasiatisch-Aegyptischen Gesellschaft* XXXI (1926) and XXXIV (1930).

context, to say that 'we are all sinners', and to conceive the idea of overcoming evil with good. They are an exciting people, therefore, anticipating the Old Testament in a number of ways and (in spite of the piety of their writings and their attractive relations with their gods) almost seeming, in their historiography for example, like precursors of the ancient Greeks. In a Pelican volume O. R. Gurney has illustrated their skilful diplomacy and skilful polemics in respect of the earliest known example of the idea of the self-determination of peoples, which they described as 'the right of the cattle to choose their own stable'.[4] One is inclined to sum up the matter by saying that the Hittites had their own style in diplomacy.

For a very long time—and in Western Europe down to the Renaissance—foreign policy was not conducted by professional diplomats, that is to say by ambassadors sent to foreign capitals for a period of regular residence. Some magnate or high ecclesiastic or court dignitary or officer of state would be sent abroad on a special mission—either to settle a particular quarrel or to conclude an alliance or to negotiate a peace treaty or to attend an important ceremony. Often an important part of the man's task would be a set speech delivered before the monarch to whom he had been sent, or before a body of councillors, or a wider assembly of the people. Texts or recommended texts or conjectural versions of such orations have come down to us from the period of the Renaissance. They have their analogy at the present day in the speeches given by delegates at meetings of the United Nations.

All this goes back to very ancient times and the early records sometimes give a nutshell account of the speeches. One of the most picturesque examples is in the Old Testament, 2 Kings XVIII; and even if it were a piece of fiction the fact would not lessen its utility to us as evidence of what diplomacy was thought to be. The event is to be located probably at 701 B.C.—a time when the kingdom of Judah was a tributary to the Assyrian Empire but had revolted, relying on assistance from Egypt. The Assyrian Emperor, Sennacherib, had disposed of the Egyptians, and then had overrun the kingdom of Judah except the city of Jerusalem, which was therefore now expecting a siege. He sent three high officials as his emissaries to try to persuade the city to surrender without a siege. These men had a meeting with three delegates from the Hebrew king, Hezekiah. The Assyrian spokesman is described as first taunting King Hezekiah for

[4] O. R. Gurney, *The Hittites* (London, 1964) pp. 76–8.

going to war when he could do nothing without the help of the horsemen and chariots of Egypt. He pointed out that no help could come from the Egyptians now, and asked the Hebrews if they thought that 'mere words' could win a war. According to the Revised Standard Version, he said that his master would offer them a wager: 'I will give you two thousand horses, if you are able on your part to set riders upon them.' He added that in any case it would be useless for them to hope for help from their God. The Assyrians, he claimed, were fighting at the command of the God of Judah, who had said to them: 'Go up against this land and destroy it.'

They were talking in the open air and some of the Jewish people were on the walls not far away, listening to what was going on. The leader of the Hebrew delegation asked the Assyrians to speak in Aramaic—the international language of the whole region at this time—because it was inconvenient to have the affair conducted in the language of Judah, and therefore understood by the populace. The Assyrian speaker, instead of obliging him in this matter, turned to the people on the walls and made it clear that it was really they whom he wanted to address. He told them that their king was treating them unfairly; for they were the ones who would suffer if he insisted on fighting. It would be far better for them if Jerusalem surrendered; for then they would at least save their lives, and for the time being they would be able to eat of their own vine and their own fig tree. It was true that they would later be taken into exile, but they would go 'to a land very like your own land, a land of grain and wine, a land of bread and vineyards, a land of olive trees and honey'. This would at least be better than death. In any case the men of Judah must not rely on being saved by their God. Let them look at the other nations who trusted their gods but were beaten by the Assyrians.

Such a mixture of reasonable argument with hoaxing and cajoling—and the addition of taunt and threat—reminds one of Napoleon when he was in a similar situation, and something of the same can be found in Hitler. This combination of ingredients is clearly very ancient, hardly needing to be treated—hardly capable of being treated—as the result of a course of 'development'.

The narrative illustrates the first point that has to be kept in mind by the student of international relations. If one begins by thinking of diplomacy as an attempt to solve problems by mere reasoning, mere discussion—all based on the assumption that the better argument will prevail—one is liable to be led seriously astray. For a beginning, it is at least better to pick up the other end of the stick, squarely confronting the fact that something more than a mere difference of opinion is involved, something more than a question of understanding, or failing to understand, the other party's point of view. Initially, at least, the need for diplomacy arises because there is a conflict of wills, resulting perhaps from the collision of interests, each party being anxious to get its own way, even though it knows all the arguments and understands the other party's point of view. Reason and persuasion may not suffice because what is needed is more than the enlightening of men's minds. It is a case of operating on men's wills, perhaps even on their wilfulness; so that other, more dynamic, factors are introduced, and the important thing is to mobilize every possible 'inducement'. Negotiators have often worked by means of promises, appeals to interest, attempts at striking a bargain, devices of cajolery. They have resorted sometimes to taunts and to bullying, sometimes to quiet blackmail or impudent bluff. Even the threat of war may be one of the counters which the diplomat uses, and this itself might be merely a piece of bluff or might call for some delicate interpretation. If one wishes to stop a big country from invading a smaller country one may have to do something more than merely reason or beseech. Diplomacy may include anything short of actual war, therefore, and sometimes the kindest thing that one can say of it is that it is better than having the guns actually firing. The leaders of labour in twentieth-century England would be quick to recognize that if they were robbed of the power to threaten a strike and reduced to convincing employers by sweet reasonableness alone they would lose much of their ability to negotiate. Bargaining strength is a factor in the game, therefore; and reason itself may have greater force when it comes from a giant like Russia than when it comes from a small state like Belgium. The total result can be unattractive even at the present day and even when it is a better alternative than actual war. In the earlier, cruder days, it was particularly true that the history of foreign policy ran too much to sensationalism and had too much of the flavour of melodrama, shocking one with its Machiavellian ruses, its confidence tricks, and its attempts at blackmail.

What is interesting is the way in which diplomacy became more refined, more civilized, though it never entirely departed from its original nature. It became so transformed that some people, who merely read about negotiations in books, became too tempted to think of it as something like an academic discussion.

II

One of the greatest factors in the evolution of diplomacy was the gradual development of the policy of sending out resident ambassadors to foreign capitals, instead of delegates appointed for a special mission. The practice emerged in Italy in the latter half of the fifteenth century; but it was curiously slow in its spread and its development, and slower still in the production of important consequences. Professor Ganshof finds a precedent in the case of the Byzantine Emperor Manuelo II (1391–1425) who accredited an ambassador to reside *en permanence* with the Ottoman Sultan.[5] Before this, the Byzantine Empire had not merely made great advances, but elaborated its own style in diplomacy—its science of managing the neighbouring barbarian peoples with the minimum of resort to actual war.

In Western Europe foreign policy was becoming more intensive, particularly perhaps after the beginning of the fifteenth century. Bernard de Rosier said in 1436 that the occasions for sending out diplomatic missions seemed to be increasing daily.[6] Even men who went abroad for specific objects (and not for regular residence) might find that they spent a long time on their missions (as Philippe de Commynes did in Venice in 1494–95). Those who had to travel great distances could already expect a lengthy absence. The new system involved the establishment of permanent embassies at foreign courts, one ambassador generally being succeeded by another after a lapse of two or three years. From about the beginning of the sixteenth century the Western European countries were following the example set by the Italian cities; though even after this the extension of the system was slow, and it has been suggested that the Wars of Religion delayed the development of diplomacy. Even in 1660 the number of resident ambassadors, etc., is fewer than one might have expected.

It would seem that an important consideration in the establishment of

[5] F. L. Ganshof, *Le Moyen Age* (Paris, 1953) p. 274 (*Histoire des Rélations Internationales*, ed. P. Renouvin, vol. 1).

[6] Bernardi de Rosergio, *Ambaxiator Brevilogus*, cap. 4, in V. E. Hrabar, *De Legatis et Legationibus Tractatus Varii* (Dorpat, 1905) p. 6.

permanent embassies was the desire for the more continuous acquisition of intelligence. Certainly those who so often opposed the new system (including Philippe de Commynes, who thought that ambassadors ought to be handsomely entertained but sent quickly home)[7] were concerned about the possible leakage of information, saying that accepting a resident ambassador was like taking a foreign spy into the bosom of one's family. But the new resident ambassadors were sometimes distrusted also by their own courts, and it is not clear that they were held in great account even at home—they were sometimes badly paid and worked with only an inadequate staff. They might find life expensive in a foreign capital, where, particularly at first, they were liable also to be dogged by spies. Furthermore, when important business had to be transacted, the resident ambassadors in the early period were still liable to be superseded by more important people sent on a special mission.

The system, however, was bound to give a great stimulus to the development of a new type of public servant; for ministers of state, court dignitaries and high ecclesiastics were hardly suitable people for residence at foreign courts. Churchmen, military men and lawyers were still important in the diplomacy of the seventeenth century; but though the 'treatise on ambassadors' is a genre which antedates the establishment of permanent embassies, the new arrangement attracted public attention, and in the later sixteenth and the seventeenth centuries there appeared a surprising number of these manuals for ambassadors. Jusserand says: 'Never was a public career the occasion of so many studies and guide-books.'[8] In treatises of this kind, Callières, one of the servants of Louis XIV, is clear that diplomacy is a separate profession.[9] And before Louis died there existed (for a few years) in France an *Académie politique* for the training of diplomats.

But, though everything moved very slowly, the introduction of resident ambassadors was to bring about a change in the conduct of foreign affairs. Some at first felt the tedium of life in a foreign capital—felt themselves to be in exile even when stationed in Paris. But it was their duty to talk to people and it was recognized that talking to other ambassadors in

[7] Philippe de Commynes, *Mémoires*, Bk. III, chap. 8.

[8] J. J. Jusserand, *The School for Ambassadors and other Essays* (London, 1924) pp. 20–1.

[9] F. de Callières, *The Practice of Diplomacy*, ed. A. F. Whyte (London, 1919) pp. 8–10, 56–7.

the capital was a way of collecting information. When there were ten or twenty such representatives in Paris they would gravitate towards one another, exchanging ideas about France or their home countries or the international situation or the art of diplomacy itself. Something almost like an *esprit de corps* tended to develop amongst the society of diplomats in a given capital, and they were on their way to becoming like members of the same club. In a work published in 1716 Callières talks about 'the freemasonry of diplomats'.[10] The result was that not only were foreign affairs conducted with the advantage of a greater amount of information —a closer knowledge of the very springs of a foreign country's policy— but the friendly relations between ambassadors oiled the wheels of the international system itself. There came to be cases where ambassadors remained friends, though their countries were quarrelling with one another. There were cases of ambassadors falling in love with the country in which they resided—open to reproach because they became too fond of their hosts and learned to understand too well the other party's point of view. At the end of the eighteenth century and the beginning of the nineteenth the court of Russia would complain of the way in which its ambassadors went native in the countries to which they had been sent. The charge was a fair one; and some of these men stayed on in the foreign country, instead of going home, when they ceased to hold their offices. Over great areas of the American newspaper press in the years 1848–49 there was the repeated complaint that an ambassador could not go to Europe without surrendering to the fascination of courts and kings.[11] Even in the twentieth century ambassadors have sometimes entered into the ideas of the host country more than their home government liked. As time went on, moreover, these ambassadors, moving from one country

[10] *Ibid.*, p. 113.

[11] See e.g. H. Butterfield, *The Peace Tactics of Napoleon, 1806–1808* (Cambridge, 1919) pp. 116–17 (Razumovskii in Vienna); p. 284 (Vorontsov in London); and pp. 285–6 (Alopeus in Berlin). Cf. *ibid.*, p. 285, where President Wilson, sending a representative to London, says: 'Now, be an American! Our men only last six months in England; then they become anglicised.' W. F. Ilchman, *Professional Diplomacy in the United States, 1779–1939* (Chicago, 1961) chap. 1, illustrates the distrust of diplomacy and permanent ambassadors at the time of the Revolution, and describes (p. 26) how the Continental Congress, fearing the corrupting effects of Europe, resolved that diplomats should be allowed to remain abroad on their commissions for only three years.

to another, accumulated a considerable amount of expertise. The diplomat very gradually became professionalized, and, in a sense, diplomacy could now have more continuous development as a technique.

The result was a change in the character of diplomacy itself, even a change in the feeling about its underlying purpose. There gradually developed the view that the prime object of the diplomat was not to collect information, not to assist in the settlement of crises and quarrels. It was rather to keep perpetual contact with a foreign country, to build up the reputation of his own nation, and, most of all, to generate confidence. This last came to be the aspect of the matter on which the profession itself came to lay the greatest stress, though, on this topic, they may have protested too much, for an ambassador does have to promote the interests and the ideals of his own country. Also some men have set out to win confidence so that they might be better able to carry off a confidence trick. Taking a different point of view, it is difficult not to believe that (particularly in a place like Venice) the habits of transaction and adjustment current in the business world, and perhaps the notions of credit and confidence which became so important there, helped to take some of the sensationalism out of diplomacy.

All this received further stimulus from the methods of Cardinal Richelieu, who in the second quarter of the seventeenth century insisted that nations should be perpetually negotiating—even when there was no issue to be settled, no tangible profit to be gained. He said that the man who keeps negotiating will know better what is going on in the world; but he had in mind also that one should cultivate the other party whenever possible, rather in the way that an English member of parliament nurses his constituency. It is true in any case that controversies between nations can arise out of little things which are quickly settled if they are caught in time; whereas a negotiator sent at the last minute would have no opportunity to feel out the ground or make useful connections, and might have little chance of stemming a crisis already far advanced. Richelieu carried his advice to a point to which the twentieth century refused to follow him. He maintained that a state should never stop negotiating even in time of war.

These developments made it necessary that diplomacy should become less melodramatic and that on the whole the diplomat should be a man of respectable character. In the reign of James I, Sir Thomas Wotton talked of an ambassador 'lying abroad' for the sake of his country. It is reported that, when in Augsburg, he wrote this down in Latin, *ad mentiendum*, and here no pun, no ambiguity, could be involved—he could only be referring to untruthfulness. In the nineteenth century, however, a diplomat who was a liar seemed to stand out as a marked man. Hitler won some initial rounds in the 1930s because he lied at levels where truthfulness was normally expected. In a settled world such a policy destroys confidence and makes all transactions enormously more difficult to conduct in the after-period.

III

In the seventeenth century scholars and writers play their part in the story, and the work of the diplomat is affected by the intrusion of perhaps a little theory, perhaps a little science. It is curious that, down to this time, the technique of foreign policy had received so little attention from the authors of books, even of treatises on government. In classical antiquity the discussion of the state (as though only a single one existed) had been carried to a great depth, but this seems to have obstructed rather than helped the parallel analysis of international relations. At the same time, certain passages in Thucydides and orations like that of Demosthenes for the Megalopolitans provide remarkable insight into particular historical situations. They seem to spring from serious reflection on accumulated experience and are more impressive than the ingenuities of fifteenth-century Italian diplomacy. In A.D. 1086 an important Muslim minister, Nizám al-Mulk,[12] produced a treatise on the art of government; but though he wrote a page or two about the representatives sent to foreign courts, he seemed interested only in the information that such people might collect. Machiavelli was anxious about the military competence of a prince and devoted much space to the art of war; but his few maxims of foreign policy are not impressive, and he seems hardly to have been conscious of diplomacy as a field for separate analysis or reflection.[13] Towards the end of the sixteenth century, a fashionable book entitled

[12] Nizām al-Mulk, *The Book of Government or Rules for Kings*, trans. H. Darke (London, 1960) chap. 21, especially pp. 98–9.

[13] H. Butterfield, *The statecraft of Machiavelli*, rev. edn. (London, 1960) pp. 116–21; and 'The balance of power', in *Diplomatic Investigations*, ed. H. Butterfield and M. Wight (London, 1966) pp. 134–5.

Reason of State—essentially a work about the art of government—examined the foundation of states, their expansion and their downfall. It gave a great proportion of its space to the art of war; but, though it had a page or two about alliances, it did not come near to dealing with diplomacy.[14] These examples are typical.

By the opening of the seventeenth century attention was being turned from Machiavelli's teaching about statecraft to his more fundamental ideas about the nature of power-politics, and also to the method by which he arrived at his maxims.[15] A little later, some of Richelieu's comments on foreign policy—for example, when he points out that small states can have greater freedom of action than larger ones—are quasiscientific or 'Baconian' in character.[16] In the earliest decades of the century the concern about war and the disturbing sense of the imminence of further conflict led to some discussion about the general problem of war and peace.[17] The 'Grand Design' of Sully, from a rather different angle, embraced a great part of the European continent and seemed to envisage a balance achieved by the creation of a body of states roughly equal to one another in size. Different again is Grotius's *De Jure Belli ac Pacis* of 1625, which marks an important stage in the development of modern international law, and raises incidentally certain points of foreign policy. In general, it was becoming more easy to extend one's survey over the continent as a whole and almost to reflect upon it as something like a 'system' of states. Nothing could have provided a better stimulus for further thought than the conception of international relations as taking place within the framework of a 'system'. Nothing indeed could have provided a better foundation for an intellectual advance in the field of foreign policy.

At the Renaissance it seemed natural to consider the states of Italy as forming something like a 'system' and to make comments on the interactions within the group. But this was not yet possible for Europe as a

[14] G. Botero, *Della ragion di stato* (Venice, 1589); English transl. by P. J. and D. P. Waley, *Reason of State* (London, 1956).

[15] G. Oestreich, 'Justus Lipsius als Theoretiker des neuzeitlichen Machtstaates', *Historische Zeitschrift* CLXXXI (1956) 31–78.

[16] Richelieu, *Testament politique*, ed. L. André (Paris, 1947) p. 354; cf. R. von Albertini, *Das politische Denken in Frankreich zur Zeit Richelieus* (Marburg, 1951) p. 188.

[17] K. von Raumer, 'Sully, Crucé und das Problem des allgemeinen Friedens', *Historische Zeitschrift* CLXXV (1953) 1–39.

whole; and Philippe de Commynes could see France watching England, Portugal set against Spain, Bavaria competing with Austria, and even England confronting Scotland, without reflecting on the composite picture. In the later decades of the sixteenth century there is almost a 'system' among a group of states that had its centre, roughly speaking, in the English Channel—France, England, Scotland, the Netherlands and Spain so closely interacting that their foreign policy (and even an event like the massacre of St Bartholomew) cries out for a single compound narrative which transcends the separate national stories. When we reach the year 1648, however, the treaty of Westphalia was so comprehensive, so fundamental in character, that, in spite of the separate negotiations and agreements that were involved, it came to be regarded as a general European settlement. Even after this, the North was still envisaged as a separate system, capable of having its own 'general' wars; and writers on the 'states-system' (Schmauss in 1741, Heeren in 1809, for example) would give a lengthy narrative of the 'balance of Europe' or the 'balance of the South', followed by a separate full-length story of the 'balance of the North'. Till 1782 England had separate secretaries of state for the southern and the northern halves of Europe. The countries of the continent had to travel a long way before practically the whole of them could see themselves as members of the same club; and, by the time they came to embrace virtually the entire continent in a single 'system', some were ready to think that overseas colonies might have to be brought into the reckoning.

It was the development of this presiding idea, together perhaps with the rage for a 'geometrical' or mechanistic type of thought, which entirely transformed the earlier simple notions of an equilibrium in international politics. In Renaissance Italy there had emerged the conception of a balance that could be produced amongst the miscellany of separate states into which the peninsula was divided. Here was a notion capable of extension to the continent as a whole; but its progress was very slow, and, during the seventeenth century, what is envisaged is a simple affair, based on the analogy with a pair of scales. The Duc de Rohan in 1638 (followed by the Baron de Lisola in 1677) was almost continental in his survey, but saw the various states as ranging themselves behind one or other of the two giants, France and Spain. Each group, he said, behaved as though it wanted the ruin of the great power on the other side, and did not see that this would mean the excessive aggrandizement of its opposite number. He asked all the states to realize that their safety depended on the maintenance of an equilibrium between France and Spain.[18] This particular version of the idea of the balance stands at an intermediate stage in the development; and here, as elsewhere, one detects a tendency to see the issues with a greater degree of relativity. (In 1624, for example, the anonymous author of the *Discours des Princes et Estats de la Chréstienté* suggested that the French would be hated as much as the Spaniards in Italy if they, instead of Spain, held the predominance there.)[19] A quasiscientific attitude to aggression became more feasible when the France of Louis XIV was seen to have replaced Spain as the menace to the continent—this from the very moment when she had the power to take the offensive.

In Fénelon, at the beginning of the eighteenth century, a number of ideas that had been appearing separately were brought together to form a coherent argument. A state that had achieved predominance, he said, was bound very soon to embark on a career of aggression however virtuous it had hitherto been. The overriding object of foreign policy was to see the danger coming, and to check the course of aggrandizement before the predominance was a *fait accompli*. The safety of the European states was so urgent a matter that it ought to have priority over the internal legislation of a country, even over the law of succession, if this were calculated to produce an excessive accumulation of power. But the opponents of a dangerous aggressor must beware of the temptation to carry their policy too far. They themselves would produce a further threat to the equilibrium if they fought for the destruction of the enemy.[20]

These ideas, together with the notion that Europe itself was a 'states-system', helped to produce a more complicated idea of balance, only partially glimpsed on rare occasions down to this time. The equilibrium was seen as distributed throughout the whole system, the various states poised against one another like the heavenly bodies in the Newtonian universe—any substantial change in the mass of one of them requiring a possible regrouping of the rest if the balance were to be maintained. All

[18] François, Duc de Rohan, *De l'Intérest des Princes et Estats de la Chrestienté* (English transl., London, 1665) Prefaces to parts I and II. Baron de Lisola, *Le Bouclier d'estat et de justice* (English transl., Brussels, 1667) pp. 227–78.

[19] F. Meinecke, *Die Idee der Staatsräson*, 2 Aufl. (Munich-Berlin, 1925) pp. 191–203. Meinecke is inclined to support the view that Father Joseph, the 'grey eminence' of Richelieu, was the author of this *Discours*.

[20] Fénelon, *Oeuvres* (Paris, 1820–30) XXII, 306–15.

this was turned in the eighteenth century into the first attempt at a general theory of international politics, involving a notion of wars for limited purposes only and deprecating ideological warfare—anything like the revival of the Wars of Religion—which ignored the distribution of power and made compromise impossible. The balance of power was extolled as the only thing which, in a world so much at the mercy of force, would enable small states to exist and to have an independent foreign policy.[21]

That these ideas entered into the practice of diplomacy can be seen particularly perhaps in the documents relating to the War of the Spanish Succession; also in the criticism directed against the Diplomatic Revolution of 1756 by the agents of Louis XV's 'secret system'—an example of something like a 'school' of practising diplomats, distinguished by the quality of its thought, and presenting Vergennes as its finest product.[22] The moderating effect of these ideas in the world of actual events was attested by Frederick the Great, Burke and Gibbon; and Charles James Fox made particular use of them when opposing the idea of a war directed against a *régime* in France.[23] The theory noted the limits to which a state could safely go either in egotism or altruism and insisted that the diplomat can never afford to ignore the distribution of power, that indeed the virtuous conduct of states might depend on this. And the pattern of the system became printed on the minds of practising diplomats—reinforcing the tendency to constant vigilance and perpetual negotiation—reinforcing also the need for farsightedness, because, once the predominance of a state is a *fait accompli*, the situation is liable to be irreversible.

IV

The etiquettes connected with diplomatic representation owe something to the Byzantine Empire and something to the ways of royal courts; but it was natural that the relations between foreign powers should call for a number of formalities and the extravagant conflicts on points of precedence, etc., were not simply due to the idiosyncrasies of the diplomatic

[21] Butterfield, 'The balance of power', pp. 144–7.

[22] L. P. Ségur, *Politique de tous les cabinets de l'Europe*, 3rd edn. (Paris, 1802) I, 211–394; III, 257–82.

[23] Butterfield, 'The balance of power', pp. 144–5; and *Speeches of Charles James Fox* V (London, 1815), e.g. pp. 28–9 on the limitation of the objectives of war.

profession. It was Louis XIV himself, for example, who was insistent on such issues; and he knew what he was about—his reign marks a further stage in the development of the organization and the procedures of modern diplomacy.[24] Precedence mattered to him because he saw prestige itself as an important factor in negotiation. The length of the preliminary discussions in Paris before a conference for Vietnam peace negotiations could really start makes it clear that, even in our century, the debate about technicalities may be a struggle about something real.

Such things as these make it easy to see why the diplomat became a handy subject for caricature; and there may be other reasons why he is vulnerable—for it is the weakness of a specialized profession that it may cut deep channels for itself and run too easily to routine. People have wondered in the twentieth century whether an ambassador, relying too much on established connections and a narrow social circle, may not have been slower on occasion than private individuals or journalists in divining the imminence of a revolution in the capital in which he resided. Occasionally there has appeared the suggestion that both historians and foreign offices may have assessed an ambassador too highly on the strength of merely the literary quality of his dispatches. In any case, democracy itself is jealous of the intrusion of professionalism into those matters of foreign policy which become so urgently important to it at critical moments. If it does not reject the whole tradition, it is liable to be intolerant of the indirect procedures or tactical moves which sometimes help a government round difficult corners. Botero in 1589 pointed out the need to 'learn like a skilful sailor to advance against a head wind by tacking'. He noted the importance of recognizing the moment for action, because 'there is a certain point of time when a fortunate combination of circumstances favours some piece of business which both before and after that moment would be most difficult'. This did not mean that he intended to promote mere cleverishness in politics. On the contrary, he pointed out that because Venice and Sparta avoided this fault they succeeded better than Florence and Athens.[25] Over a period of centuries the treatises on ambassadors have pinpointed the various reasons why princes and peoples cannot afford to despise the element of skill as a factor in negotiation.

[24] C.-G. Picavet, *La Diplomatie française au temps de Louis XIV* (*1661–1715*); *Institutions, Moeurs et Coutumes* (Paris, 1930) especially pp. 1–72, 221–79.

[25] Botero, II, 6, p. 46; and II, 8, p. 49.

They have reiterated also that the mentality of the lawyer is not appropriate for diplomatic work.[26] Furthermore, farsightedness has a special importance in foreign affairs; and democracy may produce irreversible damage if it fails to look ahead. In rejecting techniques it may show too great a contempt for the benefits of long-term experience. The twentieth century is quite capable of forgetting a device by means of which its predecessors got over a hurdle. Those greatly interested in the foreign policies of their own day would do no harm if, to their other accomplishments, they could add some familiarity with technical diplomatic history. Sometimes it has been the diplomatist who—precisely with the assuredness of experience—has given warning, as Sir Edward Grey once did, against oversuspiciousness in transactions with the foreigner; and Harold Nicolson noted that 'diplomatists have often progressed further than politicians in their conception of international conduct'.[27] But he makes also, somewhere, the disturbingly just remark that 'international intercourse has always been subject to great retrogressions'.[28]

At any rate, diplomacy should be regarded as a creative thing, capable of minimizing defeat in war, and permitting a Louis XIV to achieve his early objectives with the minimum of actual fighting. Kaunitz, Vergennes, Talleyrand and Bismarck acquired substantial benefits from it; and if Metternich held a predominance in Europe for an almost unprecedented length of time, he must have owed this to forms of persuasion and indirect inducements, for the military position of Austria was hardly commensurate with that situation. Even so, a country with a sound tradition in diplomacy may go further over a long period than one that has brilliant individuals. And one suspects that at certain moments a country has been able to turn its very weakness into a diplomatic asset.

[26] See e.g. Callières, pp. 55–6; H. Nicolson, *Diplomacy* (London, 1939) p. 50; J. Cambon, *The Diplomatist* (London, 1931) pp. 18–19; C. Thayer, *Diplomat* (London, 1960) pp. 241–2.

[27] Nicolson, *Diplomacy*, p. 38.

[28] H. Nicolson, *The Evolution of Diplomatic Method* (London, 1954) p. 2.

DAVID BAYNE HORN: A BIBLIOGRAPHY

Compiled by Hugh Dunthorne

ABBREVIATIONS

E.H.R. *English Historical Review*
S.H.R. *Scottish Historical Review*
T.R.H.S. *Transactions of the Royal Historical Society*
U.E.J. *University of Edinburgh Journal*

BOOKS

A History of Europe 1871–1920 (London, John Murray, 1927) pp. xvi, 254. This book, published first as a separate volume, was also incorporated in Sir Richard Lodge and D. B. Horn, *A History of Modern Europe, Period 1789–1920* (London, John Murray, 1927), of which it formed chapters 8–11, chapters 1–7 being reprinted from Sir Richard Lodge, *The Student's Modern Europe . . . 1453–1878* (London, John Murray, 1885), chapters 22–28.

Sir Charles Hanbury Williams and European Diplomacy, 1747–1758 (London, Harrap, 1930) p. 314.

[D. B. Horn and Andrew Browning] *Modern Europe 1648–1815* (London, Harrap, 1931) p. 287. Volume III of *A History of Europe* edited by D. B. Horn for Harrap.

Modern Europe 1789–1930 (London, Harrap, 1931) p. 408. Volume IV of the above series.

[Edited, with Introduction] *British Diplomatic Representatives 1689–1789* (The Royal Historical Society, Camden third series XLVI; London, Offices of the Society, 1932) pp. XIII, 178.

[Basil Williams, E. W. M. Balfour-Melville, D. B. Horn, Harry Rothwell, and Martin Simpson: edited] *The Edinburgh Source Book for British History 1603–1707* (London, Alexander Maclehose, 1933) pp. VII, 118.

British Public Opinion and the First Partition of Poland (London and Edinburgh, Oliver & Boyd, 1945) pp. VII, 98.

[D. B. Horn and Mary Ransome: edited, with General Introduction and Bibliography] *English Historical Documents 1714–1783* (London, Eyre & Spottiswoode, 1957) pp. XXVII, 972. Volume X of the series *English Historical Documents*, general editor David C. Douglas (London: Eyre & Spottiswoode, 1953–).

The British Diplomatic Service 1689–1789 (Oxford, Clarendon Press, 1961) pp. XV, 324.

Frederick the Great and the Rise of Prussia (London, English Universities Press, Teach Yourself History Library, 1964) pp. VII, 180.

[Edited] *English Historical Documents 1714–1815* (London, Methuen, 1967) p. 126. A selection made by D. B. Horn from volumes X and XI of the series 'English Historical Documents': *English Historical Documents 1714–1783*, eds. D. B. Horn and Mary Ransome (London, Eyre & Spottiswoode, 1957), and *English Historical Documents 1783–1832*, eds. A. Aspinall and E. Antony Smith (Eyre & Spottiswoode, 1959).

A Short History of the University of Edinburgh 1556–1889 (Edinburgh University Press, 1967) pp. XII, 228.

Great Britain and Europe in the Eighteenth Century (Oxford, Clarendon Press, 1967) pp. XI, 411.

PAMPHLETS AND CONTRIBUTIONS

Scottish Diplomatists 1689–1789 (Historical Association Publications No. 132; London, P. S. King & Staples for the Historical Association, 1944) p. 18.

'List of the principal writings of Sir Richard Lodge' in *Sir Richard Lodge: A biography by his daughter, Margaret Lodge* (Edinburgh, Blackwood, 1946) pp. 255–60.

'The Diplomatic Revolution' in *The New Cambridge Modern History* VII (Cambridge University Press, 1957) 440–64.

'Hume as Historian' [summary of a public lecture given at the University of Edinburgh on 29 May 1961] in *David Hume* [pamphlet recording the commemoration, at the University of Edinburgh, of the 250th anniversary of the birth of David Hume, 1711–1961; published as a supplement to the University Gazette] (Edinburgh University Press, 1961) pp. 25–8.

The Faculty of Arts (Edinburgh, printed for the University, 1968) p. 20.

Chambers Encyclopaedia (editions of 1950, 1955, 1959 and 1966). Contributions on *Secretary of State*, on *George I*, *George II*, and *George III*, and on many eighteenth-century statesmen, including Burke, Fox, Newcastle and Pelham.

Encyclopaedia Americana (edition of 1957). Contributions mainly on Scotland and Scottish history.

Enciclopedia Italiana (1929–39). Article on Irish history.

APPRECIATIONS OF COLLEAGUES

'Sir Richard Lodge and historical studies at the University of Edinburgh (1899–1925)', review article of *Sir Richard Lodge: A biography by his daughter, Margaret Lodge* (Edinburgh, Blackwood, 1946) in *S.H.R.* XXVII (1948) 77–85.

[Obituary] Basil Williams in *The Scotsman*, 7 January 1950.

[Obituary] B. H. Sumner in *The Scotsman*, 26 April 1951.

Commemoration of the centenary of the birth of Sir Richard Lodge contributed anonymously to the 'Scotsman's Log' feature of *The Scotsman*, 14 June 1955.

[Obituary] Richard Pares in *The Scotsman*, 5 May 1958; and in *The Student*, 22 May 1958.

[Obituary] Charles A. Malcolm in *S.H.R.* XLI (1962) 88.

'E. W. M. Balfour-Melville (1887–1963), a Memoir' in *Miscellany of the Scottish History Society* X (Scottish History Society, fourth series II; Edinburgh, T. and A. Constable for the Scottish History Society, 1965) ix–xviii.

REPORT ON MANUSCRIPTS

'Hanbury Williams MSS.' in *Bulletin of the Institute of Historical Research* II (1924) 61–2.

ARTICLES

'The origins of the proposed election of a king of the Romans, 1748–50', *E.H.R.* XLII (1927) 361–70.

'The cost of the diplomatic service, 1747–52', *E.H.R.* XLIII (1928) 606–11.

'Saxony in the War of the Austrian Succession', *E.H.R.* XLIV (1929) 33–47.

'The Cabinet controversy on subsidy treaties in time of peace, 1749–50', *E.H.R.* XLV (1930) 463–6.

'An early seventeenth-century bill for "Extraordinaries" ', *E.H.R.* XLV (1930) 626.

'The Board of Trade and Consular Reports, 1696–1782', *E.H.R.* LIV (1939) 476–80.

'Edinburgh University and the diplomatic service, 1714–89', *U.E.J.* XIII (1944–45) 27–33.

'Scottish university men in the XVIIIth century', *U.E.J.* XVI (1951–53) 169–170.

'Climbing Ben Nevis', *The Scotsman*, 14 March 1953.

'Climbing Ben Lomond', *The Scotsman*, 15 August 1953.

'The University of Edinburgh and the teaching of history' (Inaugural lecture delivered at the opening of the Autumn Term 1954), *U.E.J.* XVII (1953–55) 161–72.

'The diplomatic experience of Secretaries of State, 1660–1852', *History*, new ser. XLI (1956) 88–99.

'Principal William Robertson, D.D., historian', *U.E.J.* XVIII (1955–57) 155–68.

'Early ascents of Cairngorm', *The Deeside Field*, second ser. II (1957) 6–14.

'The Universities (Scotland) Act of 1858' [A centenary address given at the University of Edinburgh on 9 December 1958], *U.E.J.* XIX (1958–60) 169–99.

'Rank and emolument in the British diplomatic service 1688–1789', *T.R.H.S.* fifth ser. IX (1959) 19–49.

'Some Scottish writers of history in the eighteenth century', *S.H.R.* XL (1961) 1–18.

'Natural Philosophy and Mountaineering in Scotland, 1750–1850', *Scottish Studies* VII (1963), 1–17.

'The anatomy classrooms in the present Old College, 1725–1880', *U.E.J.* XXII (1965–66) 65–71.

'The origins of the University of Edinburgh', *U.E.J.* XXII (1965–66) 213–25, 297–312.

'The origins of mountaineering in Scotland', *The Scottish Mountaineering Club Journal* XXVIII (1966) 157–72.

'The roads of Moidart', *Scotland's Magazine* (July, 1966).

'The machinery for the conduct of British foreign policy in the eighteenth century', *Journal of the Society of Archivists* III (1965–69) 229–40.

'Meal Monday', *U.E.J.* XXIII (1967–68) 63–5.

'The building of the Old Quad, 1767–1841', *U.E.J.* XXIII (1967–68) 309–21 and XXIV (1969–70) 39–54.

'George IV and Highland dress', *S.H.R.* XLVII (1968) 209–10.

REVIEWS AND NOTICES

Mark A. Thomson, *The Secretaries of State 1681–1782* (Oxford, Clarendon Press, 1932) in *E.H.R.* XLVIII (1933) 332–3.

Ludwig Israël, *England und der orientalische Dreibund* (Stuttgart, Kohlhammer, 1937) in *E.H.R.* LIII (1938) 750–1.

Winifred Taffs, *Ambassador to Bismarck; Lord Odo Russell, First Baron Ampthill* (London, Muller, 1938) in *E.H.R.* LIV (1939) 192.

Britain and the Independence of Latin America 1812–1830. Select Documents from the Foreign Office Archives, ed. C. K. Webster (London, Oxford University Press, 1938) in *E.H.R.* LIV (1939) 341–2.

Lettres de Gambetta, 1868–1882 eds. Daniel Halévy and Émile Pillias (Paris, Grasset, 1938) in *E.H.R.* LIV (1939) 372–3.

Reemt Reemston, *Spanisch-deutsche Beziehungen zur Zeit des ersten Dreibundvertrages, 1882–1887* (Berlin, Ebering, 1938) in *E.H.R.* LIV (1939) 373.

Paul-Henri Michel, *La Question de l'Adriatique 1914–18, receuil de documents* (Paris, Costes, 1938) in *E.H.R.* LIV (1939) 550.

R. M. Rayner, *Britain and Europe 1815–1936* (London, Longmans, 1938); Denis Richards, *An Illustrated History of Modern Europe 1789–1938* (London, Longmans, 1938) in *History*, new ser. XXIV (1939–40) 76.

Basil Williams, *The Whig Supremacy 1714–1760* (Oxford, Clarendon Press, 1939) in *U.E.J.* X (1939–40) 153–4.

Portugal and the War of the Spanish Succession. A bibliography with some unpublished documents, ed. Edgar Prestage (Cambridge University Press, 1938) in *History*, new ser. XXIV (1939–40) 282–3.

Jean O. McLachlan, *Trade and Peace with Old Spain 1667–1750* (Cambridge University Press, 1940) in *History*, new ser. XXV (1940–41) 261–2.

Stetson Conn, *Gibraltar in British Diplomacy in the Eighteenth Century* (New Haven, Yale University Press, 1942) in *History*, new ser. XXIX (1944) 207–8.

A Lincolnshire Assize Roll for 1298 (*P.R.O. Assize Roll No. 505*), ed. Walter Sinclair Thomson (Lincoln Record Society, 1944) in *U.E.J.* XIII (1944–45) 138.

G. P. Gooch, *Frederick the Great: the Ruler, the Writer, the Man* (London, Longmans, 1947) in *E.H.R.* LXII (1947) 403.

Bibliography of British History. The Eighteenth Century 1714–1789, ed. Stanley Pargellis and D. J. Medley (Oxford, Clarendon Press, 1951) in *E.H.R.* LXVI (1951) 594–7.

G. P. Gooch, *Maria Theresa and Other Studies* (London, Longmans, 1951) in *E.H.R.* LXVII (1952) 303.

H. Butterfield, *The Reconstruction of an Historical Episode. The History of the Enquiry into the Origins of the Seven Years' War* (Glasgow, Jackson, 1951) in *E.H.R.* LXVII (1952) 447.

Markus Meier, *Die diplomatsiche Vertretung Englands in der Schweiz im 18. Jahrhundert (1689–1789)* (Basle, Helbing and Lichtenhahn, 1952) in *E.H.R.* LXVII (1952) 604–5.

Carlo Baudi di Vesme, *La Politica Mediterranea Inglese nelle relazioni degli inviati Italiani a Londra . . . 1741–48* (Turin, Gheroni, 1952) in *E.H.R.* LXVIII (1953) 484.

Two Students at St Andrews 1711–1716. Edited from the Delvine Papers by

William Croft Dickinson (Edinburgh, Oliver & Boyd, 1952) in *U.E.J.* XVI (1951–53) 274–5.

Léon van der Essen, *La Diplomatie* (Brussels, Editions P.D.L., 1953) in *E.H.R.* LXIX (1954) 146.

Guido Quazza, *Il Trattato di Torino del 1733* (Turin, Deputazione Subalpina di Storia Patria, 1954 in *E.H.R.* LXXI (1956) 494.

Guido Quazza, *Il Contrasto Sabaudo-Borbonico nella Guerra per la Successione Polacca 1733–38* (Turin, Tipografia Vincenzo Bona, 1955) in *E.H.R.* LXXI (1956) 484–5.

A Select List of Works on Europe and Europe Overseas 1715–1815, ed. J. S. Bromley and A. Goodwin (Oxford, Clarendon Press, 1956) in *E.H.R.* LXXII (1957) 179–80.

Douglas Dakin, *British and American Philhellines during the War of Greek Independence 1821–1833* (Thessaloniki, The Society for Macedonian Studies, 1955) in *S.H.R.* XXXVI (1957) 74.

C. A. Macartney, *October Fifteenth. A History of Modern Hungary 1929–1945* (two vols.; Edinburgh University Press, 1956) in *U.E.J.* XVIII (1955–57) 272–4.

'Development of the sport of mountaineering. A history of climbing in the British Isles', review article of R. W. Clark and E. C. Pyatt, *Mountaineering in Britain* (London, Phoenix House, 1957) in *The Scotsman*, 26 October 1957.

Herbert Butterfield, *George III and the Historians* (London, Collins, 1957) in *E.H.R.* LXXIV (1959) 300–1.

Recueil des Instructions données aux ambassadeurs et ministres de France depuis les Traités de Westphalie jusqu' à la Révolution française, XXVI, *Venise*, ed. Pierre Duparc (Paris, Editions du Centre National de la Recherche Scientifique, 1958) in *E.H.R.* LXXIV (1959) 349–50.

Boswell in Search of a Wife 1766–1769, ed. Frank Bradley and Frederick A. Pottle (London, Heinemann, 1957) in *S.H.R.* XXXVIII (1959) 71–2.

W. E. Mosse, *The European Powers and the German Question, 1848–71* (Cambridge University Press, 1958) in *The College Courant* [Journal of the Glasgow University Graduates Association] XI (1959) 156–8.

M. S. Anderson, *Britain's Discovery of Russia 1553–1815* (London, Macmillan, 1958) in *U.E.J.* XIX (1958–60) 215–16.

W. R. Ward, *Georgian Oxford* (Oxford, Clarendon Press, 1958) in *E.H.R.* LXXIV (1959) 532–3.

Douglas Coombs, *The Conduct of the Dutch. British Public Opinion and the Dutch Alliance during the War of the Spanish Succession* (The Hague and Achimota, Martinus Nijhoff for the University College of Ghana Publications Board, 1958) in *E.H.R.* LXXIV (1959) 733–4.

Caroline Robbins, *The Eighteenth-Century Commonwealthman* (Cambridge, Mass., Harvard University Press; London, Oxford University Press, 1959) in *S.H.R.* XXXIX (1960) 154–5.

Sir Lewis Namier, *Charles Townshend: His Character and Career* [The Leslie Stephen Lecture for 1959] (Cambridge University Press, 1959) in *E.H.R.* LXXVI (1961) 161.

Guide to the Diplomatic Archives of Western Europe, ed. Daniel H. Thomas and Lynn M. Case (Philadelphia, University of Pennsylvania Press, 1959) in *E.H.R.* LXXVI (1961) 191–2.

J. Stephen Watson, *The Reign of George III 1760–1815* (Oxford, Clarendon Press, 1960) in *E.H.R.* LXXVII (1962) 115–18.

R. A. Humphreys, *The Diplomatic History of British Honduras 1638–1901* (London, Oxford University Press for the Royal Institute of International Affairs, 1961) in *History*, new ser. XLVII (1962) 95.

Richard Pares, *The Historian's Business and Other Essays*, ed. R. A. and Elizabeth Humphreys (Oxford, Clarendon Press, 1961) in *S.H.R.* XLI (1962) 65–6.

George Elder Davie, *The Democratic Intellect. Scotland and her Universities in the Nineteenth Century* (Edinburgh University Press, 1961) in *S.H.R.* XLI (1962) 82–3.

Erika Bosbach, *Die 'Rêveries Politiques' in Friedrichs des Grossen politischem Testament von 1752* (Kölner Historische Abhandlungen, Band 3; Cologne and Graz, Böhlau Verlag, 1960) in *E.H.R.* LXXVII (1962) 562–3.

Recueil des Instructions données aux ambassadeurs et ministres de France depuis les Traités de Westphalie jusqu'à la Révolution française, XXVII, *Espagne* vol. iv, ed. Didier Ozanam (Paris, Editions du Centre National de la Recherche Scientifique, 1960) in *E.H.R.* LXXVII (1962) 781–2.

L. M. Angus-Butterworth, *Ten Master Historians* (Aberdeen University Press, 1961) in *S.H.R.* XLI (1962) 164.

Studies in Diplomatic History and Historiography in honour of G. P. Gooch, C.H., ed. A. O. Sarkissian (London, Longmans, 1961) in *E.H.R.* LXXVIII (1963) 144–5.

Alison Gilbert Olson, *The Radical Duke: Career and Correspondence of Charles Lennox, Third Duke of Richmond* (London, Oxford University Press, 1961) in *E.H.R.* LXXVIII (1963) 183–4.

Isabel de Madariaga, *Britain, Russia and the Armed Neutrality of 1780* (London, Hollis & Carter, 1962) in *History*, new ser. XLVIII (1963) 84–5.

Lesley Lewis, *Connoisseurs and Secret Agents in Eighteenth Century Rome* (London, Chatto & Windus, 1961) in *E.H.R.* LXXVIII (1963) 388–9.

Sir Charles Webster, *The Art and Practice of Diplomacy* (London, Chatto & Windus, 1961) in *E.H.R.* LXXVIII (1963) 591–2.

The Fourth Earl of Sandwich: Diplomatic Correspondence 1763–1765, ed. Frank Spencer (Manchester University Press, 1961) in *E.H.R.* LXXVIII (1963) 795–6.

Basil Williams, *The Whig Supremacy* (second edn. rev. by C. H. Stuart) (Oxford, Clarendon Press, 1962) in *E.H.R.* LXXIX (1964) 183–4.

James Bruce, *Travels to Discover the Source of the Nile*, ed. C. F. Beckingham (Edinburgh University Press, 1964) in *U.E.J.* XXI (1963–64) 347.

Herbert H. Kaplan, *The First Partition of Poland* (New York and London, Columbia University Press, 1962) in *E.H.R.* LXXIX (1964) 863–4.

The Fusion of 1860, ed. W. Douglas Simpson (Edinburgh, Oliver & Boyd for the University of Aberdeen, 1963) in *E.H.R.* LXXX (1965) 222–3.

Manfred Schlenke, *England und das friderizianische Preussen 1740–1763* (Freiburg and Munich, Verlag Karl Alber, 1963) in *E.H.R.* LXXX (1965) 360–2.

Rex E. Wright-St Clair, *Doctors Monro. A medical saga* (London, Wellcome Historical Medical Library, 1964) in *S.H.R.* XLIV (1965) 81–2.

R. W. Harris, *Absolutism and Enlightenment* (London, Blandford Press, 1964) in *History*, new ser. L (1965) 228.

Max Braubach, *Prinz Eugen von Savoyen: Eine Biographie.* I *Aufstieg* (Munich, R. Oldenbourg Verlag, 1963) in *E.H.R.* LXXX (1965) 843–4.

Max Braubach, *Prinz Eugen von Savoyen: Eine Biographie.* II *Der Feldherr;* III *Zum Gipfel des Ruhmes* (Munich, R. Oldenbourg Verlag, 1964) in *E.H.R.* LXXXI (1966) 113–15.

Nicholas Henderson, *Prince Eugen of Savoy* (London, Weidenfeld & Nicolson, 1964) in *E.H.R.* LXXXI (1966) 171–2.

K. F. Helleiner, *The Imperial Loans. A study in financial and diplomatic history* (Oxford, Clarendon Press, 1965) in *History*, new ser. LI (1966) 108–9.

Theo Gehling, *Ein europäischer Diplomat am Kaiserhof zu Wien* (Bonner Historische Forschungen, Band 25; Bonn, Ludwig Rohrscheid Verlag, 1964) in *E.H.R.* LXXXI (1966) 401–2.

Michael Grant, *The Civilisations of Europe* (London, Weidenfeld & Nicolson, 1965) in *U.E.J.* XXII (1965–66) 268–9.

Baroness Rudolfine von Oer, *Der Friede von Pressburg* (Munster, Verlag Aschendorff, 1965) in *E.H.R.* LXXXI (1966) 615.

René Albrecht-Carrié, *A Diplomatic History of Europe since the Congress of Vienna* (London, Methuen, 1958; University Paperback, 1965) in *U.E.J.* XXII (1965–66) 343.

Max Braubach, *Prinz Eugen von Savoyen: Eine Biographie.* IV *Der Staatsmann;* V *Mensch und Schicksal* (Munich, R. Oldenbourg Verlag, 1965) in *E.H.R.* LXXXII (1967) 131–2.

Forschungen und Studien zur Geschichte des Westfälischen Friedens (Munster, Verlag Aschendorff, 1965) in *E.H.R.* LXXXII (1967) 168–9.

Kyösti Julku, *Die Revolutionäre Bewegung im Rheinland am Ende des achtzehnten Jahrhunderts* (Helsinki, Suomalainen Tiedeakatemia, 1965) in *E.H.R.* LXXXII (1967) 398.

Paul P. Bernard, *Joseph II and Bavaria. Two Eighteenth Century Attempts at German Unification* (The Hague, Martinus Nijhoff, 1965) in *E.H.R.* LXXXII (1967) 406.

Edmund Heier, *L. H. Nicolay (1737–1820) and his Contemporaries* (The Hague, Martinus Nijhoff, 1965) in *E.H.R.* LXXXII (1967) 407.

Guido Quazza, *Il problema italiano e l'equilibrio europea 1720–1738* (Turin, Palazzo Carignano, 1965) in *E.H.R.* LXXXII (1967) 407–8.

Phyllis S. Lachs, *The Diplomatic Corps under Charles II and James II* (New Brunswick, Rutgers University Press, 1965) in *E.H.R.* LXXXII (1967) 614–15.

Recueil des Instructions données aux ambassadeurs et ministres de France depuis les Traités de Westphalie jusqu'à la Révolution française, XXV–2 *Angleterre* vol. iii, ed. Paul Vaucher (Paris, Editions du Centre National de la Recherche Scientifique, 1965) in *E.H.R.* LXXXII (1967) 617–18.

Repertorium der diplomatischen Vertreter aller Länder, III (1764–1815), ed. Otto Friedrich Winter (Graz and Cologne, Verlag Hermann Böhlaus Nachf., 1965) in *E.H.R.* LXXXIII (1968) 188–9.

John M. Beattie, *The English Court in the Reign of George I* (Cambridge University Press; Toronto, Macmillan of Canada, 1967) in *The Canadian Historical Review* XLIX (1968) 79–81.

M. S. Anderson, *Eighteenth Century Europe 1713–1789* (London, Oxford University Press, 1966) in *E.H.R.* LXXXIII (1968) 401–2.

Lavender Cassels, *The Struggle for the Ottoman Empire 1717–1740* (London, John Murray, 1966) in *E.H.R.* LXXXIII (1968) 402.

Max Savelle, *The Origins of American Diplomacy. The International History of Angloamerica 1492–1763* (New York, The Macmillan Company, 1967) in *The William and Mary Quarterly* XXV (1968) 643–5.

Baron W. M. von Bissing, *Freidrich Wilhelm II. König von Preussen* (Berlin, Duncker und Humblot, 1967) in *E.H.R.* LXXXIV (1969) 193–4.

William III and Louis XIV: Essays 1680–1720 by and for Mark A. Thomson, ed. Ragnhild Hatton and J. S. Bromley (Liverpool University Press, 1968) in *E.H.R.* LXXXIV (1969) 356–8.

The University of Edinburgh and Poland, ed. Wiktor Tomaszewski (Edinburgh University Press, 1968) in *U.E.J.* XXIV (1969–70) 73.

Sweden as a Great Power 1611–1697, ed. Michael Roberts (London, Edward Arnold, 1968) in *E.H.R.* LXXXIV (1969) 849–50.

Pierre Gaxotte, *Frederic II, roi de Prusse* (Paris, Editions Albin Michel, 1967) in *E.H.R.* LXXXIV (1969) 855.

Note. The bibliography is complete to December 1969. A contribution by D. B. Horn (dealing with the foreign policy of the Duke of Newcastle) will, however, be included in a volume of essays to be published towards the end of 1970.